Network Journalism

Routledge Research in Journalism

1. Journalists, Sources, and Credibility
New Perspectives
Bob Franklin and Matt Carlson

2. Journalism Education, Training and Employment
Bob Franklin and Donica Mensing

3. Network Journalism
Journalistic Practice in Interactive Spheres
Ansgard Heinrich

Network Journalism

Journalistic Practice in Interactive Spheres

Ansgard Heinrich

Routledge
Taylor & Francis Group
New York   London

First published 2011
by Routledge
711 Third Avenue, New York, NY 10017

Simultaneously published in the UK
by Routledge
2 Park Square, Milton Park, Abingdon, Oxon OX14 4RN

Routledge is an imprint of the Taylor & Francis Group, an informa business

© 2011 Taylor & Francis

Typeset in Sabon by IBT Global.

Library of Congress Cataloging-in-Publication Data
Heinrich, Ansgard.
 Network journalism : journalistic practice in interactive spheres / Ansgard Heinrich.
  p. cm. — (Routledge research in journalism)
 Includes bibliographical references and index.
 1. Journalism—History—21st centuy. 2. Journalism—Technological innovations. 3. Online journalism. 4. Citizen journalism. 5. Digital media. I. Title.
 PN4815.2.H45 2010
 070.9'09051—dc22
 2010035083

ISBN13: 978-0-415-88270-5 (hbk)
ISBN13: 978-0-203-83045-1 (ebk)

Contents

Preface and Acknowledgments   vii

Introduction to Network Journalism   1

PART I
Network Journalism: Theories and Concepts

1   The Network Age and its Footprints on Journalism   13

2   News Agencies and Telegraph Technology: The Evolution of
    Global News Exchange Networks   36

3   Network Journalism: Between Decentralization and Non-linear
    News Flows   51

4   Information Nodes in the Network Journalism Sphere   68

PART II
Network Journalism: Practitioner Perspectives

5   Studying Network Journalism   87

6   The Advent of Digitalization in Newsrooms   108

7   The Shared Information Sphere: User-generated Content
    Providers, Citizen Journalists, Media Activists   124

8   The Shared Information Sphere: Blogs and their Impact on
    Journalism   147

9   The Active User in the Network Journalism Sphere   169

10   Transnational News Flows in the Network Journalism Sphere   183

11   Reconceptualizing Journalistic Outlets as Information Nodes   207

12   Conclusion   228

Notes   233
Bibliography   245
Index   265

Preface and Acknowledgments

This book is the product of a journey through the sphere of journalistic practice and current journalism research. What started as a PhD project in 2005 became a true passion and brought intriguing insights into a profession that is undergoing profound change. It is a profession greatly affected by social, political and technological developments. The emerging pressures as well as the opportunities resulting from this stand in the focus of this work, which aims to contribute to a better understanding of current dynamics in journalistic practice.

A new kind of journalism is emerging, characterized by an increasingly global flow of news. With a growing number of news distributors entering the news production chain, information exchange is turning into an interactive conversation. A dense web of information deliverers is spanning the globe, exhilarated by digital communication technologies. It is an emerging 'network' sphere of journalistic practice in which numerous partakers gather, produce and disseminate news. Contributors of content are not only professional news organizations. Bloggers, citizen journalists or media activists feed information into this sphere and formerly silent audiences are becoming active participants in the process. These alternative news deliverers are individual information nodes and part of a dense information net spanning the globe. The interactive connections among the many nodes occupying today's sphere of information exchange constitute what I call *network journalism*.

It is at the intersections where these nodes meet, that this book identifies the challenges as well as the opportunities for professional news organizations. Journalistic outlets have to decide how they want to position themselves within this dense information net. As the power of the new network structures is changing the face of journalistic practice, news organizations have to decide which niche to occupy in the sphere of network journalism, what role to fulfill and how much collaboration with alternative news deliverers to allow. How to theoretically frame this emerging sphere of network journalism is one issue that this book addresses. Drawing on current theoretical debates in journalism studies and grounded in empirical research, this work highlights the changes and analyzes the interplay between journalistic practice and processes of globalization and digitalization. It draws upon first examples taken from journalistic practice that demonstrate how news organizations cope with the challenges of this evolving sphere of information exchange and how the opportunities on offer are being taken for the better of journalism.

The power of the global network is also the engine that drove this book. A freelance journalist for local radio in Germany, I went from practice into theory, from my home country to New Zealand, and I became what one might call a 'netizen'. Relocated into a global sphere of academic exchange, I was intrigued by the possibilities of digital communication and the perspectives that opened up with a click of a mouse. Many research trips contributed to my very own experience of global exchange. While based in Hungary and Australia, I traveled to Germany, the UK and the US to speak to media practitioners and researchers who shared their knowledge (and contacts) with me and inspired the empirical part of this book. I finished my thesis, living and working in Melbourne. As I write this I am back in Europe, now working at the Rijksuniversiteit Groningen in the Netherlands. Along these various stages of my young career, I met many great people whose thoughts and comments inspired this book —scholars, journalists and friends of whom I can only name a few here.

First and foremost I want to thank the media practitioners who opened their doors at the BBC, the Guardian Media Group, ZEIT ONLINE, MediaChannel, AlterNet, Democracy Now!, the New York City Independent Media Center, Ourmedia, Current TV, the Project for Excellence in Journalism and the International Center for Journalists. Their interviews are the heart of this book and I am grateful for their contributions. I want to thank Ingrid Volkmer for her outstanding supervision throughout my PhD. A passionate academic and inspirational mind, she introduced me to the field of journalism studies and taught me to become a scholar. A thank you also goes to my publisher Routledge and especially to my editor Erica Wetter for her trust in and patience with a young author like me. I thank the University of Otago and the Department of Media, Film, and Communication for their support throughout my PhD and for awarding me the 'Fanny Evans Postgraduate Scholarship for Women'. The Division of Humanities at the University of Otago and Education New Zealand financially supported my research travels and I owe thanks to the School of Culture and Communication at the University of Melbourne and to the Center for Media and Communication Studies at the Central European University Budapest, who both welcomed me as research fellow.

A very warm thank you goes to friends and colleagues who assisted me throughout the various stages of my PhD and throughout the work on this book. Representative for them I want to name Florian Deffner, Tanja Meyerhofer, Kim Daufratshofer and Mirle Heinzen, who offered fabulous support in the Southern Hemisphere. In Germany, I thank my friends Alexandra Kappel, Maren Puhlmann and Anke Haverkamp, who listened to academic talk numerous times without complaining and kept me focused. Iris Mojen and Jana Jakobs had patience with an impatient me (and my unfinished manuscript) and gave me shelter. A very special thank you goes to Brian McNair, who encouraged me to publish my work and offered tremendous support throughout the completion phase of this book. His comments helped improve the manuscript by miles and his moral support kept me going.

Probably the most important lesson I have learned so far in life is that an open mind is the biggest asset you can throw into your work and I want to dedicate this book to my parents Christa and Günther Heinrich, who always encourage me to travel the world with eyes and ears wide open.

Introduction to Network Journalism

Journalism is dynamic, not static. It is constantly changing and evolving to some degree.

(Executive Editor, MediaChannel.org)[1]

Neda Agha-Soltan died violently during the Iran election protests in June 2009. The amateur video footage of her bleeding to death in the streets of Tehran was broadcast across all major news outlets. Recorded with a mobile phone by a man who remains anonymous, the video made its way onto the web after another anonymous source emailed it to contacts outside of the country attached to the message 'please let the world know'.[2] The world did learn about Neda—and along with it about the opposition movement in Iran. An anonymous native from Iran currently living in the Netherlands was one of the receivers of this email and he was reportedly the first person to share the video online. From there, the images of the dying Neda were linked and referenced via an uncountable number of blogs and on Twitter, passed on and exchanged through social network sites and packaged in newsrooms worldwide. Neda's face became an icon of the reformist opposition in Iran, her violent death the symbol for repression of free speech. It was the first time that news footage authored by a person remaining anonymous received the George Polk Award in Journalism.

The case of Neda is only one of many examples of the phenomenon which this book explores: a radical change in patterns of information dissemination and newsgathering in a restructured, network system of journalistic production.

When bombs exploded in the London Underground in 2005, so-called user-generated content providers delivered the only visual materials and first-hand accounts from the scene of the bombings to various major news organizations across the globe. Bloggers gained fame during the 2003 Iraq War, continuously delivering personal accounts of the conflict situation on the ground. Along with embedded journalists corresponding from the war fields via satellite phones, independent journalists such as Christopher Allbritton traveled into Iraq, equipped with only a backpack full of technological gear and funded by readers of his website.

Putting aside breaking news stories and the reporting about so-called 'hot spots' that are of political and economic interest to countries in the Western world, the number of projects providing news from regions mainly uncovered by traditional news organizations is on the rise as well. Take the virtual community Global Voices Online that aggregates reports and provides translations of information material from bloggers and citizen journalists as an example. Founded in 2005, the website run by a nonprofit foundation provides information from regions often ignored and—as I write this—has developed a network of around 200 contributors worldwide. The Voices of Africa Media Foundation, founded in 2006 and headquartered in the Netherlands, offers a training program to support young Africans to pursue media careers. They equip their aspiring journalists with a mobile phone that has camera and editing functions (and, depending on the region, mobile broadband connections to ensure the transmission of the material) and offer training on how to produce video reports on local stories from African communities. The results of the program can be viewed online.

These examples illustrate that the way in which news and information is gathered, produced and disseminated is being altered. Since the commercial exploitation of satellite technology, news travels distances in no time from Iraq to the US or elsewhere; in addition, interactive technologies enable the delivery of information generated by ordinary people who are not necessarily journalists. This increasing number of producers and disseminators of news as well as the instantaneity of global news flows indicate that journalistic practice is changing. As I will argue in this book, this transformation is driven by two processes: globalization and technological advances in the form of digitalization.

'We are living in the middle of a remarkable increase in our ability to share, to cooperate with one another', writes Shirky (2008: 20 et seq.). Forming groups has gotten a lot easier thanks to the growing numbers of social media tools in today's digitalized environment. We are surrounded by social networking sites such as Facebook and have mobile devices such as smartphones which bring us the news when we want it and where we want it. Digital technologies enable a new level of (global) interaction with news content and the 'shape of media has shifted away from mostly passive, mass reception to more interactive, individualised modes of active engagement' (Bruns, 2006: 282). This shift has a striking effect on the production of journalism. The ability to communicate across nation-state borders in virtually no time has impacted journalism in every (digitally connected) corner of the world and expanded the reach of journalistic production and dissemination. It is this 'new ease of assembly' (Shirky: 48) facilitated by lower costs for technological equipment that has supported bloggers, Twitterers or media activists to push content online into a global arena of information exchange. News is now not fixed to a place, but rather floating through space with satellite dishes and tools such as the Internet spreading information loosened from the constraints of physical space as well as from clock time. Instead, information occurs within what Hassan calls 'Network Time' (2007: 49). News takes place in a 'digital space' which creates new relevance factors: 'speed, connectivity, and flexibility' (Ibid.: 49).

In the midst of this 'cultural chaos,' to adapt what McNair (2006) suggests as the sociological fundament of societies today, journalistic organizations are being challenged to respond. How do they adapt to this new globalized sphere characterized by a transformed time and space regiment? How do news organizations position themselves within this sphere? And last but not least: do we have models that help us define the shape of this evolution? These are the questions to be addressed in this book.

Within academic discourse, we are just at the beginning of conceptualizing journalism in relation to a sphere of communication that is profoundly enlarged through the uses of digital technology (see Volkmer and Heinrich, 2008). These innovations not only alter journalistic practice as such, but challenge journalism to incorporate cross-platform networks in various stages of the process of news production. A multi-platform structure of journalism is evolving in which boundaries between the traditional media outlets of print, radio and television are blurring. Print, audio and video are increasingly merging online as the lines between formerly distinct media platforms are becoming indistinct. Network technologies have triggered processes of convergence impacting the management of cross-platform news flow processes in day-to-day news production. Journalistic outlets in Western societies are affected by these developments and acquire new notions of journalistic practice as well as a reconfigured perception of our journalistic cultures.

In scholarly research we witness an explosion in the amount of research material that is concerned with these fundamental changes ranging from studies on alternative journalism (e.g. Atton, 2005; Atton and Hamilton, 2008) and citizen journalism (e.g. Reich, 2008; Kelly, 2009) to studies about the adaptation of user-generated content in traditional newsrooms (e.g. Hampel, 2008; Paulussen and Ugille, 2008; Wardle and Williams, 2008), the relationship between bloggers and journalists (e.g. Reese et al., 2007; Matheson, 2004; Wall, 2003), the evolution of multimedia newsrooms (e.g. Erdal, 2009; Huang et al., 2006; Avilés and Carvajal, 2008) or occupational profiles of journalists in the digital age (e.g. Deuze, 2008; Schmitz Weiss and Higgins Joyce, 2009), to name just a few. We also find literature particularly concerned with the effects of these developments on political conflicts and crises that evokes discussions of media diplomacy and about the influence of news media on foreign policy decisions (e.g. Cottle, 2009; Gilboa, 2002; Gowing, 1994; Robinson, 2003). The impacts of increasing digitalization as well as globalization furthermore raise the question of the formation of horizontal as well as vertical integrated media conglomerates, perpetuating a new 'media imperialism' (see for example McChesney, 1998; Thussu, 1998).

Yet, we are still searching for a model that not only grasps specific trends within the evolving sphere of information exchange, but also provides an overall framework that melds all of these developments—a model that unites the trends under one umbrella and encourages an understanding that these various angles in the evolution of journalistic work are altogether part of the same story. It is the story of a transformation of the journalistic sphere as a whole. This book might be a start in developing such a conceptual model.

As I will argue in the chapters to come, the key categories that characterize this evolving sphere of journalism are the *decentralization* of news production and dissemination processes of news and the *non-linearity* of news flows in an increasingly global news environment. And these characteristics of *decentralization* and *non-linearity* have far-reaching consequences for every aspect or topic discussed in any of the works mentioned above.

This book seeks to develop an understanding that entire cultures of journalism are transforming. New forms of connectivity are taking shape at the global level, enabled by the use of digital technology tools. These new forms of connectivity create a different kind of news sphere. We are moving away from the twentieth-century model of a centralized, linear media system. The monopoly of information delivery no longer lies with journalists working for major corporate or public service outlets. Digital communication tools facilitate a greater number of information deliverers, ranging from the journalist at the *New York Times* or Al Jazeera to the independent journalists (not attached to leading media conglomerates) and to what Benkler calls 'nonmarket actors' (2006: 220), including the blogger in Iraq or the citizen journalist producing for OhmyNews in Korea. They all share the same global information space. In many cases, these new news deliverers are now feeding their news pieces into established corporate or public service outlets and influencing or mediating the agenda.

Think of Neda once more. Without the far-reaching distribution of the pictures of her death, a worldwide support for the Iranian protest movement and the incredible speed with which this support was gathered would have not occurred. In cases like this, traditional news outlets rely on these unofficial sources to provide material—no foreign correspondent was on the spot where Neda was killed.

With millions of digital cameras and cell phones equipped with video devices in circulation, newsrooms have discovered their audience as information source. The number of news pieces featuring user-generated content material increasingly appears on traditional media platforms, which in the case of Neda's death served the key frame of an event for a worldwide audience. Other examples here are the uses outlets made of the visual material available on the global news market and framing the perceptions of millions of media users around the world after the 2004 Boxing Day tsunami or during and after the Mumbai attacks in 2008, when first-hand information and links spread via Twitter with accelerating speed. The former receivers are becoming deliverers of information. Journalists increasingly turn toward their audience to get footage.

These examples illustrate that not only is the number of user-generated content pieces on the rise, the whole infrastructure of journalistic work is under reconstruction, with an increasing number of news providers becoming a *constant* in the journalistic space. News is traveling into journalistic outlets via *non-linear information strings* and does not necessarily take the traditional paths of being delivered by an official source, a news agency or a reporter as former models of gatekeeping and agenda-setting have suggested with reference to the mass media system of the twentieth century (McCombs, 2005; Bennett, 2004).

For journalists working for corporate or public service news organizations, this raises questions of how to deal with these new news deliverers that include user-generated content as well as outlets created by independent journalists, citizen journalists or bloggers who all mainly use the Internet as a distribution tool for their version of the news. Gates are essentially extended, yet which of these new news sources should be counted as a reliable source for one's own news production? Should journalists contest these emerging contenders or rather seek paths of collaboration? Who could be part of one's reporting chain, and who should be not? How can a journalistic outlet deal with the masses of information floating through broadband channels? How can one filter useful information out of the billions of data bits crisscrossing the globe with the speed of light? And last but not least: How do news organizations adapt to changing needs of audiences that increasingly do not want to be restrained by the timeline of a broadcaster but are rather 'moving toward information on demand, to media platforms and outlets that can tell them what they want to know when they want to know it' (Project for Excellence in Journalism, 2008a: Online)?

This book will present a range of examples taken from journalistic practice as well as give voice to a diverse group of early adopters and media analysts from the US, the UK and Germany who have begun to rethink journalistic work and have started to develop new ways of gathering, producing and distributing news. They try to find ways to approach these changes outlined above and they view the developments mainly as an opportunity—a challenging one, but one that can serve journalistic production well if taken serious.

Notwithstanding the suggestions of the many voices who argue in favor of changing journalistic practice, among scholars as well as among journalists, the obvious shifts in the production of news toward this emerging *decentralized news sphere* characterized by *non-linear news flows* are still often viewed critically as a threat, accompanied by a fear of somewhat 'declining standards' in journalism (see for example Carr, 2005; Keen, 2007; Sunstein, 2009; for an overview of critiques see Benkler, 2006: 233–237). Some critics, for example, attest a decline in the quality of reporting and view the role of journalists as the informants of a public sphere as an endangered one. For Sunstein (2009), 'information overload' accelerated by the rise of sheer endless communication options and the increased number of actors deploying information leads to a confusing mash of disseminators. The individualization of distribution as well as consumption of news might be damaging for democracy. He fears that in a news environment where consumers can personalize what they read, view or hear they will filter the news according to their personal likes, eventually avoid viewpoints they might disagree with and instead 'sort themselves into enclaves in which their own views and commitments are constantly being reaffirmed' (Sunstein, 2009: xii). Consumers might not stumble across material that could contest whatever they have chosen to favor—the result being a fragmented individualization that eventually erases the 'social glue' of 'common experience' (Ibid.: 6) and causes the disappearance of a critical public sphere. Arguing this line, Keen (2007) proposes a cultural critique of journalism. According to him, the use of digital technologies indicates a decline in valuable knowledge dissemination and an erosion of quality journalistic work for the worse of society. Keen views the Internet as a 'killer' of culture:[3]

> Today's technology hooks all those monkeys up with all those typewriters. Except in our Web 2.0 world, the typewriters aren't quite typewriters, but rather networked personal computers, and the monkeys aren't quite monkeys, but rather Internet users. And instead of creating masterpieces, these millions and millions of exuberant monkeys—many with no more talent in the creative arts than our primate cousins—are creating an endless digital forest of mediocrity. For today's amateur monkeys can use their networked computers to publish everything from uninformed political commentary, to unseemly home videos, to embarrassingly amateurish music, to unreadable poems, reviews, essays, and novels. (Keen, 2007: 2 et seq.)

And even though at the end of his book Keen does withdraw to a (small) extent from his position, mentioning that the Internet might offer some quality journalism buried underneath piles of useless content, his polemic bluntly identifies the Internet as a threat to culture and to quality journalism.

I want to argue against this position in the following chapters.

There is no doubt that severe changes within the sphere of news production and dissemination are taking place which put pressures on the journalistic profession, but I take this phenomenon as a starting point for a discussion about the *redesign* of journalistic production and dissemination in a way that suits what we have come to call the information age—a terminology which already suggests that 'we are possibly at the beginning of an era of transition from societies organised around industrial development to societies organised around information' (Campbell, 2004: 2). Western societies have moved into what Bell as early as 1973 described as a 'post-industrial society' in which information and information-related industries take center stage. It is a move conveyed by technological advancements (Thussu, 2000: 73)—and journalism as a profession dealing with information has a vital role to play in societies in which information becomes the essential ingredient. Journalists are mediators of messages and thus play an important part within their cultural environment. Yet, at the same moment, they are also affected by the structures that surround them:

> *Forms* of media, media practices and media institutions [. . .] play a significant role in cultural production. It is *in* and *through* these that ideas are transmitted, traditions passed on, ideologies disseminated, hegemonies consolidated, and where the symbols, customs, norms and values that go to make up 'the cultural' are created, contested and manipulated. (Hassan, 2004: 3 emphasis in original)

Journalism is a commodity produced within society and is as such influenced by it. Anyone involved with journalism—be it as journalist, as scholar or as the manager of a journalistic outlet—has to be aware of this bond. Social structures shape journalistic production, dissemination as well as its reception (or the interaction with its content). I am writing in favor of an understanding of journalism that is directed by sociological premises. A sociology of journalism is

> interested in the *social* determinants of journalistic output—those features of social life and organisation which shape, influence and constrain its form and content. The sociologist of journalism assumes that his or her object of study both acts on, and is acted on by, the surrounding social environment. The journalistic text is viewed as the product of a wide variety of cultural, technological, political and economic forces, specific to a particular society at a particular time. Understanding the content, meaning, role and impact of journalism therefore requires description and analysis of the broader social context within which it is produced and of the *factors* of production which determine that context. (McNair, 1998: 3 emphasis in original)

Consequently, analyzing journalistic models of news production has to start with a close examination of the societal modes *together* with the technological conditions under which it is produced.

It is in this sense that I view digital technology as an indicator and as such as part of a larger, more complex and fundamental structural evolution that is taking place and that affects all aspects of journalism. It is an aspect so often overlooked in hastily written critiques of the Internet as a 'killer' of culture and quality journalism. It is the proliferation of a fundamentally new global news culture supported by processes of globalization and enabled by digital technologies. The critics of these practices fail to take into account the bigger picture of what Castells famously coined the 'network society' (1996). News is produced within reconfigured settings, with news structured around and carried across new routes and transmitted via different strings of information and with a new connectivity speed.

Journalism then is moving away from traditional place-based modes of production and dissemination. In my view, the ways digital technologies are adapted in today's cultures is the outcome of profound changes taking place in our cultures and societies, with transnational connectivity structures developing in a globalized world. Based on the works of globalization theorists such as Appadurai (1996), Beck (2000) or Robertson (1992) to name just a few here, I will argue that this development influences journalistic practice and opens up a new globalized geography of journalism. This new geography asks for a reconfiguration of journalism according to the new marks set by its global environment. It changes the face of journalism and puts pressure on traditional journalistic practices (Volkmer and Heinrich, 2008).

The paradigmatic shift toward a development of a global news culture then urges the central question news organizations have to address: How can journalistic outlets reorganize themselves within this new global news culture?

This book aims to identify the consequences these (globally) occurring changes have for journalistic work. I propose that the evolution of digital technologies is not a threat to the journalistic profession while more contenders are occupying the sphere of information exchange but that this is an inevitably useful opportunity—not only with respect to reconfigured production and dissemination modes of journalism. The shape of digital technology and the ways it supports journalists to connect with sources and audiences can be seen as a template for a reconfigured journalistic model: Digital technology allows journalists to connect with their environment in new ways and offers production means that create a fundamentally different structure of journalism. In the following pages I reveal these underlying structures of journalistic production and the features a reorganized newsroom carries. In essence, I develop a framework in which to understand journalistic organization today, with innovative work structures based on digital technologies changing the character and in effect replacing top-down journalism with a model that is far more complicated and resembles connections that can better be grasped in the term *net*.

This said, I anticipate that my work contributes to a better understanding of how journalism functions in the digital environment of the information age. Yet, I do not only hope to further this discussion, but also to strengthen the position of the multitude of new voices contributing at times invaluable material to our sphere of information. These new voices in the global journalistic arena—from the blogger to the Twitterer to the media activist—deserve to be heard and they have to be heard much more often by traditional news organizations, as their contribution to the journalistic field can be tremendously fruitful. This study might help to link the spaces of information already in existence into one global news culture and to conceptualize a sphere within which they all could come together and be connected.

It is an approach to define a sphere of journalism in which professional journalistic outlets are assigned the role of connectors—or *nodes*—in our information society. A new geography of journalism is taking shape that resembles the reformulation of journalistic outlets as such nodes within a dense net of information exchange. I locate *all* these various contributors who have become part of this dense net in the *same* sphere—be it the local or national newspaper or TV station, the blogger contributing to Global Voices Online, the anonymous contributor from Iran, the online radio station, the mobile journalist in Africa, you name it.

In a network society, they all roam in the same sphere of information where the question becomes which connections will be made in this dense net of many nodes—a net that I define as the fundamental structure of our new information space and as the sphere of *network journalism*.

CHAPTER OVERVIEW

Shedding light on recent developments in journalistic theory and practice, the following chapters address the implications of an emerging sphere of network journalism from various angles, considering first and foremost the consequences of this fundamental transformation for the work of journalists in the primary decades of the twenty-first century. The book is divided into two main sections: a part containing theoretical reflections and culminating in the development of the network journalism paradigm, and a part based on a qualitative study and enriched with a range of examples where the practice of network journalism is further illustrated and discussed.

Part I presents a critical analysis of background literature in the field of journalism and media and communication studies, discussing journalistic practice within frameworks of globalization and advanced technologies. I locate journalism within these contexts and identify the complex interaction patterns between technological advancements and the work of journalists. Chapter 1 will draw connections between journalistic cultures and globalization processes. Here I am particularly concerned with the question of how the paradigm of the 'network society' (Castells, 1996) translates into journalism studies. I also address how technological innovations facilitate a global flow of news and how this in turn affects journalistic production and dissemination modes. Chapter 2 builds upon a historical case study: the evolution of the telegraph and its effect on the creation of news agencies in the nineteenth century. This case study exemplifies how a technological invention of the past contributed to shaping production modes as well as the structural organization of journalistic outlets. Chapters 3 and 4 will focus on the development of a paradigm for a news culture of the information age and I will introduce the idea of network journalism. This paradigm is based on the objective of the 'network' as the central production as well as organization model for news organizations. It helps to conceptualize journalistic practices affected by global news flows and explains how production and dissemination modes are evolving in a sphere comprised of interconnected information nodes.

The following chapters make up the second part of the book, where I analyze first moves journalistic organizations have undertaken in order to reposition themselves within this network journalism culture. The basis of this analysis is a range of interviews conducted with media practitioners in the UK, the US and Germany. My sample includes experts working for BBC News, the Guardian Media Group, ZEIT ONLINE, MediaChannel.org, AlterNet.org, Democracy Now!, the New York City Independent Media Center (IMC), Ourmedia.org, Current TV, the Project for Excellence in Journalism (PEJ) and the International Center for Journalists (ICFJ). Combined with cases taken from observations of current developments in news practice, the analysis of this unique interview sample focuses on emerging structural changes in newsrooms and includes a discussion of practicing news journalism in converged multimedia newsrooms. I particularly concentrate on aspects such as the adaptation of user-generated content in journalistic practice, on the first examples of systematic collaboration between traditional newsrooms and alternative news providers and on the transformation of foreign reporting in an increasingly globalized news sphere.

Based on this analysis and the presented range of material from journalistic practice I demonstrate that a new social geography of journalism is taking shape in which news outlets become nodes in a dense network of information gatherers, producers and disseminators.

Part I
Network Journalism
Theories and Concepts

1 The Network Age and its Footprints on Journalism

> The spread of the Internet and digital communication technologies in the twenty-first century will see information confirmed as the most important global resource, and journalism as the dominant mode of cultural expression in advanced capitalist societies.
>
> (McNair, 1998: 10)

We are entering a new phase of connectivity. Information exchange now is increasingly being structured around digital communication tools. This change in interaction patterns has severe implications for our societies. Yet how exactly are societies changing and what does this mean for journalistic practice? This chapter will address these questions.

Journalism is widely understood as a vital part of democratic society, constructed on the basis of historical, technological, political and economic factors in its surrounding environment. As McNair explains, 'journalistic news is a product of the interaction of all the environmental factors within which it is formed' (McNair, 2006: 48; see also Briggs and Burke, 2005). Journalists then are actors within society, who take the role of informing citizens; they act *within* and *upon* society. It follows that if the environment in which journalism exists is transforming, the journalistic profession as well as the modes of information production transform as well.[1]

One scholar who is strongly concerned with the interplay between digital technologies and the development of societies is Manuel Castells. He introduced us to the paradigm of the 'network society' (1996), where he explains how social structures today change through the use of digital technologies and where the Internet becomes 'the technological basis for the organizational form of the Information Age' (2002b: 1). His model applies to journalism as well. For journalistic practice—just as Castells' paradigm highlights—the 'network' becomes the central pattern of connective interactions. Journalism is staged by the emergence of a 'network society' organized around 'information technology-powered networks' (Castells and Ince, 2003: 23), bringing with it a restructuring of journalism.

Castells' concept is strongly associated with the process we have come to call globalization. According to Tomlinson, 'globalization refers to the rapidly developing and ever-densening network of interconnections and interdependences that characterize modern social life' (Tomlinson, 1999: 2). Journalism as a social entity does not stay untouched when globalizing trends of whatever kind influence social, economic or political environments.

Processes of globalization push (the practice of) journalism into global settings—acting within and being affected by globally connected networks.

Much has been written about globalization. Debates circle around economic developments and discuss the shape of (global) finance and trade
systems. However, as Giddens points out, the issue of globalization is not
only to be viewed in economic terms: 'Globalisation is political, technological and cultural, as well as economic. It has been influenced above all by
developments in systems of communication, dating back only to the late
1960s' (1999: 10).[2]

This is not the place to deliver a complete overview of globalization
debates. Other scholars have comprehensively outlined the many facets and
differing presumptions of globalization (for overviews see for example Beck,
2000; Sinclair, 2004; Straubhaar, 2007; Thussu, 2000). I will instead point
at some ideas here that are useful in order to contextualize journalism within
processes of globalization. These are key resources, which assist to better
comprehend the shape of societies within which journalists interact.[3]

1.1. THE DYNAMICS OF GLOBALIZATION PROCESSES

> We live in a world of transformations, affecting almost every aspect
> of what we do. For better or worse, we are being propelled into a
> global order that no one fully understands, but which is making its
> effects felt upon all of us.
>
> (Giddens, 1999: 6 et seq.)

Globalization can be seen as a driving force that triggers changes in social,
economical and political environments, or as Straubhaar has formulated
it: 'Globalization is the worldwide spread, over both time and space, of a
number of new ideas, institutions, culturally defined ways of doing things,
and technologies' (2007: 81). With all these aspects at play, the sphere of
journalism is not left untouched.

The proliferation of digital technologies permits a global exchange of
information. Featherstone notes that globalization includes processes that
'transcend the state-society unit and can therefore be held to occur on a
trans-national or *trans-societal* level' (1990: 1, emphasis added). Globalization processes thus comprise consequences for connectivity structures
and are inevitably bound together with technological advancements: without technological tools, delivering information via distance and through
space would not be possible. Technologies facilitate what Tomlinson calls
'complex connectivity' (1999: 1 et seq.); they allow interaction across borders and lay the fundament for globalization processes. As Thussu argues,
'information and communication technologies have made global intercon-
nectivity a reality' (2000: 76). Communication technologies facilitate globalization processes 'because of the way they overcome space and time,

which thus allows individuals to free themselves from physical constraints and also to see themselves in, and adapt to, a global context, regardless of where they are' (Sinclair, 2004: 67). Or as Robertson (1992: 8) claims, the world is being 'compressed' now, as technology connects places and brings them virtually closer together. The media play a vital role here as they render it possible to execute control over this compressed, globalized space:

> The media are central to this control, not only for their technological transcendence of space and time as such but also for the interconnectedness inherent in communications, especially in their capacity to give individuals access to global networks. (Sinclair, 2004: 67)

Digital technologies thus enable us to cross time and space distanciations and lead us to a situation anthropologist Hannerz describes with the sentence: 'Distances, and boundaries, are not what they used to be' (1996: 3).

This effect of technology on the way societies act and interact as well as its effects on journalistic production should not be interpreted in terms of what has become known as 'technological determinism'. According to the purveyors of technological determinism (see for example Ellul, 1964; Negroponte, 1995, or Meyrowitz, 1985), technology is an independent power, which holds the capacity to administrate control over processes of communication. However, this view misleadingly creates the impression that technology rules over humans, when human beings are not only the users, but also the inventors of a technology.[4] Technological determinism develops a notion of 'privileging the printing press and successive technical innovations as the penultimate marker and engine of media modernization and democratization' (Hamilton, 2003: 296). But to argue with Castells: 'The fundamental lesson is that technology per se does not do good or bad to societies' (Castells and Ince, 2003: 59). No matter how strong the impact of technology on human lives might be, the most active part in the interplay between technology and people is still the humans behind the machines and not the machines in themselves: 'Because technologies are used when a use is found for them, not earlier' (Ibid.: 30; see also Castells, 2000c: 5).

With regard to journalism, this means that technologies are tools journalists use in order to communicate their information. As Schudson stresses, 'technological advances in printing and related industries and the development of railroad transportation and later telegraphic communications were the necessary preconditions for a cheap, mass-circulation, news-hungry, and independent press' (1978: 31). Technologies are instruments in the hands of humans and can affect work procedures, but do not determine them. For Braman, 'although it is true that technologies have structural effects on society as well as on individual cognition, it is also true that it is society that determines just how technologies will be used' (2004: 139).[5] Therefore, specific necessities can trigger the willingness of researchers or engineers to turn experiments into inventions (Nye, 1997).

The history of media technologies serves us with many examples relating to the hows and whens of the introduction and usage of various technologies.[6] They underline that technology alone is not capable of creating change, let alone creating a revolution. To agree with Winston, who challenges what he judges a 'myth' of a present-day 'Information Revolution' (1998): the impact of technological changes has to be viewed as the outcome of a history of developments in the social and cultural as well as economical or political environments.

Journalism is embedded within the larger framework of social, cultural, economic and political factors (see also Schudson, 1978; 2003). The evolution of journalism and the adaptation of new technologies thus has to be viewed as a constant flow in which the working procedures of journalists are developed and reshaped. Journalism is an integral part of society, and therefore it must be understood 'as a form of cultural production' (Williams, 2006: 339). Journalism is embedded in a social context and this context influences journalistic processes of gathering, processing and presenting the news. As Nerone (1987) argues, the history of the press is also a history of social or political processes in which needs and requirements of a period are answered.[7] Journalism practice thus is enclosed in and influenced by cultural, social or economical as well as technological developments.[8] Accordingly, transformations in journalism have to be analyzed and contextualized in relation to these developments (see also Hardt, 1990: 351).

One of the first scholars to analyze how technologies and their worldwide distribution impact societies was Marshall McLuhan (1962, 1964). He coined the term 'global village', and attributed this development to media technologies, which were in his view capable of 'shrinking' the world by overcoming distances. The emergence of satellite technology inspired him to think of a world connectedness and lead to the 'vision of a thus far unknown inclusion of entire cultures and societies into a 'global village', just by being exposed to the same sights and sounds which, as a consequence, transformed, i.e. homogenized, cultural habits' (Volkmer, 2003: 11). McLuhan inspired much of the discussion about a globalized world and drew attention to the role of communication technologies by stressing that media technologies affected first and foremost societies and not so much the content of media.

What McLuhan also provoked, though, was a way of thinking about the world as a place where global homogenization processes are at play and in which particular (respectively Western) ideas and practices spread across the globe that erase local colorings. Notions of a globalized society emerged, dominated by Western cultural imperialism and paraphrased with keywords such as 'Westernization', 'Americanization' (see Giddens, 1999: 15 et seq.) or 'McDonaldization' (Ritzer, 1996). Such worldviews propose a convergence of a global culture (e.g. Robins, 1991; for a critique see Beck, 2000: 42 et seq.), in which journalistic organizations become disseminators and proliferators of a 'cultural imperialism' (see for example Herman and McChesney, 1997).[9]

Appadurai on the other hand points out that 'globalization is not the story of cultural homogenization' (1996: 11). Similarly, Beck proposes a 'world society' in which difference and multiplicity are the overarching principles as opposed to unity (2000: 10). Transnational actors enter the scene, influencing society on a global as well as on a local level. Robertson (1992, 1995) has probably set the scene best in this respect by introducing us to what he calls the 'glocalizing' aspect of globalization. Here, globalization is not equated with homogenization, but resembles a much more complex idea of heterogenic movements in a globalized world in which communication technologies enable as well as foster multi-directional information flows as opposed to one-way flows of information. Robertson coined the term 'glocalization' to describe a cultural pattern, and emphasizes that this process of glocalization leads to an increased transnational interdependence. In essence the world has become part of everyday life: whatever happens on the local level has to be seen as an aspect of, and contextualized within, a global setting. The 'local' and the 'global' merge and as Beck underlines:

> From now on nothing which happens on our planet is only a limited local event; all inventions, victories and catastrophes affect the whole world, and we must reorient and reorganize our lives and actions, our organizations and institutions, along a 'local-global' axis. (Beck, 2000: 11)

Cultures thus are becoming increasingly 'glocal'—influenced by what happens locally as well as globally. The 'local' and the 'global' are interconnected—one does not come without the other.[10] The 'local' hence is not vanishing, yet to quote Hannerz:

> We are just giving up the idea that the local is autonomous, that it has an integrity of its own. It would have its significance, rather, as the arena in which a variety of influences come together, acted out perhaps in a unique combination, under those special conditions. (Hannerz, 1996: 27)

Within this setting, culture has to be seen as an entity that is not only influenced by domestic processes, but also by transcending and therefore trans-societal or trans-national movements. At the heart of this perspective lies an idea of a flow of economic as well as cultural processes that crisscross around the globe, 'gain some autonomy on a global level' (Featherstone, 1990: 1) and thereby develop a system of their own going as far as to the formation of 'transnational cultures, which can be understood as genuine 'third cultures' which are orientated beyond national boundaries' (Ibid.: 6). Cultural flows hence produce transnational cultural exchange.

Communication creates a global flow of information exchanged and traded across nation-state borders, cultural borders and continents.

Appadurai has conceptualized such flows in an increasingly deterritorialized global environment. Defined as 'scapes', he identifies the accumulation of new flows on the basis of a complex 'new global cultural economy' (1990: 296). Characteristic of this global cultural economy is a flow across the globe and Appadurai has categorized five dimensions of such global cultural flows: the flow of people (ethnoscapes), the flow of images (mediascapes), the flow of technology (technoscapes), the flow of money (financescapes) and the flow of ideas or ideologies (ideoscapes) (1990: 296–299). Especially important in the context of this study is Appadurai's definition of 'mediascapes':

> 'Mediascapes' refer both to the distribution of the electronic capabilities to produce and disseminate information (newspapers, magazines, television stations, film production studios, etc.) which are now available to a growing number of private and public interests throughout the world; and to the images of the world created by these media. (Appadurai, 1990: 298 et seq.)

Add satellite television, Internet and mobile phones to the list and the 'global flow' character of mediascapes becomes even more evident. Appadurai's scapes indicate that societies are 'on the move', creating 'symbolic' worlds, for example, through the creation of global cultural industries, and with media 'mediating' these ideas and visions from near and afar (see Appadurai, 1996, as well as Lash and Urry, 1994). These new 'flow dynamics' urge new forms of connectivity. With societies (i.e. humans) and their cultures 'on the move', the media and its journalists are 'on the move', too. 'Being on the move' opens up a new space of communication: with people, technology, money, media and ideas in motion, the ways in which humans connect change. With regard to the journalistic sphere, this means that (1) the ways in which users access the news and (2) the ways in which journalists operate within this 'third culture' are in a state of motion, too.

In effect, with globalization we have not only witnessed a reconfigured flow of information, but also the advent of a new media infrastructure that is increasingly autonomous from nation-state contexts and enables a 'transcontinental and transregional flow of political information' (Volkmer, 2003: 11). Globally distributed news channels such as CNN, Al Jazeera and BBC World embody these new flow structures. They operate differently to nation-based and nation-focused news outlets and 'with a new dimension of 'internationalization' of news, where news is not merely distributed 'transborder' but, additionally, transmitted simultaneously in various parts of the world' (Ibid.: 10). Speaking with Appadurai and his idea of disjunctive flows or scapes, such flows are the outcome of a new global cultural economy and these global flows 'are chaotic, varying in speed and intensity, overlapping, attracting or repelling one another' (Bell, 2007: 70).

As the various scapes affected by these global flows show, globalization has to be seen as a 'complex set of processes' (Giddens, 1999: 12). The information age finds journalists at the very heart of these transformations, because after all, information is their business. Their task is to inform about the world and to deliver this information to their audience. Part of their job then is to transmit information and analysis *on* globalization issues, explaining the transformations and making sense of them as well as transmitting them *according to* the new flows of economy and culture around the globe. This includes informing *about* them as well as *moving with* them. By doing so, their relationship with societal changes and global changes is twofold. Firstly, their job is part of this transformation as they act within the determinants of globalization and transformation. Secondly, they not only have to react according to transformations as a matter of adapting their profession, but also as educators and informers on it. Adopting McNair here, journalism has

> become more global, not just in the sense of bringing events in the wider world 'home' to individual members of the audience [as a nationally positioned outlet would do], but also in making the audience itself more international and 'global' in nature [as channels such as BBC World or CNN do]. (McNair, 1998: 131)

Journalists then are the *mediators* of globalization, while also being *affected* by it—globalization hits the profession at its very heart. The characteristics of globalization described above—the 'compression' of the world and the collapse of 'traditional' borders, the transcendence of space, the 'heterogenization' and 'glocalization' of issues and the new connectivity of flows—all together add to a transformation process that leaves its footprint on journalistic cultures.

1.2. JOURNALISTIC CULTURES AND GLOBALIZATION

To speak of a journalism 'culture' affected by such globalization processes in this context is to understand 'culture' as defined by Hanitzsch:

> One can generally speak of culture as a set of *ideas* (values, attitudes, and beliefs), *practices* (of cultural production), and *artifacts* (cultural products, texts). Journalism culture becomes manifest in the way journalists think and act; it can be defined as a particular set of ideas and practices by which journalists, consciously and unconsciously, legitimate their role in society and render their work meaningful for themselves and others. (Hanitzsch, 2007: 369 emphasis in original)

However, this definition should not be mistaken as a statement in favor of the existence of one 'universal' journalism culture. Notions of a journalism 'culture' or journalism 'cultures' are a contested terrain within scholarly research and as Hanitzsch attests, pointing at the 'lack of consensus on the concept of culture and the way it should be applied to research' (2007: 368), we have to be careful not to presume that there is an 'all-encompassing consensus among journalists toward a common understanding and cultural identity of journalism' (Ibid.: 368).[11] What is more, one has to acknowledge the intrinsic pluralism of culture(s) itself, as, for example, national journalistic cultures may differ from one another (Weaver, 1998).[12] Hallin and Mancini (2004), for example, talk about different 'media systems' in Europe and one can take this as a synonym for 'journalistic cultures' (Örnebring, 2009: 6), with European journalists often having a 'local culture' in mind when they produce content. Based on such findings Örnebring attests that 'national filters' might be in place and attests a 'lack of a common journalistic culture in Europe' (Ibid.: 10). In consequence: 'To speak of any journalism culture only makes sense if we assume that there exist other (not necessarily journalistic) cultures to which the former could be compared' (Hanitzsch, 2007: 370).

While acknowledging the existence of more than one journalism culture, one can find common denominators that allow us to group journalists as bearers of specific journalism cultures. Weaver (1998: 456), for example, found quite a number of similar characteristics shared by journalists, after comparing attitudes and journalistic practices of journalists in 21 countries worldwide.[13] Based on such findings, Deuze suggests that

> journalists in elective democracies share similar characteristics and speak of similar values in the context of their daily work, but apply these in a variety of ways to give meaning to what they do. Journalists in all media types, genres and formats carry the ideology of journalism. (Deuze, 2005: 445)

Accordingly, Deuze identifies a universal denominator for journalists in an articulation of a 'shared occupational ideology among newsworkers' (2005: 446). This shared ideology is based upon common agreements among journalists on certain values, such as providing a service to the public, being objective, impartial and fair, being autonomous, having a sense of immediacy and a sense of ethics (Ibid.: 447 et seq.). These shared occupational ideologies can be seen as the 'social cement of the professional group of journalists' (Ibid.: 455).

With news production increasingly affected by processes of globalization, such professional ideologies are being challenged. With the emergence of global competitions among transnationally operating media organizations, journalistic outlets find themselves catapulted into global contexts. Furthermore, they increasingly have to deal with transnational information flows that reach right into the newsroom and onto the editorial desk. The gathering, production, and dissemination of news takes place within a transformed, expanded environment. 'Global' in this sense means that news organizations are trying to operate within a *global infrastructure* and a *global setting*. This global infrastructure is characterized by *non-linear* and *decentralized*—or borderless—information flows. Not only transnationally or globally operating news outlets have been catapulted into this global space. National and local broadcast as well as print outlets have been so, too, with virtually every media organization having its counterpart present online. Through this shift into the online space, even the tiniest local platform turns global to a degree: This occurs, for example, when a local radio station allows a global audience of listeners to tune in via the Internet.[14]

The impact of globalization processes reaches even further with regard to the structural organization of the nation-state as well as with regard to the journalistic sphere, as the concept of borders set by nation-states comes under siege. On a political level 'the operation of states in an ever more complex international system both limits their autonomy (in some spheres radically) and impinges increasingly upon their sovereignty' (Held, 1995: 135). As Beck points out:

> The national state is a territorial state: that is, its power is grounded upon attachment to a particular place (upon control over membership, current legislation, border defense, and so on). The world society which, in the wake of globalization, has taken shape in many (not only economic) dimensions is undermining the importance of the national state, because a multiplicity of social circles, communication networks, market relations and lifestyles, none of them specific to any particular locality, now cut across the boundaries of the national state. (Beck, 2000: 4)

Journalism in this environment cannot be defined within national contexts, but rather within global settings. This transnational connectivity is particularly crucial for our understanding of foreign reporting. A distinction between 'foreign' and 'domestic' is grounded in traditional configurations of the world, as being divided into nation-states with news outlets placed within these borders. Such distinctions are about to collapse in an age of increasing connectivity and a fundamentally changed global structure of communication. Contextualization of news and events follow, as Stanton puts it, a 'sushi train' (2007: 3), with only a few stories being reported on in Western media outlets and contextualized solely within 'an unacceptable frame' of what he refers to as 'localization' (Ibid.: 1). Yet, with decentralization of news production and non-linear news flows gaining influence on news agendas, news production and dissemination processes are being restructured within global paradigms. Satellite signals and the ever-proliferating Internet have enabled transnational forms of communication and an exchange of news material that calls traditional concepts of 'domestic' and 'foreign' into question, triggering new modes of operations in the newsrooms and opening up spaces for new cooperation models. Journalism is no longer positioned 'conceptually in the center of one society' but integrated into the communication culture of a world 'network' society (Volkmer and Heinrich, 2008: 51).

This paradigmatic shift has crucial consequences for journalism. The repositioning of journalistic organizations within this global 'network' requires adaptive moves that would reorient journalism within a new geography.

The challenges of globalization processes for journalistic organizations then are threefold:

1. The emergence of a global news sphere contributes to a bigger number of competitors;
2. New space and time constraints pose pressure on journalists; and
3. Larger amounts of information overflowing (national) borders need to be filtered and contextualized within a larger setting.

Thus, in an era of globalization, national determining factors and the sovereignty of nationally operating news outlets are challenged. As the world leans toward a glocalized 'world society' (Beck, 2000), journalistic cultures follow suit and face the challenges of repositioning themselves within this glocalized sphere. In a world of global flows:

> The notion of closed spaces has become illusory. No country or group can shut itself off from others. Various economic, cultural and political forms therefore collide with one another, and things that used to be taken for granted (including in the Western model) will have to be justified anew. 'World society', then, denotes the totality of social relationships which are *not* integrated into or determined (or determinable) by national-state politics. (Beck, 2000: 10 emphasis in original)

Yet, what happens to journalism when it is contextualized within these transnational settings rather than based within nationally operating media systems? How is journalistic production and dissemination affected? Where do journalists position themselves when confronted with global flows of information?

This is the point where Castells' network paradigm assists in better understanding how journalistic work can fit in with this new 'global order' (Giddens, 1999: 6 et seq.). Castells' work explains how sociability is shaped by technology. He describes how social structures of 'connected' countries are moving toward a globally networked society that is supported by the necessary technology that enables those with access to them to overcome the borders of place and time. The 'network society' then is a new societal organizational form. It is built around a new communication structure and upon new patterns of communication flows. Here, information does not necessarily follow a one-to-one path, but the logic of a multi-directional roster of communication that holds the option of including more than two interaction partners. The Internet in this respect operates as the decisive instrument. It is 'a communication tool that allows, for the first time, the communication of many to many, in chosen time, on a global scale' (Castells, 2002b: 2).

1.3. DIGITAL TECHNOLOGIES AND THE PARADIGM SHIFT: THE DEVELOPMENT OF THE NETWORK SOCIETY

> The emergence of a new electronic communication system characterized by its global reach, its integration of all communication media, and its potential interactivity is changing and will change forever our culture.
> (Castells, 2000c: 357)

Castells' network paradigm explains the shape of today's developed societies and their interaction patterns. He aims to identify the key determining factors that create social change and focuses on the structural aspects that play a role in the creation of what he has termed the social structure of our times: the 'network society'. This social structure takes form on the basis of, and is powered by, digital information technologies (such as the Internet). The paradigm of the 'network society' makes for a new organization model of society in which our ability to connect beyond time and space constraints takes center stage.

One of the most important aspects Castells adds to the discussion of the proliferation of 'global flows' with regard to the study of journalistic work is his outline of the importance of digital technologies and their role in organizing such flows. He explains that without these tools, global connectivity would simply be impossible. Castells eventually makes clear that digitalization is the very foundation of our evolving social structure as it supports new ways of connectivity.[15] He thus attempts to 'make sense of this new world' restructured by digital tools in use and coined as 'cyberspace' in William Gibson's novel *Neuromancer* as early as 1984:[16]

> Cyberspace. A consensual hallucination experienced daily by billions of legitimate operators. [...] A graphic representation of data abstracted from the banks of every computer in the human system. Unthinkable complexity. Lines of light ranged in the nonspace of the mind, clusters and constellations of data. Like city lights, receding . . .
> (Gibson, 1995: 67)

Gibson draws a picture of 'unthinkable complexity' within cyberspace that corresponds with Castells' description of social structures developing in the information age. For Castells:

> Cyberspace is not a place. It is a corridor between places. You live in your place, and then you circulate in cyberspace, meeting people who live in other places. However, you can also use cyberspace to be in your mental universe. [. . .] So, cyberspace is a hyperspace, a space of the mind, that you practice every day, meeting people and thoughts from other places and from other times. (Castells and Ince, 2003: 28)

What Gibson described in 1984 was a structure of the world based upon new networks of connectivity and characterized by a flood of data running around the globe without necessarily following specific directions or strings of information flows. It is a networked world whose changing shape ineluctably has consequences and effects for the work of journalists and the ways they communicate as well as the ways they gather, produce and distribute information. What Castells adds to this notion of cyberspace is that the virtual reality Gibson might have had in mind now is merging with the 'real' reality of our lives.[17] The evolving network patterns of the information age are what Castells conceptualizes as the emergence of a new social structure—the 'network society':

> A new world is taking shape in this end of millennium. It originated in historical coincidence, around the late 1960s and mid-1970s, of three *independent* processes: the information technology revolution; the economic crisis of both capitalism and statism, and their subsequent restructuring; and the blooming of cultural social movements, such as libertarianism, human rights, feminism, and environmentalism. The interaction between these processes, and the reactions they triggered, brought into being a new dominant social structure, the network society; a new economy, the informational / global economy; and a new culture, the culture of real virtuality. (Castells 2000b: 336, emphasis in original)

With his idea of society taking on the shape of a 'network', Castells sets up the network paradigm as the basis for the information age. According to this, 'dominant functions and processes in the information age are increasingly organized around networks' (Castells, 2000c: 500). The network structure then suits 'the increasing complexity of interaction' and is capable of following 'unpredictable patterns of development arising from the creative power of such interaction' (Ibid.: 70). It is a flexible structure allowing multi-directional and non-linear (information) flows and decentralized interaction patterns with multiple points of connections within this network.[18]

The network thus is an organizational structure that corresponds ideally with a technological tool such as the Internet. As 'networks are horizontal, non-hierarchical, fluid and mobile, and their unit of work is the project' (Bell, 2007: 63), the sphere of the Internet is structured along these lines. Information crisscrosses through the spheres of the web, with a seemingly endless amount of information flowing through it as data bits.

This new connectivity model as presented by Castells holds many implications for the study of journalism and for an assessment of evolving global news flows. However, it should not go unnoted here that, although widely acknowledged, Castells' argument has its critics and the network paradigm has been contested. Especially the critical engagements of Webster (2002, 2004) and Garnham (2004) do stand out. Both highlight the importance of Castells for scholarly research and Garnham, for example, refers to the work as the 'most sophisticated' version of a theory of the information society (2004: 167). However, both Webster and Garnham also systematically challenge Castells' work. Garnham, for example, is critical of Castells' central idea of networks as being clustered around information technologies and questions the argument 'that it is the growth in the speed, reach and functionality of communication networks that is driving economic and social development' (2004: 172). Contrary to this, he points out that networks have always been in existence and Castells' 'claim of novelty, and thus of revolutionary change, is made for what in fact are long-term structures and processes' (Ibid.: 182). Thus in Garnham's view, Castells' overemphasis on the evolution of networks as drivers of social change 'exaggerate[s] the novelty of networks as forms of social and economic organization within which power is exercised, and thus at the same time exaggerate[s] both the extent and the novelty of the impact of ICTs' (Ibid.: 173). [19]

In line with this, quite a few scholars are concerned with an interpretation of social realities today who take completely different directions and who do provide somewhat 'alternative' views to Castells'. Herbert Schiller (1998) and Dan Schiller (1999), for example, offer another interpretation of the interplay between technological developments and the shape of social structures. They are far more pessimistic about the future of societies and concentrate on the impact of the economy on production modes. Herbert Schiller (1984, 1998) argues that the spread of information networks rather works in favor of capitalism and of transnational corporations, and that these networks support a strengthening of transnational corporations globally. Capitalism here is viewed as the triumphant ideology dictating over social realities (see Webster's analysis of Herbert Schiller, 2002: 124–161). Similarly, Dan Schiller (1999) centers his attention on market forces and identifies them as the major drivers of social change and respectively as the constituents of today's societies. [20] Webster summarizes their argument and points out that information networks 'have frequently been designed and put in place in the interests of these major corporate clients' (2002: 103). Accordingly, Dan Schiller is skeptic about the potential of cyberspace and warns that market-driven forces as well as other social forces are as present on the Internet as anywhere else. He argues:

> Knowledge carried through the Internet is no less shaped by social forces than it is elsewhere. Far from delivering us into a high-tech Eden, in fact, cyberspace itself is being rapidly colonized by the familiar workings of the market system. Across their breadth and depth, computer networks link with existing capitalism to massively broaden the effective reach of the marketplace. Indeed, the Internet comprises nothing less than the central production and control apparatus of an increasingly supranational market system. (Schiller, 1999: xiv)

According to Dan Schiller, today's capitalist structures thus are stronger than technological forces and do rule online as well as offline: 'Networks are directly generalizing the social and cultural range of the capitalist economy as never before. That is why I refer to this new epoch as one of *digital capitalism*' (1999: xiv emphasis in original). The Internet then follows market logics. Social inequalities here are rather exacerbated, as market-driven policies not only influence but rather govern the central communication tools of today: telecommunications systems.

On the contrary, Castells' argument for a restructurization of society on the basis of the development of digital networks implicates that transnational corporations, for example, are profoundly threatened by the changes in interaction patterns and are challenged to adapt to new communication dynamics and practices (Webster, 2002: 103). According to Castells, 'the logic of the network is more powerful than the powers in the network' (1996: 193), thus flattening power structures and favoring corporations as well as organizations who do implement network structures.

This view does significantly collide with interpretations of social reality as presented by Dan Schiller, who views globalization developments and technological advancements as market driven, arguing that transnational corporations are being empowered (1999: xiv; 37–89). The corporate-led market system is being strengthened (globally) by digital networks and according to this idea then, 'digital capitalism' concurrently aggravates already existing inequalities and enforces domination patterns (Ibid.: 209). Arguing with Dan Schiller and others, one thus could accuse Castells of underestimating the power of a capitalist-run system and especially the capitalist class system in which an elitist ruling class and class inequalities proliferate difference.[21]

This argument stands in line with Garnham's accusation of technological determinism. According to this, Castells neglects that 'it is not the technical but the social relations of production that are determinant' (Garnham, 2004: 174). Or as Webster argues, Castells

> must face the charge, irrespective of his somewhat different terminology, that he regards change as developing though [sic] a series of

hierarchically tiered stages of the sort familiar to all readers of post-industrial theory [. . .]. It follows, as it must, that he argues that a certain technological foundation is the prerequisite and determinant of all social and political life. (Webster, 2002: 120)

Taken together, the arguments that have been raised against Castells thus far range from the accusation of putting too much stress on the revolutionary character of information technologies to his overemphasis on the centrality of the 'network' for social change and social structures to the accusation of technological determinism. Yet, to argue with Webster, who is one of Castells' biggest critics but also one of his admirers: So far, the 'network society' is the 'single most persuasive analysis of the world today' (2002: 265). And even if it is contested, it inherits an inner logic that is in my view intriguingly convincing and comes as an extremely useful analysis tool in the assessment and interpretation of transformations gaining shape in the information age.

Therefore, I argue that Castells' model of connectivity accentuated in the network paradigm can be translated into the study of journalism. In effect, the amount of information in circulation creates a notion of a 'chaotic' news journalism environment at the beginning of the twenty-first century to speak in the terminology of McNair (2005, 2006). Drawing upon chaos theory, he offers a model of communication that outlines 'cultural chaos' as the underlying structure of the twenty-first century information environment. Communication systems now are 'fundamentally non-linear, and thus highly contingent. Like the strange attractors of chaos science, they exhibit structure, but of an irregular kind' (McNair, 2006: xiv). What is more, it is not only the growing quantity of information in circulation that characterizes the information age, but also the new speed of delivery fostered by digital communication tools. In relation to this, Giddens talks about a 'runaway world' (1999); a world that seems out of control. It is what McNair describes as 'an era of *cultural chaos*, [in which] people have access to more information than ever before' (2006: 199 emphasis added).

Within this sphere characterized by uncertainties and constant information flows, journalistic organizations are less controllable by powerful (political or economical) elites. McNair's 'chaos paradigm' opposes a 'control' or 'dominance' paradigm that carries the underlying notion that journalists are controlled by and act as 'agents' of political elites and institutions, which ideologically dominate news production and producers.[22] He explains:

In the context of globalised news culture, to talk about chaos is to argue that the journalistic environment, far from being an instrument or apparatus of social control by a dominant elite, has become more and more like the weather and the oceans in the age of global warming—turbulent, unpredictable, extreme. Like storm fronts, journalistic information flows around the world in globally connected streams of real-time data, forming stories which become news and then descend through the networked nodes of the world wide web to impact on national public spheres. Some stories, like some storms, blow themselves out harmlessly. Others, such as the Abu Ghraib prisoner-abuse scandal of 2004, 'get legs' and build to catastrophic political crises, despite the efforts of public relations and spin professionals to reassert elite control. (McNair, 2006: xviii)

Communication flows then have fundamentally changed. They produce 'unpredictable and largely uncontrollable outcomes' (McNair, 2005: 156), with national and global spheres increasingly being connected. What marks this quintessential change is the unpredictability of (journalistic) communication. These new dynamics of communication processes are manifest in many ways: new personnel enter the production chain and a more diverse palette of communicators adds information to the news agenda of media outlets, which shapes content output. Journalism now is practiced

within a dramatically altered information and communication environment—a multichannel, multimedia environment of unprecedented complexity and connectedness, as different from the Cold War era of the late twentieth century as that period in turn was from the coffee house culture in early modern Europe. (McNair, 2006: 105)

Accordingly, theoretical frameworks designed in the late twentieth-century Cold War era such as *The Four Theories of the Press* developed by Siebert et al. (1956) fall short of paying tribute to this 'chaos' of a global news culture, as they cluster (Western) journalism cultures into separate entities based on the notion that nation-states confine their own press systems. These frameworks do not help to reconceptualize journalistic culture with regard to the impact of changes and challenges proliferated by processes of globalization and the emergence of digital technology. What is more, professional identities of journalists are also being challenged, as journalists have to reorient themselves within a restructured global landscape. To quote Deuze,

the global picture of journalism is constantly and perhaps exponentially changing to such an extent that one has to analyze and discuss the main attributes of such (potential) changes in order to successfully study, describe and explain contemporary journalism. (Deuze, 2005: 450)

With a change in the 'picture of journalism', then, a revision of occupational ideologies and in accordance with this a revision of current journalistic practice is necessary. Reconfigured analytical frameworks are needed in order to describe an evolving global news culture.[23]

Castells' paradigm of the 'network society', with the 'network' as the key format of interaction patterns, can assist in this regard. The structure of the network is in effect just as 'chaotic', with non-linear and decentralized communication flows in action. Characterized by altered communication flows, the paths on which information travels are not as predictable. A network structure holds by far more options for connection (as well as disconnection), leading to more complex interaction patterns than in an unnetworked world. The idea of 'cultural chaos' thus corresponds with Castells' model of the 'network society'. Here, communication does not flow in a linear fashion, following consistent timelines and direction, but crisscrosses through time and space. Information is floating through space in a 'many-to-many manner'. This is what Castells describes as the 'space of flows' (see, for example, Castells, 1996: 407–459). It is a space in which communication floats over territorial borders and connects places, making them independent of their direct surrounding environments and shifting them into space. The 'space of flows', finding its realization in the networked activities of the Internet, is the model that describes 'the formation of trans-territorial complexes of activities, such as financial spaces or media production spaces or high-technology world chains of production, made of specific places that were connected with other places throughout the planet' (Castells and Ince, 2003: 25). Within this sphere, there is no such thing as fixed ways of communication or limits to the number of communicators taking part. There are also no restrictions on the ways in which communication flows—apart from the restrictions relating to the accessibility of technology. It is as simple as that: no access to technology means no access to the network.[24]

Linear structures of communication are thus being replaced in the 'space of flows' by flexible communication strings, characterized by their non-linearity within a decentralized global news culture. Geographically speaking, communication has moved out of place and into space—a space that has been made accessible via digital technologies.

1.4. WHAT THE NETWORK PARADIGM HOLDS FOR THE SPHERE OF JOURNALISM

Within societies characterized by network patterns, journalistic cultures are being shifted onto a newly defined map with altered coordinates: A reconfigured geography is taking shape as a result of the new flow and speed of news around the globe. Whereas a geographical map on paper provides coordinates of distances between certain places on earth, digital technology enables information to cross this distance in virtually no time. An Internet-based video-conference tool such as Skype, for example, moves communication into space and renders the 'real' distance between places as outlined on a paper map practically obsolete. It is with respect to such changes that the paradigm of the network can assist to sketch the journalism sphere anew—with all its uncertainties, such as the new tempo of news flow crossing national borders instantaneously and with its global shape. Digital technologies have increased the speed of information and shortened the distance to remote places on the map, laying the foundations for new connection options in journalistic space. New connectivity strings are laid out that tie places together across (physical) distance. These ties resemble the new forms of connectivity in a network age, with the Internet being the prime example of connection flows across the globe:

> The Internet, thus viewed as a metaphor for a new global communication infrastructure 'decentralizes' the advanced globalization process and creates, again following Castells' argumentation, a new social, cultural and political infrastructure, which cannot be taken seriously enough. (Volkmer, 2003: 13)

Adding to the shifts in notions of space flows is the new speed characteristic of the information age, which has led to the idea of a 'shrinking world'. Hassan and Purser explain: 'The meter of clock time that drove the industrial revolution is now being compressed and accelerated by the infinitely more rapid time-loaded functions of high-speed computerization' (2007: 11). Castells identifies this phenomenon as 'timeless time' (2000c: 460–499), and Hassan describes it as 'network time' in which 'the numberless asynchronous spaces of the network society, created and inhabited by people and ICTs in interaction, *undermine* and *displace* the time of the clock' (2007: 51 emphasis in original). Within these new parameters of time and space, notions of 'desequencing' are at play:

> As a result of living in a multimedia age with limitless access to streams of live and archived material, as well as ever more wondrous ways to predict or imagine the future, we are exposed to a montage of instants wrenched from temporal context: past, present and future are disassembled and reassembled for us and by us. (Bell, 2007: 75)

Thus, a dense net of information is spanning the globe in a rather 'chaotic' exchange of information as opposed to a linear flow of information. The information 'goes with the flow', so to speak. Yet, this new structure (of society and accordingly of journalism) is far away from lacking links placed within these networks. As Castells notes:

> The fact that a structure is flexible and decentralized in its working does not imply that there are no nodes. On the contrary, a network is based on nodes and their interconnections. The key issue is that these nodes may reconfigure themselves according to new tasks and goals, and that they may grow or diminish in importance depending on the

knowledge and information that they win or lose. (Castells and Ince, 2003: 24)

What organizes 'chaos' within this space of flows then are the *nodes* that draw together information from various points.[25] These nodes bundle information. Communication flows overlap and each node is connected to various others. A network is thus characterized by the interconnectedness of its nodes:

> A node is the point at which a curve intersects itself. What a node is, concretely speaking, depends on the kind of concrete networks of which we speak. They are stock exchange markets, and their ancillary advanced service centers, in the network of global financial flows. They are national councils of ministers and European Commissioners in the political network that governs the European Union. They are coca fields and poppy fields, clandestine laboratories, secret landing strips, street gangs, and money-laundering financial institutions in the network of drug traffic that penetrates economies, societies, and states throughout the world. They are television systems, entertainment studios, computer graphics milieux, news teams, and mobile devices generating, transmitting, and receiving signals in the global network of the new media at the roots of cultural expression and public opinion in the Information Age. (Castells, 2000c: 501)

In the context of journalistic gathering, production and dissemination, I speak of the 'concrete network' of an evolving (global) journalism sphere. Journalistic organizations represent nodes situated within global information flows or, to put it another way, journalistic outlets are repositioned as nodes according to the new geography of space. The structural pattern of the network assigns the place of an *information node* to journalistic organizations today. Journalists gather, produce and disseminate information out of information flows within a global news sphere. Journalistic nodes thus stand for connection points in space that gather, modify and disperse information material. The 'space of flows' in this context is the space in which journalistic nodes are located and able to connect to other nodes acting as information providers for journalistic organizations—be it politicians or public relations organizations, NGOs or other journalistic outlets.

However, this repositioning of journalistic outlets within a network space is not an easy step to take. The network structure enabled by technologies such as the Internet also enables a larger number of news distributors than before to form information nodes and to contribute information. Information nodes within this web can be bloggers, citizen journalists, and creators of user-generated content, as well as journalists operating independently from traditional journalistic organizations. The question is: Are the ways in which traditional journalistic outlets are currently organized in tune with the changes taking place in the sphere of information exchange? Are journalistic outlets prepared for these new information flows, and are they prepared to act as an *information node* in a network sphere? This is one of the crucial issues this book addresses and the implications of structural change for journalistic organizations will be discussed in detail in Chapters 3 and 4.

At this point, though, I want to concentrate on the pressures journalistic organizations face in the wake of globalization processes and the evolution of the structural order of the network. The changing patterns of interaction within an evolving global news sphere are characterized by the non-linearity of information flows and the decentralization of (journalistic) organizations within a network sphere of information nodes. This profound transformation goes against a notion that understands the operation of journalistic outlets as 'closed' systems.

1.5. JOURNALISTIC ORGANIZATIONS AND THE PRESSURES OF GLOBAL INFORMATION FLOWS

'Systems', according to Luhmann (1995, 2000), are the outcome of the functional differentiation of modern society, with each system fulfilling certain functions (systems include, for instance, politics, law, economy, religion, etc.). Social order is formed through the development of social systems that set boundaries against their environments:

> Modern society organizes itself by delegating different functions to specialized societal systems in order to cope with societal problems which could not be solved from other systems, or before the system has emerged. We call this phenomenon the functional differentiation of society. (Görke and Scholl, 2006: 647)

One of these systems named by Luhmann is the 'mass media', which carries the responsibility of providing information and knowledge to the members of society.[26] This is the system that looks upon and informs society about its other constituent systems: 'Whatever we know about our society, or indeed about the world in which we live, we know through the mass media' (Luhmann, 2000: 1). Journalistic outlets, as part of the mass media system, function in society as mediators who distribute knowledge and construct reality.[27] They create meaning and furthermore they decide and distinguish, on the basis of their system-specific code, what has to be counted as information and what can be considered as non-information (Ibid.: 17). In Luhmann's view, this 'mass media system' is a closed operation. Dissemination technologies are in the hands of the 'mass media' alone, disenabling the environment's capacity to infiltrate or influence the information diffusion of the mass media system:

The crucial point at any rate is *that no interaction among those co-present can take place between sender and receivers.* Interaction is ruled out by the interposition of technology, and this has far-reaching consequences which define for us the concept of mass media. (Ibid.: 2 emphasis in original)

Luhmann is very clear that a system is only stable once it has set an 'operationally produced boundary' between the system and the environment (Ibid.: 10).[28] Therefore, even though a system may need stimuli from the outside, the operations within the systems are configured internally (Görke and Scholl, 2006: 648; Edgar and Sedgwick, 2002: 400 et seq.).

However, in a network age, the task of defining clear boundaries has become problematic on various levels. The 'sub-system' journalism as part of the mass media system faces new conditions of operation. Closed systems, in the sense Luhmann understands them, no longer exist within the logic of 'cultural chaos' and the space of information in a 'network society'. Viewing media as a closed system operating without major impact from the environment in an increasingly 'chaotic' information space consequently does not hold up to the realities of societies in the information age. A closed mass media forbids interaction and necessitates a top-down communication order (with the journalist being the news disseminator and the audience being the silent receiver of information). This does not correspond with (global) information flows in a network society. A journalistic organization cannot operate isolated from such flows. These flows now transgress (nation-state) borders and reach right onto the editorial desk of a news outlet. They demand interaction. Take the case of a user who comments on a topic within the interactive spaces offered on the website of a journalistic outlet. What do you make of alternative information disseminators, such as bloggers, entering the scene? These new players are not part of a so-called mass-media system. They instead function on the same grounds, producing and disseminating information as well as commentary and opinion. How can a journalistic system be 'closed' when the structural pattern of the network and its revised 'news geography' demands the options of multi-directional information strings connecting the node of the journalistic organization with various other nodes in the network sphere?

In short: the traditional system of journalism is under heavy pressure through new modes of connectivity, with increasing levels of interaction and more actors taking part in the processes of information dissemination. These new flows are proliferated by digital technologies, which Luhmann did not have in mind at the time of developing his theory. Digital technologies enable new modes of connectivity and a high level of interactivity and impose pressures on operationally closed systems. In a world characterized by the blurring of boundaries related to neither time nor place constraints, a closed system does not function well, if at all. Instead, journalistic outlets are challenged to adapt to network structures.

This is not to say that systems as such no longer exist in a network society. The question that arises is: Does the exclusion model referred to by Luhmann hold up to the new pace, the new space and the dissolution of boundaries in the information age? The new geography in effect leads to the reconceptualization of the system, and must include a redefinition of the functions journalists may fulfill within society. With the dissolution of boundaries and with information dissemination taking place within an evolving global news sphere, journalists are urged to redefine how they operate. With digital technologies impacting the shape of societies and their connection modes, the forms and formats of journalism are reformulated as well. Journalism remains a system and it remains the system with the main responsibility of distributing information. Yet, it operates within a different societal environment—the network society. What is needed is the reconfiguration of journalism structured as what I want to call *network journalism*—a journalism characterized by new modes of connectivity, with strings of information floating through an interactive space in which journalistic outlets act as central information nodes. This structure of *network journalism* will be presented in detail in Chapter 3.

1.6. DEFINING THE TRANSFORMATIVE SPHERES OF JOURNALISM IN THE INFORMATION AGE

The development of a global news sphere within the parameters of globalization and the spread of the network affects *all* journalistic organizations. The transformation of journalism impacts print, broadcast and online news outlets alike and does not make distinctions between locally, nationally or transnationally distributing news organizations. It alters the whole sphere of journalism and with it each and every single producer of journalistic content, no matter what outlet he or she is working for—from the tiniest local radio station all the way through to global players such as CNN or Al Jazeera. Journalistic organizations operate within a new global network structure and are challenged by the effects this fundamental transformation has on their work. The evolving global news sphere is characterized by new modes of connectivity and *each and every single journalistic outlet represents a node* in this altered global information system.

Accordingly, the following three aspects demarcate the three defining transformative spheres of journalism in the information age:

1. The network becomes the model of journalistic interaction. The network pattern is the basic structure of the revised geography of news flows, allowing information flows in multiple directions.
2. Within this network structure, information strings (i.e. strands that connect various information pools and carry information in multiple directions) evolve and connectivity flows travel along non-linear paths, conveying a remapped geography of news flows.

3. Journalistic outlets transform into key information nodes within the network of the global news sphere. These nodes need to be reorganized around the new news flows of the information age.

In the following chapters I will develop the paradigm of *network journalism*. To illustrate the transformations caused by globalization processes and the introduction of new technologies, I will first proceed with a brief historical case study in which I examine the evolution of connectivity in newsrooms. An analysis of the introduction of telegraph technology to newsrooms will demonstrate how news once traveled in a journalism sphere defined by relative stability and controllability. It was a centralized news sphere, dominated by linear news flows. The case of the telegraph will also demonstrate that technologies as tools of newsgathering, production and dissemination have always been crucial to the work of journalists. Information needs paths to travel along, and these paths are dependent on technological devices. In the case of the telegraph, it took about half a century for newsrooms to adopt and adapt to the new modes of connectivity.

2 News Agencies and Telegraph Technology
The Evolution of Global News Exchange Networks

> The most important fact about the telegraph is at once the most obvious and innocent: It permitted for the first time the effective separation of communication from transportation. [...] The telegraph [...] allowed symbols to move independently of and faster than transportation. To put it in a slightly different way, the telegraph freed communication from the constraints of geography.
>
> (Carey, 1989: 203 et seq.)

A look into history is a good starting point to analyze what it is that is so significantly changing our societal interaction patterns as well as the way the public informs itself or—for that matter—the way in which news organizations inform their publics. The nineteenth century holds a great example of how the introduction of a new technology played a significant role in determining exchange patterns of news. It was the century of telegraph technology in which for the first time in history news organizations were formed that strategically built networks of global connection: It was the century in which news agencies evolved.[1] This chapter highlights the changes telegraph technology brought about for the exchange of news, especially in light of the developments we are facing today, putting these latest developments into historical perspective yet also pinpointing the very difference digital technology tools bring to today's gathering, production and distribution processes.

In many ways, news agencies can be viewed as precursors of the existing twenty-first-century journalistic networks. Their development was in large part due to the fact that businessmen such as the famous Julius Reuter in Europe understood adapting a new technology to the practice of news exchange. Telegraph technology significantly sped up the process of delivering information across distances. With its introduction, long-distance connections were made available and international information strings evolved. This decisive shift in processes of information distribution demarcates the 'starting point for the information society [...] shrinking the geographical gaps between communities, nations, and continents' (Campbell, 2004: 4). And the development of telegraph technology is the first example of a global communication network that enabled instantaneous communication over distance. The use of telegraph technology by news agencies changed the modes of connectivity among geographically dispersed news organizations. News could travel in virtually no time, creating what Standage dubs the 'Victorian Internet', trussing up distant places across a 'worldwide web of wires' (1998: 135):

> Modern Internet users are in many ways the heirs of the telegraphic tradition, which means that today we are in a unique position to understand the telegraph, and the telegraph, in turn, can give us a fascinating perspective on the challenges, opportunities, and pitfalls of the Internet. (Standage, 1998: 2)

Telegraph technology combined with innovations such as steam-powered engines, railroads and steamships laid the foundation for the evolution of international news networks. News agencies created production networks around the telegraph and formed the first highly organized outlets for journalistic news production and distribution systems operating nationally *as well as* internationally. They were arranged along the telegraph lines and relied on a network of reporters and stringers who delivered news to central agency offices.[2] News agencies in the nineteenth century operated mainly on the basis of a centralized organizational structure. They focused on the needs of the specific nation where their headquarters were located and journalistic production was dependent on the telegraph. Which places to get news from stood in direct relation to the infrastructures of the individual information network of an agency and could only reach as far as the telegraph wires. The telegraph thus only allowed for a linear flow of information from the central offices of an agency to its subscribers, as the technology could only tie one point to another (as opposed to the 'many-to-many' connections the Internet allows). What is more, telegraph technology was expensive and only a handful of organizations could utilize it for their purposes and thus develop a monopoly of international news exchange (Boyd-Barrett, 1980; Blondheim, 1994; Carey, 1989; Read, 1999; Thussu, 2000).

2.1. ROOTS OF JOURNALISTIC PRACTICE: THE EVOLUTION OF NEWS EXCHANGE

The longing for 'what's news' (Raymond, 1996: 1 et seq.) is as old as humankind, as many scholars concerned with the history of news and journalism have pointed out. The works of Innis (1950, 1951) and Stephens (2007) show that the demand for news can be traced back to ancient times, and so can the diverse technological methods supporting various forms of news deliveries.[3] Raymond has summarized this vividly in his work on the history of the newsbook:

The desire for news, with its concomitant dangers, has probably been an aspect of most societies through history. News is a constituent of communication, and communication binds together societies and cultures. It is a basic fact of sensuous human activity. (Raymond, 1996: 2)

Thussu (2000: 12) explains that 'informal networks of travelers and traders' have passed on news across distance long before technologies enabled the detachment of news from the physical presence of a human acting as the bearer of a message. What differed over the centuries, though, have been the ways in which to disseminate news. With the invention of the printing press in the fifteenth century, for instance, the written word increasingly gained influence.[4] For the first time in history it was possible to generate copies in large numbers. This reproduction technique 'prepared the ground for the mass production of books, magazines, and newspapers' (Füssel, 2001: 3). The advent of the printing press also created the fundament for more organized models of news distribution. However, infrastructures such as regular postal services were not in place just then and prevented continuous news dissemination over distance.

The expansion of international trade, though, increased the demand for news (Thussu, 2000: 21; Stephens, 2007: 64 et seq.). News was a commodity that gained importance for businesses and organizations emerged that were dedicated to gathering and distributing information, especially in centers of international trade such as London, Amsterdam or Paris. Precursors of today's correspondents operated as early as the sixteenth century:

'Walking newsmen' appeared in public places in the greater cities where people expected to hear news in exchange for a coin, similar to the *gazetta* on the Rialto Bridge. In Paris during the sixteenth century there existed about 15,000 *nouvellistes* or walking newsmen, some of them in the Tuielleries; in other cities they worked near markets or in the harbour. Gathering points for newsmongers in London were behind St Pauls; during the first half of the seventeenth century news writers used to meet near Westminster. (Høyer, 2003: 452)

Around the same time, the court in London hired private news writers (Høyer, 2003: 452; Raymond, 1996: 5). In the last quarter of the sixteenth century, occasional news pamphlets were distributed in London and around 1600 periodical publishing started, with the appearance of the first coranto in Amsterdam in 1620 and the first newsbook, a weekly periodical containing domestic news, in November 1641 in London (Raymond, 1996: 5 et seq.).[5] London also quickly evolved into the newspaper 'capital' of the world and remained so until the middle of the nineteenth century, due to the large population and a comparatively high level of literacy as well as of press freedom (Høyer, 2003: 451). Assisted by advances in transportation and mail services, 'the post office became the hub of a network for news exchange, a centre for news and rumour as well as for written newsletters distributed to a circle of subscribers' (Ibid.: 452). At the beginning of the eighteenth century, though, these loose news exchange networks were still far away from being organized. In the preliminary newsrooms of evolving newspaper and journal outlets, job demarcations for staff were not yet in place. As Smith claims, editors were mere processors of material and the printers were in charge of the outlet. Writers and correspondents delivered stories on an irregular basis, but:

> There existed as yet no professional or occupational group whose task it was to provide an unblemished version of events. There were no techniques as yet developed within the business of writing by which any form of 'reportage' was manufactured within the journalistic enterprise. Accounts of events were taken from foreign journals, from private newsletters, hospitals, prisons, markets, courts and great houses. Most material which reached the medium of periodical printed papers was placed there by its source, or direct from its source. (Smith, 1978: 158)

In the long run, though, the creation of publications such as newsbooks encouraged the structural separation of tasks in the newsroom. The work was split between editors, printers and publishers (Raymond, 1996: 21 et seq.; see also Høyer, 2003: 453). Over the next centuries, newsroom organization was to become clearly structured so that news could be delivered faster, across longer distances and in less time as the

> regularity of publication demanded a reliable supply of news through various networks and infrastructures: of readily available writers when needed, of compositors and pressmen, and of a regular functioning postal service or other form of distribution. These different functions of publishing eventually became staffed by a host of crafts and occupations within hierarchies of responsibilities for the daily routines. (Høyer, 2003: 453)

By the mid eighteenth century newsrooms had evolved into businesses selling news as a product. In the second half of the eighteenth century, reporters became increasingly specialized, the title of 'journalist' was introduced and journalism emerged as a profession (Høyer, 2003: 455). Despite these trends, though, news still traveled fairly slowly from one place to another, even though attempts were made to speed up the process of information dissemination over distance. To illustrate, at the beginning of the nineteenth century, newspapers in the United States awaiting news to report from overseas 'had increasingly tried to be up-to-date, especially in reporting the arrival of ships and in printing the news they brought with them. The New York papers began to send out small boats to incoming ships to gather up news' (Schudson, 1978: 26). Before the advent of electric communication tools, though, newsgathering and distribution processes across distance were still infrequent.

With the introduction of the telegraph, the notion of 'distance' began to change. News could now travel across the wires instantaneously, leading to the creation of a new 'sense of place' which eventually drew journalism into a 'global space', as Rantanen argues: 'Electronic news in the 19th century started to build the bridge between here and there by bringing places where events occurred to readers of news' (2003: 438). For the first time in history, 'the transmission of information and messages was separated from the physical act of delivery' (Chapman, 2005: 59) and connectivity structures started to evolve, which enabled a flow of news beyond local places. Equally important to note is the accelerated speed of transmitting information fostered by the telegraph. Nye points out that:

> Before the telegraph, information traveled no faster than a horse or a sailing ship; afterwards it moved at the speed of light. Since 1838, the speed of transmission has improved relatively little, but the distances involved and the quantity and quality of what can be sent have never stopped increasing. (Nye, 1997: 1073)

The acceleration of speed as well as the emergence of time and place distanciation thus can be considered as the main characteristics of the telegraph, which would make it not only the most advanced technology of its time in the nineteenth century, but furthermore it would proliferate the creation of international networks. The introduction of telegraph technology to the world thus has to be interpreted as a 'paradigmatic breakthrough to a new level of speed and reach' (Straubhaar, 2007: 115).[6]

2.2. THE FOUNDATION OF TELEGRAPHIC NEWS

> Like canals, railways and ocean highways, the telegraph linked national and international markets, including stock exchanges and commodity markets (cotton, corn and fish, for example). It also speeded up the transmission of information, public and private, local, regional, national and imperial, and this in the long run stood out as its most significant outcome. Distance was conquered as information relating to government, business, family affairs, the weather, and natural and manmade disasters was transmitted, much of it in the form of news.
>
> (Briggs and Burke, 2005: 110)

Telegraph became available for public use in the United States in 1844 (Blondheim, 1994: 3). Samuel F.B. Morse's invention soon grew to be what Smethers describes as a vital communication link for commerce and industry and a major force in shaping the nation's burgeoning mass media system. Most notably, telegraphy would be a preferred form of communication for over a century. (Smethers, 1998: 634)[7]

Furthered by the industrial revolution, the advent of the telegraph as well as other inventions such as the arrival of the steam printing press, which allowed for the printing of a larger amount of newspapers in less time, transformed the news sphere of the nineteenth century. More newspapers were founded and an increasing amount of (international) news became available (Briggs and Burke, 2005: 89 et seq.).[8] The improvement of transport was another factor that played an important role in carrying news over distance in Western societies:

> The development of railroads and canals in the early nineteenth century made it possible for the best equipment in manufacturing to reach a wider market. In 1810 the two-hundred-odd American papermills furnished newsprint only to nearby localities, but, during the 1830s, railroad transportation began to carry the best products of the best machinery to more distant places. In 1830 the United States had only twenty-three miles of railroad. In 1840 it had three thousand and would have thirty thousand by the Civil War. (Schudson, 1978: 33)[9]

While the means of transport improved, rising population numbers and their greater mobility as well as the growth of commercial markets in urban centers fuelled an increase in the demand for news (Blondheim, 1994: 16; Høyer, 2003: 461). Literacy grew as well as the interest of a wider part of the population in politics (Schudson, 1978: 35 et seq.). The ideas of 'time' and 'space' were redefined, as news distribution sped up and public desire for timely news increased. In consequence, the audience of newspapers as well as the competition between them grew. Blondheim points out accordingly:

> The great increases in circulation must have reflected to some extent the attractiveness of timely news for the reading public. Circulation figures of New York dailies demonstrated an additional marked expansion in the late 1840's, when the telegraph was applied to the rapid transmission of news. The timeliness of reported news was closely related to the increase in public interest. Through the accelerated pace of news gathering and transmission, newspaper intelligence was being transformed; from a history of tidings of the past it was becoming a chronicle of the present. (Blondheim, 1994: 26)

Simultaneously and furthered by industrialization processes, information on economic developments became vital for businesses, which needed information on stocks, currencies and the like (Thussu, 2000: 20). With 'global commerce acting as the main spur' and demanding to receive information as fast as possible, businesses invested in the expansion of the telegraph network and funded, among other things, the laying of submarine ocean cables (Briggs and Burke, 2005: 110). Accordingly, the telegraph spread to the business centers of the world, following major transport routes (e.g. the railway) and connecting major cities, which were the hubs of industrialization. By the 1870s, 'telegraph lines were operating within most countries in Asia and an international communication network, dominated by Britain, was beginning to emerge' (Thussu, 2000: 16). International connections between places where the telegraph was in use were made and permitted a constant flow of news.

For journalism at that time, the telegraph offered the opportunity to establish stable information connections and the ground was laid for businesses operating on a national or even international scale. News could be passed on without the 'obstacles' of distance (Innis, 1951; Carey, 1989). This allowed for reconfigured journalistic work structures. As Blondheim points out, 'news gathering by telegraph differed dramatically in its organizational implications from the editorial exchange', and was transformed 'into a dynamic process, requiring active control of a complex, interactive, and potentially continuous operation' (1994: 56).

News agencies were the first organizations to create a journalistic business model around telegraph technology: the commercial exchange of foreign as well as domestic news across distance. And: 'It was no accident that the London-based news agency which became known as "Reuters" was started in 1851, and not at any earlier period' (Read, 1999: 1). News agencies developed professional distribution and production modes through establishing an international network of connected bureaus and spanned parts of the globe with a constant flow of news running through the telegraph wires.

2.3. NEWS AGENCIES IN THE NINETEENTH CENTURY: CREATING INTERNATIONAL NEWS NETWORKS

Up through today, news agency operations are based on a complex bureau system. Journalists and stringers at local bureaus gather, produce and disseminate news. With the dispersion of bureaus nationally and/or internationally, agencies systematically braid areas with a web of reporters and correspondents and editorial control is often centralized in each agency's headquarters. This bureau system and the centralized editorial control are the two main characteristics of news agencies in the last decades of the twentieth century (Boyd-Barrett, 1980). I would argue that they also apply to the first news agencies that were formed in the nineteenth century.

Back then, the emergence of news agencies contributed to the professionalization of the journalistic occupation. First models of professional journalism were already in place, with newspaper reporters being assigned to stories.[10] However, the organizational structures of agencies commanded a further specification of job profiles to arrange for national as well as international news exchange in the most effective way possible. In order to do so, explicit tasks had to be allocated to staff. What is more, as news agencies delivered stories to a number of clients, they also had to develop a concept of 'nonpartisan, strictly factual news' in order to not collide with the ideals of their subscribers, whereas on the contrary, newspapers in the nineteenth century were known for representing partisan views (Schudson, 1978: 4). Agencies

> aimed to satisfy the news appetite of as many daily retail media as possible, regardless of political persuasion, so they promoted the idea of 'impartiality' as a valued journalistic objective. [. . .] Because they supplied the same news to clients whose individual circumstances varied they constructed a product that was at once standardized and yet flexible: the 'inverted pyramid' became the basic principle of all news reporting. (Boyd-Barrett, 1980: 19)

With the creation of a sophisticated news machinery system and a professionalization of staff, news agencies aspired to a systematic management of gathering, producing and distributing news. Telegraph technology became the backbone of an economically successful business model.

To illustrate how strong the ties between the spread of a new technology and the evolution of a complex agency network are, two news agencies will serve here as examples of such economically successful business models in the nineteenth century. The foundation of Reuters and Associated Press (AP) both coincided with the spread of the telegraphic network and the way both agencies were organized are examples of the formation of journalistic networks. In the first years of AP's existence for instance, the technology of the telegraph was used to create a national news network, whereas Reuters specialized in international news production and distribution. The birth of the two agencies shows how the technological tool of the telegraph played a significant role in shaping journalistic networks in order to gather and disseminate news.

The Foundation of the Associated Press

The first major American news wire service started as an association of leading New York newspaper editors and was created formally in 1848. Its inception 'became the most significant institutional response of the American press to the novel communication technology' (Blondheim, 1994: 47).[11] Before the emergence of the telegraph, news on the continent was transmitted by mail and thus to a large extent, it was the speed of the mail that regulated the pace of American news flow. Such speed, in turn, depended on the rapidity of post office handling at both ends, on the swiftness of the post office's mode of transportation, and on its frequency. The time consumed by the journey, and the wait for the next departure of the delivering transport, determined the interval between the occurrence of events and their being read about by newspaper subscribers. (Blondheim, 1994: 15)

Rapid circulation of news was not possible. With the advent of the telegraph, though, crossing distance became significantly less of a problem to overcome. The new technology was capable of delivering information instantaneously, be it economically related news, updates on current events and affairs in politics or score results and news events in sports from other areas of the country or the world (Schudson, 1978: 4).

Shortly after the introduction of the telegraph it became apparent to newspaper businesses in New York that having a reporter in Washington was necessary to get the latest news from the capital. Yet, only one telegraph line was in place and shared by several reporters from various newspapers. In order to allow for a more efficient use of the cable, correspondents were assigned who would deliver news accounts to a number of papers. The name 'telegraphic reporting' was applied to this new vocation and: 'The economic rationale of this new branch of business was simple. Reporters could satisfy numerous paying customers by one report, at the price of one transmission' (Blondheim, 1994: 44). First reporter networks were formed, which ultimately led to the creation of the Associated Press, after editors at various outlets came to realize that their customers' desire for news from afar was growing. As Nye elucidates:

To a considerable extent these developments were consumer driven. The Associated Press grew out of the public's intense desire, in 1846, to have news of the Mexican War. Newspapers found that it paid to make extraordinary efforts, and five New York papers soon decided that it paid even better to pool resources. (Nye, 1997: 1074 et seq.)

Correspondents were placed along telegraphic lines, connecting cities such as Washington, Baltimore and Boston. This information network soon was to be expanded, connecting at last all major cities across the country. Parallel to the extension of the telegraph network, the reporter and correspondent network was expanded, connecting cities from east to west and north to south, with New York becoming the central hub in the news gathering and distribution network of the AP: 'The New York Press, for the first time, was employing a technological system and interacting through it with an extended field' (Blondheim, 1994: 55). Telegraph technology then supported new ways of distribution. Newspaper editors saw the potential of creating networks built upon the new technology. These networks carried the promise of improving the information and story gathering machinery. The telegraph became the link between newspapers and the Associated Press, as well as for other news agencies, which were to be established in the following years, such as United Press and the International News Service (see Smethers, 1998: 635).

Within just a few decades, the AP established itself as the major distributor of telegraphic news to the American Press. Financially strong, it was not only capable of using the new technology as a newsgathering and distribution tool, but also superseding rivals. The AP managed to win the struggle over control of the access to telegraph lines and gained a market leader position by getting newspapers across the country to subscribe to its dispatches.

The Foundation of Reuters

Meanwhile on the other side of the Atlantic, a news agency distributed news *across* countries from the very start. Founded in 1849 and following the model of the French agency Havas that had already entered the stage as early as 1832, Julius Reuter entrepreneured with his agency.[12] He started small in Paris, followed by the creation of a first news hub in Aachen in 1850. Shortly after in 1851, Reuters moved to London. The British Empire was the world's leading economic power at that time and accordingly there was a necessity for commercial information from around the world. Furthermore, London was not only 'the geopolitical and financial metropolis of the world', but the city was also 'the focal point in Europe where the international cable companies were based, and where the flow of telegraphic traffic arrived' (Palmer, 2003: 483). As former sub-editor of Havas in Paris, Reuter was familiar with agency practices and could draw upon his experience:

> Reuter had opened in London, but Paris had shown him the way. From 1832 Charles Havas had developed a lithographic news service in the French capital. At first, this had simply collected and translated items from the foreign press; but within a few years Havas was employing his own correspondents to report news directly. In 1835 'Bureau Havas' became 'Agence Havas'; and by the end of the decade Havas was offering a range of targeted news services—for French Government Ministers, for departmental prefects, for bankers, and for newspapers. Eventually, he began to sell news to subscribers in other countries. Havas, in short, was the innovator who first organized the wide collection and sale of news as a marketable commodity. (Read, 1999: 6)

Systematic gathering and distribution of news was also the aim of Reuter and he used telegraph technology as well as carrier pigeons. During the 1840s, the telegraph had just started to spread over Western Europe, but not all major cities were directly connected. Pigeons filled the hole in the telegraph net, for instance between Brussels and Aachen. Since April 1851, Brussels was connected to Paris and in order to get French news across the border into Germany, the birds were sent off to deliver the dispatches with the latest news from Brussels. The pigeons bridged the gap of 76 miles to Aachen and took only two hours to deliver French news to Aachen—a quarter of the time it would have taken to deliver the information by train (Read, 1999: 11).[13]

Reuters' creativity in crossing distances, combined with an intrinsic understanding of technologies and his instinct for business (he set up contracts on exclusively delivering business news), quickly gained him and his agency fame in London as well as in Western Europe. The agency built a reputation as an independent and impartial supplier of news for its journalistic colleagues around the world. Using telegraph technology, the agency's business goal was to become the dominant supplier of overseas telegraph news to the press. Based on its financial strength, Reuters was able to buy up cable rights and spread the cost of telegraph cable space among many newspaper subscribers (Putnis, 2006: 2).

In succession, Reuters emerged as the central link between London and the continent and also established itself as news deliverer for the English dailies by providing them with continental news bulletins (Read, 1999: 20). Additionally, the network of Reuters was increasingly enhanced internationally along the stretches of the British Empire, connecting places in Asia, Africa and Australasia back to the center of the Empire in London. The British domination of the world cable network helped in that respect as it provided the technological basis upon which Reuters—an institution with strong ties to the Empire—built its dominance in international newsgathering:

> By 1880 nine cable routes were crossing the Atlantic, and by the 1890s the world was substantially united via overland telegraphs and undersea cables, although the Pacific Ocean was not crossed until the new century. About 60 percent of all cables were British-owned, and before 1914 an 'all-red route' round the globe, based entirely upon British territory, had been deliberately created for purposes of imperial defence. (Read, 1999: 59; see also Thussu, 2000: 18 et seq.)

The ownership of the foremost technological equipment at that time thus empowered the nation of the British Empire and along with it the power of the Britain-based news agency Reuters. Reuters at times even saw itself as the 'agency of the British Empire', delivering news between the center of imperial power in Britain and its colonies at the periphery (Chapman, 2005: 67; Read, 1999: 1).

2.4. AGENCIES AS MONOPOLIES OF NEWS EXCHANGE

Over the decades to come and with the purpose of gathering news from as many places as possible, AP and Reuters—and along with them a few other agencies—developed a complex (international) bureau system. Journalists and stringers would locally collect and produce news pieces and then distribute them over the telegraph. News agencies also started to collaborate with each other and divided the world into 'responsibility' zones. As the world was being organized into agency districts, Reuters and AP, for example, agreed on the exchange of dispatches across the Atlantic (Read, 1999: 38). Similar contracts emerged within Europe, resulting in the formation of a ring of news deliverers. In 1870, a cartel agreement was signed that would be 'the basis of the international news agency order until the 1930s' (Ibid.: 57; see also Palmer, 2003). Agencies of this ring cartel were Reuters (territory of the British Empire and the Far East), Wolff (Germany, Central Europe, Scandinavia and Eastern Europe) and Havas (Western Europe and the Mediterranean). The formation of these collaborative networks added to the success of agencies. They eventually became the major deliverers of national as well as international news for news organizations, capable of exercising control over the news market and forming an 'oligopolistic and hierarchical structure' of the news sphere (Boyd-Barrett and Rantanen, 1998: 26).

The exploitation of the telegraph lines was crucial to this development. The telegraph was the basis on which nationally or internationally operating news empires were built, 'concentrate[ing] power in the hands of a few dominant companies' (Chapman, 2005: 65). A news deliverer elite was established, formed by very few news agencies—or conglomerates—who controlled the national as well as international news flow. News agencies thus created a 'monopoly of knowledge' based on their power over the telegraph lines (Blondheim, 1994).

Such 'monopolies of knowledge' are according to Innis (1951: 190) made possible through the existence of technology that can be exploited in favor of a powerful group of people. As Thussu points out, there is a correlation between inhabiting communication instruments and being in charge of power: 'Communications networks and technologies were key to the mechanics of distributed government, military campaigns and trade' (2000: 11). This exertion of power over the telegraph was a result of two factors: the linear character of the telegraph as well as the financial strength of news agencies. The telegraph was a communication tool enabling communication from point to point. It could only operate sequentially with messages sent one at a time. Furthermore, the 'channel-like' nature of telegraphic communication supported the creation of monopolies over the wires:

> Turnpikes and canals also restricted communications to a channel, but unlike them, and very much like the railroad, the telegraph was a single unit that was both the road and the vehicle. Control of telegraph lines implied control of the message traffic flowing through them. When information was moved along canals and roads, numerous vehicles could compete over a variety of channels; but there was only a single conduit

for instantaneous communications, and it could easily be monopolized. (Blondheim, 1994: 4)

Also, as telegraph technology was expensive, only financially strong organizations such as news agencies could afford to use it. Reuters had the financial means to build telegraph lines, for example, in Ireland (see Read, 1999: 40). In the United States, the AP was the biggest customer of the telegraph by the 1870s, with ten percent of Western Union's revenues. By the 1880s, more than 80 percent of the copy contained in Western American newspapers consisted of AP dispatches. In 1875, AP even started to set up its own network of leased wires connecting member newspapers (Coe, 1993: 123). Thus, AP was able to create a monopoly in the national distribution of news.

The ability to control telegraph lines therefore has to be identified as a key element of gaining influence within the news sphere of the nineteenth century. Telegraph technology was a *tool* that became a *power instrument* making news agencies the dominant players in national and international news markets. These agency services furthermore introduced a *professional organizational network structure* to the gathering and distribution of journalistic products that had not been in existence before: The dissemination of journalistic content took place on a *global scale*, with news being produced in various corners of the world and delivered by correspondents and stringers arranged in bureau networks. The headquarters of the agencies located in the (national) centers of each agency were the central hubs within this network of bureaus.

The formation of news agencies in Western journalistic systems facilitated the creation of a monopolized news industry for the century to come in which subscribers became dependent on the news dispatches distributed by agencies. As Putnis elaborates with regard to the European news market:

> A global system of news distribution [was created] in which the major international news agencies—Reuters of Britain, Havas of France and Wolff of Germany—would have a dominant role and national presses would be relegated to being mere retailers of international news within a wholesale/retail distribution system. (Putnis, 2006: 1 et seq.)[14]

Those agencies set the agenda for their clients and reduced the journalistic tasks especially at provincial newspapers to 'cut-and-paste' jobs, with stories being composed from agency material (Palmer, 2003: 482). They 'inevitably became pre-selectors and pre-processors of news' (Chapman, 2005: 66) and newspapers as well as (smaller) national or regional agencies grew to be heavily dependent on news agencies. Especially the 'big' players in the field of news agencies named above, which later came to be known as the 'Big Four', were able to exercise central monopoly power over the distribution of international news, creating a 'media dependence on the world agencies' (Boyd-Barrett, 1980: 15).[15]

Agencies functioned as central agenda setters and gatekeepers within the (national) journalism sphere of the nineteenth century. Services such as AP produced one report on a news story for the entire country, defining what was going to be news in the first place: 'They held the yardstick that measured news value and news definition of politically relevant information, and they sifted through it and edited it before supplying it to the country' (Blondheim, 1994: 174). Reuters, for example, was the 'unofficial voice of the Empire, giving prominence to British views' (Thussu, 2000: 22). News selection as well as framing were processes with few people deciding on what was 'news' and how it was going to be presented. Telegraph technology enabled agency editors to act as gatekeepers. As Blondheim explains for the case of the AP:

> The function of the AP in the news industry may be linked to that of a giant funnel. From the vast network of wires of the nation's (SIC) telegraph monopoly it gathered information from all over the country in its headquarters. There, the news was consolidated to a single report and, again through WU's vast facilities, distributed throughout the country. Not all information that reached those headquarters went out, and what did was necessarily transformed in the process. (Blondheim, 1994: 174)

News agencies established an organized system of news production and dissemination. Building upon far-reaching national as well as international networks, their operational structures established monopolized systems of newsgathering, production and distribution and transformed the news sphere of the nineteenth century. The connections between agencies, their correspondents as well as their subscribers were characterized by linear information flows, with headquarters and editorial offices as centralized hubs in which stories delivered by correspondents were gathered, revised and then distributed to subscribers around the world. The ability of agencies to control the telegraph lines was a key element in gaining worldwide influence in (and power *over*) the sphere of journalism in the nineteenth century and, in succession of this, for a century to come. Telegraph technology was the tool that became the power instrument of news agencies to position themselves as the dominant players in national as well as international news markets.

2.5. FROM CONTROLLED NEWS FLOWS TO NON-LINEAR NEWS NETWORKS

The introduction of telegraph technology to nineteenth century newsrooms had a severe impact on the working procedures of news producers and disseminators. As the above analysis has shown, the telegraph constituted the 'first global information structure' (Braman, 2004: 134). It enabled instantaneous connectivity across distance and thereby the formation of an international network of news distribution (i.e., through news agencies) as well as an international network of customers (i.e., subscribing news outlets). Technology laid the foundation for the emergence of an international network of news exchange and inevitably influenced the (net)work of journalistic organizations. The technology of the telegraph assisted in and thus modified the gathering, production and dissemination of news. In Braman's words, 'the use of that infrastructure was limited because there were relatively few points of access, technical expertise was required, the length of messages was limited, only text messages could be sent, and it was expensive' (2004: 134). News agencies operated along the wires of the telegraph, transforming the news sphere of the nineteenth century and laying the fundament for a highly organized, centralized news exchange infrastructure that would remain more or less stable until the late twentieth century. Journalistic networks displayed *controlled flows of information*, with agencies monopolizing production and distribution processes. International connected news flows evolved, with the power to control them in the hands of a few news organizations such as Reuters or AP. The sphere of journalism had the character of a *closed system*, with a limited number of active producers and disseminators taking part in the news exchange process. The sphere of news exchange was centralized, dominated by linear news flows.

I will argue in the following chapters that the character of the news agencies' operational modes that used to dominate the sphere of information exchange is decisively different from that of the evolving *information nodes* located within a complex (digitally) connected global journalistic network of the twenty-first century. Expanded through digitalization, today's journalistic sphere displays significantly different characteristics. The evolving global news sphere of the information age exceeds communication systems based on technological devices of point-to-point communication. Information now travels instantaneously via digital paths and multiple places in various parts of the globe can simultaneously be connected. Digitally created communication networks are much denser, with an indefinable number of information strings crisscrossing and overlapping within virtual space. Whereas the example of news agencies and their relation to the introduction of telegraph technology displays the development of monopolistic centers dictating the (global) flow of news, digitally created networks display a significantly different character. They are *decentralized* networks, characterized by a *non-linearity* of information flows. This transformational shift quintessentially redefines the shape of our evolving global news sphere.

3 Network Journalism
Between Decentralization
and Non-linear News Flows

> Now, the real change is where the information comes from. Information in the current Internet age comes from people, people producing their information and exchanging it over the net. This is the true revolution. We do not have too much information (as we do not have too many books in a library, just more options to find the one we really want). It is the endless collective capacity of society to produce its own information, to distribute it, to recombine it, to use it for its specific goals, that transforms social practice, through the transformation of the range of possibilities for the human mind.
>
> (Castells and Ince, 2003: 139)

The relative stability and centralized control of linear news flows, which characterized information exchange among journalistic outlets in the nineteenth century, remained a feature of news media until recently. Side by side with news agencies controlling news flows, corporate and public service news outlets were the leading (and often sole) distributors of information nationally and internationally. A 'one-way, hub-and-spoke structure, with unidirectional links to its ends, running from center to the periphery' (Benkler, 2006: 179) would dominate journalistic information exchange throughout the twentieth century. A very small number of outlets controlled this sphere such as national public service outlets in many European countries or corporate stations in the US, securing journalism production as 'broadcasting to the masses' (Chaffee and Metzger, 2001: 369). Journalists operated within a closed system, characterized in terms of a fairly simple structured sender-receiver model or a top-down organization of journalistic work (Bardoel and Deuze, 2001: 98; see also Beckett and Mansell, 2008: 93). This allowed only a relatively small number of actors such as politicians or public relations organizations to influence journalistic news agendas, for example, during humanitarian crises (Robinson, 2002).

Today's journalistic sphere is organized in a significantly different way. Take some examples that demonstrate how the system of information exchange has opened up: The first images of the Virginia Tech Shooting in April 2007 aired via national or international news programs were produced on a cell phone and shot by a graduate student. The story of British Prince Harry being assigned with a military unit in Afghanistan broke on the news aggregation website Drudge Report in February 2008. In the same month the protests in Tibet reached a climax. While Western journalists of corporate and public service outlets had been expelled from the site and cut off from direct access, Tibetan dissidents, tourists and bloggers stood in, driving international news coverage. The Mumbai terror attacks of November 2008 were covered all across the World Wide Web. One could find breaking news on Twitter streams, follow bloggers from Mumbai who delivered accounts and comments on the situation in the city, or access multimedia coverage (including coverage of the aftermath in the months to come) on sites such as NowPublic.com, an open-platform news magazine where anyone can upload stories, photos, videos or tweets and that according to their homepage counts five million readers visiting the site each month.[1] And whenever a story breaks, one can almost immediately find a current events page set up on Wikipedia that includes links to updates on the unfolding story, as was the case during the Mumbai attacks of 2008, the Iranian protests in 2009 or when the devastating earthquake hit Haiti in January 2010.

News coverage in each of these cases has been significantly influenced by a greater degree of global connectivity, and professional journalists have been affected by the input of alternative news deliverers. Gillmor refers to them as 'non-standard news sources' (2006: xx). Benkler uses the term 'nonmarket actors' (Benkler, 2006: 220) and Bruns identifies a 'paradigm shift' away from 'industrial-style content': 'the collaborative, iterative, and user-led production of content by participants in a hybrid user-producer, or *produser* role' (2006: 275 emphasis in original). Yet, what are these new voices adding to the news sphere, how are they impacting news production chains and how are traditional gatekeeping modes being challenged? We do not have a conceptual approach that would help to understand the role of these new news deliverers, and how they fit in with traditional models of gathering, production and distribution as the object of research—in this case the journalism sphere—is 'in a state of hyper-growth and permanent transformation' (Lovink, 2008: xxiii).

With such transformational shifts in information exchange, methods of information gathering, production and dissemination of global news have to be scrutinized, customized and re-organized. Organizational structures in today's print, broadcast and online media need to be reassessed accordingly (not least through developing a 'new sense' of connectivity). Journalistic outlets are *information nodes* within this evolving global news 'network' sphere—and if they acknowledge the wide range of other nodes available within a dense net of news exchange, they can serve as central contact points tying together multi-directional information strings, including journalists at other journalistic outlets and news agencies as well as user-generated content providers, freelance stringers and the like. A paradigmatic shift toward a global *network journalism* structure is taking shape and here I will outline its specifics and identify its key parameters.

3.1. CHANGING NOTIONS OF SPEED AND CONNECTIVITY IN THE NEWSROOM

The increased speed of news flows and new connectivity levels demarcate this evolving global news sphere from a closed journalism sphere. Accelerated by the introduction of digital technologies as many scholars have recently pointed out (see for example McNair, 2006; Pavlik, 2000; Straubhaar, 2007; van Dijk, 2004; Volkmer, 2007), the capacities of digital media support instantaneous transmission of information as well as allow a greater number of information deliverers to contribute to (global) news exchange. What Boyd-Barrett described as the pressure of a 'continuous deadline' (1980: 74 et seq.) affecting the work of agency journalists in international bureaus has become a general feature of all news organizations. 'Stories break at the speed of light, circling the globe instantly via the Internet' (Pavlik, 2000: 231). Journalists feel the pressure of keeping up with the pace of news delivery, which at times leads to a neglect of in-depth coverage or fact-checking (Thussu, 2000: 244; Seib, 2002: 3). Within the online digital space, deadlines are nonexistent. What is more, as journalistic outlets now mostly have their online counterparts, the pressure formerly affecting mainly agencies now applies to all journalistic organizations. Seib points out that because the

> delivery of the news product has become constant rather than periodic, the newsroom's rhythm has changed, as have its procedures. Consider the routines of the newspaper newsroom and how it has been altered: from a measured pace of gathering, analyzing, verifying, expanding, verifying some more, and refining a daily product; to instead delivering whatever is available at a minute-by-minute pace. (Seib, 2004: 12)

This new work routine is furthermore reconfigured by the sheer volume of information in circulation. Chaffee and Metzger explain:

> More than any other technologies for mass communication, contemporary media allow for a greater quantity of information transmission and retrieval, place more control over both content creation and selection in the hands of their users, and do so with less cost to the average consumer. The Internet serves as the best example and, through digital convergence, will form the backbone of most future mediated communication. The Internet was designed to be decentralized, meaning that control is distributed to all users who have relatively equal opportunity to contribute content. The increased bandwidth of the Internet further enhances users' ability to become content producers and to produce material that is fairly sophisticated at low cost. In addition, many of the new technologies are more portable and, therefore, more convenient to use compared with older mass media. (Chaffee and Metzger, 2001: 369)

News flows used to be more or less fixed, being gathered, produced and disseminated almost solely by journalists working for corporate or public service outlets and news agencies. Information traveled along a one-to-many path and was 'pushed' toward audiences (Schoenbach et al, 2005: 248), allowing the consumer no form of interaction with content. The Internet, in contrast, supports selective 'pulling' of content as users can actively search for desired information (Ibid.). The Internet is a 'push-pull medium' (Volkmer, 2003: 12), allowing not only journalists but every Internet user to 'push' information into the virtual sphere as well as to selectively 'pull' information from an almost uncountable variety of sources accessible online. Furthermore, users now increasingly follow links provided on stories. Instead of following a storyline, for example, on frequently updated television newscasts throughout any given day, it is possible to break with this linear model of receiving information. Users can browse through the web, hear an update on radio, read a comment in a newspaper the following day and of course follow links on a story that can possibly lead them all across the web from one source to another comment or another update in a non-linear fashion.

What is more, digital technologies have assigned power to the masses. As Shirky asserts: 'When we change the way we communicate, we change society' (2008: 17). A 'new ecosystem' (Ibid: 60) of social interaction based on the use of digital technologies is emerging. Through a rapid decline in the costs of digital technology, 'we now have communications tools that are flexible enough to match our social capabilities' (Ibid.: 20). Gathering and processing of information, forming communities and pooling knowledge from diverse backgrounds has gotten a lot easier, as the success of Wikipedia and social networks such as Facebook with 500 million active users worldwide at the time of writing this book prove.[2] Tapscott and Williams (2008) attest a fundamental shift in societal (and economic) organization characterized by collaborative production modes and based on a new economic logic. About the benefits these new possibilities and potentials are bringing about and how they signal new structures and modus operandi for corporations, the authors write:

> The new promise of collaboration is that with peer production we will harness human skill, ingenuity, and intelligence more efficiently and effectively than anything we have witnessed previously. Sounds like a tall order. But the collective knowledge, capability, and resources embodied within broad horizontal networks of participants can be mobilized to accomplish much more than one firm acting alone. (Tapscott and Williams 2008: 18)

What Lévy (1997) termed 'collective intelligence' is the heart of this emerging level of 'peer production'. This idea builds on the premise of proactive group interaction and that a big enough and diverse enough group can come up with great ideas and decisions that are best for the masses—it is what Surowiecki (2005) terms the 'wisdom of crowds'.

Taken together, the possibilities for mass collaboration and the 'push-pull' characteristic of the Internet challenge journalistic practice in an online digital space. The impact on the sphere of news gathering, production and distribution is incredibly profound and the effect on the work of journalists can be attested on three levels:

1. The number of news disseminators increases and is not limited to journalistic outlets. A greater number of actors can take part in the gathering, production and dissemination of information, producing four categories of 'online actors' as McNair defines: the 'professional-institutional actors' (professional journalistic organizations), 'professional-individual actors' (journalists operating individually without attachment to news organizations), 'non-professional-institutional actors' (such as government agencies, NGOs, political parties or terrorist organizations disseminating information online) and 'non-professional-individual actors' such as bloggers (2006: 119).[3]
2. The plurality of information online offers more sources than ever for journalistic outlets and 'reporters can now effectively use online tools to gather news and information, check facts and even find sources off the Web' (Pavlik, 2000: 230).
3. The online environment allows for instantaneous feedback and active participation of users, eroding the structure of a one-to-many information flow and supporting a form of horizontal networking, 'offering instead one-to-one and many-to-many at once' (Bell, 2007: 78; see also Castells, 2000c: 341).

The challenge for journalistic outlets lies in the question of how they adapt to each one of these impacts. The transformation of a global news sphere with more actors taking part in the news production process and more information in circulation as well as the options of instantaneous feedback and active participation of users demands a repositioning of news organizations. A structural transformation of journalistic outlets needs to take place to appropriately equip journalists to navigate through this (global) information sphere. This structural transformation (Volkmer, 2003: 12) has to form on grounds of a reassessment of the journalism sphere in which news organizations operate. Within an emerging global news sphere, information flows are *multi-directional*. A *network* character of communication is taking shape based on a *network* structure of journalism in which *decentralization* and *non-linearity* are the key parameters defining news flows at the beginning of the twenty-first century. The basis of this evolving journalistic practice is the structural pattern of *network journalism*. A complex collaborative network of national and transnational information gatherers, producers and disseminators is developing that allows the integration of a great variety of voices. The paradigm of *network journalism* can be a starting point to explain our emerging global news sphere. Along with the reshaping of our social structures in an increasingly globalized world, professional journalism is undergoing profound changes in styles, formats and ways of reporting.

Journalistic organizations then are urged to adopt network dynamics and accordingly need to identify corporate models to work within the global *network journalism* sphere characterized by a new transnational space in which information is exchanged. As Hassan and Thomas note: 'Networks are open structures, able to expand without limits, integrating new nodes as long as they are able to communicate with the network' (2006a: xxiii). This openness of network structures allows for a greater level of connectivity and thus significantly transforms news gathering, production and dissemination procedures. Failing to understand these significant structural changes might ultimately lead to failure in repositioning within this redesigned sphere of journalism.

3.2. THE USE OF THE TERM 'NETWORK JOURNALISM' IN CURRENT RESEARCH AND PRACTICE

The term 'network journalism' is of course not new. It has been used at times by scholars and journalists over the past few years, so far infrequently, within different contexts and embodying various connotations (for example, Bardoel and Deuze, 2001; Beckett, 2008; Beckett and Mansell, 2008; Jarvis, 2006: Online; Wardle and Williams, 2008). A set definition of 'network journalism'—and its variation 'networked journalism'—however, does not exist. With the implications of digital technology for journalism being almost erosive and scholars as well as journalists trying to make sense of the changes occurring with such rapidity, the term 'network' has been applied in various contexts in the (scholarly study of) journalism. Especially in North America, 'network journalism' has furthermore often been used as a substitute for 'television' or 'broadcast journalism.' Closer to my understanding of 'network journalism', however, are various other definition suggestions. Let me sketch some of these meanings that seem to stand out at this point.

Especially within the blogosphere, the term 'network journalism' has at times been utilized as a synonym for 'citizen journalism' or 'participatory journalism' (for a list of synonyms, see Cohn, 2007: Online), and refers to the active role of citizens who are not working professionally as journalists and report news on various web portals from private blogs to citizen journalism sites such as OhmyNews and Global Voices Online. 'Citizen journalism' here is defined as having the potential to transform news reporting and production 'from journalism as a lecture to journalism as a conversation or seminar' (Gillmor, 2006: xxiv; also see Lasica, 1996), with a greater variety of voices taking the opportunity to be heard on a global scale. Cohn tries to establish 'citizen journalism' as an 'umbrella term' and defines 'citizen journalism as follows: 'citizen journalism is when a person who does not make their living as a journalist engages in an act of journalism' (Cohn, 2007: Online). 'Network journalism' can be classified according to Cohn as one type of citizen journalism and refers to a certain model of information exchange between journalists and their audiences:

> 'Network journalism' is when groups of people come together through the Internet to work on a single story. Like stand-alone journalism it is a conscious decision, but the work is not done by a lone reporter. Instead, it requires a group of people. Network journalism rests its fate on two principles: First the 'wisdom of the crowd,' the notion that a large network of people will have a collective intelligence that is greater than any single reporter. The second is 'crowdsourcing' [. . .], in this case crowdsourcing is the idea that a group of people will be able to tackle a large investigation in a more efficient manner than a single reporter. (Cohn, 2007: Online)

On the contrary, Jarvis applies the term 'network*ed* journalism' and uses it as a replacement for 'citizen journalism' (Jarvis, 2006: Online). He suggests that 'networked journalism' describes a partnership between the public and journalists that lays the grounds for a conversation between journalists and their publics. The journalist here becomes the moderator of an open news production process. According to Jarvis, 'networked journalism' describes collaborative models between citizens and professional journalists, who would network together to gather topics, gather information, produce news stories, reflect upon the journalistic product and if necessary correct and revise it once it is published.

> 'Networked journalism' takes into account the collaborative nature of journalism now: professionals and amateurs working together to get the real story, linking to each other across brands and old boundaries to share facts, questions, answers, ideas, perspectives. It recognizes the complex relationships that will make news. And it focuses on the process more than the product. (Jarvis, 2006: Online)[4]

Wardle and Williams (2008) use Jarvis's definition as backbone in their analysis of the BBC and how the public broadcaster makes use of content gathered and shared by its users:

> Networked journalism can empower the audience in direct ways. Using a grassroots, public journalism-influenced, model which emphasizes local meetings and community reporters, it can reconnect mainstream media with the local communities. Or [. . .] by connecting with expert

communities within the blogosphere, it can empower audience members with particular specialist knowledge or experiences to become directly involved in the research and production of a news story or item. (Wardle and Williams, 2008: 18)

Beckett and Mansell agree with Jarvis, defining 'network*ed* journalism' as a 'kind of journalism [which] continues to involve the journalist as a professional who is becoming more a facilitator of on- and offline news production for media institutions' (2008: 92). In his book *SuperMedia*, Beckett furthers this definition and outlines the opportunities of 'networked journalism' for collaborative gathering and production models: 'Networked Journalism is a hybrid of Citizen Journalism and Mainstream "professional" journalism' (Beckett, 2008: 86). For him, the social role of journalistic outlets is based on the premise of dialogue, and journalists are facing major changes in the way they go about their work with new tools at hand:

> It [networked journalism] is a recognition that mainstream professional journalists must share the very process of production. Networked Journalism includes citizen journalism, interactivity, open sourcing, wikis, blogging, and social networking, not as add-ons, but as an essential part of news production and distribution itself. (Beckett, 2008: 4 et seq.)

What these definitions listed above have in common is that the central characteristic of 'network(ed) journalism' is the interplay between civic participation and journalistic action. All these authors refer to journalistic production methods by outlining the potential of network building. However, they utilize the term in a fairly broad way, and do *not* apply it to design a conceptual model of professional journalism and its organization as such. Their focus is strongly tied to observations of how citizens can make an impact on journalistic production relying 'on a growing array of new media platforms' (Beckett and Mansell, 2008: 93).

Rather than concentrating on exchange modes between professional journalists and citizen journalists, Karp draws attention to the general ability to link information online—to sources, to journalistic content produced by citizen journalists, to content produced by a variety of professional journalistic outlets, you name it. He views the option of 'linking' as the primary new characteristic of today's journalistic work and it is within this context that he coins the term 'networked link journalism'. 'The standard journalistic technique for providing context and support for assertions is to quote sources, but on the web, the "link journalism approach" is to link to other actual reporting' (Karp, 2008a: Online). In addition: 'Link journalism is linking to other reporting on the web to enhance, complement, source, or add more context to a journalist's original reporting' (Karp, 2008a: Online). By adding the term 'networked' to his model, Karp wants to underline the ability of the web to do more than merely link to sources.

In his view, these links tie the whole sphere of journalism and its information outputs together:

> Networked link journalism is combining all the links created by journalists practicing link journalism to determine that most important, interesting, and newsworthy content that journalists are linking to. In the simplest form of networked link journalism, one link = one vote. The stories with the most votes rise to the top. This is the newspaper of the future—or rather the newspaper of today. This is how Google works, and how Digg works, by combining the power of many links. What's on a Google search results page? Or Digg's homepage? A bunch of links. But not just any links—the 'best' links. Why do some [sic] many people go to Google and Digg to click on those links? Why do they drive so much traffic on the web? Because those links are determined by networks, not individuals—and networks are the most powerful force on the web. (Karp, 2008b: Online)

The term 'networked link journalism' as defined by Karp (2008a, 2008b) thus refers to ways of content distribution on the web and how journalists can best navigate through information flows in order to provide users with the best possible overview on important news information. Based on his idea of sharing and exchanging information through links, Karp has founded the project Publish2 together with his colleague Robert Young. On the Publish2 website, news organizations and journalists can share, collaborate and curate their work among each other and with readers. The platform thus serves as a pool of online news sources chosen by journalists. It is the perfect example of what Karp has in mind when using the phrase 'networked link journalism': He suggests that instead of monopolized distribution models, journalism should turn to collective distribution platforms and share information, knowledge and stories: 'Remember the rule of networks on the web—the bigger the network, the more powerful it is' (Karp, 2008b: Online).

On the contrary, Bardoel and Deuze have applied the term 'network journalism' (without the suffix *ed*!) in the context of 'online journalism' or—as they repeatedly name it—'journalism on the Net', referring to implications of digital technologies and their uses for the roles of journalists in the information age (Bardoel and Deuze, 2001; Bardoel, 2002). Here, 'network journalism' describes a form of journalism, news production and distribution developing 'online' and next to the traditional forms of print, radio and television journalism. This 'online' journalism according to the authors also carries implications for journalism in general. 'Journalism on the Net' threatens old media and existing business models (Bardoel, 2002: 504 et seq.) and in accordance with this, new technological tools as well as changed audience expectations necessitate 'a redefinition of the core competencies of journalism' (Bardoel and Deuze, 2001: 92). Bardoel and Deuze aim to characterize the work environment of the 'converged' journalist of the future and 'network journalism' here describes 'a journalism for any medium, genre, type, or format' (Ibid.: 99). They view the emergence of online journalism as the core example—if not the form as such—of 'network journalism' as it in effect converges competencies of old and new media professionals (Ibid.: 99). 'Online journalism' according to the authors is marked by three key characteristics, namely (1) interactivity 'relinquish[ing] increasing levels of control to the user, instead of the producer, of content' (Bardoel, 2002: 504), (2) hypertextuality as a specific nature of journalism online offering the user to access in-depth reporting or further reference material and (3) multimediality describing 'the convergence of traditional media formats—(moving) image, text, sound—in one story online' (Ibid.: 505). Bardoel also adds a fourth characteristic: asynchronicity. This refers to the options for consumption, as online material is available on demand. Accessing news hence becomes 'a matter of individual choice and not mere producer-driven media logic' (Ibid: 505), whereas on radio or TV news content is scheduled at an appointed time. These key characteristics are, according to Bardoel and Deuze, not only carried by the 'journalism on the Net', but are impacting all forms of journalism. It is within this context that Bardoel and Deuze define 'network journalism':

> We propose a turn towards what we call 'network journalism'; the convergence of core competencies and functions of journalists, the blending media modalities in a fully wired and digital (working) environment, and an exploration of enhanced civic potentialities of journalism. This new, 'network' journalism can be seen as a potent factor in empowering citizens, overcoming digital divides, and establishing a critical rather than utopian foothold in the near-future media sphere. (Bardoel and Deuze, 2001: 92)

This 'reality' of 'network journalism' reveals, however, changing interdependencies between journalists and society. Bardoel and Deuze argue that the journalistic role has been transformed into that of a mediator of information. They are especially interested in professional identities of journalists—with the journalist giving orientation to citizens, filtering information and guiding users through information overload:

> The journalist of tomorrow is a professional who serves as a nodal point in a complex environment between technology and society, between news and analysis, between annotation and selection, between orientation and investigation. (Bardoel and Deuze, 2001: 98)

Bardoel and Deuze mainly focus on competencies of professional journalists, though, on their individual roles and the implications of a changing environment. 'Network journalism' for them describes one form of journalism. I absolutely agree with their analysis of a converging media space. However, the implications I connect with the term 'network journalism' reach far beyond journalistic roles and rather build on Deuze's and Bardoel's idea that 'network journalism' holds implications for the whole sphere of journalism.

3.3. THE PARADIGM OF NETWORK JOURNALISM

Network journalism as I define it describes a completely revised organizational form of the entire media system as such—including all platforms from print, via radio through to television as well as online journalism. The sphere of *network journalism* is 'organized in a radically more decentralized pattern than was true of this sector in the twentieth century' to use the words of Benkler (2006: 3) and characterized by *non-linear* information flows. *Network journalism* then is not a term that relates specifically to roles of journalists or that should be used solely to describe changing relationships between users and journalists, or a term that defines the evolving partnerships between citizen journalists and professional journalists as Jarvis and others understand it (Jarvis, 2006: Online; Cohn, 2007: Online). *Network journalism* rather stands for a model of changing connectivity modes and interaction patterns in today's global journalism sphere. Instead of using the phrase as a synonym for citizen journalism or as a concept that mainly focuses on roles of journalists or on one specific form of journalism, I understand *network journalism* as a *structural* concept, referring to the whole of the global journalism sphere in which roles of journalists de facto change, but even more importantly a new organizational framework is taking shape in which journalistic outlets operate. *Network journalism* on the level of organizational structures refers to changes that create a completely revised journalistic sphere. *Network journalism* is the underlying *structural concept* that refers to the structural organization and the connections not just within one form of journalism (e.g., print or online), but to the emerging connection modes within the whole sphere of journalistic work as such. Digital technology enhances the options of news gathering, changes production modes and impacts news dissemination not only for online media, but *for every single journalistic platform that operates within the network society*. Within this network society, new connection modes and information flows then influence the structural organization of journalistic outlets just as well as the day-to-day work of gathering, producing and disseminating news within a global network sphere.

Network journalism then can be understood as the paradigm for a dynamic structure of the global news sphere that has superseded the traditional media system. Thus, all the characteristics listed by scholars and journalists mentioned above belong in the context of *network journalism*. The characteristic features of 'network(ed) journalism' mentioned by Bardoel and Deuze, Karp, Jarvis, Cohn, Wardle and Williams and Beckett and Mansell all are absolutely appropriate. Network structures are characterized by an increasing level of interactivity, hypertextuality, multimediality and asynchronity as mentioned by Deuze and Bardoel. Network structures do support collaborative exchange between journalists and the public as Cohn, Jarvis and Beckett point out. Network structures do severely affect and alter content distribution as Karp argues. The role of journalists is being redefined and they become mediators of information who, as highlighted by Bardoel and Deuze, function as a nodal point within a complex information sphere.

But all these characteristics need to be drawn together, as they altogether characterize not just one transformative aspect of journalism, but are elements of a *completely revised structural pattern evolving in a global journalism sphere*. Using *network journalism* to describe just one part of this severe structural change of our entire journalism sphere is insufficient.

My argument is that the societal changes brought about by the 'network society' impact organizational structures and support the development of a whole new 'global network journalism culture'. The *network journalism* concept expresses the paradigmatic shift in a journalism sphere that is 'going global', delineating former temporal and spatial distances as described in Chapter 1. The structure of the global journalism sphere is supported by digitalization as the digital tools support network building. Its evolution is inseparable from its cultural, political and economic base: the network society as described by Castells, supported by globalization processes and proliferated by digitalization. *Network journalism* thus explains as a basic principle the structure of journalistic systems in the digital age, implying that journalistic work as well as the structural organization of journalistic outlets is being fundamentally altered.

Within this *network journalism* sphere, new ways of information flows and new forms of connectivity emerge. This sphere is characterized by a complicated or—even though it might sound like a paradox at first glance—a 'chaotic' organization of information strings running to and from journalistic outlets and thus offering journalists the opportunity to draw upon innumerable sources. The news sphere has undergone a shift from a fairly organized, linear news flow structure to 'chaotic' information flows produced and disseminated globally by an uncountable number of information transmitters. The 'quantity of (political) communication, the speed of its flow, and the extent of its reach as it flows down a billion pathways to TV monitors and computer screens all over the networked world' is increased (McNair, 2006: 133). The more or less static flows of a highly controlled, closed system of journalism are being replaced by dynamic exchange modes.

A network according to the Collins Australian Dictionary is 'an interconnected group or system' (2003: 1094). The Oxford English Dictionary characterizes a network as a 'work in which threads, wires, or similar materials, are arranged in the fashion of a net' (1989: 345). Watts refers to our times as 'the connected age' and explains that a network is 'an integral part of a continuously evolving and self-constituting system' (2003) in which slight changes in one part of the network affect the rest of the network as well. Such networks carry two significant characteristics:

> First, real networks represent populations of individual components that are actually *doing something*—generating power, sending data, or even making decisions. Although the structure of the relationships between a network's components is interesting, it is *important* principally because it affects either their individual behavior or the behavior of the system as a whole. Second, networks are dynamic objects not just because things happen in networked systems, but because the networks themselves are evolving and changing in time, driven by the activities or decisions of those very components. In the connected age, therefore, *what happens and how it happens depend on the network*. (Watts, 2003: 28 emphasis in original)

Networks thus constantly evolve and reshape. They are dynamic and because of the interconnectedness of all nodes in a network, what happens to one node will inevitably affect the other nodes to some degree.

The journalistic system constitutes such a network system, which is characterized by a dense net of connection nodes that are linked with each other in multiple directions and in which the forces hitting just one single node can be felt in the other nodes as well. The journalistic sphere viewed as a network is thus made up of a complex system of information strings organized in a 'chaotic' way. And as networks are aligned in a multi-directional fashion, they carry the characteristics of functioning in a *non-linear* matter. This goes against the notion of a strict one-way flow of information coming from a standard news source to the journalist who processes the information and passes it on to the (silent) audience. Instead, the connection points within a *network journalism* sphere are organized in a *decentralized* fashion and more abundant, with information flowing into news outlets via a multiple number of strings, being processed and then either pushed toward or pulled out by the active user. This *network* characteristic not only applies to journalistic outlets operating on online platforms, but impacts the work of *any* journalistic outlet and any journalism form as they all operate within the distinctively new global *network journalism sphere* and are all affected by this new level of connectivity. They are thus consigned to adapt to the information flows of the network age.

A network structure is also permeable and allows for information flows in and from multiple directions, including alternative media outlets as well as users feeding information back into a sphere of journalism that once was almost solely occupied by traditional journalists working for corporate or public service news outlets or agencies. The idea of the permeability of

networks also corresponds with an understanding of a network in a technical sense. The structural setup of a computer network is constructed 'to link
(computers) together to make possible one or more of several functions, such
as the transfer of data, the sharing of processing capability or workloads,
and accessibility from many locations' (Oxford English Dictionary, 1989:
346). Sharing and exchanging information within a structure of flows is
the key idea within the framework of the *network journalism* paradigm.
Journalistic outlets in this sense are not closed environments, but rather act
within a complex sphere of (global) networks connected via multiple information strings running multi-directionally to and from information deliverers and producers—and this can of course be good as well as bad. Watts
explains: 'Networks share resources and distribute loads, and they also
spread disease and transmit failure—they are both good and bad.' (Watts,
2003: 303) Good in the sense that a piece of valuable information can be
spread in multiple directions via digitally connected strings; bad in the sense
that a news fake can spread along the same paths just as well as a computer
virus that might infect all connected computers (if they are not properly
protected by the necessary software). Or thinking of the Iranian protest
case once more: The power of the digital information network spreading
the news of the protests was good viewed from the perspective of those who
value free exchange of information as the highest good and want to find out
about what happened. At the same time, one can be sure that for the Iranian
government the power of the network was anything but good. The interconnected communication infrastructure enabled information providers such as
the person who shot the video of the dying Neda during the protests or the
anonymous distributor of the content in the Netherlands to lift the curtain
and to reveal an insight into Iran and onto the political situation that the
regime wanted to see covered from the eyes of the global public.

3.4. RECONFIGURING GATEKEEPING MODES

The global network journalism sphere carries powerful implications for
news flows around the world, as traditional modes of gatekeeping seem to
shift away from corporate and public service news outlets—and this goes
for journalistic work on a local or national as well as on an international
level. As Volkmer remarks:

> The traditional meanings of 'gatekeeper' and 'news factors' become
> obsolete. A new translocal reference system of news selection and pre-
> sentation replaces the domestic and foreign news angle with a global jux-
> taposition of internal and external perspectives. (Volkmer, 2003: 313)

The connectivity flows of the information age thus foster the emergence
of a 'translocal reference system' that delineates former borders of news

production restricted by local and/or national borders. As traditional borders vanish within an online space, 'deterritorialized and globalized online zones for news and political discussion' (Reese et al., 2007: 236) emerge. The distinction between 'foreign' and 'domestic' news in this online space is to a degree collapsing. Volkmer argues: 'This conventional parallelism [of foreign and domestic news] is challenged by the fact that transnational channels and their particular political angle reach the same audience as national channels' (2003: 11). Consumers of news now have a choice of channels and access is not limited to only one or two (national) channels distributing newscasts. Along these lines, Thussu notes that: 'In a multi-channel era, a viewer can have simultaneous access to a variety of local, regional, national, and international channels, thus being able to engage in different levels of mediated discourses' (2000: 200). News exchange and the ways in which it is delivered to news consumers thus cannot merely be seen within a national setting, but has to be seen within a system of constant flows and in terms of a global exchange of information. This poses significant change to traditional modes of reporting and especially challenges our understanding of foreign corresponding—after all, the supposedly 'foreign' is not so far away any longer as it becomes increasingly accessible on a variety of platforms online. News consumers from Germany, for example, can access their daily fix of news from abroad by watching the newscasts on national television or read the daily newspapers. They can also choose to view the program of the BBC or CNN via cable or they can follow coverage on websites of literally every news organization in the world, read the accounts of a blogger who is based in another corner of the globe or jump on Facebook, check through the so-called 'news feed' feature and see what articles their friends link to, recommend and share.

Our traditional concept of foreign reporting is strongly tied to the idea of the modern nation-state in Western Europe and 'the 'domestication' of 'foreign' news in the first era of 'mass' print media', as Volkmer vividly explains (2007: 65). The creation of 'foreign journalism' derived from a nineteenth-century nation-state perspective, supporting the definition of identity of each nation and reflecting national perspectives (Volkmer, 2004: 210: see also Volkmer and Heinrich, 2008). Media thus played a crucial role in the process of nation-building, creating what Anderson (1983) famously coined 'imagined communities'. As Waisbord explains, 'the media need to be understood as a set of institutions involved in the creation, maintenance, and transformation of cultural membership' (2004: 377). With regard to this, identity building of nations took place within the reference system of 'We' as a nation against 'Them' as other 'foreign' nations (Volkmer, 2005). The idea of foreign journalism is thus deeply rooted in the notion of internationalization and sketches relationships *between* nations. News from the foreign country is reported through the lens of domestic perspectives.

Within a global space, though, the boundaries of Here and There are collapsing and journalism does not operate within clearly identified national borders. An analysis of the development of foreign reporting conducted by Volkmer (2007: 63–66) gives an overview of the changes the concept of foreign reporting has undergone and is the basis of my analysis of the shifts I observe. She argues that technological advancements of the past eighty years beginning with the introduction of shortwave radio technology supported a 'transborder flow of 'news'' (2007: 65) and challenged narrow national worldviews expressed in the news. Satellite technology marked the next step in the evolution of transnational news flows, while still supporting the interpretation of news stories within national settings:

> It seemed that a new dimension not only of transborder but transcontinental news flows had emerged: the coronation of Queen Elizabeth II, Armstrong's first steps on the Moon. These were the same images being distributed 'live' not directly (and this is an important point) to worldwide audiences but to national newsrooms, which *then* constructed domestic frames for their national (and to remain in my metaphor) 'place-based' audiences. Whereas Armstrong's first steps on the moon were interpreted as an accomplishment of science in the Western world, the same 'live' images were framed differently in Arab nations. Algerian Television commented on the globally broadcast 'live' images of the moon landing, Armstrong's first steps on the moon, in local frames. The 'live' coverage was associated with comments of Algerian television, that Armstrong heard the voice of the Muezzin while taking his first steps on the moon, in order to 'domesticate' this global event for local Islamic audiences and provide a religious framework for this unique scientific achievement. (Volkmer, 2007: 65 et seq.)

With transnational operating news outlets such as CNN, foreign news became a commercially exploitable product, 'creating trans-national communities not around national but topical contexts. [. . .] CNNI has been viewed as the inaugurator of a new phase not only of transborder (or transcontinental) but globalized news flows' (Volkmer, 2007: 66). It is not necessarily the foreign correspondent or the news agency providing stories, but multiple *networks* of deliverers providing the information on news events, which is then tied together in the newsroom. In a sense, journalistic (net) works are freed from geographical constraints obscuring the work of journalists and complicating stories (as there are more voices and positions to be heard). Journalism faces a 'global complexity' (Urry, 2003) in which multiple story angles (as opposed to pure national perspectives on issues) present themselves. Simple or linear explanations to stories—be it about a war or about a different culture—within the framework of 'we' versus 'the other' do not withstand transnational cultural flows—and neither do they withstand transnational information flows. Cause and effect are not linear notions (see Urry, 2003). The world—and thus reporting about it—has become far more complex (for this argument see also Featherstone and Lash, 1999: 1–13).

This shift of news into a transnational global sphere also needs to be identified as a shift of gatekeeping modes in a transnational reference system. Advanced digital technology does not only support the creation of transnational communities and thus a globalized journalism sphere, but also impacts the control mechanisms of transnational news flows. With cheap digital technology tools available not only to corporate and public service journalists, the content provided by news channels does not only consist of material gathered in traditional ways, for example, by foreign correspondents or news agencies. Even more important: Whereas the role of the gatekeepers of information traditionally was assigned to officials and journalists with information 'being selected in and out of the public sphere constructed by the press and political actors' (Bennett, 2004: 283), digital technology enables anyone from the professional journalist to the citizen journalist to publish footage and comments. This marks a shift in the power structures of gatekeeping dynamics. After a 'period of relatively stable gatekeeping patterns' (Bennett, 2004: 293) within a highly organized and controlled closed media system and with very few players (i.e. officials and news organizations) taking part in this process, the dispersion of first satellite and then digital technologies has shaken up these traditional top-down gatekeeping standards, 'creating complex interactions and correspondingly puzzling changes in news content and press-government relations' (Ibid.: 284). Traditional outlets have lost the full control over the content and over the gates and are just one voice among many in a sphere of *network journalism*.

4 Information Nodes in the Network Journalism Sphere

> Instead of having some kind of control over the flow of (meaningful, selected, fact-checked) information in the public sphere, journalists today are just some of the many voices in public communication, including but not limited to professionals in public relations and marketing communications, advertisers, and citizens themselves through weblogs, podcasts, and using all kinds of other online publishing tools.
>
> (Deuze, 2008: 12)

In a sphere of network journalism characterized by its permeability and the non-linearity of information flows, the control gates for the dissemination of information are wide open. Journalists now compete with a range of voices in the gathering, production and dissemination of news. This chapter will draw upon some cases to outline how the gates are being crashed in various corners of the world and how the dynamics of a network journalism sphere are impacting the reporting of traditional newsrooms.

One example is the coverage of the protests against human rights abuses and against Chinese occupation in Tibet. The images of the protests and the information about police forces violently afflicting demonstrations as well as evidence proving the abuse of human rights did not initially come from foreign correspondents, news agencies or official sources. Images and comments on the situation were delivered by non-standard news sources that used dissemination platforms on the Internet such as weblogs or online video-publishing sites like YouTube.

Other examples of the changing dynamics of journalistic practice in a network journalism sphere can be found on a continent that often serves as the prime example of a technologically lacking and underrepresented spot on earth: Africa. Despite fears of a digital divide, the cases of election coverage and the coverage of its aftermaths in Zimbabwe (Moyo, 2009) and in Kenya (Mäkinen and Kuira, 2008) show that the changing structural organization of information dissemination based on the use of digital technology tools impacts even this corner of the world. These cases also indicate that in line with a significant change in the way information gates are being opened, news agendas are increasingly being influenced through non-traditional sources. In addition, just as traditional notions of gatekeeping are under scrutiny, agenda-setting processes now increasingly follow different rules. How the story of British Prince Harry and his deployment to Afghanistan broke is just one more example of these agenda-setting powers of non-traditional sources.

All these cases provide a glimpse of how journalistic work is undergoing profound changes these days and how journalistic routines practiced in newsrooms over the past decades are under revision. Deuze explains (2007, 2008) that journalists are used to routines and standardized news sources such as PR officials, politicians or fellow reporters and furthermore are influenced by what he calls 'operational closure'. It is the

> internalization of the way things work and change over time within a newsroom or at a particular outlet. Outside forces are kept at bay primarily by the rather self-referential nature of newswork, as expressed through the tendency among journalists to privilege whatever colleagues think of their work over criteria such as viewer ratings, hit counts or sales figures. (Deuze, 2008: 18)

This 'operational closure' is increasingly harder to apply to journalistic work in the sphere of network journalism. The cases outlined in this chapter reveal that the structure of network journalism is carried by a dense net of information nodes and these include not only traditional sources and professional journalists, but also an increasing number of new news deliverers and informal sources. And whereas each node is entangled with others, impacting the way information flows and how stories are being covered, the process of news work increasingly follows a decentralized pattern: neither are traditional news organizations the sole providers of information any longer, nor do they have the power to centralize and thus control information dissemination. As a consequence, the routines of journalistic work are being altered.

4.1. GATEKEEPING REVISITED

In the wake of the anniversary of the failed uprising against China in 1959, a series of demonstrations marked March 2008 in Tibet and in other Chinese provinces with Tibetan populations. Hundreds of monks were the first to take the streets in Lhasa during peaceful protests, calling for the release of their fellow monks who had been arrested in demonstrations a few months prior. What followed was a period of severe unrest in various provinces, including riots as well as police abuses. Chinese authorities had banned foreign journalism staff from the affected regions and the story of the unrest might have never gone public worldwide without any news coverage from the scene. However, the news of the events unfolding in Tibet and elsewhere did break and the images of violent intervention of Chinese police forces against the monks did spread across the globe. Yet the stories of the incidents did not come from official sources, nor were journalist witnesses on the spot.

The German broadcaster Deutsche Welle explained in an online article that while mainstream reporters were expelled from Tibet and while China was censoring websites that distributed content on the protests, the only sources leaking information about the situation in Tibet were activists and tourists who delivered eye-witness accounts, photos and videos on the situation, often bypassing firewalls and censorship.[1] In another article online, the British *Guardian* named major news organizations affected by the Chinese censorship including BBC World and CNN. The *Guardian*'s source of information on the censorship crackdown in China and Tibet was a Chinese technology blogger.[2] The only footage professional news organizations did have came from so-called 'amateurs'—and it was used in international as well as national news programs around the globe to cover the story. The BBC, for example, organized a major part of its Tibet coverage on its interactive 'Have your Say' pages online, providing personal perspectives on the situation in and around Lhasa gathered from users and blogs.[3]

Major news organizations *reacted* to this information, opened the gates and started gathering information from these non-standard sources, as mainstream journalists (such as foreign correspondents) were either denied access to the protests by the Chinese government, or their access was limited to official sources and press releases often filled with propaganda.[4] The information distributed by news organizations around the globe relied heavily on alternative news sources drawn together from blogs and citizen journalism sites or by approaching users traveling through or living in the affected regions directly. Digital production and distribution technology available to these non-standard news sources as well as to corporate and public broadcast journalists allowed a *networked* connection between journalists and sources that was previously unimaginable.

Citizen journalists as well as independent journalists and bloggers also made extensive use of the microblogging tool Twitter, bypassing Chinese censorship gates and delivering constantly updated information on the protests in Tibet to the outside world. Described by Carr as 'the telegraph system of Web 2.0' (Carr, 2007: Online), the service allows users to send short messages and links of no more than 140 characters. With numerous independent journalists, activists and citizen reporters using Twitter as a communication tool during the protests in Tibet, journalists could receive constant updates on the current situation. Similarly, Twitter worked as a breaking news and information tool during events in other spots of the globe such as during the protests in Iran and during the Mumbai attacks.

With an uncountable number of tech-savvy bloggers or citizen journalists, with tools such as Twitter and with software that helps users to bypass firewalls or remain anonymous while surfing the net, controlling the information flow within a tight system of gates becomes an almost impossible task. It is much easier to control a few mainstream news organizations clearly identifiable for a political apparatus such as the Chinese government than to control independent journalists, tourists, dissidents or activists in the possession of a mobile phone (with camera function) or a video camera and with access to the Internet where they can publish their material, with tools at hand to work around censored gates to sneak information through. Even when China cut the Internet connections and blocked sites such as YouTube in order to restrict the global information flow about the demonstrations, the protests made headlines in an indirect way, with major news organizations reporting on the information crackdown in the regions.[5] McNair notes, 'the attempt to control has a tendency to become part of the story', turning 'the ban into a story of global reach and resonance' (2006: 190). The network journalism sphere is a permeable, open space, providing breaches and gaps in the gates with information traveling via multiple paths and eventually getting out, thus indicating power shifts with regard to the dissemination of information and its constant flows. 'In the chaotic communication environment of the twenty-first century, the cultural marketplace tends to self-adjust and work around state control apparatuses faster than those apparatuses can adapt to a rapidly evolving environment' (Ibid.: 192). It is the new level of connectivity that enables the bypassing of gates that is the typical characteristic of the network journalism sphere in which informational strings crisscross the globe and eventually get picked up by major news organizations as in the case of Tibet.

Similar cases where bloggers or citizen journalists gave voice to information suppressed by government officials or unheard of by traditional news organizations can be found in Zimbabwe and Kenya. Within these countries gates were crashed by an army of citizen journalists and bloggers and the impacts shook up the political situation. Moyo (2009), for example, has researched the role of citizen journalism on the information flow during the Zimbabwe elections in 2008. In his study he focused specifically on the use of text messaging and blogs to exchange information during the controversial delay in releasing the 2008 general election results. While information flows were being disrupted, controlled and restricted by President Mugabe and his government, traditional media relying on their routine work processes barely had any information about the outcome of the elections or were heavily influenced by spin through official sources. The information gap was filled by alternative news deliverers who spread rumor or misinformation in some cases, but mainly fostered critical engagement, delivered comments and breaking news and disseminated all sorts of information that possibly could shed light on the state of affairs:

> In a situation where information flows are restricted and the mainstream media are unable to fulfil the citizens' informational needs, the 'parallel market of information' became the dominant source of a mix of information and disinformation—attributes that used to be the monopoly of professional journalists and mainstream media. (Moyo, 2009: 553)

Some traditional media outlets did tap into the information circulated via text messaging, email and blogs. Similar to the Tibetan case where news organizations worldwide tried to gain a picture of the situation through following the information provided by alternative news providers, the Zimbabwean media started monitoring its fellow citizens for further background information (or in some cases for rumors).

Moyo also reflects on the problem that limited access to the Internet in Africa does hinder the majority of the population from engaging with and making use of digital technology tools in favor of citizen participation (Ibid.: 555). However, two factors played an important role in regard to alternative coverage of the situation and did lay the grounds for information flows. Firstly, quite a number of Zimbabweans live in the Diaspora, 'creating a situation where those who have remained at home post compelling eye-witness accounts, while those who are in the Diaspora both amplify and comment on what they read from home-based bloggers' (Ibid.: 559). Such accounts were, for instance, gathered on the Global Voices Online website. Secondly, the so-called 'single-owner-multi-user' phenomenon in West Africa (Nyamnjoh, 2004, cited in Moyo, 2009: 555) plays a vital role. African communities still function as word-of-mouth cultures, and while the number of Internet cafes in urban centers is on the rise and the increasing number of mobile phones in circulation is remarkable, users with access eventually distribute messages by 'word of mouth' among other citizens. So even though Internet penetration is still low, alternative voices disseminating information in digital space do exist and as Moyo explains: 'This is a common pattern across the continent and serves to illustrate that access may not necessarily be defined by ownership' (2009: 555).

Mäkinen and Kuira (2008) observed similar evidence for the increasing impact of citizen participation on political discussion and election coverage in Kenya. They analyzed online discussions and media coverage during the violent postelection crisis in 2008 and observe that social media tools and in particular text messaging—despite the problems of the digital divide—increasingly function as delivery tools for citizen participation and alternative news coverage. While both participating political parties stated they had won the polls, violent clashes among the population occurred across the country. During this crisis, media coverage of the election as well as of the clashes was partly banned, censored by the government or by journalists themselves. To access information, citizens increasingly turned to text messaging and the Internet. Mäkinen and Kuira note: 'Social media tools like wikis, weblogs, Facebook, Flickr, YouTube, Twitter, and "mashups" were increasingly used to organize and share information about the crisis and violence, and to raise funds' (Ibid: 329). Bypassing censorship, a range of blogs covered the situation online, generating what Mäkinen and Kuira refer to as the 'alternative public sphere' in Kenya.

The social media offered narratives by citizen reporters and digital activists that were more diverse than the views presented in the mainstream media and represented grassroots reactions during the crisis. While the international media only scratched the surface of what was happening, and the traditional media partly resigned to censorship due to fears of repression, the social media offered swifter, more subjective, and more detailed coverage during a fast-moving and changing situation. (Mäkinen and Kuira, 2008: 330)

Similar to Moyo's findings, Mäkinen and Kuira also underline that expatriates play a vital role in this process and that even though access to digital media is still low in Kenya, there is strong evidence that with a rise in penetration rates, a growing middle-class population and growing awareness of digital media and its tools, citizen participation via digital platforms will play an even more profound role in the near future.

Taken together, these examples from Tibet, Zimbabwe and Kenya offer firm grounds for the observation that gatekeeping modes are being revisited in our emerging sphere of network journalism. Traditionally, newsgathering and production used to follow restricted paths, usually relying on a foreign correspondent who would pick up information at the scene or mainly through official channels. The correspondent decided on the newsworthiness of such content and delivered the story to the news organization. In accordance with this, Sigal analyzed in 1973 with regard to traditional gatekeeping schemes that direct access to news material is often not given to the journalist and the reporter mainly turns

to official channels to provide him with newsworthy material day after day. To the extent that he leans heavily on routine channels for news, he vests the timing of disclosure, and hence the surfacing of news stories, in those who control the channels. (Sigal, 1973: 119)

In the network journalism age, news stories bypass these traditional news flows. Information travels along new paths and reaches news organizations and journalists via digitally connected information strings. The interaction processes between sources and journalists consequently are undergoing profound change. Digital technology marks a shift from 'highly managed institutional settings providing the framing' and the 'gatekeeping practice of "officiating"' to an increasing number of 'unmanaged event[s]' (Livingston and Bennett, 2003: 363, 365) as in the case of wars, crises, protests et cetera.[6] In a journalism sphere increasingly structured as a network of information nodes, traditional gatekeeping relations are losing grip. Material is neither solely controlled by official sources nor by mainstream journalistic outlets, but instead information flows through various channels and affects what gets in front of the lens of journalistic outlets in the network age.

Especially with regard to so-called 'event-driven news' as in the case of Tibet, the impact of digital technology tools on gatekeeping dynamics becomes obvious. Lawrence characterizes 'event-driven news' as being 'cued by the appearance of dramatic news events and the 'story cues' for reporters that arise out of those events' (2000: 9). According to Lawrence: 'In institutionally driven news, political institutions set the agendas of news organizations; in contrast, as event-driven news gathers momentum, officials and institutions often respond to the news agenda rather than set it' (Ibid.: 9). Applying this argument to the model of the emerging network journalism sphere, journalistic organizations now increasingly pay attention to alternate voices delivering these 'story cues' and connect and refer to non-mainstream deliverers of information. The power to control is neither resting solely in the hands of officials acting as gatekeepers nor solely in the hands of the foreign correspondent.

In my view, this development is a major opportunity for journalism. The 'chaotic' flow of information is far less predictable than the flow of news in times of mass media and hierarchical, fixed communication systems with only a few players affecting the information flows, namely professional sources and journalists. If the media aims to exercise the role of the fourth estate in the information age and aims to act as an 'institutional source of political and cultural power which monitors and scrutinizes the actions of the powerful in other spheres' (McNair, 1998: 19, 20), this increase in non-standard sources accessible for journalists around the globe can be interpreted as a fruitful development. With the growing quantity of information in circulation enabled by the use of digital technologies, 'the growing unpredictability and irreverence of news media [and the possible contents it can carry] provides grounds for relative optimism about the democratic, watchdog role of the journalist in the new millennium' (Ibid.: 18).

Without bloggers, activists, tourists and independent journalists being digitally connected to the rest of the globe and without leaks in the censorship systems of the countries in which the protests were held (in effect leaks in the digital systems), who knows if the information would have ever passed Chinese censorship. Civic participation in Zimbabwe or Kenya most likely would have been toned down to an absolute minimum—with the public spheres in each of these countries being much less informed about the election outcomes and with political regimes being much more powerful in spinning election results in their favor. These stories may never have made headlines within their respective national communities or around the world without the wide coverage of the protests on alternative information sources distributed via mobile phones and the web.

4.2. AGENDA-SETTING REVISITED

Just as gatekeeping processes are under revision, the agenda-setting powers of news organizations are altered in the sphere of network journalism. As the examples cited above have shown, with an increase in the number of platforms powerful enough to scoop stories, more information providers are able to place stories on the (global) news agenda. Accordingly, traditional notions of how agenda-setting works are increasingly coming under scrutiny.

Our current understanding of agenda-setting processes was formed with reference to a media system in which relatively few news outlets had the power to define 'what to think about' for the public. Entman explains:

> The distinction between 'what to think' and 'what to think about' is misleading. Nobody, no force, can ever successfully 'tell people what to think.' Short of sophisticated torture or 'brainwashing', no form of communication can compel anything more than feigned obeisance. The way to control attitudes is to provide a partial selection of information for a person to think about, or process. The only means of influencing what people think is precisely to control what they think about. (Entman, 1989: 76 et seq.)

But just as the gatekeeping dynamics are under revision in a digitally networked sphere, agenda-setting dynamics are shifting out of the hands of a few. As a consequence, argue Chaffee and Metzger, 'the key problem for agenda-setting theory will change from what issues the media tell people to think about to *what issues people tell the media they want to think about*' (2001: 375 emphasis in original; also see Delwiche, 2005: Online). Professionally operated journalistic platforms are no longer the sole definers of news.

An illustration of this is how the story about British Prince Harry in combat in Afghanistan broke and how it was placed on the news agenda around the globe. In the run-up to the story, the plan was to suppress the information and British mainstream media paired up with officials aiming to control the agenda. They had signed into an agreement with the Royal family and the British military not to report on the story until the Prince was going to return to Britain, arguing that this was to protect the prince from becoming a target for the Taliban while on his deployment.[7] Yet, the news broke in a matter of ten weeks—bypassing traditional outlets—via the Drudge Report, the news aggregation website that had previously gained fame when breaking the Clinton-Lewinsky scandal.[8] After the Drudge Report broke the news, traditional media could not withhold the story any longer. It was out in the open; the formerly secure gates of a closed mass media system had been crashed.

The Drudge Report scoop carried another implication: It sparked a discussion on the web as well as in print and broadcast news outlets, with commentators questioning the legitimacy for journalists to suppress a news story and pair up with official sources. The story did cast a negative light on corporate and public service media, as Friedman comments:

Fleet Street's finest are feeling proud lately for cooperating with authorities and keeping Prince Harry's whereabouts in Afghanistan a secret. They should be ashamed, instead. [. . .] It's never a good idea for the media to play ball with the rich, famous and powerful, regardless of whether they're royal family members, government officials, corporate executives or celebrities. The practice establishes a potentially dangerous precedent. How can the public believe what we say and write if they suspect we're willing to suppress news? (Friedman, 2008: Online)

With the scoop on the Prince Harry story, established media received a wake-up call regarding the suppression of agendas and the failed attempt of controlling the gates of (free) information flow. In the global network journalism sphere, information travels via a dense net of information strings and eventually hits a node that is strong enough to break the story and push it into the global information arena.

Journalism companies used to control the megaphone—and therefore had a monopoly on who got heard. New technologies such as satellites, cable, fiber optics, and, of course, computers have destroyed that world forever. (Fulton, 1996: Online)

In another recent incident Twitter showed its powers in breaking news and established the frame for a story in the form of an iconic image that made it onto the number one pages of newspapers, into television newscasts and onto numerous websites. In January 2009 a commercial US Airways flight ditched into New York City's Hudson River. A passenger traveling on a commuter ferry that went to the rescue of the stranded airline passengers was one of the first to break the news via Twitter and he also provided the iconic picture of the plane in the river, showing passengers and crew standing on top of the wings and on the escape slides.[9] Just as Wikipedia was instantly updated and filled with information and links, Twitter lead the way in the coverage of this breaking news story.

All the above-mentioned examples—from the protest coverage in Tibet, the election coverage and the aftermaths in Zimbabwe and Kenya to the breaking of the story on British Prince Harry and of the Hudson River Plane crash—are just a few out of many indicating a power shift. The gates that formerly restricted access to a small elite of politicians, PR people and media organizations are now being challenged by changing interaction patterns and connectivity structures. With more deliverers of information and the availability of a variety of dissemination platforms, journalists working for major news organizations and official sources are no longer the only gatekeepers controlling the flow of information in a decentralized information sphere:

New intermediary practices arise, in which journalism is just one of many 'middlemen', whereas at the same time disintermediation—as a result of an increasing self-service facilitated by the combination of new technologies and active, information-seeking individuals—becomes possible. This is not to say that the end of mediated communication is near, but only that, due to new technology, the exclusive hold of journalists on the gatekeeping function to private households is reduced. (Bardoel and Deuze, 2001: 96; see also Singer, 1998)

This is also not to say that media organizations are completely losing their gatekeeping functions, as some journalists and academics presume (see, for example, Lasica, 1996).[10] Not all structure is 'lost'—to paraphrase Bennett (2004)—within the more complex, non-linear journalism sphere of the digital age, but a new structure is taking shape, a network structure that allows for more open gatekeeping mechanisms in a globalized news sphere. Alternative sources and information deliverers become *part* of the newsgathering and production chain and thus macerate traditional gatekeeping modes.[11] This should also lead news outlets to carefully consider whether the gates they use are adequate to cope with incoming information flows and new connection modes. Outlets that attract large audiences are still powerful and widely consumed platforms. But a more flexible gatekeeping dynamic within these organizations allows for expanded source opportunities and a more diverse information inflow. As Bennett indicates:

> Instead of a one-way information flow shaped by varying patterns of press-government relations, new technologies offer the potential for multidirectional press-government-citizen gatekeeping relations. It is possible to imagine a gatekeeping system in which each set of players contributes meaningfully to the selection and construction of news. Perhaps the greatest challenge for journalists and politicians today is to learn how to use this technology to include citizens more fully in the public sphere. (Bennett, 2004: 311)

Becoming aware of and using the multiple connection options given in the global network journalism sphere is essential for news organizations. Developing a deep understanding of the new dynamics of newsgathering and dissemination will assist them to reposition themselves in this new sphere.

4.3. INFORMATION NODES IN THE DIGITAL AGE

A complex (global) network journalism sphere consists of an uncountable number of information nodes that vary in size. Just as our social structure is a 'network of nodes' (Castells, 1996; Volkmer, 2003), so is the journalistic system of our age. The nodes within this system are the information outlets—from a news aggregation site such as the Drudge Report to a transnational broadcast news corporation such as CNN. Within this sphere, professional journalistic organizations carry the potential to act as major players of information production and dissemination, as they 'have access to a broader network supporting processes of gathering, producing and distributing information. In a system of connected nodes, they act as the 'supernode" (Volkmer and Heinrich, 2008: 55). Journalists working for major journalistic organizations provide portals that attract huge user traffic online as well as over the traditional portals of radio, print and television. Even though studies indicate that audiences are increasingly turning to the web for information, public service and corporate media outlets are still in favorable positions as their brands attract attention to stories.[12] News outlets can use this position in order to survive and strive in a global news network, but the situation demands a structural reorganization. With more producers and disseminators being part of the global network of information delivery, with technological devices that support a diffuse dispersion of information in multiple directions, new connection modes need to be put in place that correspond with this structure. Journalistic outlets need to find their new role—a role that pays its dues to the network dynamics and still needs to evolve (Pavlik, 2000: 236).

The proliferation of digital technologies has supported dynamic exchanges between newsmakers and whoever is connected within our global network society. The process of 'making the news' does not only happen within the closed environment of the newsrooms at traditional news outlets and among professional correspondents in the field. News production takes place within a *multi-channeled, multi-layered information network* fed by an uncountable number of news deliverers. In an information space characterized by 'chaotic' information flows, information seekers (i.e., users) will search for orientation, for help in filtering which sources are legitimate and which are not. There exists a need for a guide and users will most likely turn to information sources that are common knowledge (Schudson, 1995; also see Singer, 1998). Journalists who understand the dynamics of a decentralized, nonlinear sphere of global information flow can adopt the role of news accelerators, generators and commentators guiding and navigating their consumers through the information space of the twenty-first century.

Approaching and collaborating with alternative sources can assist journalists to apply a structure to the chaotic information flows. *Networking* is also a navigation tool: The bigger the network of the journalist and the bigger the network of collaborative partners in the journalistic network, the better. Journalists then can play the role of the filterers of information who navigate their recipients through an increasingly complex information environment in which *networking* becomes an inevitable part of the job. As Bardoel predicted as early as 1996 when digital technologies were just about to kick-start a revision of journalistic working tools:

> More than ever, the task of journalism [in print and every other medium] will lie in filtering relevant issues from an increasing supply of

information in a crowded public domain and its fragmented segments. Journalism evolves from the provision of facts to the provision of meaning. (Bardoel, 1996: 297)

A journalistic outlet constitutes only one node within this network. This node manages non-linear information flows. In order to 'make sense' of these flows, to distinguish 'valuable' from 'useless' content, journalists need to identify reliable sources within these non-linear information flows. As nodal points in a dense net of information providers, they need to position themselves in between these non-linear strings, allowing for input across various paths and thus in a way decentralizing themselves. In the context of network journalism, nodes mark the interconnection points of the network. The node is the point within a networked system of information flows that allows intersections of information floating through digital space from various destinations.

The paradigm of network journalism thus outlines a revised structure of journalism (on an organizational level) that takes into account and allows for revised information flows within the network society. It suggests an open model of journalistic contacts (i.e., linking to a wider variety of sources) and takes into account the new geography of news production and dissemination in which the complex information flows are knitted together.

This is not to say that journalists have not networked with sources before—but never in such an extended sense. The structures and the body of the network (who is involved, who belongs to it) are changing. New producers have entered the production chain. The significant change within this production environment is an adaptation of journalists' work sets, a structural reformation in the newsroom.

Restructurizing the newsroom then needs to be accompanied by a revision of several features of 'traditional' journalism:

(1) a revised journalist–source relationship,
(2) a revised journalist–audience relationship and
(3) a revised journalist-to-journalist relationship including revised attitudes toward colleagues working for formerly distinct journalistic outlets from print through to radio and television and online portals.

With regard to the journalist–source relationship, digital technologies offer new connection modes in order to support proliferating flows of information within a radically changing global news culture. With digital technologies, new strategies of information management open up. The creation of new outlets of expression (such as blogs, citizen journalism websites and channels such as YouTube and Flickr) and new opportunities for access and participation inevitably means the *reconfiguration* of traditional outlets. The traditional mass media system was characterized by a compartmentalization of the communication process into senders and receivers, authors and readers, producers and consumers or media and society, with resulting questions about the relationship between the two. (Hamilton, 2003: 295 et seq.)

Network journalism functions upon different grounds and within different parameters: It is characterized by a 'chaotic' structure of information flow, fed by a vast number of optional news sources ranging from the official at a governmental institution such as the White House providing information on the war in Iraq to the political activists and independent journalists critically reflecting upon governmental positions via platforms such as Democracy Now!. It includes the independent journalist like Christopher Allbritton providing reporting pieces from Iraq or the Iraqi blogger Riverbend, who provides an inside perspective on the situation from a local point of view. It includes the sources of news agencies with stringers in the field as well as vlogging platforms such as Alive in Baghdad, where an independent foreign reporter team provides stories and comments on the current situation in Iraq.[13]

In addition, sources of information are no longer only an outlet's own reporters, news agencies, official sources, globally operating television stations or foreign correspondents. The segments in the news production chain are far more diverse and within the sphere of network journalism, outlets need to open up to these diverse input channels. Strategies of information gathering have to become more complex, checking not only the day-to-day press releases and whatever reaches journalistic outlets through 'official' channels. This change in information gathering needs to be accompanied by a change in awareness of the digital tools—from Twitter to news aggregation sites targeting journalists like the upcoming Publish2—that journalists can use in order to advance their reporting and widen their net of sources to gather information. The outcome is a set of connections shaped in the form of a multi-channeled, multi-layered information network fed by an uncountable number of news deliverers that supports a multiplicity of voices.

A second significant transformation within the global news sphere is the changing attitude of audiences toward news consumption. A new journalist–audience relationship is taking shape. This relationship needs to be viewed in terms of the ways recipients consume news. Audiences can no longer be viewed as passive consumers. They are rather active users of news content (Deuze, 2004: 146–147). Users have a wider variety of news providers to choose from and are increasingly technologically adept. With personal digital assistants (PDAs) and smartphones at hand, by setting up RSS feeds online specifically designed for the taste and need of the individual user, news recipients create their personalized news sphere:

> The paths for obtaining information are characterized by a 'networked individualism' (Castells, 2001). Which path and provider—be it for

local, national, or transnational topics—are up to the user to decide, and he or she has a wide choice. (Volkmer and Heinrich, 2008: 52)

The new technological tools provide 'an appropriate material support for the diffusion of networked individualism', enabling individuals to 'build their networks [. . .] on the basis of their interests, values, affinities, and projects' (Castells, 2002b: 131). The consumption of news in this respect is 'demand-led, rather than supply-led' (Bell, 2007: 78) and a 'see for yourself' culture takes shape as Benkler describes it (2006: 218). It is the vision of Negroponte's customized 'Daily Me' (1995) becoming reality. Instead of the traditional push mechanisms with news organizations setting the daily information agenda of their audiences, users can pull their desired news dispatches and organize their very own personal news worlds. Journalistic outlets need to be aware of these new forms of news consumptions, the on-demand reality of news usage, which is altering the relationship between journalists producing news and the users of their products.

Third, network journalism demands a revised attitude among journalists with regard to their journalist colleagues. Journalistic outlets today do not only compete with their presumably 'equal' contestants along the lines of traditional demarcations between print, radio, broadcast and online platforms. Almost every media outlet has its online counterpart, which 'provide[s] global access to news from all parts of the world. Suddenly, newspapers, television, radio and other news providers all find themselves in head-to-head competition' (Pavlik, 2000: 233). Furthermore, in an increasing number of journalists' work, crossmedia and multimedia competence is becoming a necessary requirement for the journalistic profession in the digital age (Barnhurst and Nerone, 2003; Kawamoto, 2003; Pavlik, 2000). These developments will eventually lead to the creation of converged news outlets with 'formerly distinct media operations' (Deuze, 2004: 141) drawn together into one newsroom. This development corresponds with the attitudes of users toward media, as according to Regan

> people use one medium to complement the other. In other words, they like having a choice. In the future, new media outlets that work hand in hand with old media counterparts will be the ones that prosper. That's because the secret to making money with new media is for media companies to see themselves as content providers, and not just newspapers, radio stations, etc. (Regan, 2000: 8 et seq.)

Network journalism corresponds well with such 'hand-in-hand' operations as its very basis is the vital exchange of information across platforms—network connections do not stop just because the output medium changes. The converged newsroom is a new management model for newsrooms that supports the nodal functions of a journalistic outlet sphere as:

- it corresponds with the shift from audiences to technologically adept users of media who actively seek news on various media platforms;
- it enhances the capabilities of networking between journalists formerly operating in distinct media,
- it increases the opportunities of drawing more participants into the news production process from outside the newsroom, and
- it makes possible distribution of content via various platforms in ways that are appropriate for each medium.

(Volkmer and Heinrich, 2008: 55)

Among journalists, thoughts of converging newsrooms are often accompanied by fears of increasing workloads, or fears of job cuts and of employers trying to save money through drawing together differing media platforms and depending on a smaller staff body (Avilés and Carvajal, 2008; Deuze, 2004 and 2008; Huang et al., 2006; Paulussen and Ugille, 2008; Singer, 2004). Furthermore, high degrees of competitiveness among journalists often characterize the relationships differing media outlets (Deuze, 2004: 148 et seq.). Yet, collaboration is needed in organizing the informational 'chaos' of the digital age. With digital tools affecting all forms of media in a 24/7 news flow environment, journalists need to have a deep understanding not just of one medium. They need to learn 'to "see the news" through more than one medium' (Volkmer and Heinrich, 2008: 55) and to think 'crossmedia'. Viewing news production and dissemination not just within the closed-up environment of one platform such as print or television is becoming a necessary requirement for journalists. Journalistic practice today requires multimedia competences, as journalistic work is increasingly characterized by a 'shift from individualistic to collective and cross-departmental team-based newswork' (Deuze, 2004: 148).

These three revised relationships listed above, between journalists and (1) their sources, (2) their audiences and (3) their journalistic colleagues, demarcate the new flow structures and new collaborative working models for journalists in the sphere of network journalism. Journalistic outlets are nodes within this evolving sphere. Their function is to filter the newsworthy out of the information flow while having the technological tools to access as much information as possible. Within a 'space of flows', as Castells refers to the new structural patterns of societies, journalists can get in contact with virtually anyone. As 'people of all kinds, wishing to do all kinds of things, can occupy this space of flows and use it for their own purposes' (Castells and Ince, 2003: 58),[14] journalists can make this information flow work *for* them. The new 'space of flows'—in which virtually anyone can provide whatever he or she defines as news—need not lead to a 'death of media', with journalistic outlets being endangered as informants of a public sphere (see Keen, 2007, or Sunstein, 2009). Some journalistic outlets might die, yes, but it will be because they have not understood the dynamics of the network society and with it the ways in which information flows are being altered. The current developments increase the accessibility of information and are an opportunity for journalistic outlets to reposition themselves as news accelerators and navigators. If outlets do understand and adapt, they will have a chance for survival. Working *with* the new digital tools and embracing the opportunities given, adjusting work sets and organizational structures is a necessary part of the adaptation process for news organizations to align themselves for the digital age.

4.4. DEVELOPING A GLOBAL NETWORK JOURNALISM CULTURE

The rapid evolution of digital information technologies and the shake-up felt in newsrooms across the globe is reminiscent of the times when telegraphic reporting struck journalistic outlets. In the nineteenth century, newspaper business also faced drastic changes accelerated by new technology. Some editors were overwhelmed by the impact telegraph technology imposed on their work, with more news items being accessible and news agencies such as Reuters being formed that posed a threat to the ways reporting had been practiced up to that point in time. As Blondheim notes with regard to the creation of the Associated Press:

> The prospect of an all-telegraphic newspaper could have dampened the enthusiasm of even the most affluent editor. With the volume of American news expanding rapidly with the growth of the nation, with more and more localities being brought into telegraphic communication with New York, and with the development of ample facilities for telegraphic transmission, the future promised an exponential rise in telegraph bills. Witnessing the growing public interest in distant events by reason of their timely reporting, the individual editor must have been intimidated by the idea of singlehandedly satisfying an ever-increasing, seemingly insatiable appetite for news. Rising expectations deriving from the telegraph industry and from systematic news gathering thus dictated that cooperative telegraphic arrangements had arrived to stay. (Blondheim, 1994: 67)

If one replaced 'telegraphy' with 'Internet' in this quote, structural parallels between the interplays of technology and journalism appear. To the editor practicing journalism in the second half of the nineteenth century, the environment in which news was produced must have seemed similarly as 'chaotic' as the global news sphere at the beginning of the twenty-first century might seem to journalists today. The introduction of technologies from the telegraph to the Internet challenged and challenge journalists to integrate them in newsgathering and production techniques in order to organize news flows and to enhance reporting procedures. It was absolutely impossible to reverse the flow of history and to ignore the proliferation of telegraph technology and the revised information flows the technology brought along—and so it is today as digital technology tools have entered virtually every sphere of our social lives.

As outlined in these last two chapters, the transformation of the journalism sphere is characterized by a decentralization of information exchange as well as by the non-linearity of information flows. The key parameters of the evolving global news culture are the increased speed as well as the transformed levels of connectivity. Within this sphere, journalistic outlets are just a few of many nodes disseminating, sharing and exchanging information. In accordance with this transformation, gatekeeping as well as agenda-setting modes need to be revisited. Traditional notions of foreign correspondence have become redundant and instead innovative collaborative approaches with regard to newsgathering and production are emerging. Relationships between journalists, their sources, users and journalistic colleagues are being altered. All these factors taken together form the key parameters of an evolving global news sphere, transforming a closed journalism system into a global news sphere characterized by the paradigmatic shift toward the structure of network journalism.

The second part of this book will be dedicated to analyzing a range of examples and will give voice to practitioners and media analysts from the UK, USA and Germany who in one way or the other have been concerned with these structural changes in newsrooms. Their insights into day-to-day practices provide valuable information on the current state of journalism and help to show a path into the future of the profession.

Part II

Network Journalism

Practitioner Perspectives

5   Studying Network Journalism

The reality is that the elements that make good journalism, and good journalists, will never change. Ignoring the future doesn't mean we can escape it. But paying attention to it means we can shape it.

(Regan, 2000: 9)

Journalists, regardless of what platform they are operating on—be it broadcast, print or online—are realizing the pressures of having to adapt their practices of newsgathering, production and dissemination. Yet the question remains for many: what to make of these changes, if and how they should adapt their media presence and how much interaction with users as well as with alternative sources they should allow. The reactions toward the introduction of digital technologies to newsrooms have been extremely dispersed, ranging from an attitude of viewing them as both 'a blessing' and 'a curse' (McNair, 1998: 125).

As part of the research for this book, I talked to a number of practitioners and analysts and witnessed trends that suggest a movement toward a future for the journalistic profession that will be much more interactive, crossmedial and less top-down in its organization, less patronizing in its approach toward news exchange and with news organizations acting more like information nodes carrying multiple voices and story angles. This second part of the book gives voice to some early adopters and media experts who shared their insights with me in personal interviews. I conducted in-depth interviews with thirteen producers, executives, media analysts and media educators in the UK, the US and Germany who are concerned with the implementation of digital tools.[1]

The central theme of these interviews was: How is journalistic work being reorganized in the age of network journalism? I wanted to find out how journalistic organizations can be reinvented as communication nodes within the complex, decentralized network journalism sphere in a transnational context. The organizations and interviewees I chose to be part of this unique sample can be considered as either (a) forerunners in applying network journalism structures in newsrooms, with some outlets being traditional media platforms where digital tools were adopted and other outlets being founded on the premises of digital news production and dissemination or (b) organizations that monitor the journalism sphere and analyze trends in journalistic practice as well as offer training programs. The experts who shared their knowledge at the time of my visit worked at the following outlets in the UK, the US and in Germany as shown in Table 5.1:

Table 5.1   Interview Partners

Outlet	Expert	Abbreviation
AlterNet.org	•Executive Editor	•AlterNet
BBC News	•Editor for Interactivity	•BBC
Current TV	•Vice President of 'Vanguard Journalism'	•Current TV
Democracy Now!	•Senior Producer	•Democracy Now!
Guardian Media Group	•Director of 'Digital Structure and Development'	•Guardian
International Center for Journalists (ICFJ)	•Vice President 'Programs'	•Interviewee 1, ICFJ
	•Senior Program Director	•Interviewee 2, ICFJ
MediaChannel.org	•Executive Editor	•Interviewee 1, MediaChannel
	•Executive Director	•Interviewee 2, MediaChannel
New York City Independent Media Center (IMC)	•Volunteer and Producer	•(Indymedia)
Project for Excellence in Journalism PEJ (Journalism.org)	•Senior Associate	•(PEJ)
Ourmedia.org	•Video Blogger and Volunteer	•(Ourmedia)
ZEIT ONLINE	•Editor for Web 2.0 Applications	•(ZEIT ONLINE)

I will now briefly introduce each outlet and interviewee and briefly explain why I chose a qualitative approach as the method of analysis.

5.1. METHODOLOGY

Professionals who deal with the effects that the transition from a closed journalistic system to an open network structure imposes on journalistic practice are the most vital source of insight. Their views and experiences help us to understand how journalistic outlets are being repositioned. The interviewees who shared their knowledge here provided 'expert' interviews in the best sense of the word: They shared details of their professional realities and—to adapt Glesne's and Peshkins's view of qualitative research—helped to 'understand and interpret how the various participants in a social setting [i.e., journalism culture] construct the world around them' (1992: 6). Qualitative research approaches aim to provide an insight into lifeworlds—or in the case of professionals, provide an insight into the construction of professional reality from the perspective of the actors. In this sense, qualitative research adds to a better understanding of social—in this case professional—realities as well as to a better understanding of processes, interpretative models and structural features (Flick, von Kardoff and Steinke, 2000: 14).

As journalistic organizations find themselves in the midst of searching for solutions to adapt to revised modes of communication in societies, choosing a methodology that allows an understanding of an emerging phenomenon that cannot be narrowed down to a specific time period in the past seems logical. Surveys as provided by institutes such as the Pew Research Center do indicate, for example, that an increasing number of users log on to the Internet to receive (political) news or that users now increasingly consult online platforms of independent media or citizen journalists and bloggers as sources of information.[2] The market research company Nielsen frequently provides updates on global Internet usage, surfing behavior of users worldwide and the most frequented sites on the net.[3] This kind of research is vitally important to diagnose trends. However, these statistics do not explain how journalistic outlets react to increasing non-linear news flows proliferated by digital technologies, how they handle the vast amounts of information available on- as well as offline and how journalistic outlets are reorganized in the wake of an emerging global news sphere. Statistical data provides arguments for the view that digital technology tools support the growth of an alternative sphere of information providers with an increasing number of alternative news outlets or citizen journalism sites and the like, as the technology is cheap and thus lowers the barriers to produce and disseminate political information (see Benkler, 2006: 212). Yet, these figures do not explain *how* the work of journalists in the newsrooms is affected and *how* journalistic organizations adapt to these significant changes.

As Baur and Lamnek (2005: 241 et seq.) point out, qualitative research enables us to comprehend a (sociological) phenomenon as a whole, in all its depth and with all its facets and dimensions. The openness of qualitative approaches also allows 'the researcher to approach the inherent complexity of social interaction and to do justice to that complexity, to respect it in its own right' (Glesne and Peshkin, 1992: 7). Asking media practitioners how they value the transformation of journalistic practice in its interplay with digital technologies lets the researcher in on the perspective of insiders and allows access to material gathered right in the center of transformation: the newsroom. The knowledge of the interviewees who agreed to participate in this study is vital for a further conceptualization of an evolving network journalism sphere.[4]

The experts whose insights you will read here are involved with journalistic practice in one way or the other and many of them need to cope with the transformations described in the first part of this book on a day-to-day basis. They are the ones directly concerned with the effects this transformation has on journalistic practice. They stand in the midst of this evolution and with their willingness to be interviewed deliver the raw material out of which to generate a further conceptualization of network journalism—and to gain an exemplary picture of the current state of the art in journalism. They share their notions of audiences, notions of collaboration as well as of competition with other journalistic platforms and their thoughts on the role journalists have to fulfill today. Their views illustrate the realities of newsrooms and open a level of analysis that in the following serves to reflect upon the advantages as well as struggles journalists have to cope with in a digital environment.

What is more, as the network becomes the inevitable model for a structural change of journalistic systems, crossmedia analysis becomes absolutely essential. The structural transformation of the journalism sphere takes place *across* media platforms and affects print as well as broadcast and online media. The Internet in this respect should not be viewed as a separate medium in opposition to other media (Sterne, 1999). As Thorburn and Jenkins explain, the emergence of digital technology 'resist[s] notions of media purity' (2003: 11) and 'each medium is touched by and in turn touches its neighbors and rivals' (Ibid.: 11). With an increased convergence of 'traditional' as well as 'new' media (Bell, 2007: 13), media platforms do not function in opposition to each other or separate from each other anymore. In effect, platforms are merging online and this form of media convergence 'is more than simply a technological shift. Convergence alters the relationship between existing technologies, industries, markets, genres and audiences' (Jenkins, 2004: 34). This has a crucial effect on anyone who is part of the journalism sphere: With virtually every media outlet—be it a television outlet or a news magazine—having its online website counterpart, with online research tools being used by print journalists as well as radio journalists, with journalists working for more than one medial platform producing written reports as well as video pieces, and on the other hand with media users consulting a variety of outlets—across the whole spectrum of available media (!)—to draw together their information, a study of structural and organizational reconfigurations of journalism needs to take into account media outlets from across the existing range of platforms. As 'newspapers, television, radio and other news providers all find themselves in head-to-head competition' (Pavlik, 2000: 233), singling out the Internet as study object becomes redundant (Bell, 2007: 13; Marshall, 2004) and blocks an open and realistic view on trends in the development.

Consequently, the media experts heard here work across the spectrum of content platforms, with some of them being employed or volunteering for print and others for broadcast and others working for solely online-based outlets or yet again others monitoring outlets across the spectrum of available media platforms. This approach resembles the change in the journalistic environment. Here it is not only television outlets competing with television outlets or newspapers competing with their print counterparts. In the evolving journalistic sphere information is key and the outlet choosing the best way to deliver it and to connect with the users of news is what is at the center of interest. Here, broadcast, print and online platforms do very much stand in direct competition.

Every single one of the outlets represented here is part of the evolving sphere of network journalism, with each of them carrying specific structures, intentions and organizational models. In their unique features, each organization represents an individual node within a complex system of information gatherers, producers and disseminators. Each targets specific segments of users, and produces and disseminates news content in its very own ways. Each organization also exhibits various connection nodes, with a vast number of news deliverers connected within their individual new source spectra. And each organization stands for an increasing number of non-linear news flows, which add to the content produced and disseminated within a global news sphere.

What all organizations have in common, though, is that they are adapting to the network journalism sphere through adopting cutting-edge models of how to connect with their users, their sources and other journalists or by monitoring, analyzing and training journalists to work within this news journalism culture. They all have experimented with different approaches to information gathering, production and dissemination.

5.2. THE RESEARCH SAMPLE

For the sample presented here, thirteen media experts from the United States, United Kingdom and Germany were chosen.[5] As all three countries stand for a long tradition of journalism, are considered technologically advanced nations and are located within the Western hemisphere, the ways to practice journalism in each of these countries are broadly comparable and the sample allows for a comparison of opinions and views.[6] Each media organization serves either as an example of an outlet adopting network journalism practices to newsrooms or plays an international leading role in journalism education and monitoring. Using digital technologies for news production and dissemination, or for that matter using the World Wide Web as a platform for training programs and/or to collaborate with alternative news providers such as citizen journalists or bloggers is a regular feature at each of these outlets.

As the paradigm of network journalism is based on the premises of a shared information sphere, the sample includes not only journalists working for traditional news organizations, but also so-called media activists and media educators. To make the sample more comprehensible, I have identified four groups:

(1) Traditional print and broadcast outlets with an international reputation who have adopted digital tools in their everyday practice in order to enhance their source network and allow for user interactivity (BBC Interactive, Guardian Media Group, ZEIT ONLINE)

(2) Alternative or independent media outlets providing a 'counterbalance' of news content to traditional media outlets (Democracy Now!, Current TV, Ourmedia.org, Indymedia NYC)

(3) Online-based independent news aggregation sites drawing together and selecting content from various media platforms and including commentary and original reporting (MediaChannel.org, AlterNet.org)

(4) Media monitoring, training and education organizations who look into the everyday work of journalists (Project for Excellence in Journalism, International Center for Journalists)

When selecting interview partners, the following staffers were of special interest for the sample: personnel responsible for either producing content (i.e., experienced journalists who could provide content-related viewpoints), personnel responsible for strategy planning within news organizations (i.e., staff in a leading executive role who could provide information on organizational structures and future strategies), staff working for media monitoring organizations (i.e., experienced journalists, trainers and commentators who focus on the current state of the art in journalistic practice) or people with extensive practical experience in the field of alternative media. The following paragraphs provide a brief overview of the organizations visited and briefly introduce each interviewee.[7]

5.2.1. Traditional News Organizations

BBC Interactive and the Guardian Media Group in the UK as well as ZEIT ONLINE in Germany are organizations that build on a long tradition of journalistic practice in the field of either print or broadcast. With the proliferation of digital technologies, all three outlets early on began to alter their newsroom strategies and launched additional online counterparts, where they started to experiment with new formats such as blogs or to embed user-generated content, to build online communities or implement external links on their websites. All three outlets thus now complement their one-way news flows and top-down reporting methods with interactive features. Of special interest here were the first-hand experiences of journalists and executives working for these three outlets who are familiar with the structures and organizational models of a traditional outlet as well as with (interactive) models that are evolving in the global news sphere.

BBC News Interactivity Desk

With its cutting-edge approach toward the use of digital technology in news production and dissemination processes, the British public service broadcaster BBC makes for an interesting case in regard to studying the evolution of network journalism. The outlet was one of the first major global news organizations to adjust its work sets in accordance with revised schemes of connectivity and early on started to work with bloggers and user-generated content. First analyses of the BBC's digital strategy moves have been published (e.g., Lee-Wright, 2008, or Wardle and Williams, 2008) and will inform the interview analysis in the following chapters.

Originally called the British Broadcasting Company, the BBC started as a radio service for the UK in 1922 and the history of the organization shows that the BBC has played a role as a prototype for journalistic practices ever since its inception.[8] In November 2007, the BBC as the first major global news player announced plans to merge into a multimedia newsroom, maintaining the BBC News website, the radio summaries and bulletins (except for Radio 1), BBC World Service News, BBC News 24, BBC World, BBC Breakfast and the bulletins on BBC One at one, six and ten, melting television, radio and online into one entity.[9]

The online services of the BBC were launched in the 1990s and quickly rose to become one of the world's leading providers of information disseminated via Internet. The BBC regularly tries out new digital tools and interactive features on its online platform and offers services such as podcast downloads and mobile phone-friendly versions of BBC content. The BBC also distributes its content via various external platforms such as Facebook, YouTube and Twitter. Bloggers from across the globe in such locations as Iran, China or Saudi Arabia have been regularly featured on the website in the past years and in addition, the BBC repeatedly tests co-operative news production processes with alternative information providers. One example was a two-week team-up with Global Voices Online, the nonprofit network of more than 200 bloggers from around the globe.[10]

Of particular interest in regard to the relationship between the BBC and its users is its move to generate debates and embrace user-generated content material online on its 'Have Your Say' website. This interactive arm of BBC News allows users to comment on current affairs and deliver video or photo footage or to suggest story ideas. The desk is located at the Television Center of the BBC in London.

The Interview Partner: The Editor for Interactivity at BBC News

At the time of the interview, the Editor for Interactivity had been with the BBC for 20 years. She is an experienced television news producer who used to work for BBC's flagship programs and as researcher for a BBC current affairs program after starting her journalistic career at local newspapers. In 2001, she moved to the BBC website to work on interactive programs involving audiences in the coverage of the UK general elections. After the elections, she stayed at the website and with a team of initially five journalists administered a web feature called 'Talking Point' that hosted user debates on current affairs. 'Talking Point' developed into the 'Have Your Say' site where journalists now administer user-generated content and moderate multiple debates.

Guardian Media Group

Like the BBC, the Guardian Media Group has a pronounced interest in online journalism and started implementing digital technology tools in the late 1990s. As early as 1997 the *Guardian* appointed a readers' editor responsible for creating a stable link between the *Guardian* and its readers, who would respond to complaints and queries. The newspaper itself was founded in 1821. The printed version is the flagship of the multimedia business Guardian Media Group, which consists of a range of media outlets such as newspapers, websites, radio stations and magazines. The online counterpart Guardian.co.uk was launched in January 1999. Owned by the Scott Trust as the sole shareholder, the Group preserves its financial and editorial independence.

Guardian.co.uk today is one of the most popular news resources on the World Wide Web and offers a range of digital tools to its users, from RSS feeds or podcasts to mobile versions of the *Guardian* content. It can be found on Twitter, Facebook and other social networking services and the Guardian also provides a number of interactive features designed to deliver niche content on demand or to enhance community building around the Guardian website. In its section 'Comment is Free', the Guardian has, for instance, created an open space for debate around content published in the *Guardian*.

The website also hosts an extensive collection of blogs on topics ranging anywhere from arts and entertainment to politics, sports, technology and media. A number of these blogs infrequently serve as platforms for liveblogging. Depending on actuality and priority of topics, users can follow frequent updates about unfolding events and breaking news. The liveblogging services are provided for topics ranging from season finales of popular TV shows to coverage of political debates, the aftermath of the Haiti earthquake or the protest marches in the streets of Iran. Apart from the talkboards that are built as hubs for open discussions (a platform created already in the late 1990s), in February 2010 the Guardian also started to test an activity monitor called Zeitgeist.[11] The tool fosters the idea of crowd-powered recommendations and provides a visual record that tells users what is currently being viewed on Guardian.co.uk. Zeitgeist aims to assist site visitors to find out which topics are attracting users of the Guardian service most.

The Interview Partner: The Director of Digital Structure
and Development for the Guardian Media Group

Before he was appointed as Director of Digital Structure and Development in 2001, the interviewee worked as a trade press journalist and in 1996 became member of staff in various positions at the *Guardian*. At the Guardian Media Group he is responsible for the digital activities of the outlet. His work is concerned with the development of strategies affecting the Group's digital activities in the national press, as well as in the regional press, radio and classified businesses of the Guardian Media Group.

ZEIT ONLINE

ZEIT ONLINE is the web platform of the German weekly newspaper *ZEIT* and was launched in 1996. Over the past few years, the online arm of the print outlet has become one of the most important multimedia platforms for news and information in the German media landscape. The weekly magazine *ZEIT* was founded in 1946 and since 1996 the ZEIT Verlagsgruppe belongs to the Publishing Group Holtzbrinck, one of the biggest German media companies.

ZEIT ONLINE has its own editorial department running independently from the editorial department of the weekly paper. Similar to the Guardian.co.uk, ZEIT ONLINE hosts an extensive range of blogs concerned with various issues such as politics, arts and entertainment or travel and has managed to built a community around its website. The majority of the stories published on ZEIT ONLINE are produced exclusively for the site. The content is not only produced by freelancers and ZEIT ONLINE editors, but also involves staff working for the traditional arm of the weekly magazine. Roughly a third of the articles published in the weekly are also published on ZEIT ONLINE. Since 2006, the outlet cooperates with the online arm of the German newspaper *Tagesspiegel* and it produces a news ticker that complements the news services of both websites. In its commentary sections, ZEIT ONLINE also offers direct links to the op-ed pages of the *New York Times* and the *Washington Post* as well as to the Guardian's 'Comment is Free' section.

Beginning in 2010, ZEIT ONLINE appointed a community editor responsible for looking after its users and monitoring activities in the commentary sections and on the talkboards of the site. The community editor works together with a team of moderators and runs the debate and commentary sections including the ZEIT community.

Apart from offering various mobile services including RSS or Twitter, ZEIT ONLINE also offers a range of audiobooks and produces audio feeds of selected articles that are available for download for a fee or can be listened to via telephone.

The Interview Partner: An Editor and Blogger at ZEIT ONLINE

A specialist for web 2.0 topics, the interview partner worked as an editor for ZEIT ONLINE until 2008, where he developed user-participation features ranging from user-generated content applications to navigation tools. Until the end of 2007, he also ran a blog on the site concerned with current IT developments, interactive media formats and social software. He started his journalistic career in 1998 and freelanced for various German online portals such as Heise and Netzeitung as well as ZEIT ONLINE and is an active blogger in his spare time.

5.2.2. Alternative or Independent Media Outlets

The alternative and independent media outlets that are part of this surveyed group were not created as 'spin-offs' or online counterparts of traditional media outlets, but rather formed on the explicit basis of providing a 'counterbalance' to the latter. Part of the sample are staff at four media outlets, with each of the organizations following different aims and holding differing organizational structures. Included in the research were the daily broadcast news program *Democracy Now!*, the citizen journalism website Ourmedia.org, the New York City arm of the activist group Indymedia and the interactive television and web-based platform Current TV, which broadcasts non-fictional user-generated video stories.

Each of these outlets makes extensive use of digital tools in order to produce and disseminate content and apart from *Democracy Now!* the outlets were originally launched on the web, with the online platform being the inextricable part of their medial appearance.

Democracy Now!

Democracy Now! is a New York City-based national independent radio and television news program operating as a non-profit organization. Its online counterpart has over the past few years fully transformed into a multimedia platform, carrying audio and video streams of its full news program as well as of each story. The news programs are also available as downloadable podcasts and written transcriptions of news stories can be accessed on the website. *Democracy Now!* also translates its program into Spanish and offers it as text or in MP3 format, distributing it to Spanish-language community radio stations in North and Latin America. Apart from being present on social network platforms or Twitter, *Democracy Now!* reaches out to its users through calls for commentary and story ideas.

Democracy Now! started its broadcasts as a daily election radio show in 1996 as part of Pacifica Radio aired on community radio stations. In 2000, the program began a multimedia collaboration between non-profit community radio programs, satellite and cable television and an Internet based-service that developed into a radio and television newscast aired daily on independent radio and television stations across the United States as well as overseas. As of February 2010, its programs are aired on more than 800 radio and television stations in countries ranging from the US to Uruguay, Colombia, Kosovo, Spain, the UK, El Salvador, Spain, Honduras, Japan and New Zealand.

Democracy Now! aims to provide an alternative to corporate mainstream news programming on politics and current affairs in the US. Its news program concentrates on delivering a variety of perspectives on US foreign policy and draws among other sources on independent journalists, grassroots and peace activists, academics and analysts for its information. *Democracy Now!* has been presented a range of awards, including the Associated Press Award for Best Enterprise Reporting, the George Polk Award for Radio Reporting and the Webby Award Honoree for Podcasts and Politics in 2007. The station is funded through audience contributions and foundations and its production studios are located in the Downtown Community Television Center in New York City.

The Interview Partner: A Senior Producer at Democracy Now!

The interviewee started working for *Democracy Now!* in 2002. As Senior Producer, he is mainly responsible for editing and providing newscast material and works for the daily program. Previous to his work for *Democracy Now!* he volunteered for the New York City Independent Media Center (Indymedia NYC) and co-founded *The Indypendent*, the newspaper arm of the Independent Media Center. He is also the founder of the RNCWatch website, which covered the 2004 Republican National Convention. Prior to his work at *Democracy Now!* he worked for two daily newspapers in Massachusetts.

Ourmedia.org

Ourmedia.org is a web-based community of more than 150,000 members that provides video producers and podcasters with a space to publish and share their work. The multimedia platform is part of the grassroots media movement and is designed as a converged media space. Ourmedia's aim is to effect local and global change through the use of social media tools. Users can join the network as so-called 'changemakers' and contribute productions ranging from video to podcasts, texts or images. The media pieces published on Ourmedia range from documentaries to music videos, grassroots political ads, original music and ebooks.

The platform is divided into content channels and users can contribute their pieces relating to specific causes they support or topics that are of particular interest, such as environmental coverage or digital technology developments. Ourmedia also aims to provide an interactive discussion platform on which users can not only share their produced material, but also learn from each member of the community. In its so-called 'Learning Center' section, Ourmedia runs topical features on varying subjects, offers producer tools and teaches users how to create content and improve their multimedia performances. Their website also offers information resources on media law issues such as copyright, libel or defamation rules.

Ourmedia is an open-source project and partners with a number of other open-source applications such as Creative Commons, the Internet Archive and the San Francisco-based social media company Outhink Media, which supplies software and social networking tools. The organization also collaborates with the non-profit Internet Archive, which was founded to build a lifetime-lasting library of free online content around topics of interest.

The Interview Partner: Volunteer and Moderator at Ourmedia.org

The interview partner works as an independent video blogger and at the time of the interview volunteered as moderator for Ourmedia.org. He started his career as a television journalist, working in local news for several years as a writer and producer until he joined CNN International in Atlanta as a producer of daily news shows. After having worked for CNN for two years, he became involved with independent media outlets and citizen journalism organizations. Since 2004 he has collaborated in various online video projects, launched several online portals, taught video journalism online and co-authored a book on video blogging.

Indymedia NYC

As one of the biggest decentralized global activist networks, Indymedia has been widely researched and thus is a well-known case in the field of alternative media (for examples see Atton, 2004; Downing, 2002; Garcelon, 2006; Kawamoto, 2003: 15; Powell, 2003; Wall, 2003). Established by independent and alternative media organizations and activists in 1999, the Independent Media Center originally was designed to provide grassroots coverage of the World Trade Organization protests in Seattle. The aim was to create an open source and publishing information 'clearinghouse' (Kawamoto, 2003) for journalists with audio, video and print material on the protests distributed through the website:

> Media activists believed that the corporate media would not tell the whole story of the protests, so they set up a Web site to give the other side with a particular emphasis on volunteer participation and on representing the marginalized voices of women, people of color, the economically disadvantaged, and so forth. (Wall, 2003: 118)

Out of this initial set-up grew a collective network of independent media organizations around the globe. Indymedia outlets now can be found on every continent and in cities such as Vancouver, Mexico City, Jakarta, Istanbul, Beirut, Sydney and Budapest. The activist sites are connected via the Indymedia.org website. According to the site, as of February 2010 there were more than 150 Independent Media Centers in operation around the globe. Several outlets also produce their own newspapers, distributed as paper versions, on a local level, or globally as downloadable versions via the World Wide Web.

Because each center operates independently, the agendas of the outlets can differ and each outlet manages its own finances.[12] The aim of Indymedia activists can, however, be considered similar around the globe: They intend to provide independent views on issues concerning human rights and global politics and consider themselves as counterbalance to corporate media. Indymedia does not have fixed staff and is built on the principle that anyone can contribute to the site. Along with original reporting pieces stand articles pulled from other sources.

The New York City Independent Media Center (IMC NYC) is one of the most active arms of the Indymedia movement in North America. The center has monthly meetings and runs various print, online and television productions. IMC NYC currently has six media production teams, including a team working on a bi-weekly published newspaper called *The Indypendent*, a team for the Spanish version of the newspaper *El Independiente* and a team for the newspaper *Indykids*, which carries a collection of current news and world events packaged for children. The IMC NYC also has a team responsible for editorial and technical questions, a photojournalist team and a team that produces a weekly TV show.

The Interview Partner: A Volunteer With the New York City Independent Media Center

The interview partner started working for Indymedia NYC in 2001 shortly after September 11. At the time of the interview, he worked as a moderator of the Indymedia news wire, monitoring posts and hiding offensive publications on the open publishing platform. He was also responsible for the design of features on the Indymedia NYC website that are created out of individual stories that reach the organization across its news wire. The interviewee also infrequently wrote for the IMC newspaper arm, *The Indypendent*. As an experienced activist with Indymedia, he acted as advisor and assisted with organizational questions occurring throughout the Indymedia network.

Current TV

Current TV was launched in August 2005 on the premises that citizen journalism productions contribute to the original reporting of professional journalists. The so-called 'peer-to-peer' news and information network is a 24/7 multi-platform media company and its content is programmed and produced in close collaboration with users. As a fully integrated broadcast and online platform, the outlet combines television and web, with the latter being an inevitable part of the production process. Current TV is aired via cable and satellite channels on television across the United States and screens an ongoing news and information stream.

Users of the website can just read or watch items, but the participation of community members is vitally important to the service. Individual users are, depending on their level of activity, identified as contributors, commentators and producers and encouraged to participate in the content creation for the program. Users can submit non-fiction video pieces of one to eight minutes in length, a feature the station refers to as 'interactive viewer-created content' (VC2). Users can also submit so-called 'viewer-created advertisements' (VCAMs). An algorithmic blender assists the staff to determine popular stories and videos. Once these short videos—also known as 'pods' in the jargon of Current TV—have made it on the website, users are encouraged to vote for and comment on the pieces. These votings add to editorial decisions on pods that are integrated into Current TV's television schedule. Approximately one third of Current TV's on-air broadcasts are composed of this content, with topics ranging from political comment, satire and music journalism to news stories featuring current affairs stories from around the globe. Producers of full-length pods and VCAMs chosen to be aired on television receive payments. Current.com also hosts a range of other interactive features such as embedded social networking tools, comment options and discussion boards where users can add text, computer files or webcam pieces.

Embedded in the staff body is the so-called 'Vanguard Journalism Department' that is responsible for the production of original journalistic features. The department consists of a team of reporters and producers who travel internationally. The department also coordinates the citizen journalism arm of the outlet and collaborates with users who submit content pieces. Users whose pieces are aired on television are viewed as partners and might be contacted directly for future assignments.

The outlet mainly targets young adults and aims to deliver news stories on national as well as global issues from the perspective of young viewers. Current operates as an independent media company financed by private investors and individuals. The headquarters are based in San Francisco, yet Current also runs a studio in Los Angeles, an ad sales office in New York and international offices in London and Milan. In September 2007, Current TV received an Emmy Award for its interactive television services.

*The Interview Partner: The Vice President of the
Vanguard Journalism Department at Current TV*

The interview partner was at the time of the interview Vice President of the Vanguard Journalism Department. She had started working for the channel from its inception in February 2005, where she started to manage the department as well as produced stories and documentary pieces. Prior to her work for Current TV, she was a news producer at Channel One News, a television channel aired in high schools across the United States. She also produced a documentary series for MTV on the issue of covering hard news for the so-called MTV generation.

5.2.3. Independent News Aggregators and Media Commentators

In addition to traditional and alternative media organizations, two online-based news services are included in the sample that have specialized in a mix of commentary, original reporting and the aggregation of news stories from across the web. Staff at the web magazine AlterNet.org based in San Francisco and at the self-proclaimed 'media-supersite' MediaChannel.org based in New York City were interviewed. Both outlets are solely online based and perceive themselves as alternatives, creating counter-narratives to corporate media. As web-based platforms, both are inescapably dependent on the use of digital technology in order to produce and disseminate their content.

MediaChannel.org

MediaChannel aims to monitor the state of journalism and the political, cultural and social impacts of media across the globe. The organization is a global online community that cooperates with about eleven hundred affiliated groups worldwide, such as university journalism departments, professional media organizations and trade publications. The platform entails a mix of original reporting, opinion pieces and commentary on the current state of the media as well as a selection of international publications (such as investigative reports and stories on media issues) gathered online. Alongside articles taken from print and online publications, the site features video material, blogs and an archive for research and article material as well as a newswire that links to the latest news and articles on the state of the media. In addition to original news and reports, a large part of the content is drawn from affiliates and selected by MediaChannel-staff who keep a database of media-related news that circulates on the web. MediaChannel thus is a multimedia news aggregation site as well as a media commentary page that views itself as a self-proclaimed watchdog of the global media sphere.

The MediaChannel website aspires to enhance citizen participation as well as to assist media professionals in their everyday work and to provide users with an overview of the media scene and current debate about journalistic work worldwide. The platform can also be used as an information research pool for professional journalists as well as for activists or citizen journalists. Starting in early 2010, the outlet also launched a so-called 'Student Journalist Network'. The rubric is produced with support from the Park Foundation and designed as a social network that serves as a collaborative platform on which journalism students and media makers can connect, exchange questions, share knowledge or promote their own work.

Produced by the independent media firm Globalvision New Media, the headquarters of MediaChannel are based in New York City. It was set up as a non-profit organization as a project of two foundations: the UK-based global information network OneWorld—an organization developed to support media worldwide and concerned with human rights and sustainable development issues—and The Global Center, a New York-based foundation that supports independent media. MediaChannel has received support from several foundations such as the Rockefeller Foundation, the Open Society Institute and the Reebok Human Rights Foundation as well as grants from individual donors.

The Interview Partners: The Executive Editor and the Executive Director at MediaChannel.org

At MediaChannel.org, two separate interviews with leading executives were conducted.

The Executive Editor is one of the founders of MediaChannel and an experienced broadcast and print journalist. He worked as radio newscaster, reporter and news program producer for several outlets and as producer at CNN and ABC. He also took up assignments as print editor in London and his writings have appeared in outlets such as *Boston Globe*, *Columbia Journalism Review*, and *Z Magazine*. A former Nieman Fellow in Journalism at Harvard University, he has published a wide range of books, he blogs frequently on global media issues and he has received several prizes for his journalistic work, including two national Emmy Awards. He is also co-founder, vice president and executive producer of the independent media firm Globalvision Inc.

The second interviewee was at the time of the interview the Executive Director and New Media Director of MediaChannel. He draws upon a variety of new media experiences and was the co-producer of the Internet's first streaming media news show called *The Cyber City News* in 1996. He is the cofounder of the production company Speakeasy Productions and has worked as a content consultant and producer. He left MediaChannel in 2007 shortly after the interview and now works as independent media producer specializing in video production. As an internationally exhibited visual artist, he has displayed paintings as well as photography and video art pieces.

AlterNet.org

AlterNet.org is an alternative online-based news magazine and syndication service that started operating in 1998 and describes itself as an 'infomediary portal' brokering and filtering information out of the masses of information in circulation. The website entails news, opinion pieces and investigative reporting on a variety of topics, ranging from environmental, human rights or economic issues to media critique. Apart from original reporting pieces compiled by staff, the AlterNet website works as an information aggregation site or amplifier, providing information and news stories from other mainly independent news sources such as alternative newspapers and magazines and non-profit organizations. Its multimedia content ranges from investigative reports to blogs, video and audio material.

AlterNet has a strong focus on user participation and community building and explicitly addresses its audience to actively comment and provide news to the site. According to the outlet, it currently has 30,000 registered commentators, with some stories receiving hundreds of individual comments. In a so-called 'SpeakEasy' section, users can sign up as commentators and are also encouraged to create their own blogs that are embedded into the AlterNet website. The outlet views itself as a progressive news organization providing a counterbalance to right-wing as well as to corporate media reporting and aims to draw wide attention to what it refers to as failures of corporate media. The use of digital technology is perceived as a tool to promote a diverse range of progressive voices and part of Alternet's philosophy to remain a competitive outlet in today's media sphere and to spark citizen action and advocacy.

AlterNet is a project of the non-profit Independent Media Institute, an organization that supports independent journalism projects. Based in San Francisco, the site is funded through a range of private foundations such as the Open Society Institute, the Arca Foundation and the Schumann Center for Media and Democracy and receives funding from individual donors. The online platform has among other prizes received two Webby Awards for Best Web Magazine.

The Interview Partner: The Executive Editor at AlterNet.org

As Executive Editor of AlterNet, the interviewee is responsible for the daily operations at the web magazine, including supervision of the site and of staff. He is also the Executive Director of the Independent Media Institute. Before joining AlterNet, he worked as publisher of *Mother Jones Magazine* and has edited several books as well as newspapers. Especially concerned with political issues and media criticism, he has written and published a range of articles for a variety of print outlets. He was organizer of the Media & Democracy Congresses held in San Francisco and New York City in 1997 and 1998 and in the past has taken up assignments as political campaign manager.

5.2.4. Media Educators and Monitors

This interviewee group comprises staff at two organizations dedicated to monitoring as well as to training and educating professional journalists around the globe. Included in this sample are the Project for Excellence in Journalism (PEJ) and the International Center for Journalists (ICFJ). As these organizations aim to enhance journalistic work and improve professional journalistic skills as well as to screen and comment on current processes, they can provide extensive expertise on cutting-edge developments. Their broad knowledge of the current state of journalism helps to identify changes relating to organizational matters at journalistic outlets as well as to identify challenges journalists face in their daily work. Both outlets employ staff members who previously worked at professional news organizations or are still working as journalists.

Project for Excellence in Journalism PEJ (Journalism.org)

The Project for Excellence in Journalism (PEJ), also referred to as Journalism.org, is a research organization that monitors and evaluates the performances of the press. PEJ describes itself as non-partisan, non-ideological and non-political and specializes in quantifying empirical methods to study journalistic content. With its publications, the project aims to assist journalists in their day-to-day work as well as to provide insights into the current state of journalism for consumers of news.

PEJ is probably best known for its annual publication, the 'State of the News Media' report. The report covers content studies of American journalism and press performances of key events such as elections. PEJ also provides a so-called 'Daily Briefing' that contains a daily mix of articles on media performance and media issues aggregated by PEJ staff out of stories provided in major press organs in the United States as well as overseas. Aggregated articles are also collected in an online archive. All content produced by PEJ—including daily briefings, reports, empirical research and featured content as well as the PEJ archive—are accessible via the website. PEJ also links to the website of the Committee of Concerned Journalists (CCJ), a consortium of journalists, publishers, media business owners and academics that offers a range of tools and information relating to the craft of journalism for journalists as well as for citizens, students and teachers of journalism. On its own website, PEJ also features a so-called 'News Coverage Index' among other similar applications, where news agendas at a number of print, broadcast and online news outlets are examined in real time. These indexes provide information to determine what stories currently receive coverage in the American news media.

The project originally started in 1997 as an affiliate of the Columbia University Graduate School of Journalism. In July 2006, PEJ separated from Columbia and joined the social science research center and public opinion polling organization Pew Research Center (Pew). Pew hosts a number of other projects such as The Pew Research Center for the People & the Press, providing national surveys on public attitudes toward the press, politics or policy issues, and the Pew Internet & American Life Project, which explores the impact of the Internet on individuals as well as institutional processes and civic life in the United States. As part of Pew, the Project for Excellence in Journalism is funded by the Pew Charitable Trusts. The project is based in Washington, DC, and has received several awards for its research projects, including the Sigma Delta Chi Award for outstanding research in journalism in 2000, 2002 and 2004 granted by the Society of Professional Journalists.

The Interview Partner: A Senior Associate at the Project for Excellence in Journalism (PEJ)

A researcher, writer and editor, the interviewee worked as Senior Associate at PEJ at the time of the visit. He was responsible for a variety of the project's reports and also wrote a range of articles and essays for PEJ. His journalistic background is mainly rooted in print media. Until he joined the project, he worked for the *Christian Science Monitor*, and when I visited PEJ he was still freelancing as media columnist for the outlet as well as for a range of other publications. His writings have appeared in press organs such as the *Washington Post Magazine* and *Columbia Journalism Review*. From 1994 to 1997, he also worked as a reporter and researcher on the National Affairs Desk at *Newsweek Magazine*.

International Center for Journalists (ICFJ)

The International Center for Journalists is a non-profit organization that specializes in the provision of journalistic training for media workers. The center aims to foster the development of independent media outlets and to raise the standards and skills of media professionals worldwide. Founded on the belief that quality journalism can contribute to the improvement of human conditions, the center so far has worked with journalists in nearly 180 countries. ICFJ started operating in 1984 and since then has provided hands-on training programs, workshops and seminars for journalists in various corners of the globe. ICFJ also runs fellowship programs and in addition fosters journalistic fellowships in all corners of the world and promotes international exchange programs for reporters, editors and media management staff.

ICFJ works across the whole media spectrum including print, broadcast and online, yet specifically stresses teaching digital tools. Its website provides a range of educational material, including free-of-charge online training courses in a variety of languages such as English, Spanish and Arabic. The courses cover a variety of topics such as the practice of investigative journalism, freedom of expression, digital reporting and training programs for citizen journalists. ICFJ also focuses on specialty journalism and targets environmental journalists just as well as health journalists or business reporters.

Headquartered in Washington, DC, ICFJ is funded by a range of foundations and in addition finances itself through corporate sponsorships, various organizations and US government agencies as well as individual donors. One major project of the center is the International Journalists' Network (IJNet), an online-based media development monitoring system and clearinghouse for information on global media issues. Supported by foundations such as the Open Society Institute and the John S. and James L. Knight Foundation, the portal is an online service for media professionals from across the globe and assists in tracking and disseminating information on media training opportunities. The site is available in five languages and offers research and training material and information on matters such as media law and ethics. The site also provides a blogging guide for citizen journalists.

The Interview Partners: The Vice President 'Programs' and the Senior Program Director at the International Center for Journalists

At ICFJ, two separate interviews with leading staff members were conducted.

The Vice President 'Programs' is responsible for the development and execution of training programs at ICFJ. He is also responsible for the supervision of staff. Before joining ICFJ in 1999, he worked as a print journalist starting in 1986 and wrote for newspapers including the *San Jose Mercury News*, the *Herald Journal* and *The State* (Columbia, SC). In 1999 he was appointed as a Knight International Press Fellow in Nicaragua for five months.

The Senior Program Director previously worked as a broadcast journalist. At ICFJ he runs the center's programs in Latin America and the Caribbean and is responsible for project development as well as conducting training programs and conferences. In 1988 he received a Fulbright Scholarship and in 1997 a fellowship at the Louisiana State University's Manship School of Mass Communication. In between the fellowships, he worked in his home country of Panama as a morning newscast producer, host and television reporter for Televisora Nacional and took up assignments in Colombia, the United States and Europe.

5.3. ANALYTICAL GUIDELINES: SOME KEY PARAMETERS FOR THE FOLLOWING CHAPTERS

The interviews were conducted in 2007 and the themes and issues raised during the interviews are in some cases even more acute today. Since I conducted the interviews, the number of examples that prove the point of this book has grown massively and in academic research we are still lacking conceptual approaches that tackle the trends in journalistic practice that emerged with the advent of digital technologies in newsrooms. The interview partners reflect upon notions of speed and revised connectivity modes in the information age and how the introduction of digital technology affected journalistic work procedures. They discuss how the emergence of user-generated content, citizen journalism and blogging has affected self-perceptions of journalists as well as supported the creation of collaborative models that integrate these new news deliverers into journalistic production processes. They provide extremely valuable information on the use of blogs, podcasts or forums, digital production formats often adopted by professional journalists as a reaction to the growing number of information material and opinion pieces produced by citizen journalists and media activists. And they discuss the role that user-generated content features such as the BBC's 'Have your Say' website play in the news sphere of the information age. They talk about the personalization of news services and the evolution of an 'active' news user as opposed to the 'passive' consumer of news. Issues of gatekeeping and agenda-setting are also broached as the aim was to gain insight on how transnational news flows affect newsroom practice, how global connections are created via digital technology tools and how transnational networks with news deliverers are taking shape, challenging and reshaping the business of traditional foreign reporting. Along these lines the case of covering the Iraq War serves as an example throughout the discussions of the development of innovative collaborative approaches in newsgathering, production and dissemination.

Last but certainly not least, the interviewees envision the future of journalistic organizations in what this book phrases as the sphere of 'network journalism'. Their reflections on the role of journalistic organizations in a revised news sphere and how the emergence of multimedia newsrooms might assist in collaboratively gathering, producing and disseminating news in the information age contribute to a profound understanding of what is happening to the journalistic sphere today. Enriched with examples taken from current practice, the voices of the interviewees will dominate these following chapters of the book and illustrate the realities of journalistic production today, how the environment for gathering, producing and disseminating journalistic content has changed and how we have now entered the sphere of network journalism.

6 The Advent of Digitalization in Newsrooms

What are the implications of an evolving sphere of network journalism for journalistic practice? The first part of this book was mainly concerned with highlighting the theoretical underpinnings of the network journalism concept. I will now turn to the realities of information exchange and analyze how this concept fits in with the present state of journalism and what it might mean for its future. The following analysis of newsroom practices is grouped into six chapters, each dedicated to different aspects that highlight how the interplay between the emergence of digital technologies and news-gathering, production and dissemination processes transforms the practice of journalism.

This first chapter will chart the terrain by starting with a brief historical overview of the advent of digital technologies in the newsroom, provided through the eyes of the interviewees. The chapter will address how non-linear information flows started to challenge journalistic practices and how self-perceptions of journalists are being affected by this. Within a little more than a decade and especially with the launch of the first free browser in October 1994 and the introduction of the Internet to a greater public, (global) communication practices in general and communication practices in the newsroom in specific began to change and the interviewees reflect on their first encounters with digital technologies as well as on what they perceive as some of the great changes and challenges to journalistic work as a result of that.[1]

6.1. DIGITAL PRODUCTION ENVIRONMENTS AND THE COMPLICATION OF JOURNALISTIC WORK

> The new media is basically a bombardment of information.
>
> (Interviewee 2, ICFJ)

Digital technology has fundamentally transformed information gathering, production and distribution modes. All interviewees note that the introduction of digital tools to journalistic practice has been perceived as a severe intervention, challenging and changing the notions of how to practice journalism. When asked to describe the impact of digital technologies on day-to-day practices, interviewees replied with a variety of comments describing the effects the introduction of these technologies had on their work. First and foremost, the speed at which technological advancements are made almost seems stifling, demanding media practitioners to react. The Executive Director of MediaChannel recalls on his personal experience:

> As someone who started doing this from the first moment you could do it: When you couldn't do video yet, we could just barely get audio to go across a 56k, 58k telephone line. That was a big deal! And then you could get video, but it didn't work so well. And then suddenly every year you are like 'okay, what are the new codex, the compression things, that are going to come out to make the files. And then [. . .] flash video, the technology behind YouTube.' [. . .] Suddenly for the first time you can easily publish, watch and stream a video online. Like super easy! It went from being a difficulty level of eight to a difficulty level of 1 point 5. I mean, boom! Totally changed! (Interviewee 2, MediaChannel)

Producing content has not only become easier, but the ability to stream online has also assisted news outlets to increase their reach. Via the World Wide Web, the wide (and global) dissemination of programs has become possible and even news outlets that formerly operated solely on a national level, can now—at least in theory—enter the global market of information exchange. Formerly almost exclusively occupied by large media corporations that could distribute content via costly satellite platforms, a global information trade bazaar is gaining shape. And whereas journalists used to produce and circulate their stories mainly within the restraints of national or local settings and to a specific audience within a certain locality frame, content is now increasingly exchanged *transnationally*.

One case in point, taking advantage of these new news dissemination options, is the independent news outlet Democracy Now!, which originally started as a radio program aired on a couple of dozen community radio stations. Its Senior Editor explains how the station eventually transformed from a radio outlet into a multimedia platform that distributes its program not only to specific radio communities located in specific spots, but via the net across the globe:

> If you didn't hear *Democracy Now!* on the one-hour news on your local station: that's it! And eventually we went on to the web and we started streaming it on real audio. But again, unless you had an hour to spend at your computer, listening to the stream, assuming the stream doesn't break up, that was your chance to listen. And then, over the years we've expanded to MP3s where you obviously can take it anywhere, you can

share it. We now have video downloads. We started transcribing every single segment so people can just go on to the website and read it or they can email it to friends or print it out. A lot of blogs and other websites now run portions of our transcripts on their sites. [. . .] We also translate the headlines every morning into Spanish. Both in text and we record the headlines in Spanish as an MP3. So then those headlines are distributed to Spanish language community radio stations around this country and also in Latin America. (Democracy Now!)

In the digital era, the radio station-turned-multimedia platform now incorporates digital technologies to reach as many users in as many countries as possible.

Yet apart from the introduction of transnational dissemination options to news outlets, the Internet has also had a significantly strong impact on the communication between journalists and their sources. When the Guardian Media Group Director of Digital Structure and Development started as a journalist, he 'had nothing but a telephone. There was no Internet, only telephone and press cuttings and that was your life. And so everything was very much based around your contact book' (Guardian). And even though the contact book is still important, the Internet now provides

an enormous database of information [. . .] to search from. So I think that's something that's changed completely. In our times no one had mobile phones, so you were trying to get people in their offices. No one had emails so it was all very different. (Guardian)

The technology thus has changed the processes of gathering information, offering journalists research tools and access to a seemingly endless plethora of information—and the Internet has become an inevitable research tool, altering, for instance, journalistic investigation methods:

The way I write stories, you use the Internet a lot. Because it is, if nothing else the world's greatest phone book. And it is the way to get a hold of anybody. And when you use it skeptically, it's an excellent tool. It can be a wonderful tool. It can mislead you. You have got to be very careful. But when it's used properly it's a wonderful tool. (PEJ)

An observation by Paulussen and Ugille (2008: 34) supports this statement. In their study about the use of user-generated content in newsrooms, they note that journalists seem to mainly use the Internet as a background research tool and rarely as a primary information source. Yet, digital technology comprises far more than just the Internet and has changed not only content distribution options but also widened the ways of gathering information. It also influences production processes and has widened the options of accessing news content produced in other parts of the world. Democracy

Now!, for example, collaborates with stringers worldwide. Digital production tools allow 'video makers around the country and around the world to send video to us that we can use on the program', as their Senior Editor points out. The introduction of digital technologies at Democracy Now! has permitted direct access opportunities to spots in parts of the world that the independent outlet previously did not have. Take this example as a vital illustration and a case in point:

> I think the first time we started was right before the Iraq War. We had a correspondent in Baghdad, named Jeremy Scahill, and he was working with a filmmaker named Jacquie Soohen of Big Noise Films. And they were able to produce five-minute pieces from inside Iraq and then they were able to manage to essentially sneak the material out via the Internet. Saddam Hussein actually had a very strict firewall within the country. You couldn't send any large files. So obviously you couldn't send video. But they managed to be able to split the files into five hundred pieces and send each individual piece, and then back in New York we could connect the pieces together and we would have a five-minute piece. So we were able to broadcast video records from Baghdad at a fraction of the cost that it would take under traditional means of satellites. (Democracy Now!)

The advent of digital technologies hence allowed even a small outlet such as Democracy Now! (that does not run overseas bureaus) to invest in a correspondent team that provides direct coverage from elsewhere on the globe. Stories traditionally assigned to foreign correspondents operating for national and transnational corporate outlets, public service organizations or news agencies now can also be covered and distributed by independent news crews freelancing, for example, for small-scale news outlets.

What is more, the dividing lines between journalistic platforms are collapsing. To name just a few options that come with digital technology: former radio-only programs such as *Democracy Now!* now distribute additional video broadcasts, newspapers such as *ZEIT* provide video on their online portals, the Guardian.co.uk offers a range of podcasts to its users on demand and last but certainly not least, almost every outlet in the Western hemisphere has decided to appear on social network sites such as Facebook and at least quite a number of outlets—no matter if they originated in broadcast, online or print—collaborate with YouTube. This also urges a revision of the traditional roles of journalists. The MediaChannel Executive Editor mentions how roles of journalists are increasingly transforming and this seems to be the result of a change of news media itself:

> So traditional journalism that is which we used to think of as somebody who worked for a newspaper was assigned stories or a beat. And cover that beat is becoming increasingly a smaller part of the

whole media 'mix', because of radio, because of television, because of the Internet, because of websites, because of blogs—because of all these new forms of communication and information. (Interviewee 1, MediaChannel)

In addition, the emergence of global news flows proliferates a revision with regard to the expectations connected to the journalistic work profile. Whereas local topics used to be dealt with on a local level, globalization not only impacts international news, but also local news. Journalists are challenged to work within a 'more complex world' as the Senior Program Director at ICFJ suggests. This 'more complex world' demands an understanding of the global impacts on local stories:

> I would say that journalists now have to be more global. I mean: before it was very local. Now they have to be able to make connections between the local and the global issues. If you don't do that nowadays, you will certainly be reporting things out of context. So having said that, the skills also would require more cultural awareness. You wouldn't think about that before, maybe just on the local level. But now you have to project that into the international level. What does that mean for people here and overseas and where can connections be made of that? I think the skills are quite more complicated now and certainly a journalist has to master all of them if he or she really wants to play a good role in society. (Interviewee 2, ICFJ)

Accelerated by the process of digitalization, journalists therefore now gather, produce and disseminate news within 'global' rather than within 'local' settings. Not only has the world around them become more 'complex', journalistic work *as such* has become more 'complex' or 'complicated'. This 'complication' of journalistic work is aggravated by the emergence of new information disseminators.

6.2. THE REVISED SPHERE OF INFORMATION FLOWS

> This was impossible ten years ago! There was no way that that was going to happen! My investment is a 1200-buck computer, and other stuff of course. But that just lowered the threshold to get in. And I know so many really excellent producers and writers who got in that way.
>
> (Interviewee 2, MediaChannel)

Easy-to-use, affordable technology has widened the circle of content distributors as well as supported the creation of countless news outlets in a global news sphere. A transnational sphere of information exchange is evolving, consisting of traditional media organizations *as well as* an unmeasurable number of news dissemination platforms varying in size. New players have entered the field of news production and distribution and so-called 'alternative' platforms have emerged such as Ourmedia or Indymedia, providing content online and competing with traditional news outlets. 'Alternative' media according to O'Sullivan et al. (1994: 205) and Atton (2005: 15 et seq.) are concerned with social change, seek to involve citizens and aim to innovate media forms and/or content. The 'alternative media' movement is of course not new (Ibid.), but through the introduction of digital technologies, alternative and independent producers have found more options to gain a stronger voice on a greater public scale, as the alternative producer and videoblogger from Ourmedia points out:

> The big 'Aha' moment was when we learned that we could distribute our work online. Because up until that point that was the one boundary. I could take video, I could tell stories, I could write it, but I couldn't get it out there. And now that we can—I mean, does a journalist have to be a part of the BBC to do what he or she does? (Ourmedia)

The opportunities provided by digital technologies also draw media personnel into the news sphere who were formerly not producing journalistic content, with one example being the career path of one of the MediaChannel interviewees:

> I've certainly come into contact with a fair amount of people with the same sort of story as me, which is not journalist background, but who got [...] involved in political journalism online. And most of the people I know [...] got into it from just getting so disgusted about things politically, just started saying: 'I'm going to start doing something myself!' [...] I'm definitely from that camp where I'm someone who wasn't a journalist and went: 'Oh, what are these new technologies?' It's more like: I just found myself knowing how to use some of those technologies and being like: 'All right, I need to say something here! And here is a way to do it.' (Interviewee 2, MediaChannel)

This career path is just one case in point, indicating that a growing number of tech-savvy users are becoming involved with news reporting who do not necessarily have a background in traditional journalism. This new media personnel adds information layers to increasingly altered global news flows. Hence digital technology has lowered the threshold to enter the sphere of news production and distribution and news providers do not need to be attached to large-scale corporate or public service outlets any more in order to gain access to news consumer markets. The online sphere provides the option of disseminating independently at a low cost—and on a platform on which user numbers can vary anywhere between zero and millions, or as MediaChannel's Executive Director highlights: 'There are a lot of people who write blogs that get ten people a day on them. Some of those people end up getting hundreds of thousands eventually' (Interviewee 2, MediaChannel).

With more personnel entering the news production sphere, we also witness an increasing flow of information that is created to counterbalance news stories disseminated by corporate and public service media. Supported by digital technology tools, the 'balance of power' is shifting, as Shirky remarks (2008: 164). The online sphere provides space for alternative viewpoints that otherwise might go unheard in the coverage of traditional news outlets and not only supports the emergence of new alternative news outlets, yet for that matter enables alternative news organizations to amplify their voices and increase their reach. Take the example of Democracy Now!:

> We definitely try to bring out voices and viewpoints [...] that aren't heard in the mainstream media or aren't given enough coverage. Especially in the lead up to the Iraq War we were probably the only national program that consistently had experts on the show that were skeptical and critical of what the Bush Administration was claiming was going on in Iraq and the threat they posed to the United States and the Middle East. (Democracy Now!)

The ability to cover stories and provide space for alternative voices has also attracted a number of media practitioners to leave corporate media and turn toward outlets located in the independent spectrum of information platforms, such as the Executive Editor at MediaChannel or the volunteer at Ourmedia. The Ourmedia volunteer, for example, left traditional media in the wake of new platforms created on the Internet. He turned away from his corporate employer and started working independently when he realized that there were platforms on which he could distribute his content autonomous of a traditional news outlet:

> I kind of left the professional journalism world when I was 26. I was just burning with passion to tell the stories around me and I was in a position, you know, I was very excited. I was at CNN! This was the news—I imagined—that world leaders would turn and watch when events were happening to kind of keep up with what's going on. [...] But being inside of that, I just realized that no one was ever telling lies. I was never told to say something I didn't think was true. [...] There was just a general feeling in the environment that certain things were not allowed. Certain questions just shouldn't be brought up. The way to approach stories. [...] It was a self-censorship almost. And it was just very stifling. So yes, I was gatekeeping; and [...] it was 2000 when I left and that was just when the powerbooks came out with firewire cables and digital video and Finalcut Pro. So I would do my day job or I would write news

and help make news and then I would go home and I would learn on my computer how to use this new technology. (Ourmedia)

The ability to distribute content to a wider audience via independent news platforms eventually drew the Ourmedia volunteer to leave CNN and work for a number of independent outlets, where he felt that he was in control of the 'gates'—and where he felt that he could open them to stories he was interested in. As argued in Chapter 4, using the case of Tibet: The emergence of an increasing number of independent news outlets is stirring up the conventional idea of gatekeeping and allows access to stories otherwise suppressed by traditional media. In line with this, the Executive Editor at AlterNet remarks: 'There's a larger level of distortion in the corporate media and then underneath there's almost everything you need to know if you know how to find it' (AlterNet). Along with independent outlets working on a highly professional organizational level such as Democracy Now!, activist platforms such as Ourmedia or Indymedia hence are now capable of producing and disseminating stories for a wider public—and they can be heard:

> In theory [. . .] something on the Indymedia website has just as much of a chance of being seen and noticed as something on CNN. At least in theory. Now that's not how it actually works, because of various network things. But in theory at least we're all equal. So I think, the technology really serves as a threshold lowering thing when it comes to distribution. When you have a mobile phone you can take photos at a protest or you have small recording devices like this one, with which you can record in new ways.[2] But I don't think that's as big a step as the distribution side of it is. You could always get media. Now you can just get more people to see it. (Indymedia)

Many cases in which individuals were able to impact the news coverage of corporate and public service outlets through online reporting have occurred over the past few years, with the story of the dying Neda in the streets of Tehran or the information provided by citizens and activists during the protests in Tibet being just two examples. Another striking example that provides a case in point on how a fully fledged activist platform can influence news agendas of corporate outlets is the story of Indymedia and how its activists drove the coverage during the Republican National Convention that took place in New York in 2004:

> It was, I think, one of the high moments of the Indymedia movement where they had probably over a hundred whether you call them journalists or activists. But people with cameras, people that were taking notes and really chronicling what was going on in the streets to an extent that no other media outlet could even accomplish. And they were

just breaking story after story about people being arrested on minor charges, being held for 36 hours, 48 hours. Hundreds of people that were arrested were held in this former bus depot that was filled with toxic chemicals. The IMC managed to get photos from inside of this bus depot before any other news outlet could. The photos ended up being published in all of the daily papers. [. . .] Indymedia was all over the story as it was happening. And the rest of the media really just had to follow the story from there. (Democracy Now!)

In cases like these, alternative and independent news outlets serve as a nonstandard news source for traditional news outlets—widening up the source opportunities and confronting journalists with an almost uncountable number of research and story opportunities unthinkable before the advent of digital technologies. This is exactly what is meant when I talk about the 'decentralized' character of digital media, offering more opportunities to social movements, for example, to publish, distribute and mobilize support. Indymedia is one prime example of that (Garcelon, 2006).

Another example of how alternative news platforms can impact the coverage of traditional media was the political coup that took place in Haiti in 2004. Until the major earthquake hit in January 2010, Haiti was pretty much non-existent on news agendas of traditional media outlets. In 2004, however, the Caribbean state did get its share of international news coverage, when Democracy Now! eventually exposed the involvement of US governmental organizations in a coup against the first democratically elected president of Haiti, Jean-Bertrand Aristide, who had been exiled from the country:

Initially the US denied any role at all. They even denied there was a coup. They said he left voluntarily. We received a call from a congresswoman, Maxine Waters—I think it was a day or two after the coup occurred, saying that she had just spoken to Aristide. That he'd been flown to the Central African Republic. That it was a coup. That he was forced to leave the country. We put her on the air right away. That afternoon, Donald Rumsfeld was questioned based on that report as to what happened in Haiti. It really started the ball rolling of journalists questioning the Bush Administration over the role and what happened in Haiti. (Democracy Now!)

As a matter of fact, independent outlets are gaining influence in the (global) news media sphere and are being recognized by traditional media. The latter have begun to realize that an increasing number of emerging alternative news deliverers have the potential to become competitors. The Vice President 'Programs' (Interviewee 1) at ICFJ explains:

I think part of their role [independent media] is to shake up the traditional media and to say: '[. . .] everything is changing. You are not the only ones! You are not the only gatekeepers! You are not the only guardians, the ones who can decide what is news and what isn't!' And they're exercising that role and I think they are winning the argument, because young people are not reading traditional news organizations. (Interviewee 1, ICFJ)

Younger people seem to be turning away from traditional media and instead search for information from an increasing number of platforms online, especially on social networks such as Facebook.[3] In addition, platforms such as YouTube, easy-to-handle blog software or various websites that offer comment functions provide the tools for individuals to publish their content. Traditional media outlets are challenged to consider how to incorporate the material produced by these non-standard sources. Ignoring them would be a fundamentally wrong approach, argues the Senior Associate at PEJ:

> YouTube is a really interesting thing. A lot of it is ridiculous and worthless. But […] some of it is really interesting and it's like anything else: it really depends on the person. What is the role of those people? Increasingly they will be providing content or providing raw material that will become content. I think that's going to happen. If you're the editor of a newspaper or a producer of a newscast and you get incredible footage from somebody who's out there, are you really just not going to use that at all? And then I think you're going to get it more and more often. You're going to get stuff from out there. (PEJ)

A transnational sphere of participation is emerging in which the amount of information strings crisscrossing through the information sphere is growing. This information can be delivered by alternative or independent news outlets just as well as by private citizens or independent producers. Each of them constitutes a (smaller or larger) information node within a complex net of information disseminators and producers. And each of them constitutes a possible source for journalists within the complex sphere of network journalism.

Yet, this diversity of sources comes as a challenge, as journalists struggle to navigate through a restructured global news sphere. As the Senior Program Director at ICFJ explains, there are not only more sources available, but journalists need to identify ways to find them and how to verify them as reliable. The questions are:

> Where do we get that source? What tools do we use to get the source? With technology, with the Internet, where you might have very good sources, you can also have blind sources there. So, where do we go for that source? How do you weigh the importance of the sources in a heating environment? That basically changes the value of a source

and changes the way we use sources for information. So, that's why the skills of the journalists have changed so much, because the sources have gotten more sophisticated as well and you might perceive something that is not necessarily real when you deal with a source today. And before you were pretty sure that the source was representing what the source said it was representing. (Interviewee 2, ICFJ)

Or to put it another way: 'It used to be [. . .] the source that is in favor, the source that is against. The expert source or the government source or the civil society source. They were extremely well structured. Now, I don't think that line exists' (Interviewee 2, ICFJ).

The revised sphere of information flows also carries another implication apart from diversification and confusion with regard to the relationship between journalists and sources: Journalists seem to fear that the growing competition through alternative and independent outlets disseminating information might cost them their jobs. This is a scenario the Indymedia volunteer is also concerned with. Even though he does support the idea that alternative outlets seek to add more voices and therefore broaden 'the streams of information that sort of flow into the journalistic reservoir', these alternative platforms, in his view, cannot serve as substitutes for traditional media. He fears that 'when you have an army of unpaid freelancers providing information, you can then no longer pay real journalists [. . .]. I don't necessarily think that an army of bloggers should necessarily cost all the journalists their jobs!' (Indymedia) His argument reflects just one of many concerns articulated by journalists in the wake of the transformation of the journalism sphere—and it raises the question: Are journalistic outlets and their staff prepared for the challenges the sphere of network journalism holds for them?

6.3. THE JOURNALISTS' STRUGGLE WITH SELF-PERCEPTIONS

The attitude is: 'Who do these people think they are that they can tell stories better than us?'

(Ourmedia)

With the emergence of an increasing number of news disseminators, journalists seem to be not only afraid of losing their jobs, but at times these new news disseminators are identified as threats to trained journalists who fear for their position of being the leading purveyors of news production:

If you were a mainstream journalist and you've gone to a school and you've worked on three different newspapers and you've built your career and you have certain skills and you have a certain sense of yourself and your credibility, it's a bit threatening and aggravating if somebody who doesn't know what they're doing suddenly is a journalist here at a press conference. Somebody stands up and asks questions who's from the local parent teacher association, okay? [. . .] You resent that! You say 'How is that possible? Why is this person here and blocking my chance to get access to the decision makers?' (Interviewee 1, MediaChannel)

Journalists seem to feel as if they were in competition with these new players. A certain self-perception of journalists is under siege, as one of the interviewees at ICFJ points out:

Journalists sometimes tend to think of themselves as, you know, the ivory tower thing: 'We are the ones who know how to take the information, interpret it for the public and give it to the public.' And I think that's not a healthy attitude. I think it's good for there to be more sources of information and more ways for people to express themselves. (Interviewee 1, ICFJ)

Such self-perceptive views of traditional journalists as being the purveyors of truth is also highly criticized by the Ourmedia volunteer, who argues that even though corporate journalists might perceive themselves as the sole information disseminators, they might not necessarily attain journalistic standards. Producing investigative journalism pieces, for instance, can be considered an ideal form of journalistic production. However, the room given to investigative journalism is declining in the reality of the day-to-day corporate newsroom work:[4]

That's something that when I was in journalism school, those were the books we read. This idea of a journalist who would go out and find stories. Would like, you know, have a beat, and they would have like a neighborhood or the crime scene. And they would get to know people in that community and people would tell them tips. That's what I wanted to do. Then when I ended up at CNN, which I thought was like the top of journalism, [. . .] it was like working at Burger King. I had a schedule, I had a couple of shows that I helped to produce and it was very rote. I didn't do any journalism. I put together news. I didn't actually help find them. (Ourmedia)

This type of attitude among 'elite' news producers disturbs a number of independent producers who would prefer to see a dialogue evolving between news consumers and journalists *as well as* between independent and corporate news producers:

They [corporate journalists] come out there very authoritative! And so when they aren't telling the truth or when they're wrong, people get angry! And I think those of us in the grassroots who are bloggers, we don't really take the attitude of 'We are the authority'. I take the attitude of: 'You know what? I'm a person, I've gone out, I've asked these things of people, here is what I found out and these are my sources. What do you think?' So it's more of a conversation. (Ourmedia)

This 'authoritative' attitude of traditional journalists as described by the Ourmedia volunteer seems to be even further pronounced in countries with less access to digital technologies. In countries with a 'closed' media system still in place, traditional journalists often still occupy the role of the dominant news distributor and are not necessarily being challenged by independent or alternative competitors. ICFJ, for example, trains journalists in countries where news production and dissemination is still very much an 'elite' business and ICFJ's staff has observed that journalists working in such environments are often unwilling to adopt digital tools. When I visited the ICFJ headquarters, one of their trainers had just been to Colombia for nine months, working with management staff at newspapers in the country. Reflecting on her stay, she revealed to the interviewee that the attitude

> was very much a 'head in the sand attitude'—much more than there is here [US]—among newspaper owners, publishers, top editors, about the need to change to accommodate new technologies. Because fewer people are connected to the Internet in many of the countries where we work, it's easier for traditional media to say: 'We don't need to pay attention to that!' In countries where connectivity is very high, you can't ignore it and you're losing readers very quickly. So I think that in many of the countries where we work that there is a fear—or even more fear—of the changes and a refusal to accept it and to change. (Interviewee 1, ICFJ)

The reluctance to introduce digital technologies to newsrooms is met with incomprehension by quite a few of the interview partners as the emergence of a greater number of news producers and disseminators is viewed as a necessary wakeup call for traditional journalists:

> Journalism is an insular, scared profession that needs to open up a bit. And there is too much going on in the world for journalists to be as covered in their shells as they have been. It's helpful that things are getting stirred up and mixed around and they are kind of back on their heels a little bit. (Indymedia)

Instead of trying to fight for a right to exclusiveness or an 'elite' position within the global news sphere, the interview partners stress that journalistic outlets should rather alter their newsgathering and production processes and incorporate these evolving global news flows. These new paths to material and sources allow for a dynamic process of information gathering as well as for a greater accessibility to more spots around the globe. Journalists, according to the interviewee at PEJ, should be much more open toward these new sources. The Internet in this respect comes as a valuable tool that provides journalists with the means to research further details on stories:

> I can read about what's going on in the world by just a few clicks with my mouse. [. . .] If I really want to find out what's going on in Myanmar I can do that. I mean that's up to me. And there are people out there who are posting on it and there are news agencies out there that cover it and I can go get that stuff. (PEJ)

The Internet provides an enormous amount of background information and according to the Senior Associate at PEJ this is one of its greatest assets:

> Part of being a journalist is: You have to acknowledge that you just don't know everything. And when you get an assignment . . . I particularly think about this as a magazine writer, but I get assignments and I don't know about the topic. And I just basically spend a month or two just informing myself on the topic and I read everything I possible can on it and you find out when you do those stories: there is this entire network of people who only care about this topic that to you seemed utterly obscure. And those are the people you kind of have to lean on to get the thing done right. (PEJ)

This statement can be interpreted as a call for more transparence and it is a call for journalists to pay attention to non-standard news sources.

However, the evolving global news sphere in which information flows multi-directionally and in which information strings produced by traditional as well as alternative news disseminators overlap does not only impose challenges on traditional journalists. The Indymedia volunteer points out that alternative news providers are struggling to adapt as well. With some traditional media outlets starting to monitor the alternative media sphere to pick up stories, the boundaries between these spheres seem to disappear. Two formerly antagonized spheres of news production are moving toward each other. This demands not only a repositioning of traditional news outlets, but also requires reflection on the side of alternative media:

> Indymedia was sort of founded on this opposition between 'Them' and 'Us': 'We are the radical amateurs doing crazy things and you are the boring professionals who do things this way!' And that is not the way it is anymore! (Indymedia)

The 'balance' between traditional and alternative news outlets is—in the words of the Indymedia volunteer—becoming 'somehow modeled and mixed up and confused'. Furthermore, outlets such as Indymedia struggle with the growing number of other alternative competitors. Platforms such as YouTube as well as the proliferation of user-generated content portals on corporate and public service outlets offer individuals more choices to publish their material. Accordingly, Indymedia is challenged just as well as traditional media outlets to reposition itself within this network journalism sphere, as

> the absorption of these formerly amateur forms into the mainstream world potentially draws users away from Indymedia. It's finally dawning on the people in the network that: 'Holy crap! You don't have to be the media just by going to Indymedia any more! You can be the media and send your little video to CNN!' (Indymedia)[5]

Thus one has to note that not only traditional journalistic outlets have to find their position within this revised structure of information exchange. Both traditional as well as alternative news producers and disseminators are starting to realize that our information space is shared by a number of outlets—or *nodes*—that contribute to (global) news flows, no matter how small or big each individual outlet is.

All in all, one can say that the transformation of the information sphere seems to have a severe effect on self-perceptions of traditional journalists as well as on self-perceptions of alternative news disseminators. Traditional journalists are urged to abandon their supposed 'elite' status. Accordingly, the Indymedia volunteer advises journalists:

> Not to be so damn serious for one thing. [. . .] They will have to bring the skill of not having to have the last word. Kind of this perpetual openness to revision, which I think mainstream journalists now have a hard time with. [. . .] I think we'll start to see this become more and more of a web, kind of a seamless web as more and more young people enter the field. (Indymedia)

The journalism sphere is being altered into a network of many nodes, including traditional, alternative or independent news producers and deliverers. They all add content and are *nodes within this network journalism sphere* in which traditional and non-traditional streams of information merge into one sphere of (global) news flows. This also includes the (formerly silent) news consumers as information deliverers and conversational partners for journalists: 'Journalism has evolved in a way that feedback is not an option. It's not an option, it's not a choice—it's a requirement for journalists now!' (Interviewee 2, ICFJ)

As these first remarks on the state of journalism after the advent of digital technologies already show, journalists now have the company of a variety of new news deliverers within the space of the global news sphere. Alternative platforms such as Ourmedia or Indymedia and independent new outlets such as Democracy Now! are just three out of many demanding a place alongside traditional journalists.

7 The Shared Information Sphere
User-generated Content Providers, Citizen Journalists, Media Activists

Among the new news deliverers adding to (global) news flows, four groups seem to stand out at this point: media activists, citizen journalists, bloggers and user-generated content providers. However, there is no set definition as to what is behind each of these groups or if and how they differ in their character and in the ways they produce and distribute content (for a number of terms currently in use see Kelly, 2009: 17). This conceptual lack of terminology also became obvious throughout the interviews. The interviewees often had differing types of content deliverers in mind when talk came to any of the groups mentioned above. Some would, for example, not divide between citizen journalists and user-generated content providers whereas others would stress that these were two very distinct types of information deliverers.

Instead of treating these information deliverers as a somewhat unspecified 'bunch', though, I will draw lines here as each of these groups carries specific characteristics and impacts journalism in differing ways. This chapter as well as the following will explain what each group can deliver. Each one constitutes a specific form of information node in a network journalism sphere. Making clear distinctions as to what kind of material each of these groups can contribute to information exchange will assist in understanding what kind of node they represent and how they fit into this dense communication net. Therefore I am treating the groups as separate entities—or as distinct information nodes. In the following sections I will characterize each one and analyze its specific impact on the transformation of the journalism sphere, starting with one group that encompasses individuals who deliver story ideas, video material or comment to traditional outlets. I call this type of information deliverers the group of user-generated content providers.

7.1. USER-GENERATED CONTENT PROVIDERS AS INFORMATION NODES

> The phrase we use, somebody in the World Service used, was: 'It's a global network of stringers.' And that's what we've got really. I mean they're not journalists. They're just people who happen to live in parts of the world who've emailed us, want to tell us their story.
>
> (BBC)

Part of these new news flows journalists deal with are users who do not necessarily intend to add content on a regular basis to news organizations, but more likely happen to be on the spot of an event and more incidentally than intentionally witness a story that might seem of interest to journalists. The Executive Editor of MediaChannel clarifies one fundamental difference and attempts to draw the line between user-generated content providers and bloggers or citizen journalists:

> A lot of what's been talked about as citizen journalism is like the guy with the cell phone who's outside the subway station in London when the victims of the bombing are brought up and he gets some images of it. That doesn't make him a 'journalist'! That makes him an amateur photographer who's selling his images or giving them to the BBC or somewhere else. A 'journalist' is 'reporting' on something: That takes reporting and that's what's not happening. The World Trade Center here in New York, there were thousands of people with cameras who took pictures of it. Some of them got in newspapers, some didn't, okay? But that didn't make them all journalists. (Interviewee 1, MediaChannel)

User-generated content then rather refers to the 'ordinary' person from the street who happens to be an eye witness on the spot when a supposed 'newsworthy' story appears. One ICFJ interviewee characterizes this user-generated content as an important part of the increasing information flows reaching editing desks, becoming

> one of those new sources that we need to start dealing with. [. . .] [The user] is a new breed of sources that could be anyone anywhere that has changed the face of journalism. So I wouldn't call him a journalist, because he doesn't do that on a regular basis. [. . .] I would call him the new breed of sources that the media is relying on. (Interviewee 2, ICFJ)

The use of footage or information provided by the man or woman from the street is of course not a completely new phenomenon. Journalists have always been interested in hints and story tips. The Guardian interviewee explains:

> There are normal, non-professional, amateur people who get access to information, which could be of interest in normal media whether it's on the web or in print or TV. There's nothing new about it. You happen to catch Prince William snogging in a nightclub, snap a picture on your mobile phone. That would have been a story ten years ago, that will be a story now, it will be a story forever. It's just that the technology to label that is much greater. [. . .] It's sort of adding in some cases a rich tapestry to news, because of catching frequencies and that's fine. (Guardian)

What is revolutionary and a challenge to routine journalistic work processes is the sheer mass of user-generated content that reaches newsrooms today. With digital cameras and broadband access at hand, getting access to footage from a spot where a supposed story occurs without a journalist on the site at that very moment has become much more likely. Furthermore, the barriers to getting in touch with a journalistic outlet and providing comments on a story or pictures and videos from the spot of an incident are lower than ever before. Users can easily upload a picture or video on various online platforms or email content directly to news outlets. The content they add to the newsgathering chain is an addition that is viewed mainly positively by the majority of the interviewees, for example by the Senior Associate at PEJ:

> If it's used properly, I think it's a wonderful thing to have. Particularly if you're talking about the camera. If there is something big that happens and you get like fifty different emails from people sending you video or photos. The thing that comes to mind is the bombing in Spain. [. . .] You have got to be careful obviously about the content, as you don't want it to be too disturbing. But what are the odds that you're going to have somebody there when something like that is happening. It can't be a replacement of other coverage. But in terms of adding something to the coverage you have: Yes! It can add a lot! It can really add a lot! (PEJ)

The ICFJ Senior Program Director furthermore points out that users do not only add content, but in a number of cases have become the *first* source of information for journalists. In his view, this changes the nature of the information gathering process, with the importance of official sources and the like declining: 'The people are the source now. The traditional ways of gathering the news are not functioning how they used to function. The people are beating the official sources and the traditional sources' (Interviewee 2, ICFJ). The gathering process is actually being inverted, with users being the first source in an increasing number of cases: 'You start with the locals, with the people. It could be through the blogger, through online, through anywhere. But you have got to start there. And from there you double-check all the facts with the traditional sources' (Interviewee 2, ICFJ).

Illustrating his train of thought, he uses an example he encountered while traveling to Panama. During his visit, a bomb exploded in front of his sister's house, tearing apart the car of a neighbor who works as a Supreme Court Justice:

> Her [my sister's] son, who is twelve years old, goes out with his cell phone. He filmed everything: the car on fire—everything! The police came afterwards, the investigators sealed the place, the kid went out. He

found a bottle of gasoline spread in the bushes afar from the place and another gallon that had contained gasoline. He pictures everything, films everything, he calls the investigators. They came: 'Oh, I didn't know this!' [. . .] They left—no reporters! No one was there, nobody came! The car was left there. It was still there! And I said: 'Is this any news?' No! Her neighbor, her next-door neighbor is one of the Supreme Court Justices! An extremely important guy in the country! No security came. And I said: 'He got it on tape!' My nephew came to my house, showed me the film: clear film on his cell phone. The whole fire—amazing! [. . .] I mean, forty feet high, the flames! With audio! 'Send it in. I will give you the name!' He sent it to the TV station. The people is the news! It's not the officials anymore. (Interviewee 2, ICFJ)

The twelve-year old boy thus became a source for journalists. In this case, the roles of the news gatherer and the receiver of news are reversed, with the little boy being the informant and deliverer of news and journalists or officials such as the police being the receivers. Users can now deliver information either before or simultaneously with official sources, or provide background information and footage once a story breaks. This marks a significant turn in the process of news gathering, underlining the increasing importance of stories reaching news desks from multiple directions and indicating an increase in the number of possible information deliverers a journalist can work with: 'The good side is that all the sudden we're getting information that we never would have gotten before. Journalists can't be everywhere. Citizens are' (Interviewee 1, ICFJ). Other examples of citizens turning into content producers include the Boxing Day tsunami when mainly tourists in affected regions provided footage of what happened. Their stories, pictures and videos revealed the devastating effects of the wave. Journalists were rarely at the place when the tsunami hit. Another striking example the interviewee mentions is this one:

People recording police abuses against private citizens. [. . .] Before there might be an allegation that that happened, but there was no proof. Now we've got the evidence right there. So that's a good thing that this kind of information is getting out. There is a multiplicity. (Interviewee 1, ICFJ)

The increasing amount of content being sent in by users has inevitably led to the creation of new news divisions at traditional news outlets, responsible for utilizing user-generated content. Some big-scale examples are the creation of an Interactivity News Desk at the BBC or CNN's iReport platform. Here, users are perceived as potential participants in the news production chain. This indicates a change in attitudes toward audiences, who were formerly first and foremost known as (silent) receivers of information, but not as content deliverers. The example of the Interactivity Desk at the BBC illustrates how this traditional perception of audiences no longer holds up.[1] Wardle and Williams (2008) have conducted a study of the BBC's user-generated content hub and illustrate how the awareness among journalists grew after 9/11 that citizens contribute content and how a turning point was reached with the Boxing Day tsunami and the London bombings in July 2005. The user-generated content hub is now responsible for the 'Have Your Say' website of the BBC.[2]

One of the interviewees worked as Editor for this division at the time of my visit. She provided insights into the work processes of the Desk and gave some figures indicating the dimensions of user-generated content streaming into the BBC: In 2007, 12,000 emails reached the Interactivity News Desk on a quiet day; bigger stories usually gathered around 15,000 emails. During the Lebanon War in 2006, all in all the BBC counted about 150,000 emails on the subject sent in by users. Such emails make up the content the Desk provides:

> We're doing multiple debates. Not a debate on every story, but we do about say seven or eight debates on the key topics of the day. We get hundreds of pictures every week. [. . .] You've seen something appear on the wires, something's happened and you put what we call a 'post form' on a story on the news website which because it's so huge—the BBC website—because it's running about 6 million unique users every day, and because people now traditionally come to the web, because it's instantly updated to find out what's going on, your net of people who could give you information is pretty enormous. So all you need are one or two people to say what's going on. (BBC)

For the BBC Editor, this kind of content delivered by non-professional 'amateur newsies' (Allan, 2004) has become an inevitably useful pool of information—and it is a gateway to news content as well as to background information:

> I mean basically they're giving you the most fantastic access to a story as a journalist. And the July 7th bombings in London sort of was the turning point in all of this. People were showing us what was going on under ground and there was no professional journalists or cameramen down there. They were the only way we could get what was going on on that day. We had 20 thousand emails, and a thousand pictures or something to tell that stories—so fantastic! They didn't see themselves as journalists. We've gone back to a lot of them after and said: 'Why did you do it?' And they thought they did it, because they wanted to tell people what was going on. And that's quite a normal thing now. People caught up in a huge event, they want to pass on the story. And predominantly [. . .] not for payment. (BBC)

Through connecting and *re*connecting with its 'informal' information sources from around the globe, the BBC Interactivity Desk has since its inception in 2001 developed a contact database of its users. The database provides an opportunity for editorial staff to directly connect with users living in various countries in case a news story breaks. The BBC refers to them as their 'global network of stringers' who—even though they are not (!) perceived as journalists by the BBC—provide direct access to a number of stories and background material. The systematic development of relationships with users eventually has become part of the overall BBC coverage. One example underlines how this means access to spots that might be hard to cover:

> There was a coup in Thailand last year [2006] and we had a few people who'd messaged us in the past from Bangkok about other stories. So as soon as we heard tanks are rolling down the streets in Bangkok we emailed these people. And they looked out of their window and said: 'Oh yes, tanks are rolling . . . ' Straight on to world television, straight on to the website! And these were people who we can go back to. And that's instant access to stories, which is transformational! (BBC)

With the inception of the BBC's Interactivity Desk solely dedicated to the content provided by users, the outlet has embedded a number of new content deliverers. This innovative form of gathering news and converting parts of the audience into 'informal' news reporters marks a turn away from the sender–receiver model, and a turn toward more interactive information structures within the BBC. The specific way of partnering with news users—the opening of gateways that allow for more news flows apart from the use of traditional information strings such as news agencies or correspondents—is an example of how a traditional news organization is adapting to the revised dynamics of news exchange. The case of the BBC shows how an outlet provides its users with a platform where they are encouraged to contribute content and to a certain extent be part of the public service broadcaster. Users become individual information nodes not only receiving, but sending content to the BBC; they serve as a source within the network journalism sphere in which collaborative interactions between journalist outlets and users have become possible.

Another example that outlines how network collaborations are evolving, with users as stringers and information deliverers, was the coverage of the Virginia Tech shooting in April 2007. The interview at the BBC took place the day after the shooting and the Editor explained how news reached the Interactivity Desk on that day. User-generated content was a vitally important part of the BBC coverage as users contacted the BBC directly to either comment on the story or to provide further background material as some users had been directly involved with the shooting. The content they provided was generated at the Interactivity Desk and forwarded to various production arms within the BBC—a typical way the hub collaborates with other BBC arms. The Desk was, for example, contacted by an engineering student who had been caught up in the shooting:

> [He] had barricaded the door against this gunman [and] wrote the most compelling story on email and then, of course, we call him back and it' s on all our radio outlets.[3] It was on our *Today* program this morning, which is our flagship radio program, it makes stories for the website and he's all over. And that happens, that's not just a one-off. Every day something will happen and we'll put a form on and we'll get response. And that is amazing: From being a very small little unit and not many people knew about us, it's now universed and the BBC understood that user-generated content, which is what we call it, will help your programs from the most average story. (BBC)

With the creation of an Interactivity Desk, the BBC hence has assigned a team of journalists responsible for systematically distributing news stories and background information within its organization. What is more, the desk is a newsgathering pool. Here the BBC receives story hints that otherwise might have gone unheard. An example:

> Let's say there's a story today about student nurses feeling under pressure to do the work of senior nurses, because of pressures in the health service. Then we get case studies from nurses saying: 'Yes, that happened to me.' They can not only make stories for the website, but they can be on our radio broadcast or television broadcast. We can go and film them for our packages. In the past if you were making a television piece or a radio piece, you would have rung up the charity or the Union or the Health Service or whatever involved and say: 'Can you give us a case study.' We don't have to do that anymore. We've got them! And over the years since 2001 the database we've built up of people who have stories to tell is just fantastic! So now, anything that happens we can get eyewitnesses, because they write in, say what's happening. (BBC)

This is a perfect example of what has become known as 'crowdsourcing': using the audience to deliver story hints and background material.[4] This works on an international level as in the cases of Thailand or the Virginia Tech shooting, on a national level as in the case of the story about student nurses in the UK and it works just as well on a local level, as Wardle and Williams (2008) have found. The BBC Wales, for example, has launched the 'Here For You' project (for a detailed analysis see Wardle and Williams, 2008: 27 et seq.), a community outreach project that is committed to building a closer relationship with the people of Wales by promoting digital literacy. Story suggestions from users are most welcome here and users can even take part in the production process of news about the community:

The results of these collaborations are quite striking. These relationships produce stories which would otherwise stay under the radar of the BBC and would probably remain untouched by the mainstream media. Also, because stories come directly from communities, they are often more relevant to a wider range of audience groups. (Wardle and Williams, 2008: 14)

Be it with the creation of a community project such as the one in Wales or through the inception of the Interactivity Desk that provides stories for all arms of the BBC, both examples illustrate how the BBC values user-generated content as an additional option in covering news stories. According to the BBC Editor, active users are far more than a resource, and rather a group of active citizens who can 'educate' journalists. Asked if users are actually able to 'teach' journalists, she replies:

Of course you can learn from them. Some people tell you the most vivid stories; they send fantastic pictures. Often the pictures and the video quality is as good as any professional has made. I mean they maybe not doing it professionally themselves, but their picture quality and things like that. [. . .] They're as good as any you might get from a professional. And if it's the only picture of that story, then you'll take that whether it's wobbly or blurred or whatever. (BBC)

As user-generated content has become an inevitable part of the BBC coverage, one part of the routine work of journalists at the Interactivity Desk is to build relationships with these informal stringers, not least to ensure that they send the material to the BBC and not elsewhere. This requires a careful handling of content provided by users and the establishment of mutual trust:

If they're going to send you the material they have to trust you. That you're not going to abuse it or use it in any sort of offensive way or misuse it or say things about them which clearly distort their story. So what's important for us is the audience trust us. If they want to tell their story via the BBC, we'll treat them fairly. We're completely clear: 'You come to us. We're a publicly funded organization. We can't pay you for it.' We're not like some newspaper groups. We couldn't afford to get everybody fifty quid for their pictures [. . .], but we will treat you absolutely fairly. We'll be very open with you. We'll say what's happening to your material. If we're publishing it, we'll show you it and you'll get a massive audience. And then—in picture terms—if you send us a picture and we've used it and then some organization, too, would pay. Come and say: 'Hey, we'll buy that picture!' We'll go back to you and say: 'You own the copyright. If you want to sell your picture you can do.' We may buy the copyright if it's a one-off picture and it's fantastic. As we've always done; as journalists have always done.

But because there's so much now we can't afford to buy everything by the copyright. So they own the copyright. If they wanted to sell it they could do. So that's sort of a basis we've worked out. To have that relationship they need to trust you, they need to realize that the BBC is going to be a massive audience for their material. (BBC)

However, the interview partner also points out that the number of contributors is still by far smaller than the number of mere news consumers:

And in all this excitement about user-generated content you must remember it is still a sort of minority of the audience who were doing it. It's a really good minority and really fantastically important to our job, but more people are watching and reading the news than taking part in it. (BBC)

This goes with what Horowitz (2006: Online) defines as the '1—10—100 rule' of user participation: In general only one percent of the user community can be defined as 'creators' who deliver content. Ten percent make up for the group of 'synthesizers' who do participate and send comments or share links to material produced by an outlet, yet 100 percent of the 'consumers' will benefit from the actions of the group of contributors and 'synthesizers'.

While the BBC has developed a systematic approach toward collaborating with users on a range of stories, this is not an accepted practice at every journalism outlet. User contributions are in the majority of cases limited to breaking news coverage and incidents such as bombings, disaster and crime. Wardle and Williams have found that even at the BBC and despite efforts to collaborate, the material provided is in many cases 'little more than a novel alternative source of raw material among many. As one journalist stressed, newsrooms could be doing more to encourage audience members to have more impact on the final product' (2008: 16). This corresponds with many interviewee replies and is an indication that as of now, 'amateur' content is first and foremost only incorporated in journalistic practice as a resource when covering a somehow 'unusual' event:

You talk about the same handful of things. We had a whale down in the Thames and everyone has got that picture. All we have is sort of: Fire up at Buncefield and everyone has taken photos of that. So everyone's got all this stuff, but actually it doesn't amount to the day-in-day-out routine coverage of everything that's going on. (Guardian)

However, what does amount to the day-in-day-out routine is, as this interviewee also mentions, that journalists are confronted with a much larger quantity of information in circulation and that editors have to filter this vast mass—the result being in the ideal case a much better product because there are many more resources at hand:

And if you're doing your job, you're making a much more creative package by bringing this information in. But at the same time you're still making a package and you're using it as another source. (Guardian)

The central question for journalists at news outlets then becomes: What filters do they want to agree on? They also have to decide whether they want to follow the example of the pioneering BBC and launch a completely new arm of their organization devoted to user-generated content. The BBC is still one of a few organizations that has created a team solely responsible for the generation of user-generated content. This might be an indication why apart from the BBC's systematic approach to forming relationships with users, the relevance of user-generated content mostly is reduced to breaking news coverage. In addition, studies on the practices of traditional newsrooms and their adoption of user-generated content also indicate that journalists still often perceive their news outlet as the gatekeeper (Thurman, 2008). An extra arm of their outlet dedicated to user-generated content material might collide with their understanding of who is allowed to generate and produce content. What is more, journalists are often concerned, for example, over 'the news value of some user generated content; its standards of spelling, punctuation, accuracy and balance; and the influence of blogs on the mainstream news media' (Ibid.: 144).

However, the problem might not necessarily lie with the quality of the content. As the example of the BBC shows, there are many cases in which the outlet gains and not loses. The general problem rather lies with the organizational contexts existent in newsrooms that hinder the adoption of user-generated content as Paulussen and Ugille (2008) have found in their comparative study of two Belgian newspapers and a local community website. They conclude that the biggest problem in regard to user-generated content is an often-felt resistance against opening up in traditional newsrooms that is a result of the daily routines, work practices or organizational structures of newsrooms. Unless staff members are assigned to the task of monitoring content provided by users as in the case of the BBC's Interactivity Desk, news routines at traditional outlets often do not allow for active user participation. Journalists are too busy with their day-to-day work and there is barely space left (let alone do they have the training) to embrace user-generated content as a valuable addition to reporting. This echoes a statement made by the Indymedia volunteer who signals that the value of user-generated content and the possibilities it could provide if used not only as a 'one-off' source for breaking news are often completely underestimated. He refers to CNN and the major chunk of content gathered and uploaded on its iReport portal and criticizes that this material often represents not much more than a collection of 'odd' home videos:

'iReport'! Now, what is that? [...] I mean, what is that like: 'Hey, send us footage of your dog and like he did crazy tricks!' [...] That's like 'Americas Funniest Home Videos' or something. [...] Here is when we will be able to say there is a real change. When those organizations are accepting footage that's simultaneously both serious and not breaking. Okay? So, when they're taking footage that has actual serious public value and political content and isn't: 'I'm on the scene and saw the London subway bombers five minutes before they were dead.' If they ever take serious footage that's not got this aura of 'On-the-spot': that's when there will be a legitimate change. This other stuff is just sort of like: 'Wow, we know there is this technology out there and we know there are all these crazy cameras doing their stuff. So we have got to incorporate them somehow! So let's make it fluffy; or if somebody has something that we don't have, let's get that, too, and if we can, let's get it for free!' If there ever is real footage being provided by people and it's more than just 'I saw the volcano explode kind of as I was walking by and I just had my camera out.' That's I think when there will be a real difference. (Indymedia)

Another point of criticism is raised by the Guardian interviewee and concerns the handling of user-generated content during disaster coverage. Footage sent in by users can shift attention solely to spots accessible for tech-savvy users, whereas other parts of the world, where you might not find eyewitnesses with a camera at hand, are being ignored. Journalists who solely focus on user-generated content as a gathering method then are running the risk of neglecting technologically 'underdeveloped' areas. The interviewee refers specifically to the Boxing Day tsunami of 2004:

Actually that was completely skewed towards where there were affluent Western tourists in most cases, where you had sort of clusters of tourists. In Sri Lanka and places in Thailand: People with video cameras to the hand. You had a ton of information coming from that. Information, the video footage: Absolutely gripping! It would have found its way into any media outlet. Banda Aceh, which is actually where the worst atrocities were held, none of that! Actually there, everyone had to depend on the fact that news organizations were going. 'This is where we're going. We're going to send reporters out, because it's not a tourist set.' (Guardian)

News coverage of regions such as Banda Aceh was solely provided by traditional journalists. This stresses that journalistic organizations—apart from relying on an increasing number of users providing material—definitely still need their networks of professional correspondents:

And I think the job of a newspaper is to go: 'Where are things happening in the world and how we're going to cover it and what resources can we bring in to help tell that story most effectively?' Those might be blogs from other people, it might be pictures sent in by citizens et cetera et cetera et cetera. But that's part of a broader sense of 'How to tell the story.' And I think if all you do is skewed by where people already are, where this sort of amateur activity is happening, you're probably not doing your job. Now, just after the tsunami there was this earthquake on the India-Pakistan border. There was no bloggers there! No one snapping things with their mobile phones. (Guardian)

As this statement illustrates and as the interviewees repeatedly point out, there needs to be a level of critique that accompanies the practices of implementing user-generated content in the day-to-day business. This also refers to the ways in which corporate news organizations use the footage and which at times seems questionable:

> You know, if something happens I would want to see it. I guess what we all hate about television especially in America is that then that picture will get flashed every ten minutes. Or it gets flashed, flashed, flashed and that becomes the only piece of news people hear. (Ourmedia)

This corresponds with a statement of one of the ICFJ interviewees, who hints at the dangers of flashing the same picture over and over again as

> their impact is multiplied ten-fold, hundred-fold, thousand-fold over the impact of words. So for example [...] police abuses: Yes, it's shocking and people see that and they're outraged and they want something done about it. And those images get replayed over and over and over again and their impact is compounded in such way that sometimes the other context is lost. And I think there we have to be very careful in using those kinds of images and video to be sure that we're seeing the whole story. (Interviewee 1, ICFJ)

The handling of user-generated content then also raises ethical issues. Which kind of footage provides added value and which kind of footage could stir a story in the wrong direction or spin it in inaccurate ways? Whereas in general the interviewees signal a positive attitude toward the use of amateur material, they also repeatedly point out that the way news organizations deal with user-generated content at times seems to lack reflection as to appropriate standards of handling the footage:

> I think there's a dangerous territory around privacy! It's a sort of stop. Just because a minor soap star goes to the shop doesn't mean that people should be paying two hundred quid just so everyone can snap them with their mobile phone. And these two things of risk and privacy pose longer-term ethical debates for how we might engage with this content. Because you resume and say: 'Well, we don't want paparazzi.' Then we

have a press commission where we talk about: 'Actually we don't want paparazzi doing this.' But actually, what about amateurs? What about: does anyone have a right to not be snapped by a complete amateur with a mobile phone and someone buying it up? (Guardian)

What is more, digital material can easily be faked—and some users might have good reason to simulate a story or forge a video: 'A lot of the people who are using this kind of citizen journalism stuff taken by cell phones are paying for it. And that means that people have an incentive to go out and find stuff that maybe isn't really accurate' (Interviewee 1, ICFJ). Similarly reacts the ZEIT ONLINE Editor, who does welcome user-generated content but views parts of it critically, though, especially thinking of the dangers amateurs might get themselves into. As he puts it, 'journalists who were educated to work as journalists do have a definitive advantage. And this being, that they take a professional risk they know and can estimate' (ZEIT ONLINE). Amateurs on the other hand might underestimate the risks of certain situations just for the sake of snapping a picture and getting their footage and their name into the news. He refers to an incident that took place in 2006 during a school rampage in the German city of Emsdetten where students tried to take pictures of the unfolding events:

So they [the students] turned on their little mobile phones, switched on the video mode and walked towards the school, while all others were storming towards them to flee to the schoolyard. That's misunderstood citizen journalism, completely misunderstood citizen journalism! This human being puts himself in danger in that moment, forgets about his flight reflex. That's one of the things I find very, very alarming about that. I'm not saying that every professional journalist is much better in this respect. Someone might surely have gone there as well. There are enough examples in professional journalism. But in the case of a professional journalist, I would say, that's a professional risk. Also, to determine this risk evaluation. I can't expect this from an amateur. (ZEIT ONLINE)

Similar incidents have been reported, for example, during the Buncefield fire in 2005, when a series of explosions at the Hertfordshire Oil Storage Terminal destroyed large parts of the surrounding area and hundreds of nearby homes had to be evacuated. Lee-Wright notes that during the incident kids with mobile phones ran toward the danger field to take close-up pictures and offer them to reporters (2008: 255). The Guardian Director comments:

If you take something like Buncefield: That was a dangerous fire! But you don't go and sit there and say to people: 'We've got five-hundred quid if you can fancy getting your toes singed.' You have to be quite careful! [. . .] One of the things is: professional journalists in positions of risk. They are professionals who are able to manage those positions. You don't want suddenly get everyone doing it just for the hell of it! (Guardian)

What seems to be missing then are general guidelines for journalists that deal with standards of how to handle such content. With a greater range of source opportunities emerging, journalists are challenged by situations that are not addressed in standard ethical codes of journalistic organizations. The confusion in the wake of an increase in user-generated content therefore requisitions a revision of such guidelines and encourages a discussion about how to handle the material. Some news organizations now provide guidelines for their staff on how to deal with such content or how to perform in social networks. Reuters, for example, set out its social media policy in February 2010 and provides a manual for journalists on social media. The Radio Television Digital News Association (RTDNA) has also released Social Media and Blogging Guidelines.[5] Yet, whether guidelines already exist and whether journalistic outlets like it, hate it or are insecure as to how to handle it, the transformation of our sphere of news exchange is inevitably taking place and user-generated content is part of this. And as one interviewee concludes: 'The more cameras the better! I think the more people are out there that are following what's going on in this country, can hold those in power accountable. I think, that can only be a good thing' (Democracy Now!). Accordingly the Executive Editor at AlterNet comments: 'Well, you have to tell the stories the best you can and if that's the only images that you have and you can verify them, of course' (AlterNet). Besides this, the emergence of user-generated content can challenge journalists not only with regard to the question of how to use it as source material. It can also provoke them to improve their own coverage:

> Once you lose the fact that you are the only people with access to a mass audience, because now everyone can have access to a mass audience, you have to opt your gain! You have to prove what you're doing. You have to provide something that can't be done just by an amateur. And I use the term 'amateur' by the way [. . .] not in a derogative way. It's just a sort of monitory thing. Actually, someone doesn't make their living from this. Some of the most important astronomers are complete amateurs. They're just obsessives. And they achieve breakthroughs, because that's what they're obsessive about in a way that someone who's paid a salary. Einstein was an amateur mathematician. He really was and they paid his office when he came out with the theory of relativity. (Guardian)

This statement supports the argument that journalists should view user-generated content as another resource and a legitimate option to gather news material. Dealing with this content and with these alternative sources of news—or *individual information nodes* for that matter—should also be taken as an incentive to improve the coverage provided by journalists themselves—a perception that is also applicable with regard to content produced and disseminated by two other groups of alternative information providers: so-called media activists or citizen journalists.

7.2. MEDIA ACTIVIST AND CITIZEN JOURNALIST PLATFORMS AS INFORMATION NODES

> The point is amateurs—enthusiastic amateurs—have a valid role to play in pretty much every endeavor. And enthusiastic, motivated—heavily, highly motivated—amateurs are very often a fantastic force to be working with, because they are different to professionals who sort of deliver between nine to five.
>
> (Guardian)

Media activists as well as citizen journalists are two groups of new news providers who carry the potential to severely impact (global) news flows. The Indymedia coverage of the Republican National convention in New York City in 2004 when activists gathered and distributed material to traditional news organizations and drove the coverage has already been mentioned as an example in the preceding chapter and there are many more examples of how citizen journalists make their impact felt on news coverage. Before I turn to other examples and how the interviewees perceive the relationship between citizen journalists, media activists and traditional journalists, though, I want to clarify the difference between user-generated content producers and media activists or citizen journalists. Media activists as well as citizen journalists differ from user-generated content producers in so far as they generally do not just happen to be on the spot when, for example, a bomb explodes. The ambitions of citizen journalists or media activists reach far beyond snapping a picture with a mobile phone coincidentally. Media activists and citizen journalists are concerned with a *continuing* coverage of issues they are interested in and they choose various methods to provide such coverage: They adopt traditional news formats and, for example, publish print magazines or newspapers or launch TV channels, often focusing on local communities as the Indymedia NYC group demonstrates, and of course they use the most powerful technology at hand that helps them to distribute content locally and nationally as well as globally: the Internet.[6] Via the World Wide Web they can publish and distribute in whatever format they prefer: They can share audio or video, write articles or become bloggers and publish on a stand-alone website or join a citizen journalism platform or an activist network. Accordingly, some interview partners do consider citizen journalists as legitimate journalist 'colleagues':

> As long as they are providing information where they can provide sources and that is a continuing information-interactivity sharing-process, I

think we have to call it journalism! [. . .] You are not a journalist just
because you went to school or because you work for the mainstream
media. You are a journalist, because you are in a process of seeking
information in a balanced way. You are using sources, you are putting
things in context, you are getting feedback, you are in the communication industry and being part of it. It's just that there are different ways
of doing it now than ever before. (Interviewee 2, ICFJ)

Even though the interview partner here also argues that 'mainstream media
might be probably the most powerful' and the 'most recognizable form of
journalism', citizen journalists as well as media activists have the potential
to eventually drive stories and therefore have to be considered journalistic
partners:

Now, you can call it 'civic', you can call it 'social', 'public journalism'.
You can call it 'one person journalism' or there are people that say
it's 'angular journalism' or 'grassroots journalism'. You name it, but
you got to have 'journalism' in there, if you are providing information
that people want to know and someone wants to hide. If someone is
sending information to a wider audience—to more than one person—
and that information is valuable, uses sources and is something somebody else wants to hide: it's news! And if it is news, it is journalism.
(Interviewee 2, ICFJ)

Citizen journalists and media activists have produced and disseminated
content long before digital technology arrived. However, these alternative
voices used to be less powerful within the (global) information sphere. The
advancement in technological tools, though, has enabled a greater number
of citizens to participate and produce acts of journalism. Drawing upon an
example taken from the history of alternative media, the Democracy Now!
producer stresses that

Frederick Douglass was a citizen journalist in many ways. When he
started his first newspaper advocating against slavery he had no journalism background at all. But he had a message that he felt had to get
out. And he started his own newspaper and I'm sure he would have
started a blog if he was around today. (Democracy Now!)[7]

The improvement of dissemination technologies then has empowered citizen journalists and media activists to provide a wide variety of information
and to feed many more stories into the information sphere. As Bennett has
pointed out, their coverage goes 'beyond standard mass media in terms of
the extent, the depth, and (potentially) the quality of information about a
vast range of political subjects' and they 'provide citizens with information
on demand, rather than when it is supplied in sufficiently dramatic fashion

by officials and prominent sources along organizational beats' (2004: 310 et seq.).

These 'organizational beats' that mainly drive the journalistic practice at traditional news outlets often stand in contrast to the coverage provided and sources used by citizen journalists or media activists. In a comparative study on websites of traditional news outlets in Israel and their citizen journalist counterparts, Reich (2008) weighs production processes of citizen journalists against those of traditional journalists and finds that citizen journalists are often hindered in having access to news sources. He uses this as an argument that citizen journalism can complement but not replace traditional journalism and critiques that 'the sources in citizen journalism are largely defined by the serendipitous encounters and idiosyncratic choices of lay people as well as their inability to access better-positioned sources' (Reich, 2008: 742). According to him, because of such access problems citizen journalists make limited use of human sources and thus 'are freed of the burden of having to confront, negotiate with, and come to terms with fellow human beings. Instead, they are more inclined to show up at the news scene and use the web as a news source' (Ibid.: 749). However, even though Reich does have a valid point to make here, he does also miss the point of what citizen journalism is and what it has to add to the sphere of network journalism. His argument can be turned on its head; journalistic routines at traditional news outlets also invite charges that often journalists too heavily rely on official sources and news routines. And although Reich rightly points out that PR reps and spokespersons tend to ignore citizen journalists and rather talk to journalists working for traditional news organizations, the question remains, though, whether this routine way of gathering is always the 'better' way to do journalism. According to the Ourmedia volunteer, the 'alternative' voices of citizen journalists or activists accumulate otherwise narrow news agendas of the traditional media:

> I think a good experiment is when you wake up, go down to the store and you buy every paper, every major paper there. Put them side-by-side and you'll notice that most of the front-page stories are the exact same. Everyone's covering the same thing. And I think that's why grassroots media has kind of been flowering, because people know that those five stories are not the only things going on in the world. (Ourmedia)

An impression shared by the MediaChannel Executive Editor:

> I think this is one of the problems today that a lot of news templates, ways of covering stories, are similar in many different outlets. So you'll find the same stories often set by the news agencies. By the AP or Reuters. What they lead with, other people pick up or other websites pick them up. It's cheaper and easier to do that than maintaining your own stringers and your own people from around the world and have

confidence in your news judgment as opposed to their news judgment. (Interviewee 1, MediaChannel)

Often disagreeing with coverage provided by traditional media organizations, citizen journalists and media activists are capable of delivering different perspectives—or another layer of information—to stories. In addition, they often perceive themselves as 'oppositional' to traditional journalists, as this MediaChannel interviewee reflects. However, they do not only contest traditional media views and thus are opponents, but represent much more. In a sphere of network journalism, they are nodes just like each traditional journalistic outlet represents a node. Citizen journalists, media activists and the outlets they choose as distribution channels have already become part of a global news sphere—be it oppositional or consensual content they gather, produce and distribute. They should be viewed as valid additional nodes and working together with citizen journalists or media activists could add value to the output produced by news outlets.

Traditional media organizations are starting to realize the growing importance of such platforms. One of the first examples raising the attention of traditional news media was the Korean-based OhmyNews.com. Now, platforms such as MoveOn.org, GlobalVoicesOnline.org, OneWorld.net and NowPublic.com also increasingly become known among journalists. However, independent media outlets are still far more open to collaboration with citizen journalists or media activists:

> Historically Democracy Now! has had a close relationship with a lot of people connected with Indymedia. But I would imagine that in more mainstream newsrooms around the country they're realizing that whether it's Indymedia or these blogs—that they are consistently breaking important stories and it has to be looked at and they have to be given the credit they deserve! (Democracy Now!)

Corporate and public service news outlets seem to be just getting aware of the potential usefulness of material produced and disseminated by activists and citizen journalists. As mentioned in Chapter 5, the BBC, for example, collaborated with the blogger network Global Voices Online as part of its so-called 'SuperPower Season', a program special dedicated to highlighting how the introduction of the Internet has changed people's lives worldwide. All interviewees agree that these new voices are a 'valuable' (PEJ) addition to the traditional news media coverage. Media activists and citizen journalists can provide

> insights into a whole other part of the world that you wouldn't see otherwise. Global Voices is a really interesting site. I think OhmyNews is a really interesting site. These are interesting experiments in how to bring citizen journalists into the process. (PEJ)

One corporate outlet extensively collaborating with citizen journalists and media activists is Current TV. The organization is apparently designed as an integrated web and TV platform on which both—original reporting produced by journalists as well as material produced by citizen journalists and activists—find their place in the day-to-day news schedule. Current TV hence represents an information node within the evolving network journalism sphere in which traditional journalists work *side by side* with citizen journalists and media activists. This is a distinctively different approach compared to the collaboration model of the BBC's Interactivity Desk. Primarily, Current TV is not interested in user-generated content, but rather asks for fully fledged reporting pieces to be sent in by its users:

> Current is more about people who have personal access or insights into a particular situation as opposed to 'I just happen to have my camera . . . .' Now, we've had people send us those things and we certainly highlight it. But I think that's sort of the playing field that the traditional outlets are on. They want to call out for those breaking news images. And we're looking for really unique personal reports from people in our demographic, because we think that that's what is sort of missing from the news and journalism that younger people are really wanting. (Current TV)[8]

By incorporating alternative voices in its daily schedule, Current TV aims to provide angles to stories not necessarily found at other outlets. And even though its basic journalistic concept differs from the BBC's Interactivity Desk, the general aim of both outlets is quite similar: While the BBC views its user-generated content providers as 'stringers', Current TV builds a database of 'stringers' through collaborating with media activists and citizen journalists. This has eventually led to the evolution of collaborative story productions. Even though Current TV has a very limited number of staff and offices only in the US, UK and Italy, the outlet operates transnationally. As it combines web and television, it is able to disseminate its content globally and attract users as well as producers from various countries. In addition, Current TV might send correspondence teams overseas to cover stories, but in many cases it relies on citizen journalists. The interviewee explains:

> We try to do a collaboration of stuff where our reporters will reach out to citizen journalists. You know, we might not have money to travel to Venezuela. But we've been working on this report on Hugo Chávez and there happens to be a citizen journalist out there who is filming the protests because of the TV station being shut down and that person is capturing that as a collaborative process for this journalist, in some sense. So there are ways to incorporate citizen journalism into traditional journalism, I think. (Current TV)

Current TV not only looks for individual viewpoints or statements provided by its citizen journalists. These stringers are often also producers of complete individual reports. In addition, the outlet is on the lookout for story angles that differ from the coverage provided by traditional media outlets. After the fatal shooting at Virginia Tech, for instance, Current TV did not send a correspondent team, but approached Virginia Tech students via email and listservs and encouraged them to provide their own account of the event:

> When the campus was flooded with news media so much so that the students actually had to tell the media to leave, we never sat foot on that campus. But what we did do was we gave the students a platform to tell our viewers what was going through their heads through web cam stories. They sent vlogs, in a sense, via the web cams. We had a student who was sitting on the bunk bed in his dormitory saying that he just heard those shots and he just told us what was going through his head. It was very intimate; it was in his own words. There wasn't a reporter going like this [interviewee approaches interviewer up close]. Kind of like a feeding frenzy. (Current TV)

These reports carried very personal views and some students also used their web cam stories as an opportunity to critically reflect upon the coverage of the shooting provided by corporate news outlets:

> One guy sent us a report. It said: 'I did an interview with somebody from CNN and at first I told the reporter what I was thinking and then I started thinking that this reporter doesn't care what I'm going through. They just want to hear more details, more of the gory details. And I got really upset and I heard that there was this network where I could just tell you what I feel. So I'm sitting here in my room and this is what's going through my head right now.' And at the end of his conversation—his web cam thing—he says: 'You know, I'm really sad right now, but I feel a little bit better doing this.' And he submitted it. We aired these vlogs in a very like 'raw' and unvarnished way and I feel like it was about letting these people, who'd been affected, speak in their own words for themselves without engaging in that feeding frenzy. (Current TV)

Such coverage features very personal viewpoints and accounts for quite a number of stories produced and reported by citizen journalists or media activists and indicates that their 'rules' and 'standards' might at times differ from traditional understandings of how to cover the news. Opinionated reporting often seems to be favored over somewhat 'objective' or 'factual' news reporting proposed by most traditional news organizations. These highly personalized reporting styles at times also target traditional media. One example is the coverage provided, for example, by Indymedia:

They have a critique of the media. They think media is an important issue and they want to be the media. They want to offer another narrative about what's happening. There is a demonstration taking place and [. . .] newspaper guys are standing on the police side of the line and reporting on the numbers and the signs and what they can see. The Indymedia person is *in* the crowd. And he's actually a participatory journalist. He's participating in what's happening and giving a perspective on the people who are in. (Interviewee 1, MediaChannel)

To this interviewee, Indymedia's global online production and dissemination system is an 'impressive' model of organizing a transnational activist network on the basis of digital technologies. However:

That doesn't mean some of the reporting isn't just what I would call 'Fuck You!-Reporting'. Basically saying: 'They lied . . . ' It's sort of 'Point-Of-View-Reporting', which has a validity. It's more commentary than it is news and information. But there is good news and information there, too. (Interviewee 1, MediaChannel)

Yet, this turn toward personalized reporting also indicates that dealing with such content and allowing alternative news providers to become part of the production chain raises questions of journalistic standards an outlet such as Current TV sets for its contributors—or criteria outlets such as Ourmedia or Indymedia establish for content disseminated on their platforms. Obviously, traditional journalistic criteria such as 'impartiality' as promoted by many public service or corporate news organizations are hardly applicable when reporting is personalized to a certain degree—a dilemma Current TV tries to solve as follows:

I do think that some of the values of traditional journalism need to be understood by citizen journalists on the other end! Which is why [. . .] we have this code of ethics and standards that we apply to our citizen journalist reports. And we really do hold them to a high standard. And I think that that's important. (Current TV)

The Senior Program Director at ICFJ goes as far as to state that a debate is evolving especially concerned with the issue of standards for citizen journalists or media activists:

You might need standards, of course. [. . .] Whether or not they want to use the traditional journalism standards. I don't know if they are actually going to do it. If they do it—I know there are some new media people doing it—that's journalism! Now, if they don't want to use it, would they create new standards [. . .] so people know what to expect? That's being developed right now. However, I feel that journalism standards will prevail and they will definitely remain as a core value of journalism. Whether or not everybody uses it: we don't know. (Interviewee 2, ICFJ)

The problem of introducing general standards or guidelines for alternative media producers is an issue that also urges discussions among citizen journalists and activists. The interview partners volunteering at Ourmedia and at Indymedia already had their share of struggling to deal with some material uploaded on their platforms. The Indymedia interviewee comments that eventually 'you have a lot of "dreck" in Indymedia which are the re-prints and the rants and the kind of crazies' (Indymedia). This highly biased material can at worst call the reliability of an information node such as Indymedia into question, because it overshadows that Indymedia is also capable of providing valuable information or background material:

> The best stuff, the stuff that is what I think Indymedia is supposed to be, is: 'I was at this thing and this is what I saw and this is what I heard and this is how I felt about it and I'm now going to tell you and I'm going to share it with you!' So I'd say a lot of it is direct sort of first-person engagement with either situations or activities. (Indymedia)

However, these 'rants' disseminated via media activist or citizen journalist portals do eventually cause problems. The Ourmedia volunteer describes a general feeling circulating in the sphere of alternative media, where the ideal of freedom of speech has repeatedly collided with radicalism at times proposed within the spaces of alternative media networks:

> We have this ideal, this vision of what we want it to be. To empower people! But it gets a little dirty when you actually start trying to do that and things are happening that you don't always expect. Like, you know, people will be dirty and nasty, and [. . .] people will start ranting. Free speech is great, but sometimes people don't know what they are talking about. They'll start talking about politics in a way that just makes no sense. Or sometimes there is hate. People, when they have free speech, they start saying what they hate. And sometimes their hate is other people or other genders or whatever. (Ourmedia)

Citizen journalism and media activism hence seem to entail two sides of the medal: Whereas these platforms allow the circulation of more perspectives as well as information and opinion in addition to material provided by traditional media, they also struggle to control their producers and to ensure that the quality of reporting meets professional standards. The Ourmedia volunteer comments:

Of course, I have got to say that I love grassroots journalism, because, my ideal is that everyone has a voice and we can all take part. But the reality is that: They drive me crazy! I think there's not enough humbleness in the grassroots scene. You have some guy that has a camera and suddenly he thinks he is the best or that he is an authority! You know, sometimes he is as bad as a mainstream journalist. And Indymedia—which I love and I think it's a great thing that got started and I think Indymedia like in Manhattan, they do a very good job for events—[. . .] but there's so much in-fighting, they fight amongst each other. [. . .] I definitely don't go to them for information of the world. Only if there's an event I will read what they say. Other than that there's so much politics and stuff that I don't even understand. (Ourmedia)

Another important aspect mentioned with regard to citizen journalists and media activists is that the German interview partner was struggling to find examples of any widely known platforms operating within Germany. Whereas, for instance, the concentration of alternative dissemination platforms seems to be fairly high in countries such as the US, the German national media sphere looks quite different. This might indicate that media spheres, for example, in Germany do in some sense differ. Here, platforms such as Indymedia have so far failed to attract the wider attention of traditional news outlets or large audiences. The ZEIT ONLINE Editor believes that because of a structural difference of national media spheres, a platform such as OhmyNews would not work within a pluralistic media sphere as existent in Germany:

I can't see them at the moment, but don't want to exclude [the possibility] that they could also work in Germany. I only see one minor structural difference. If one has looked at the South Korean media system before OhmmyNews appeared, then I would simply say that was not a pluralistic media system in that sense. But we do not have that system in Germany. In spite of this we have—in spite of many one-newspaper-districts and similar [situations]—a relatively pluralistic system still. There are many published opinions; there are many different published opinions and hopefully additionally many different published facets of one topic. (ZEIT ONLINE)

A valid point made. However, the material gathered here can only serve as an indicator that structural differences of specific national media spheres might be the reason why citizen journalist or media activist platforms flourish in one country, but might go unnoticed in others. This is a question that cannot be solved within the parameters of this study and further research comparing (national) media systems is needed to shed light on this aspect. However, there is one group of 'new' news disseminators that definitely has gained fame in many countries around the world, including those with pluralistic media systems: bloggers.

8   The Shared Information Sphere
Blogs and their Impact on Journalism

Bloggers are the group of new information deliverers that so far has gained the most attention from journalists and in scholarly research (e.g. Lasica, 2003; Matheson, 2004; Reese et al. 2007; Wall, 2005). How many blogs there are on the web is not exactly measurable, with new ones created virtually every minute while others are abandoned yet still present on the web. Blog search engines such as Technorati try to keep track of their numbers and provide lists of blogs most read or quoted. As of April 2010, Blog-Scope, for example, an analysis tool for the blogosphere developed as part of a research project at the University of Toronto, was tracking more than 44.2 million blogs worldwide.

The range of topics blogs are concerned with is vast. Blogs can be personal diaries created for friends and family or they are dedicated to a special area of expertise such as technology blogs, corporate blogs run by companies, fashion blogs or entertainment blogs. The blogs of interest here are the ones that focus on the coverage of political issues and daily news, monitor journalistic performance or comment on emerging trends in journalistic practice. These blogs can be categorized as the 'commentariat' of the information age and this is the characteristic feature that makes this group of content providers so special with respect to this book. How such blogs constitute information nodes in the sphere of network journalism and how the relationship between blogs and traditional journalism can be described will be discussed on the following pages.

It should be mentioned here that citizen journalists and media activists often use the format of the blog to raise their voices and blogging aggregation platforms such as Global Voices Online are proof of that. However, as blogs do support a specific style and form of writing that has also been adopted by journalists working for traditional news organizations, they do deserve special attention.

8.1. BLOGGERS AS INFORMATION NODES

> Very little gets by the blogosphere anymore. And in that sense you got to be more careful. I think journalists are much more careful about

their facts. They are more thorough in their research. They may not show their biases so easily, because they can't back them up.

(AlterNet)

Bloggers who dedicate their websites to commenting on and interacting with content produced by media outlets often critically reflect upon the daily news coverage. In the words of the Ourmedia volunteer: 'The mainstream media are kind of like the foundation that all of us [bloggers] build around. A lot of blogs, again, aren't journalism. They're more commentary. It's a blog post about a story that they read' (Ourmedia). Bloggers do not necessarily have direct access to a news story, but use material already accessible online as well as offline for discussion and critique. As the Senior Associate at PEJ enunciates, 'a lot of them [bloggers] don't do a lot of reporting, some do. But a lot of them are just putting forward kind of opinionated interpretations of what's already going on in the news' (PEJ). Accordingly, most of the interviewees draw a line between traditional news organizations and the blogosphere. One interviewee at ICFJ explains:

As a consumer of news myself, I'm interested in blogs, I read them, but I distinguish between that and a traditional news organization. Because often I think, the newer media, blogs and that type of thing, have their benefit and I know what I'm getting when I read them, which is opinion. It's often not reporting. The reporting is still traditionally often done by the more traditional news organizations. (Interviewee 1, ICFJ)

This does of course not mean that producing commentary or opinion pieces is not part of journalistic work. Pamphleteering, for example, has played a vitally important role in journalism since the French Revolution (Stephens, 2007). And 'commentary' reminds one of the interviewees of a historical case in point in the United States:

There was a period in our history, I think it was right before the revolution, where pamphlets became all the rage. You could easily, cheaply, print small pamphlets. [. . .] Basically little magazine type things. And I think that's sort of what's going on with the blogging right now. It's like suddenly everyone realizes: 'Oh, I can have a voice to! I can make something!' (Interviewee 2, MediaChannel)

With the emergence of the Internet as a platform to easily publish and distribute such comments, the engagement with news topics has reached a climax: Commentary is not only found in the paper or as a segment of TV shows; everyone can now set up a blog and discuss his or her topic of choice. And the topic of choice for a whole group of bloggers is the work of professional journalists: 'Now any time someone will write a story or make a TV story about something, there are blogs that fact-check; that document the problems; that put the word out' (Ourmedia).

Critically reflecting upon the work of journalists has become the focus of numerous bloggers. They feed off of mainstream journalism (Reese et al, 2007; Wall, 2005) and are establishing themselves as fact-checkers who hold journalists accountable for what they write or broadcast:

> It [blogging] holds the mainstream media to open to criticism in a way that it never has been before. People are watching them and commenting on them and their fuck-ups are not going unnoticed. Not that that can change things over night, but it is changing things. They realize: 'Oh, people are scrutinizing us more.' And they're going to have to justify more how their coverage is. And that's definitely good. (Interviewee 2, MediaChannel)

With the appearance of blogs in the US, for example, the Ourmedia volunteer asserts that:

> You can tell in this country that that affects the coverage! That journalists now for traditional media: They know when they tell a story, their feet are going to be held to the fire! And I think that is good! So it's not always that bloggers compete and tell parallel stories, one is more right than the other. It is more like the bloggers will fact-check the mainstream media and keep them more honest. (Ourmedia)

This specific group of bloggers described here has taken the role of watchdogs, monitoring content provided by news organizations and delivering critical reflections on the coverage of both commercial and public service outlets. Bloggers constitute information nodes in the network journalism sphere and function as commentators who in many cases provide feedback for traditional news organizations.

The proliferation of blogs has also sparked a reciprocal effect in the emerging relationship between journalists and bloggers. Not only do bloggers monitor journalists, but journalists vice-versa monitor bloggers now: 'An increasing number of journalists is going to start to follow what is happening in blogs. Especially with regard to their respective fields of expertises' (ZEIT ONLINE). Both are reversibly feeding material into each other's production chains and they are increasingly interconnected online. On the web, 'another level of interacting with content' is taking place and 'people are interacting with our [Guardian] content, but not on our site. [. . .] I think there's a broader sense which is the sort of tactile engagement with content' (Guardian). As described by the interviewee, interactive conversations evolve around content produced by news outlets. Bloggers initiate discussions and trigger conversations through commenting on news coverage. As a result of this, they foster a wider dissemination of content originally produced, for example, by the Guardian. Online tools such as link or trackback functions make it possible to follow the path such conversations take while they crisscross through the World Wide Web.

Blogs furthermore do not only link to traditional media publications. They are also becoming research pools for journalists, easily traceable via search engines:

> Never underestimate Google as a research tool and blogs per se are simply always at the top of Google in terms of topics due to their extremely good ranking because of their clear labelling and so forth. If there's anything [to be found], blogs are generally amongst the first hits. Whether they [journalists] surface on Google or whether they actually went as far as using a blog-search engine to effectively form an opinion. There are those situations where it really works when journalists explore blogs. There are always a few occasions where it happens, that one positively starts looking [for these things] systematically. [. . .] One investigates, if there is anything related [to the subject matter]. And this shows that this is already being taken advantage of. (ZEIT ONLINE)

However, taking aside the connections developing between the traditional journalism sphere and the blogosphere, both blogs and traditional news organizations are in essence very distinct in character. The striking distinctive feature between traditional journalism and the blogosphere is the often-observed level of partiality. Whereas journalists working for traditional news organizations in general perceive themselves as impartial, many bloggers do promote a more personal tone:

> What they publish, how they publish [it], according to which standards they publish, if they adhere to classic journalistic ethic principles, or if they like a relatively well-known German blogger [the German blogger Don Alphonso], who is actually innately a journalist, in fact abandon those principles and essentially do nothing other than to become very polemical and really write their opinion very explicitly—more explicitly, than he would have ever been allowed to do as a journalist, including corresponding choice of words and so on. It's up to the individual, of course. He also takes full responsibility for what he or she writes and that is certainly a small deviation from the traditional media company. (ZEIT ONLINE)

Independent bloggers typically carry this personal tone in their writing, while journalists—attached to a news organization—are bound to act in accordance with institutional guidelines, as

> at the end of the day the institution is jointly responsible for what happens in it. [. . .] It is also held accountable for it by the reader. If we

publish a bad article as a rule it then doesn't say: 'What has such and such written?' But rather: 'What have you [plural] written?' Now if a blogger writes something—okay, that's when they say: 'Why did you [singular] write it like that?' (ZEIT ONLINE)

This is just one of the differences between independent bloggers and traditional journalists. However, traditional news organizations have begun to acknowledge (at least some) bloggers as information providers and perceive them as part of the (global) news sphere. The BBC, for instance, has integrated bloggers on its website and regularly features blogs from countries such as Cuba or Iraq:

I mean the BBC has to be an impartial news organization. You know what our charter tells us to do. So that is what we do. A lot of these bloggers are very partial! A lot of these people come with strong views. Now we can display all those views so we get a range of voices. We get all sorts of different people with different views adding to the story. And what we hope is: We can display all this and then whoever is reading it or viewing it or listening to it can make their judgment. We're telling the story as best we can with comments from all sides of the argument and let people make up their own mind. (BBC)

Besides such approaches to integrating bloggers into traditional news operations, the evolution of blogging has also been met with fear. One of the ICFJ interviewees worries that blogs might be misunderstood as a replacement for traditional media—a role that according to him bloggers are unable to fulfill. Traditional media outlets see it as their duty and social responsibility to uncover stories, to, for example, reveal abuses of power or breaches of privacy rights. Bloggers on the other hand are 'not the ones going out and filing a freedom of information request to get that information, working the sources, doing the role of traditional journalists. And that's the danger' (Interviewee 1, ICFJ). The interviewee gives an example:

New York Times won a Pulitzer for its stories revealing governments' wire-tapping of US citizens. Not just foreigners, but Americans. We've always had sort of a belief that in this country we have a right to privacy and that there needs to be a check on governments' ability to investigate citizens and that traditionally has been through courts who give permission for invasive procedures to get information from citizens. And the *New York Times* reported on a program that is secretly wire-tapping Americans and getting information from them without any oversight from courts really. The *Washington Post* won a Pulitzer also for its investigations of secret prisons in countries in Eastern Europe and South East Asia and Afghanistan where people who were arrested by US Forces were sent to these secret prisons and methods could be used on them that would not be allowed under US jurisdiction. I think those are both important stories! They were again uncovered by traditional journalism. Bloggers have commented on them of course quite a bit. But I think that what I fear could happen is that we are sort of discounting the role of traditional journalism at our peril, because we haven't yet found a way for the kind of reporting that finds that kind of information to be supported financially through new media and bloggers. (Interviewee 1, ICFJ)

In line with this, traditional journalists do seem to feel the urge to incorporate bloggers in their coverage as they are part of the evolving global news sphere, however, not for the sake of sacrificing the responsibilities they carry as journalistic outlets. The blogging tool as such, though—initially only used by alternative media—has found its way into traditional journalistic outlets and almost every organization now has set out one or more staffers to blog.

8.2. JOURNALISTS AS BLOGGERS: THE ADAPTATION OF AN ALTERNATIVE MEDIA TOOL

Some of their blogs have become essential reading and in some cases they are more important than a lot of the coverage that's actually in the paper.

(Democracy Now!)

In the wake of the increasing popularity of blogs, media organizations have not only started to monitor them or feature certain blogs on their websites, but they have assigned some of their staff members to blog. They now appoint 'their own journalists to use the same techniques that the citizen journalists were using' (ICFJ Interviewee 2). Blogging offers journalists a 'vessel' (Indymedia) to transport information in a digital space. It is a tool that in the eye of the Guardian interviewee constitutes an 'evolutionary step in online publishing' and a news organization can benefit from using it:

Actually it means we don't have to write stories, we can update what we want, we can have comments immediately, people can link to an individual thing et cetera et cetera, plus it is all happening in one place. It was just the perfect form for working on the web. It just had everything: it's all there, the whole kit and caboodle and it is very search engine friendly. So really, it's just a passive thing. A blog is just an entity and a journalist will use it just in the same way as my Mum might use it to describe the activity of her cat. The debate about 'What is a blog? What isn't a blog?'—sort of meaningless! I think that the software that came with blogs and then what has emerged: this is how content is meant to work on the web. And I think journalists were right to seize it as a tool. Who then uses it and how they use it is another matter. (Guardian)

The majority of interviewees are blogging themselves or have blogged at some point in their journalistic careers. Active bloggers at the time of the interviews were the Ourmedia volunteer, the ZEIT ONLINE Editor and the MediaChannel Executive Editor. The latter explains that he uses his blog

> as a way to write a counter-narrative about the news everyday. So I'm actually offering an analytical take. What's in the news, what's not in the news, what other people are covering, what we're covering here et cetera, et cetera. (Interviewee 1, MediaChannel)

He perceives himself as a commentator, especially analyzing the work of his journalist colleagues:

> Because my feeling is that our news system is not doing a good job of covering the news and covering what's happening. And so I want to point that out and I want to also give people other resources, links. You know, the *New York Times* said this, but the *Guardian* of London said something very different. (Interviewee 1, MediaChannel)

Such a turn toward blogging marks a (re)turn toward 'opinionated' journalism within the 'professional' sphere of journalism, making 'mainstream journalists more like the journalism in the 60s in a sense, because blogs have personal voices' (AlterNet).[1] The Indymedia interviewee comments that 'one of the reasons why political blogging has taken off so much in the United States is because there isn't an outlet for that unabashedly partisan political perspective' (Indymedia). However, this (re)turn is also challenging journalists with respect to their work routines—especially in regard to their tone and style of writing:

> If you're going to be a good blogger you'll have to share your own experience! If you're an objective journalist you're not in the story! You typically are not. So, I assume for some journalists this is uncomfortable. But for other journalists it's very exciting, because they've got so much that they want to express that doesn't fit easily into the confines of the traditional journalism story. [...] Now, blogging requires a certain kind of personality. Especially if you're going to be a serious blogger, because you basically do it all the time! I mean you have to be a manic personality. You have to be really energetic, and you have to be paying attention all the time. You can't just like dapple once in a while. You won't get any audience paying attention to you! Blog every once a couple of days—who cares. (AlterNet)

Another characteristic of blogs that differs significantly from the traditional work practice of journalists is the invitation to users to participate in a conversation. Blogs are much more than an author's commentary page: They encourage readers to add their opinion or even add additional information. Reese et al. explain that the very characteristic of blogs is that they 'provide the connectivity lacking in the professional media' (2007: 239). Through their embedded commentary function, blogs allow interaction. Linking and trackback functions support the development of a net of information sources around a news story. Their 'ease of use, low barriers to creation and maintenance, dynamic quality, easy interactivity, and potential for wide distribution' (Ibid.) are their foremost characteristics.[2] Some bloggers, for example, use the commentary function of each blog as crowdsourcing tool (Briggs, 2010). Asking questions in a blog and inviting users to participate and deliver additional information or comment on a story is the true added value of blogs. It embraces Surowiecki's (2005) idea of using the 'wisdom of crowds' in favor of a better end product.

However, the interactive opportunities the format allows often go unrecognized by journalists who blog on websites of traditional news organizations:

> If you look at a lot of newspaper blogs, there won't be links. Their blogs are basically articles, they are done in blog format. But a good blog will have links that go off. But a lot of newspaper and TV's websites don't want links off their site, because that gets them off the site! Which is a little crazy. (Ourmedia)

Thurman (2008) conducted a study of blogs at professional news organizations and his findings support the above comment. He reveals how some organizations try to exercise control over a sphere that has interactivity as its main characteristic and thus should allow for engagement rather than restrain users and command them to silence. Thurman found that 'amongst the mainstream British online news media, only the Guardian.co.uk allowed comments to be posted to its blogs without pre-moderation' (2008: 145). Such handling of content does neglect the social conventions of the blog format and is lead by a 'desire to retain, and in some cases reclaim, control over the editorial content of the publications in question' (Ibid: 151). The ZEIT ONLINE Editor argues along these lines, similarly criticizing that the options a blog offers might often not be used in their entirety:

> From a journalist nowadays publishing at least online I expect that he/she is able to compose salient links. From a journalist, who publishes online I expect that he/she [. . .] addresses relevant user answers personally. If he/she responds to them himself/herself in his/her next article; if it's a column for example, which lends itself to this. If he/she's administrating a blog, then maybe it also lends itself to him /her seizing it that way. As

an example we do have this in our [publishing] house, too, very differing ways to treat this [subject matter]. I, for instance, react directly to user comments on my blog. But for example my colleague Jochen Bittner [. . .] responds to user comments later on. Basically when he enters an item pertaining to a similar topic, he picks up [previous] issues. But in his own comments, hence those comments regarding his blog entries, you can't find anything [written] by him. Therefore he still draws a clear distinction: 'I am the one here, who writes the text. You are the ones posting the comments. I read them but I do not leave comments.' (ZEIT ONLINE)[3]

Journalists ignoring typical characteristics of blogs fail to acknowledge what Jarvis (2009) proposes as the main ingredients of today's production sphere: engagement with users and the ability to link to other content provided across the web. He takes Google as an example of a company that has best understood the dynamics of the information age. Google has according to him learned that sharing and collaboration are the most salient values. Ceding control to customers and letting them become partners in the production chain are important. The blog format with its interactive features allows exactly that: to let the users in on the thoughts of the individual blogger and to take on board information, advice and links to other sources.

The Indymedia volunteer adds another point of criticism. Although he more generally welcomes blogs as an addition to the journalistic toolkit, he questions whether journalists are capable of being 'good' bloggers:

There was a day and the *Times* like a year ago [2006], when their blogs dealt with the Oscars, food, wine tasting and the most ridiculous, stupid things. Now, that's changing. They are starting to have blogs about politics now, finally! I guess the question for me is what's the value added there? [. . .] What value are they adding to what the *Times* already does? I don't necessarily think that they're adding all that much. First of all [. . .] these people don't know how to blog! That's the first thing! They do not write like bloggers, most of them. They write like journalists trying to blog. They just sound stilted! They just sound so damn serious, still! [. . .] They just can't get into that casual smirkyness like a good blogger can. (Indymedia)

Taken together, the critical reflections on the work of journalists who blog for traditional news organizations indicate that although the blog format has been adopted, there is room for improvement in regard to the ways journalists utilize blogs. Traditional news organizations, for example, need to learn how much 'blog' is actually useful for the outlet:

Everybody has a blog now. Every outlet has a blog. They have several blogs. They can be good and they can be bad. The bad thing is when the outlet is so eager to have something in the blog that they just have people constantly filing to their blog, because they want to have something fresh all the time. And there is nothing bad about that except that ultimately what it means is the person who's doing that is probably spending less time reporting. (PEJ)

With regard to this, the interviewee draws an interesting parallel between television news coverage and blogging:

It's like the cable news phenomenon. You don't really see much on cable news, because they keep going back to the correspondent every twenty minutes. How can that person do any reporting? He really can't. But their job is to stand in front of the camera every twenty minutes and say: 'You know, this is what's happening. There is a courthouse behind me and there is a chaos going on there. We're going to have more for you in twenty minutes.' And there is never anything they really say, because the fact of the matter is: You can't just spend all your time typing in a blog or staying in front of a camera. A lot of journalism isn't what's on the paper or on the screen! It's all the stuff that goes on behind the scenes and when you start telling somebody to put more and more of that stuff out there, they have less time to do the reporting that really makes journalism complete. (PEJ)

According to this statement, blogs are an add-on in which extra layers are provided in addition to conventional coverage, but they should not replace the traditional fields of work. What is more, if blogs are used, their full potential should be seized as well. This includes linking to sources, listening and reacting to user comments and writing in a more personal tone. To allow the blog format to seize its full potential, ZEIT ONLINE, for example, handles its blogs slightly different from regular news stories. Its bloggers are allowed to write more personally and the interviewee explains: 'We do not edit blog posts. Concurrently the author is responsible for his/her blog's content. There is no second check. [. . .] It really is purely that author' (ZEIT ONLINE).

Blogs also can provide a space for journalists to incorporate stories and topics that might otherwise not get any attention, for example, in a newspaper (as the newspaper can only provide a limited number of pages) or on television or radio (as the clock time frame limits the amount of coverage). The ZEIT ONLINE interviewee explains that ZEIT's blogs are often used to delve into special topics more deeply, a procedure that at times can attract users to regularly follow a particular blog:

Blogs are fast, they are authentic, and above all they offer this immediate user connection. We observe this on all our blogs, that certain communities are formed within these blogs. Those are often the same ten people that react to every blog entry. To illustrate we have this marvellous 'How capitalism works' blog. It's called 'Herdentrieb'. A terrific blog, I think. Personally I know very little about economics and I don't understand many of the contributions [to the blog]. But the level of the comments on it is sometimes unbelievable! It has thereby become a professional platform. And it's our usual ZEIT financial correspondent, stationed in Frankfurt, who elaborates on topics he just can't tackle in the paper. Either because they're too specific, because they're simply too long. He can do so much more there! He has so many more options! He can insert more pictures, stats, graphics. That's left up to him. That's his highness. And nobody interferes with how he ultimately wants to design it. (ZEIT ONLINE)[4]

Blogs thus can offer niche rooms for stories that usually do not have priority on journalistic day-to-day schedules. Current TV, for example, uses blogs to give its users insights into its production processes. This includes that journalists write about the story *behind* the story as Current TV aims to be transparent about what is happening throughout the making of the program:

Because we think that that is not only interesting to watch and clues the viewer in into the whole, the bigger picture of the story. But it also sometimes can affect the story [. . .]. The audience deserves to know about those sorts of things! And some of those things have to do with what the reporter is thinking or feeling at a particular time or their observations, which come out in the blogs. So we do feature a lot of our reporter blogs and I try to blog when I can and when I feel inspired. And I think that that connects the audience to the reporter, the producer a little bit more and builds that more personal connection with this person who is out investigating a story. (Current TV)

The introduction of blogging to traditional newsrooms thus has opened up entire new paths of telling stories, adding more variety to the content delivered.

Yet despite adopting the blogging format, for some journalists it still seems important to draw a line and perceive themselves as 'different' from the blogosphere. While Rosen as early as 2005 optimistically headlined an article on his blog with the title 'Bloggers vs. Journalists is Over', it might be more applicable to note that it *should* be over, but still is not. Some journalists still view themselves as somewhat 'superior' to bloggers—a distinction that might be owed to the 'declining sovereignty' Rosen attests and that translates into the fear of losing power over a system of information dissemination that is increasingly opening up to a vast number of information providers.

In the sphere of network journalism, independent bloggers and traditional journalistic outlets are sharing the same space. The links created between the blogosphere and the traditional journalism sphere inevitably tie them together. Bloggers reference the content produced by journalistic outlets and professional journalists adopt blogging as a legitimate format. These are indicators of a transformation process. Bloggers have understood to position themselves in the sphere of network journalism. However, quite a number of traditional journalists seem to measure the supposed distinctiveness between the journalism sphere and the blogosphere along the lines of values such as 'accountability' or 'credibility', with blogs being perceived as less accountable or credible. This straight-edge needs critical reflection.

9.3. BLOGGERS VERSUS JOURNALISTS? ACCOUNTABILITY AND CREDIBILITY IN THE SPHERE OF NETWORK JOURNALISM

> There are people who are worried about standards. I think that there's hysterical media out there already! Fox News, I mean how many millions of people watch O'Reilly and he puts out the dreck! Ridiculous, hysterical stuff that they make up. So nothing that any blogger could create could be as bad as Fox. So that's where you're stuck! There's already loads of crap out there that you can't trust. News you can't use from people you can't trust.
>
> (AlterNet)

The turn toward personalized journalism accentuated in blogs has often been criticized by journalists as interfering with the role of a journalist as an impartial observer. In many cases, though, the argument that bloggers or citizen journalists lack accountability or credibility because their stories carry points of view, that they deliver opinionated stands and are not produced by 'professionally' trained journalists, lacks foundation. Journalistic outlets are vulnerable to failures and flaws just as well as bloggers who take their business seriously.

One example mentioned frequently throughout the interviews with regard to failures of traditional news media was the run-up to the Iraq War and how traditional media especially in the United States reported on the unfolding conflict. The Executive Editor at AlterNet points out that

> the ability to invade Iraq was partially eased by the inability of the media to ask tough questions or to do their job essentially. In fact they did the opposite. They fed the information that helped the war happen. (AlterNet)

Similarly, the Current TV interviewee criticizes that values such as accountability or credibility cannot only be called into question when discussing the material provided by bloggers, activists or citizen journalists. According to her, audiences today have less trust in traditional outlets. Using the same example of the run-up to the Iraq War, she states that the lack of trust in this case was caused by the failures of traditional media:

> Why didn't we know that there were no weapons of mass destruction in Iraq? Why didn't the public know about Osama bin Laden before September 11? Why didn't we care about Afghanistan before September 11? Why did Americans know so little about the rest of the world and why does the world know so much about the United States? There is a lack of emphasis that's put on places like Afghanistan. Even today coverage of it is very limited! So that's the job of the media whether you are a professional or you're not! The job of the media is to inform and enhance and expand the knowledge of what's really going on out there. We can blame politicians, but the fact is that the American public is very ill informed. The American public wasn't at fault, it's the media's job to keep its people aware of what's going on. So some people are doing that well in the professional world and some people aren't. But I think that an average citizen—and especially in the 18 to 34 demographic, which is what we target—is kind of seeing through that. Not only seeing through that, but wanting to make a difference and become more of a leader in journalism or reporting. And now people can, because they have the outlets to disseminate information. (Current TV)

Along these lines argues one MediaChannel interviewee:

> There are certain journalistic values that are important. Honesty, truthfulness, balance to some degree, ethical values, accuracy. These are all issues that are in dispute. In other words: The people who report on the march to war in Iraq, they all claimed they were being accurate. Secretary Rumsfeld said this and they reported what he said. But they didn't then also speak to other people saying that Secretary Rumsfeld is lying to you. He's wrong! He doesn't have accurate information. In other words: The duty of journalism is not just to be a stenographer, to report what they're hearing, but to add value, context, background and other information from other sources to be more diverse! (Interviewee 1, MediaChannel)

Instead of discussing journalistic standards only with reference to bloggers or citizen journalists, this debate then should rather be deployed to the whole information sphere that is shared by professional journalists *and* activists, citizen journalists or bloggers. Every information provider adding content has to be held accountable. The argument of a lack of credibility or accountability then can be held against traditional media just as well as it can be held against alternative media:

> I think it's debatable whether even the mainstream media is living up to the values that students are taught in journalism school. I never went to journalism school, but I imagine they teach you that fairness and accuracy are two of the most important things. And it's also informing, giving your audience the information that they need to make informed decisions. I think it's debatable whether especially American media is fulfilling that promise. [. . .] I guess we can question whether bloggers are living up to these values, too. But I don't even know if the people that we see as the journalists in this country are living up to it. (Democracy Now!)

Users now have options to complement the information provided via traditional outlets with information accessed via alternative platforms. The turn away from (or at least a critical approach toward the coverage provided by) traditional media might very well be the outcome of increased information flows in circulation. What the interviews cited here sense with respect to this is supported by recent research into audience behavior: The trust in corporate or public service outlets is declining and users are increasingly critical of news coverage. A 2009 survey conducted by the Pew Research Center, for instance, finds that the press accuracy rating has hit its lowest point in more than two decades, with 63% of Americans stating that they view news stories provided in the news media as often inaccurate.[5] As the MediaChannel Executive Director asserts, accountability is not a value automatically guaranteed by some journalist working for a specific outlet, but the product of an informed consumer who is capable of searching for different angles to a piece of information:

> Just because they're mainstream doesn't mean there is accountability. In a sense maybe it's not such a big deal. Maybe that idea that they somehow know what they're talking about is bullshit anyway and maybe it's better that people don't put any difference between what I write in my blog or what you write in your blog or what the *New York Times* or *Washington Post* or *Time Magazine* write. Then it gets put on to you. Then it's just maybe up to you as the consumer. 'Does this guy ever cite sources? No!' Well, maybe that's a problem. Maybe he's making it up out of his head. On the other hand: What if somebody starts just citing sources that don't exist? Can you sue a blogger for . . . ? It's hard for you to know. There are a lot of grey areas. (Interviewee 2, MediaChannel)

Criticizing alternative media as being less credible or less accountable therefore seems to be a questionable debate in light of recent failures of traditional media outlets and should not be held as an argument against alternative media, bloggers, citizen journalists and the like. This is in line with what Rebecca Blood frequently advocates for. In one of her blog entries she argues to finally put the discussion around trustworthiness and credibility that has evolved around blogging to rest. Instead, she points out that whoever provides 'good' journalism is the one users should consult:

> When a blogger writes up daily accounts of an international conference, as David Steven did at the 2002 World Summit on Sustainable Development, that is journalism. When a magazine reporter repurposes a press release without checking facts or talking to additional sources, that is not. When a blogger interviews an author about their new book, that is journalism. When an opinion columnist manipulates facts in order to create a false impression, that is not. When a blogger searches the existing record of fact and discovers that a public figure's claim is untrue, that is journalism. When a reporter repeats a politician's assertions without verifying whether they are true, that is not. (Blood, 2004)

Another important argument in favor of citizen journalism and blogging is that their publications usually do not go uncriticized. The interactive character of digital communication spheres already allows for control mechanisms or as Shirky remarks, 'amateur publishing relies on corrective argument even more than traditional media do' (2008: 65). The AlterNet interviewee explains:

> Just like almost every journalist has an editor, every citizen journalist has an editor. Because if you have your own blog, then people comment there or edit for you. [...] The OhmyNews model, I guess, is similar. So it's not like all the sudden people who aren't trained are getting access to huge audiences and changing people's minds. It's not possible! The system has all the safeguards. So, I think it's all healthy! (AlterNet)

Within a restructured and decentralized sphere of information production and dissemination, a discussion of journalistic values and standards thus needs to address *all* participants who add their portions to the information flows. It cannot be used as an argument against the utilization of alternative sources at traditional newsrooms; and it is too unreflective to be counted as an argument to generally treat alternative voices as unreliable sources or unacceptable partners for news services. So-called spin doctors, for example, can be found in any arm of the information exchange chain. News spinning is not an exclusive terrain of a specific journalistic medium or format or of a certain group of information providers. It could be PR representatives spinning the news, it could be politicians, it could be activists—but it might as well be traditional journalists themselves. The AlterNet interviewee:

I trust the blogosphere a lot more than I trust most journalism, because it's so transparent. And as soon as somebody says something wrong—if they are in any way prominent—there are dozens of people, who will correct them. It's kind of like the Wikipedia in that sense. There may be some falsehood out there for a brief moment, but there's a kind of fierce debate that goes on and in the end you generally come out knowing more than you did before. (AlterNet)

Accordingly the interviewee is convinced that this 'group process' of news production has a lot of advantages. Even though it might not be a 'foolproof or failsafe' system, he has little sympathy for journalists who attack the blogosphere as being inaccurate and the like:

Somebody just did an essay saying he would be happy to see if blogs were all gone by tomorrow. Some prominent journalist, I forgot who he was. Silly! So many more people are involved, engaged, excited, courageous, expressive, finding stuff out, holding people accountable. That's great! Before, there were just a bunch of elite people who often wrote stuff without really doing much reporting. Or when they did reporting they talked to their friends. It's so typical of the *New York Times* to have an article where some person who went to some fancy college talks to a handful. And this is often with women's issues around women and work and stuff like that: They talk to a handful of people who are all kind of the same corner, the same niche and then they come to a conclusion about a pattern. Like: 'Women are staying home and not really going back to work after they have their kids.' But they're only talking to women who are quite wealthy, whose husbands have their hedge fund. Directors or something like that. So a lot of the stuff that the corporate journalism system produces is very class centric. And that really doesn't know that much or tells stories about poor people or people of color or people that are on the coasts. (AlterNet)

From this point of view, alternative media have 'the right' to reciprocally criticize traditional news media, hold them accountable and challenge journalists to improve their work—a notion that seems to gain ground especially in countries with an extremely centralized news media system, as one of the interviewees at ICFJ explains:

We run some programs with editors from around the world. And an editor from a very important paper in Liberia told me last year for example: 'You know that my paper'—which is one of the mainstream media there—'if my paper provides some sort of information that is not confirmed, that is something that we think is happening or might happen, people will be less likely to believe what we wrote about that fact than if they read it on the web!' So what it tells you is, that in certain countries the web is more reliable than the mainstream media! In this country [United States] I doubt it and I doubt it in Europe as well. In certain cases they might provide a scoop, but in general the mainstream media still prevails credibility, and also are the main source of information of the people. But in certain countries—unbelievable! Citizen journalists are more reliable than the mainstream media! (Interviewee 2, ICFJ)

Credibility and accountability thus are becoming the determining values to which corporate and traditional as well as alternative media need to measure up. They seem to become the central values for content produced and disseminated, especially in light of increasing amounts of content provided by a vastly growing number of information deliverers online. However, this does not come without dangers. One interviewee at ICFJ reflects on his experience as a journalism trainer and on certain risks the Internet as a research tool does involve:

Even among journalists, traditional journalists—and this is in countries where we work, not necessarily in the United States—[...] a lot of young journalists do tend to just take whatever they read on the Internet at face value. They don't take certain steps to figure out: 'Okay, how reliable is this source? What can I do to check whether this website has any accuracy? Is it endorsed by anybody that I trust? Does it have a track record of reliable reporting in commentary?' Even young journalists who should be more aware of that don't do that! They just see something on the Internet: 'Wow, I didn't know that!' And then sometimes it ends up in traditional media as well, because somebody saw it on the Internet. (Interviewee 1, ICFJ)

The issue of how to handle the content floating via various information strings into outlets is seemingly affecting traditional as well as alternative news outlets. As the interviewees frequently point out: With a growing quantity of information circulating around the globe, the central task journalists have to fulfill in order to hold up to claims for accountability and credibility is fact checking. It has become the most central and an inevitable task of journalism. Fact checking is especially important when digitally produced content provided by unknown sources is used. The *Guardian* apparently learned its lesson through an editorial blunder, which lead to the publication of falsely labeled user-generated footage:

There were some fires in the South of England and we published a photo we got sent in by a user. There's woods, blazing, spectacular photo! No one noticed that in fact there was an elk in the middle. Now, there haven't been elks in England for about 700 years. Because it was actually a photo taken in Canada about five years earlier. (Guardian)

The elk example is a reminder of the most important task journalists have to fulfill in newsrooms today:

> You've got more information coming in, so you need to check it much, much better. And I think that, again, it's a journalistic skill and the first thing is: if something is too good to be true, it often is too good to be true! And I think we just have to keep a calm head around that. It's just one of those things that you have to deal with. (Guardian)

Yet, even though fact checking has always been an inevitable part of producing journalism: In the wake of an increasing amount of information streaming into news outlets as well as considering the speed at which information travels via digital wires and the sheer volume of accessible information, the modes of how to fact check every single bit of information are challenged: 'It's just whether having to apply them at a greater pace [. . .] we're slightly in danger. We push a lot of content out, a lot more than ever before. And being able just to verify that on a regular basis gets much, much harder' (Guardian).

Similarly, the AlterNet interviewee views fact checking as the inevitable part of journalistic work when dealing with the increasing amount of information in circulation. This holds advantages as well as disadvantages:

> Well, the proof is in the pudding. It's what they write and whether it holds up! You can make your argument based on 'according to the sources' or statistics that you can go back and check. Now, we have Google and LexisNexis and so many different things. (AlterNet)

A tool such as the web hence does provide a journalist with more options to fact check. However, one also finds inaccurate information here or pieces of information that were not meant for a wide audience. As it runs at a much faster pace and is disseminated at a bigger rate, problems arise:

> So there is where there is a risk and there is an interesting case where one of our writers was interviewing a woman and she revealed something about her habit and medical condition and there was some confusion whether she was just inexperienced—the woman who was talking to the journalist was just inexperienced—or she thought it was off the record, was unclear. But the article was printed and of course it went into Google and the woman called and, in fact, more so her husband who was a lawyer called and said that this is terrible. That people in her family don't know about this and it would be very devastating if they did. So we took the story down, which is easy to do. But then he said: 'You have to get rid of it in Google!' Well, fifty hours of work later it still hadn't been taken off Google, because it's like an endless train. Because somebody else links to it and it's all over. So it's on Google

again in another way. So this is like one of the undersides of the web and citizen journalists in that if something gets out there, it's hard to get it back into the box. (AlterNet)

Yet, who is the one who makes such mistakes or causes editorial blunders just as well as who gets it right and provides useful pieces of information is not determined by the form of the outlet; it can be an independent blog or it can be a traditional news organization. Most importantly, though, is that either way they hold up certain standards:

> I think that the role of a reporter should be: Report on things accurately and honestly. And that can happen from all different levels as [. . .] we've seen here at Current. Some reports that come from non-professionals are some of the most authentic and honest pieces about things that you might not have heard of versus professional reporters who might be regurgitating a headline that they read here and there or have already sort of figured out the story before they've left the office. (Current TV)

Current TV is one of the best examples that shows that these supposedly distinct spheres can work together. Intersecting the blogosphere, citizen journalism and traditional media outlets, using information strings that connect all of these nodes in favor of better coverage is what the sphere of network journalism holds for the better of the journalistic profession as such.

An interesting case from Germany exemplifies that information flows from various angles—be it user-generated content footage, stories provided by professional news organizations or commentary submitted in the alternative media sphere—increasingly intersect. The case demonstrates how bloggers, traditional journalists and user-generated content providers now are part of one sphere of information exchange and how control mechanisms unraveling accuracy breaches are part of this. During Hamburg street riots on May 1, 2008, user-generated footage of an incident made its way onto the online platform of the German tabloid *BILD*. The footage provided screen shots taken from a user-generated video and apparently showed how a supposed radical, hooded man tried to set a car on fire by pushing a cloth soaked with a flammable liquid through the car window. *BILD* titled it, 'Slobs are setting cars on fire'. Footage of the same incident taken from another angle was also uploaded on YouTube. Watching the complete video piece, the incident appears completely different: The supposed 'slob' does not push the burning cloth into the car, but pulls it out. The story was covered by one of Germany's leading media criticism websites, BILDBlog. The authors held both *BILD* and YouTube footage against each other and suggested to their readers to make up their own minds on questions of accurate reporting and the use of user-generated footage.[6]

Apart from disclosing how easily information can be manipulated, this example also shows how supposedly counterflowing media spheres such as the traditional press and the platform BILDBlog as well as the video portal YouTube are now connected to each other. Content and comment get pushed and pulled from one site to the other and they feed off of each other. This indicates a level of interconnectedness between the blogosphere and the formerly closed system of journalism that marks a turning point toward an open field of information exchange. Information dissemination has become multi-faceted.

This does bring with it dangers and an independent blogger is to a certain degree much less controllable than a professional journalist who has an editorial board in his or her back. One MediaChannel interviewee comments:

> Anyone with access to a computer can start writing a blog. And there are no rules! You don't have to fact-check your blog if you don't want to. You can be accused of being a bad blogger and say: 'Great, I'm a bad blogger, so fuck off!' [. . .] Your editor is not going to come and talk to you about if you are an ethical journalist. So there is a danger and that has already happened, too. (Interviewee 2, MediaChannel)

However, the interviewee also points out just like others cited above that this is a general problem of the whole information sphere. Despite these inherent dangers and given that the corrective elements are also part of this sphere, the greatest potential of blogs lies in their openness, allowing for an interactive conversation—a feature traditionally produced news does not offer:

> I know a lot of really smart, dedicated people who are writing great blogs and just having a facilitating dialogue that needs to happen. There are also hacks out there who are writing horseshit of every political persuasion. So there is big danger. I mean, for me this is the other thing! For me this almost has less to do with journalism than it has to do with civics. [. . .] Anything connected to media is under radical change. But for me even more important isn't that the media is changing, but what I see as the whole blogosphere phenomenon and even what I do producing video and media pieces. For me the importance is more that it's a dialogue! (Interviewee 2, MediaChannel)

Who to trust within this sphere then might depend on how the relationship between journalists, bloggers, media activists and citizen journalists is going to develop. Mutual trust between these information providers evolves, according to the ZEIT ONLINE interviewee, over time. Such trust can be put into a traditional news outlet just as well as into an alternative news disseminator:

Dependability is indeed usually defined over a period of time. Hence let's take any given blogger: If I believe that he/she truly works neatly, then eventually my [. . .] threshold of scepticism will decrease. At some point I will start believing him/her. And once I trust him/her, then I will verify to a lesser degree what he/she is doing. (ZEIT ONLINE)

Along these lines, the credibility of an outlet develops over time. Media-Channel's Executive Director once more:

The credibility is a delicate thing. Credibility is not something you can easily wrap your head around. And usually you get credibility through time. The reason that the *New York Times* and the *Washington Post* and the *Boston Globe* and a few other newspapers carry more weight than others here in the United States is because they've been around for a long enough time and they have withheld a certain amount of attacks you would assume over the years that they've been around long enough. It's like they seem to know to print things that haven't gotten them sued enough that they're not here anymore! (Interviewee 2, MediaChannel)

The sphere of information thus has become far more complex, decentralized and filled with non-linear proceeding strings of information floating through digital connection wires. If more journalists will start to disperse links across the web, if more of them will reach out and engage in dialogues with their users, remains to be seen. Accuracy and credibility, though, are qualitative attributes that should not be contextualized with either 'traditional' or 'alternative'. When asked if journalists can learn from bloggers or citizen journalists, one interviewee states:

They should. I am not sure if they are really doing it. Yet you can at least learn a lot from amateurs with regards to user-participation and the like. [. . .] That you do not need to take everything personal. That you maybe not even necessarily should. I think this is an area in which one [the journalist] could learn a lot. (ZEIT ONLINE)

This might be just one other advantage of the network journalism sphere: 'traditional' as well as 'alternative' news producers can *learn from each other*. They should neither be understood as competitors nor should blogs be kept at bay with the argument that they are less credible or less accountable. Lasica (2003) and Reese et al. (2007) stress that bloggers and journalists do complement each other. In the sphere of network journalism they intersect and push content back and forth—something that traditional journalistic outlets can profit from (!) as bloggers are not only promoting 'the circulation of public dialog' (Reese et al 2007: 257). Through linking back to news organizations, they do offer users the opportunity to engage with material: 'In fact, much of what these blogs do is push readers to other information that they would not have otherwise read' (Ibid.). Bloggers have understood to use information strings running toward and away from their platforms—and they draw connections between the nodes.

Within the network journalism sphere, then, all news producers and disseminators eventually share the same information space. They merge into one global information sphere and can make this interactive sphere work in favor of a more comprehensive coverage, tied together in a dense web of useful information. And the information can very well be provided by bloggers.

9 The Active User in the Network Journalism Sphere

With the number of platforms disseminating information via the net on the rise and with journalism turning more conversational, the way users engage with content is also changing. Users now have a greater choice of who to prefer as their information providers. As receivers of information and thus customers of news organizations, they decide who is going to be watched, listened to, read and therefore trusted—and the group of users eventually decides on the fate of a media outlet.

The importance of users as content providers for journalistic work has already been discussed in Chapter 7 of this book. Whereas in the past the only option to interact with a news organization directly was through the letter to the editor or an enquiry over the phone, users today have the means to get in touch with news outlets and engage with the content produced on a much larger scale. Commentary functions or user-generated content platforms integrated into the web appearance of a news outlet allow users to leave statements or discuss issues of interest. In this chapter the focus will not so much be turned on the issue of user-generated content and what a journalistic outlet can do with it, but on the changing behavioral patterns of users: How do they receive information, where do they search for it and how do they engage with it?

Users are increasingly distributors of news themselves. The 'people formerly known as the audience', as Rosen (2006: Online) refers to them, actively seek content. Even more than that, they are the prolonged distribution arm of news outlets as they recommend their choice of news stories to their peers. The passive receiver of the past has become the active user who engages with stories, links to them, tells friends, delivers critiques. On their Facebook pages or Twitter accounts, users can post links to their favorite news stories or critically engage with content provided by news organizations. This changing dynamic of information exchange with users becoming an important arm of information distribution networks is a key characteristic of the network journalism sphere.

9.1. JOURNALISTS' PERCEPTIONS OF USERS

> The relationship is no longer completely passive. [. . .] It used to be
> an adult feeding children. But I think now it's much, much more of a
> dialogue, much more information passing both ways.
>
> (Guardian)

As early as 1971, Toffler introduced the term 'prosumer' to define the
relationship between news audiences and news organizations. In his
view, the consumer of news is a more informed citizen 'who would need
to be kept content by allowing for a greater customizability and indi-
vidualisability of products' (Bruns, 2006: 275). In the digital age where
consumers have the technological means to draw upon a wide range of
news sources and to engage with content, this definition holds more truth
than ever before. McNair explains that users today are 'media literate,
relatively suspicious and disbelieving and increasingly cynical. Informed
skepticism about what is read, seen and heard in the journalistic media
can be assumed to be a common feature of the contemporary reception
environment' (1998: 39). Traditional news outlets accustomed to a closed
system of journalistic production are challenged to decide how to deal
with users who demand options to engage with the content disseminated
on these platforms. As the Guardian interviewee explains:

> I think the single biggest challenge we face as news organizations is
> that [. . .] a decade ago [. . .] pretty much all our processes were
> about outgoing information. It doesn't matter if it was our marketing,
> our publishing: everything was about outgoing. Trying to actually
> phone in: nightmare! We kept the roots into the organization down
> to an absolutely minimum: 'Write a letter!' That was pretty much it.
> And over time, if there was some way you measure it, the volume of
> information coming in has multiplied enormously. (Guardian)

In his view, this development is a result of the transforming (global) information sphere in which citizens (as well as journalists) can access more
information. The introduction of comment and feedback sections or the
inception of positions such as a reader's editor at the *Guardian* or a Community Editor at ZEIT ONLINE highlight the reactions of news organizations to cope with the new situation.

> The reader's editor every year gets more and more letters. Not be-
> cause we're doing more things wrong, but just because more people
> feel it is their right to question and challenge what we're doing! Our
> journalists are getting more emails, or we set up things on the website
> where we would get more response. (Guardian)

Similarly, the work of the BBC at their Interactivity Desk reflects an attitude change toward audiences. In his assessment of the BBC's strategies for its digital future, Lee-Wright outlines that BBC News chiefs are 'striving to find better ways of communicating with them [their users], more in the way of dialogue than demagogue' (2008: 255). Forming an interactive producer–consumer relationship and tapping its full potential is a point also made by the BBC Editor interviewed for this study. She recalls her encounter with interactivity during the 2001 elections in the UK. This was the first time she was assigned to the task of building 'conversational' relations with users:

> I came along and thought it was absolutely fantastic and it was in a way a bit of a revelation to me: That we started off saying what were people interested in the election and what did they want to talk about and we would get all these emails back instantly. And having been working in traditional broadcast this was fantastic! You had instant response to what was going on and you could really engage what the public wanted to hear about. (BBC)

What she describes is the creation of an engagement relationship between journalists and users. Accordingly, traditional journalistic outlets such as the BBC now are not merely platforms disseminating news content. In the 'Have your Say' sections users become part of the production chain and the BBC facilitates discussions *about* its content and cultivates conversations among its users. The high level of acceptance of sections such as the Guardian's 'Comment is Free', of the ZEIT ONLINE talkboards and the BBC's 'Have Your Say' site reflects this demand for conversational formats:

> On the Lebanon War last year we got like a hundred and fifty thousand emails on that topic alone. Shilpa Shetti: It was a big brother racism row, do you remember that? A celebrity TV program. Thirty odd thousand emails. Individual stories. Usually a bigger story gets about fifteen thousand emails. We have engaged them. And when it goes over that we know [. . .] people are going mad [laughs] about a story. So we've got all this information to deal with, we just then have to pass it on to others. And News 24, which is our digital television channel, they trail all the time: 'Send your emails, have your say! We've got an mms number, send your pictures and things.' And they all come in to us and we process them and send them back. (BBC)[1]

Other than seeing the audience as a 'herd' of mass consumers, journalists are starting to learn to change their attitudes toward them—especially with regard to younger users who are pulling the plug on traditional news dissemination models:

That's happening, young people are not reading traditional newspapers any more. So, traditional news organizations I should say including broadcast, need to find ways of reaching those people, need to convince those people that you do want somebody responsible making decisions that what you're reading on blogs in many cases and seeing on news websites, that you shouldn't just take it at face value. And that what you read in the traditional news organization, although mistakes are made there, too—but for the most part you can trust it. [. . .] I do—but I'm an old person [laughs]—I tend to believe something that I read in the *New York Times* more than I would something that I see on a blog. Because I feel like there definitely are people there who are checking it and who are very careful about what information they put out. (Interviewee 1, ICFJ)

This argument does remind one of the discussion of credibility and accuracy raised in the previous chapter. Gaining the trust of young users is closely tied to a change in attitude toward audiences. Responsiveness here is not an option, but a *must* because, according to the Current TV interviewee, especially young users are reluctant to accept the traditional sender–receiver model of news distribution and consumption:

I think that's one of the reasons why the younger audience is sort of disenchanted. Because it's been very top-down and it's been very much about the same headlines on the same channels, sometimes at the same moment! I mean it's crazy how they can time things to a tea [. . .]. I think what exists today is sort of like the same regurgitation of the same stories told in the same ways—until now. (Current TV)

In order to regain trust especially with younger audiences, journalists are in need of reforming the relationship with their users. As the Guardian interviewee points out: 'What we going to have to learn and get better at is: We need—as an organization—to be as good at managing incoming information as we are at managing outgoing information' (Guardian).

This incoming information can reach a news outlet from all corners of the world because consumers are not necessarily restricted to accessing news content distributed within their specific geographical locales.[2] The new relationship with users is formed in an online space that allows readers from virtually any connected spot within the global sphere to engage with content. The potential dialogue between news producers and users is taking place in a transnational arena and the group of users is not limited to a national audience. AlterNet, for example, counts according to the interviewee roughly between ten and fifteen percent of users accessing the website from outside the US. The BBC's 'Have Your Say' site receives comments from users who post their messages from virtually each continent. Current TV receives submissions from around the globe and MediaChannel operates with affiliating groups based in a number of different countries. These are just a few examples of how the production and dissemination as well as the reception of information has to be contextualized within an emerging global setting today and how users engage with content produced and disseminated online.

It is also important to note that users increasingly use multiple platforms to get their news. A survey of the Pew Internet and American Life Project published in March 2010 found that 92 percent of Americans use a variety of different platforms to get news, with 46 percent stating that they consult four to six different platforms for news and information on a typical day, from sources including national TV, local TV, the Internet, local newspapers, radio and national newspapers (Purcell et al, 2010: Online). News organizations are facing much more competition with a rising number of news providers who deliver information across numerous platforms. The report stresses that:

> The internet is at the center of the story of how people's relationship to news is changing. Six in ten Americans (59%) get news from a combination of online and offline sources on a typical day, and the internet is now the third most popular news platform, behind local television news and national television news. (Purcell et al, 2010: online)

The community of news consumers thus is adapting to the networked structures conveyed by digital tools. While the group of news consumers for a single platform can potentially comprise users from different parts of the world, users in addition seek information across platforms, potentially engage with content or provide feedback. In this transnational exchange pattern, interaction between producers of news and their costumers has become an important part of the development:

> Interactivity now is a requirement to do journalism. [. . .] We need to develop new strategies to improve it. We need to implement new ideas to straighten it. So it's a whole new field for journalists that I don't think was there before! Before it was a decision that we made in an outlet. It was something you wanted to do. But I think it's a requirement now. It goes beyond the choice of the journalist or the media. (Interviewee 2, ICFJ)

The active user demands a change in attitude toward audiences and the level of participation and engagement with content a news organization allows. In line with this, Jenkins's characterization of how consumers function in the digital era summarizes this argument greatly:

> If old consumers were assumed to be passive, the new consumer is active. If old consumers were predictable and stationary, then new consumers

are migratory, showing a declining loyalty to networks or even media. If old consumers were isolated individuals, then new consumers are more socially connected. If old consumers were seen as compliant, then new consumers are resistant, taking media into their own hands. If the work of media consumers was once silent and invisible, they are now noisy and public. (Jenkins, 2004: 37 et seq.)

And they can be 'noisy and public' because they have access to instruments that enhance the reach of their comment or content provided: Digital technologies offer excellent tools to assist users in raising their voices. These tools can foster interactive conversations. How a journalistic organization uses these voices strategically and in favor of one's own outlet will be of crucial value to the survival of journalistic organizations.

9.2. THE DEVELOPMENT OF INTERACTIVE CONVERSATIONS

> Obviously in Utopia journalists would actually have a relationship with the audience. And it would be a partnership, where someone would write a story and they would listen to comments maybe on a blog. And would get back and forth!
>
> (Ourmedia)

Journalists 'need to be more conversational. They need to be willing to listen to people', claims the Ourmedia volunteer, who signals that this is the only way to pay tribute to changing interaction patterns in a network society. The ideal medium to facilitate such conversation is currently the Internet. It is the first platform that allows direct interaction between a news disseminator and his or her audience. The BBC Editor points out that journalists need to react to the users' demands of engaging in an interaction with journalists and the content they produce:

> I think the consumption of news has completely changed in the last ten, twenty years. That it used to be something you noted, you listened to and you just sort of 'all right, great, that's what it is.' Now you think: 'I want to be part of it.' [. . .] So it was a monologue before and now it's a dialogue. 'I want to have my say in that. Yes, I understand that. I've got a story similar to that or I'm caught up in that. Let me tell you what really happened.' Or just a very simple thing: 'I feel strongly about something. I'll vote online.' It can be a very basic non-time-consuming participation as well. And then we adapted to that. We suddenly thought: 'Yes, that's what the public are wanting to do, and we can in a way capitalize on it. Because they can help us do our jobs.' (BBC)

Here, the BBC Editor describes the ideal relationship between journalists and users. The Indymedia volunteer accentuates that the willingness of journalists to engage in a conversation about content will be key to binding users to a news platform. Such conversation would eventually include journalists, citizen journalists, bloggers, activists or audiences alike:

> Ideally it means that journalists and amateur journalists and readers will engage in a conversational process to create better journalism. Someone will say something is wrong and they will provide their own expertise on something that's already written. (Indymedia)

One way of doing this is to carry online chat sections. The Guardian's 'Comment is Free' format, for example, is designed as an open space for debate and invites users to engage with the articles provided by Guardian authors. It hosts a range of blogs and contributions from Guardian commentators and also carries the main commentary articles or editorials from both newspapers of the Guardian Media Group. This idea of facilitating a conversation is also behind some rubrics carried on the BBC's 'Have Your Say' platform. The BBC provides the topic (as well as encourages readers to contribute a topic) and the users provide their input:

> Yesterday we did a story about mental health, whatever. It could be French elections, whatever. So we ask for people's comments. Clearly we don't verify everyone's comments sent in. People could be sending in, saying something that we can't check. But it's a message board. I think that's fine. We put them up there and we make it very clear: These are not the views of the BBC. This is just what people are sending us. (BBC)[3]

The Guardian has also given room to communities that specialize in certain topic areas. Its travel site 'Been there', for example, is composed of user-generated content. Here, Guardian users can submit travel tips, videos and photos or create individual travel guides for fellow users. As the Guardian interviewee explains, 'the user-generated content is there, but it's given a definition and shape by us.' The Guardian uses the full potential of its crowd to create a unique travel forum run by a professional news organization, yet with content fed in by users:

> And our role there is: We're like a campfire that people gather around. And I think this shift in that case really is interesting. We are no longer the people who are responsible for all the content. We sort of shepherd it and herd it a bit, but we are very minor, but the whole thing wouldn't exist in its format unless it was us doing it. (Guardian)

As first studies indicate, the interactive possibilities of the net to contribute to the blurring of the roles between consumer and producer are welcomed by some journalists. In a survey of online journalists from Latin America, North America and Europe, Schmitz Weiss and de Macedo Higgins Joyce find that feedback options as well as active contributions made by readers are acknowledged as useful material in the newsroom (2009: 593). Yet the range of participatory devices does not only entail chats or sections where users can, for instance, make story suggestions. The Current TV model shows that interaction with and participation of users can be a whole business model on the information market:

> Current is all about allowing our audience to interact. So we consider it a two-string experience. We are always calling out for feedback, not only highlighting the work of our audience and our viewers through VC^2 or viewer-created content, that's what we call it. [. . .] You can go on our website, you can vote for pieces, you can comment on them. You can call them out if they're inaccurate, the pieces that are online. We feature those pieces on our air. It's kind of a cycle between the TV and the Internet. So for Current, we think that interactivity is key, it's a huge part of our network and involving our audience is a huge part of what we do. We don't see our audience as passive viewers, though they can be if you're just sitting in front of the TV and you just want to watch it [. . .]. But there is also an opportunity to engage and to get off the couch and do something and react and know that your opinion, your comment is just part of this bigger conversation. (Current TV)

This conversational idea is accentuated in the blog format and the adaptation of this format at traditional media outlets as shown in the previous chapter is one striking example of the way interaction patterns are changing. The MediaChannel Executive Editor:

> What's happening is increasingly mainstream journalists have added blogs because of their popularity. I mean you've gone to a situation, I don't know their current number, but 50 million people blogging! That's a phenomenally successful number of people! What does that say? It says people want to participate in media; they just don't want to be recipients of media. Okay? And as a result we see that the circulation of newspapers and the TV ratings of news shows have fallen significantly. People are turning away from it; they're turning away from traditional media. So traditional media is now adding video to websites, is adding blogs, is adding more opinion columns et cetera trying to keep the audience and therefore also keep the advertising. So this is the crisis that the media is in. This new media in some cases is not just supplementing old media; it is the media for many people. That's all they read. [. . .] This is a profound cultural problem that's deeper

than just journalism. It's about people being citizens and can they as citizens learn what's going on in their world or not? (Interviewee 1, MediaChannel)

Learning what is going on in the world can be a process resulting from a conversational exchange of information. The phenomenon of crowdsourcing through interactive online conversations as practiced in parts of the blogosphere is an example of this. Some bloggers use the comment features of their blogspots as such crowdsourcing instruments (see Briggs, 2010: 70ff). They gather information on a topic through actively asking the audience to participate and engage with their readers on a whole new level. The Ourmedia volunteer:

> I think that those of us that have been on the web, we realize that the people know as much as we do. Or the person that watches my video knows as much as I do! And so it's important for me to get comments or emails or to get voices back. Either telling me 'I got my facts wrong' or suggesting another way I could go on that story. It's very important! (Ourmedia)

The blogosphere holds one prominent example that proves the point of collaboration and the opportunity to draw upon the knowledge of users in order to improve or check a storyline. In 2007, blogger Joshua Micah Marshall asked his readers to send him information on US attorneys being fired in various districts across the US. The story broke on his blog 'Talking Points Memo'. It turned into a massive controversy and the publication eventually lead to congressional investigations by the Department of Justice and the White House, where it was checked whether the state offices were firing attorneys in order to gain political advantages:

> [Joshua Micah Marshall] basically said that: 'It seems like something weird is going on in my district.' It really reached out to the community. 'Is anything sort of fishy going on in your community or are you seeing any unusual activity regarding US attorneys and things like that?' And it was these people who happened to be in those little districts that were noticing that their attorney was being fired and that's how it broke. Who knows if it would have happened or happened as soon as it did if it wasn't for this site. I thought that was fantastic! [. . .] That was community involvement that actually broke this big story. (Current TV)

The AlterNet interviewee refers to the same case and argues that forming information circles and partnerships through a blog brings with it the option to improve the quality of journalistic content. A positive development in his view:

I think that the journalism has approved and will continue to improve because of the blogs. And there are journalists who are brave enough to kind of—or smart enough—to open their process up. [. . .] Joshua Micah Marshall has been able to break stories by asking his readers to do research for him. And suddenly the power of one is the power of fifty! [. . .] They're able to call the congressperson in fifty different places and get the answer and that adds up to this. And he [Marshall] couldn't possibly do that by himself! The journalists that put their emails on their articles or allow people to comment on it and then go back and engage with them are I think better journalists for it. (AlterNet)

Participating with content thus holds advantages for both sides: The user can interact with content and the journalist in return receives useful feedback and information:

For me relevant interactivity begins with participation. [. . .] Participation really means, that the user actively decides to do something that will yield a reward in some shape or form for him. So not simply typing in zeit.de, but that for example he/she actually sits down to read an article and then thinks: 'Mhmm, maybe the author's not quite right about that. Or whatever, or perhaps there's another perspective to this.' And sits down to write a comment in response to the article. That's true interaction to me. However, interaction is not entirely one-sided for me. Subsequently [. . .] for me it's part of being a good journalist to accommodate the interaction and actually involve oneself. (ZEIT ONLINE)

With the World Wide Web in place, the tools to facilitate this conversation are right at hand—and journalists using them acknowledge that the society they cater to carries (digital) networking as a defining principle of its interaction patterns.

Web 2.0 is probably the original intention for the web, which was a desire for people to use it for their own creative expression. [. . .] I kind of believe in the 'wisdom of crowds' notion and that the readers out there know a lot and that should be taken advantage of. I think the blogging revolution has given a lot of people who had no way into the world of radiant journalism the avenue. And many of them have surfaced as being great writers or tenacious trackers of information. On AlterNet right now we have about twenty thousand people who are registered to make comments. And some stories get five or six hundred comments. (AlterNet)

Yet, this does not come without a price. An increased level of interaction does have its downsides as well: 'Tricky road however, because there are trolls and there are nasty people and we don't have the staff to monitor those comments nearly as much as we would like' (AlterNet). Instruments have to be in place to secure the accurateness of information and organizations need strategies for how to deal with offensive comments or false information. Sites like the Guardian, Current TV, ZEIT ONLINE and the BBC's 'Have Your Say' do carry sections in which they explain the ground rules of engagement. Users usually have to agree to terms and conditions and ensure that they do not post any offensive comment or fake material. Some organizations also take their customers on board to monitor the commentary sections and offer users opportunities to rate the content of their fellow commentators, for example, at AlterNet:

> So we're trying without imposing censorship, without being heavy handed [. . .], we're trying to get the behavior shaped by the people themselves, even though some people will attack this claiming that we are taking away their First Amendment rights even though we're not. But we are probably being more conscious of taking away . . . deleting people's stuff if they're really abusive. Sexist, racist, any of those things. (AlterNet)

The problem of trolls trying to invade a site or abuse it to spew radical comment is also well known to grassroots platforms such as Indymedia. 'Interactivity' in this sense involves a whole other contextual dimension:

> At least in the Indymedia world, interactivity means dealing with trolls [laughs]! Dealing with disrupters. There is not a very high dialogue level on the Indymedia website. There is some! There is some, but you're dealing with very committed political people with passionate positions on things and I find that the conversation on Indymedia any way more often resembles kind of scrawling things on a bathroom wall than it does any sort of engaged interactive dialogue. If you step back and you kind of look at the website as a whole, there is obviously some interactivity and some conversation going on. But if you look at the comments people make to individual stories, maybe you'll get five really good comments right away that are actually useful and then you'll just get this pure nonsense. (Indymedia)

Dealing with offensive postings, generating high-quality information and conversations and setting rules for each individual platform are the tasks every journalistic organization operating within the space of the World Wide Web has to fulfill. The facilitation of conversations with users and the inclusion of interactivity features is becoming an inevitable part of journalistic production in the evolving network journalism sphere and how to manage these conversations online is just one emerging task journalistic organizations have to deal with.

Another important point refers to what users do with the content provided by news organizations away from the actual website and at some other place in the networked space. Online tools such as RSS feeds support the personalization of news services and social bookmarking tools or social networks such as Facebook are places where users exchange links, recommend stories or discuss issues they personally have an interest in. How to engage with the spaces created by social networks is probably one of the most important lessons to learn for news organizations today.

9.3. SOCIAL NETWORKS AND THE PERSONALIZATION OF NEWS SERVICES

> The reality is: There is a difference between reading a newspaper that has to show up every day and that is going to be held accountable in ways that somebody blogging in his underwear in his living-room isn't. And so the question becomes: How do people make those choices? People reading the news or watching the news or consuming media. How are they going to figure out who is full of shit and who is not!
>
> (Interviewee 2, MediaChannel)

The first generation of computer-literate users especially in Western countries such as the US, the UK or Germany is growing and this generation is completely unfamiliar with a time before the Internet.[4] Young media users can hardly relate to a non-interactive, closed journalism sphere, or as the AlterNet interviewee explains, 'a lot of young people are not interested in that top-down model! That's going back to the web 2.0. They are much more interested in communicating with each other, and using tools and being creative and creating their own multimedia-mashups' (AlterNet). These digital natives have found their online homes on Facebook, MySpace, the German StudiVZ or on any of the numerous other platforms that supply space and the necessary tools for the creation of online communities. Social networks are by definition communities where peers exchange personal updates or photos as well as viewpoints or recommendations. And with respect to the latter, these social network sites are becoming the extended distribution arm for online information.

For example, two of the easy to use tools Facebook offers are the 'Share' application and the 'Like button'. Within a matter of a few seconds, users can indicate that they like a certain status update of a friend or a news article they found somewhere on the Internet. They can recommend links to articles or videos and to their favorite news websites. Applications such as these can have a significant impact on user behavior and news consumption patterns. As the Pew study about 'The Participatory News Consumer' in the United States suggests:

> To a great extent, people's experience of news, especially on the internet, is becoming a shared social experience as people swap links in emails, post news stories on their social networking site feeds, highlight news stories in their Tweets, and haggle over the meaning of events in discussion threads. For instance, more than 8 in 10 online news consumers get or share links in emails. (Purcell et al, 2010: Online)

This kind of social interaction with peers does determine to a certain extent what users read, listen to or view on the net. The same survey also finds that '50% of American news consumers say they rely to some degree on people around them to tell them the news they need to know' (Ibid.). Such recommendations can be found on social networking sites through applications such as the Like button.

Many news outlets now are realizing that attracting especially the young generation of Internet users does not only work through one's own homepage. With users growing up partially in the interactive world of social networks, a new marketplace for content has emerged and, in addition, many platforms now do not only use their own homepages for the distribution of their content, but share information or links via YouTube, Facebook or Twitter. Delivering content on a variety of (interconnected) platforms across the net is one step toward securing that the content of an outlet finds wide distribution. Other ways are to embed social bookmarking tools, Like buttons and easy-to-use functions that enable users to send an article via email with not more than a click of a mouse.

These options do help news organizations to ensure that users find their content in many network nodes across the web—and not only on the homepage of the outlet. With the move into the online spaces potential users might visit, news outlets acknowledge the power of networked communication: They tap in to the opportunity of social networks where users can share the content they find the most interesting. As Briggs points out: 'It's important to understand the collateral benefits of social media distribution and participation. [...] Journalists can earn social capital—the concept of becoming the trusted center for a community—by engaging in multiple channels' (2010: 332 et seq.).

This type of engagement acknowledges the power of recommendations and links. Users who share their favorite stories or point their peers to topics of interest are important individual information nodes in the sphere of network journalism. They push links into a widely connected sphere and secure a wider distribution of information. Users who actively engage with content are a force to be reckoned with. Their power to distribute information should not be underestimated as they potentially drive web traffic back to the sites of journalistic organizations or for that matter discourage their peers from following the coverage of certain news organizations if they have proven it to be insufficient or inaccurate. Outlets that acknowledge the power of social networks and pay tribute to it through their presence in these online communities—just as well as outlets open to feedback or stories delivered by users—do use the potential power of the interactive conversation in a networked world. They recognize that the position the 'receivers' of information take toward journalism has changed.

In accordance with this, asked how the media usage might look like in ten years' time, the BBC interviewee replies:

> I think integration and interactivity will just be absolutely part of people's everyday lives. Because say, in ten years time did you say, people who are now teenagers, who are the sort of MySpace, Bebo people will be the generation. That is just how they live now! Everybody will be getting their news where they want it, when they want it, how they want it. There will be no sit-down-appointment to view stuff. It'll all be when people want it. It'll be sort of there and we just have to adapt to that. And there'll be a load of changes. We might have to go through some rocky times and maybe not spend as much on our traditional services. We've got to give the audience what they want on the platform. (BBC)

And—in addition—on any platform users favor, including social network sites. Developing a strong social media presence will help news organizations to connect with users in many virtual corners online and enhance the reach of distributed content.

10 Transnational News Flows in the Network Journalism Sphere

The impacts of digitalization and globalization are maybe strongest felt in the field of foreign reporting. Within a sphere of global news flows, the contextual settings in which foreign news stories are presented are under scrutiny. At the same time, the emergence of transnational networks such as CNN and the new access opportunities even to remote spots on the globe are changing the practice of corresponding across borders. New job profiles have emerged, with so-called parachute journalists sent on short assignments to hot spots or backpack journalists traveling without staff or a crew to points of interest.

As argued in Chapter 4, the traditional focus of reporting from afar mainly concentrates on foreign perspectives and the angles from which a story is told are often limited. However, while more people across the globe digitally connect to the news from afar and while events in one world corner might very well impact the life of people in another corner, local insights gain importance. What is more, with the help of digital technology, journalists in many cases now have access to a larger number of local information sources and can extend their network of information providers. These sources do not only include foreign correspondents or local fixers. Citizen journalists, bloggers and the users of news services to a growing extent are becoming part of the production chain as the international operations at outlets such as Current TV or at the BBC's user-generated content desk demonstrate. These new news deliverers feed local perspectives into the global coverage of news and do contribute to a coverage that is rather 'transnational' than 'foreign' in its nature.

This chapter will highlight how these dynamics of foreign corresponding are influenced by today's network structures. Drawing upon examples taking from coverage of the war in Iraq and its aftermath, I will highlight some opportunities digital distribution methods and the growing number of source options offer in the field of foreign corresponding.

10.1. PARACHUTE JOURNALISM AND THE TRANSFORMATION OF FOREIGN JOURNALISM

> I think the move towards new media is almost accelerated in people who care about the world, because the traditional media do such a bad job of covering the world. So people who care about the world are often more likely to turn to some Internet sources, new sources of information, because there's so little available.
>
> (Interviewee 1, ICFJ)

Asked about the interplay between foreign correspondence, globalization and digitalization, the interviewees did reflect on some major trends and identified a number of changes in and challenges to the profession. One of the strongest concerns expressed is about the financial pressures newsrooms are suffering from. As the PEJ interviewee explains, in order to save money numerous overseas bureaus, for example, of US news outlets have already been replaced by so-called parachute journalists, that is, journalists who are flown to spots of interest especially in the event of elections, political crises, war or natural disasters:

> Whenever they started closing these bureaus, the first reaction of many of the major news organizations was: 'Well, we'll parachute people in.' Which is: 'We still have correspondents. They're all based out of New York.' And when there's a hot spot, they fly into the area and they find out what's going on. (PEJ)

This development does at times jeopardize the quality of foreign reporting. It can, for example, contribute to a fatal loss of context for news stories:

> What you lose when you don't have the person there is: a) you have none of the backstory. You really don't know how the situation got to where it is. The way you find that, the way you know that stuff is: You have somebody who has experience there. [. . .] If there is a topic you know a lot about and you see somebody write about it: Eight times out of ten, maybe nine times out of ten you're going to be unhappy with it. And you'll be like: 'This person completely missed this angle, this angle. How could they ignore this factor.' And when news organizations stop having correspondents on the ground they sacrifice that. That was what they had. They fly people in; maybe they are excellent writers. Maybe they are even excellent reporters. But you know, when I fly into an area I can be the best reporter of all, but if my story is really this event and the background of this event is actually like several hundred years of history: That's going to be hard for me to capture in a week, two weeks, in a month. Having somebody on the ground makes all the difference. They can get the nuances. (PEJ)

What the foreign correspondent used to deliver was background to the story. Being 'embedded' in a country gave the journalist access to locals, enhanced his or her knowledge of the country. Now that news outlets often rely on the same reporters to cover event sites in numerous different countries, the foreign correspondent permanently based in a bureau in one specific locale appears to be a dying species. Dying with this professional profile are the contacts a correspondent established—contacts a parachute journalist cannot set up on the ground in a matter of a few days or weeks. What seems to be missing is the link to a specific country and the inside knowledge. The majority of the interviewees argue, parachute journalists are not capable of filling this gap the vanishing institution of the foreign correspondent leaves behind:

> Parachute journalism is definitely not a good trend. You're losing so much context when you have somebody who doesn't know a country drop in for a week to do a reporting and then disappear again and not show up again until the next crisis happens or something like that. As opposed to having somebody there who really knows the country, knows the context, isn't going to make mistakes, isn't going to have misinterpretations of something. So I do think that's a bad trend. Sometimes it's necessary because you just don't have anybody in the country, but again, this idea of having people that you have relationships with in countries around the world—even if you're going to send one of your own experts in as a parachute journalist—but just team them up with somebody who's there, who's local, who knows the situation is very important so that you're not misreading things. (Interviewee 1, ICFJ)

Along those lines argues the ZEIT ONLINE interviewee with respect to parachute journalists:

> There are people who are very, very, very, very good at this. But I believe these are very, very, very, very few. And of course it's just extremely dangerous! And in case of doubt they are indeed essentially vastly war and crises experienced. But what I view as exceedingly critical is: They mostly aren't experts on the subject matter, educated on it. You can't really be overly familiar with all conflict areas around the world. And obviously it's nice if somebody knows the ropes in Iraq, or possibly even in Afghanistan, but then we send him to the Congo and the situation might seem completely different there. (ZEIT ONLINE)

The AlterNet Executive Editor draws an interesting parallel between parachute journalism and fictional representations of reporters. The glorification of the journalistic hero is a stereotypical image that according to him corresponds with the unrealistic approach of parachuting journalists around the globe:

Well, you know, we have these classic characters that show up in movies. This journalist who shows up and figures out the problem and is the hero. But, I don't know. Parachuting anybody in for anything is really not the way to find out what's going on! They do that in politics here. They try to win an election and then parachuting experts from another round who are supposed to know what they're doing, but they don't pay enough attention to people on the ground who really do know that. (AlterNet)

The general tone of the interviews is that parachute journalism does not appropriately replace foreign correspondents based in permanent overseas bureaus. To add a comment from the Ourmedia volunteer, he finds that this type of reporting is also 'boring very often, because they don't really give any local color or depth. I mean it's in and out. Unfortunately that's a lot of the journalism that we see on TV or read in the paper' (Ourmedia).

Another more general problem identified with respect to foreign corresponding in general is reflected in the argument that the story a reporter wants to deliver is often not necessarily the story news outlets want to see on their news agendas:

Well, a foreign correspondent is there to cover a story for their outlet. And most of these correspondents who go there are very frustrated because they can do the story, but they can't get it on the air in America. They don't make the decisions about what gets reported and what doesn't. And a lot of their reporting tends to look the same, because somebody in Washington has seen or somebody in New York has seen a story from Iraq on another channel. They say: 'Get me that story! Give me the casualty, give me the dead . . . another American soldier is dead.' Is that the story of Iraq? Or not? (Interviewee 1, MediaChannel)

The argument raised here goes with what the Dutch foreign correspondent Joris Luyendijk expresses as the main driver that got him to write a book about his experiences as news correspondent in the Middle East. In an interview, he notes that while on assignment he could hardly report the stories he wanted in the way he wanted. What to cover and in what manner to present a story were largely subject to factors outside of his control such as the agendas set by wire services or chief editors. As a correspondent, he often found himself 'at the end of the news-production assembly line. By the time I got involved, it had usually been decided already whether to cover something and also how' (Kester, 2008: 502).

Back to the discussion of parachute journalism in particular, though, there is one positive outcome mentioned by some interviewees. Even though parachuters might miss local knowledge or the necessary depth in coverage, they at times do accomplish one important mission: Parachute journalists can create awareness for crisis regions that might not receive enough attention globally.

For someone like Anderson Cooper to go to Sudan [. . .]: He's become like one of the best-known journalists on CNN. And he was recently in Darfur and I guess that's an example of parachute journalism. But it also did raise the issue of what's going on in Sudan better [. . .]. I guess, journalists have been there for a long time. But he does have the star power, so I guess it helps a little bit. Maybe it takes someone like him to go to a place to actually start getting attention on this country. (Democracy Now!)

Parachute journalists also directed the attention of a global audience, for instance, after the Haiti earthquake in January 2010 or after the Boxing Day tsunami in 2005. Their ability to point audiences to certain events is a quality stressed by the BBC interviewee; however, she also notes the flipside of such coverage. In many cases, foreign correspondence in general and parachute journalism in particular do concentrate on breaking news, but fail to follow up on stories:

Journalism has always gone where the story is and reported it. And let's say the tsunami where a whole load of people were sent and then they came away again. But they covered the story and the devastation caused there was revealed to the world. So I think it's a derogative term to say 'parachute journalism' when it is just really showing what was going on there. What I think we might be guilty of is: We don't go back and follow up stories enough. (BBC)

Bearing in mind the criticism noted with regard to parachute journalism and a declining quality of foreign correspondence coverage in general, users wanting to find information about the world might have to seek other options.

One option to replace traditional foreign corresponding is to follow the coverage provided by so-called backpack journalists or multimedia reporters. In many cases, they work freelance and instead of going where the majority of foreign correspondents travel, they often cover spots where other journalists rarely show up.

10.2. BACKPACK JOURNALISTS ON INTERNATIONAL TERRITORY

Our people, when we send them out, they're lean. Sometimes it's one person, mostly it's two, just because they have a partner to help with all the stuff. But they're shooting their own stuff, they are writing for our website and blogs and filing stories. They're editing on the road and we have editors who will help out on editing as well. But it's sort of like that one-man-band backpack journalist.

(Current TV)

Training journalists as backpack journalists or multimedia reporters for corresponding tasks could be one option for filling the gap the foreign journalist leaves behind. Backpack journalists are in general much more independent than the majority of their colleagues. They often travel alone, comparatively light and on a fraction of the budget needed for traditional foreign correspondence operations. Equipped only with a bag full of digital technology gear to shoot and edit video, produce audio and send text files via digital connections or satellite links, the backpack journalist does not rely on a rather expensive crew of technicians or a number of producers.

ICFJ's Senior Program Director notes, however, that practicing backpack journalism is not necessarily new. During a visit to the French television channel TFI in the early 1990s, one of the managers introduced him to the at the time new editing suites and pointed out that TFI staff were also trained to handle a camera, do the voice-over and so forth. For this manager, this was 'the journalist of the future'—for the interviewee, this practice described the day-to-day routines and journalistic realities in many countries:

> I was working [. . .] in Panama [at that time], which is a developing country where the media don't have that many resources. There are few reporters in the networks. There are not many cameramen. And I had done that in a developing country! I had used the camera once, because we had no cameramen. I had asked the questions myself, I had written, I had edited my story. And I was in a developing country. And she [TFI manager] was telling me: 'This is the journalist of the future!' When I went back to my newsroom in Panama I met the reporters. They all were: 'How was your trip to France? You visited all the news media!' So I said: 'Yes, it was great! But let me tell you, guys: you are all the journalists of the future!' I think that is nothing new in the developing world where resources are scarce. (Interviewee 2, ICFJ)

Assigning journalists to not only write a story, but also produce it thus is not necessarily a new development, but a fairly atypical practice at traditional news organizations, especially in the developed world where journalists are often specialized to concentrate only on the task of reporting. In times where financial pressures increasingly demand the cutting of costs, preparing journalists to work as a one-man-band, however, does seem like an option. In alternative journalism, though, where financial resources are often limited, this practice is much more common. The Senior Producer at Democracy Now!, for example, points out that journalists trained on multimedia devices can produce stories with a fraction of the budget compared to traditional foreign corresponding operations. This comes as a true advantage, for example, when reporting from war zones, where the highest flexibility is asked of journalists to produce under extremely difficult circumstances:

During the Lebanon War one of our video producers went to Lebanon and was filing reports from Southern Lebanon. And she managed just with a video camera and a laptop and a microphone to be able to produce and edit five-minute reports from Lebanon, send it back over the Internet. That's all the technology she had. And then we would play it on the show the next day. (Democracy Now!)

Yet there are more factors apart from lacking financial resources that do support the assignment of backpack journalists. As the boundaries between formerly distinct media types are blurring and with crossmedia operations at news organizations in increasing demand, journalists are required to develop multimedia skills. Training journalists as multimedia reporters and sending them out as backpack journalists is one response:

I think that this is something that the mainstream media is exploring, because they never had to deal with it. Just in the last ten years. It just happened that technology has forced the mainstream media to think that way. That news is not only the recording, the audio, or the text, or the pictures, or the video. That news is now everything together. It has to be together. (Interviewee 2, ICFJ)

Viewed from this perspective, the backpack journalist almost seems to be the inevitable professional profile. It already implies that a journalist works 'across media', that is, produces content for various media platforms. Accordingly the BBC interviewee notes:

People have to be multimedia now! Journalists have to be multimedia! The days when I worked a long time ago in television news, we used to go with the producer or correspondent, a cameraman, a soundman and sometimes a lighting man. So a three-man crew, three-person crew. That's way gone! Now the cameraman often edits and shoots, edits and maybe does a bit of production himself. And the correspondent does his radio piece, does a television piece and writes for online. That's absolutely part of the business now and they have to be multimedia. We're a multimedia world! There's no question that our correspondents who are out and wherever don't write a piece for online as well as do their normal job. So they just have to do it! (BBC)

Current TV is an example of a commercial outlet that operates mainly with backpack journalists when it sends its staff on overseas assignments. This practice does according to the interviewee not only save costs, but has another advantage in certain situations. Whereas large journalistic crews often appear invasive, backpack journalists might get closer to the people who can best provide insight and background information:

I think some of it is very imaginative and creative. It sometimes goes places where ordinary media outlets don't go. And actually lives with the people and kind of can recount what's going on there. It gives you that kind of contacts, the human interaction that's missing in a lot of reporting where somebody is standing and saying: 'In the building behind me so and so has just said such and such.' (Interviewee 1, MediaChannel)

For the Current TV interviewee, this is the main advantage of the backpack journalist. The unobtrusiveness of the equipment and a small-size team allows to reach out to sources who are more likely to pass on information in a less 'staged' environment:

I feel like it breaks down some of the barriers when you're in a place. You're not rolling in with a big crew and you seem very intimidating. You're able to integrate more with your surroundings and that's the way I usually work when I'm out in the field and I find that the easiest way, because you can really develop relationships more easily. So that's sort of how we function here! (Current TV)

The prospects of assigning backpack journalists to the task of foreign corresponding, however, are also viewed as rather controversial by some interviewees. One major point of criticism expressed is concerned with a rather personal tone of stories provided by backpack journalists. The PEJ interviewee, for example, notes that there is a danger that the journalist him- or herself becomes the center of the story and might personalize the reporting to a degree in which the attention is drawn away from the initial object of reporting:

I think that if you're talking about somebody who goes around, who's the backpack journalist and who is like hitting hot spots, hot sites; what is that journalism ultimately going to be? It's ultimately going to be about the person. It's not going to be about the places as much as they want it to be. Because that's not the way it works. It's going to be everything filtered. It's kind of like: 'If it's Tuesday then I must be in Kabul.' What you're really doing is getting this person's kind of instant impression of what's going on. And you're getting his unique view of what's happening and that's fine. But it's not the same as like having somebody there whose focus is to get as much as possible to the bottom of the story. Those are two different things. (PEJ)

Along these lines, one of the ICFJ interviewees fears that the reduction of a foreign corresponding team to a one-person-crew is hardly capable of delivering the same quality reporting for different media formats. The backpack journalist might be an option as the journalistic profile of the future, yet it should be regulated and restricted in the amount of the assigned workload. Otherwise the quality of reporting might suffer:

> I think it's a necessary thing in the way that [. . .] traditional media have to be changing and adapting and that means having multimedia websites, so that you've got your journalists in a country or wherever they are in this country, too, are able to do audio, sometimes video, to take pictures. But there is an impact! It does mean that as a journalist if I'm doing that, then I don't have as much time to focus on simply reporting the story, getting good information and writing a good story. I'm distracted, I've got to get some video to match my story, I've got to take some pictures, I've got to get audio, whatever. (Interviewee 1, ICFJ)

He rather wants to see both, traditional foreign correspondents and backpack journalists, as part of staff at media organizations. In accordance with this, one ICFJ interviewee also demands that backpack journalists and traditional foreign corresponding crews should work side by side and feed different story angles into news coverage:

> Larger news media have the ability to send different people in, have the basic reporter and then somebody in. We have a trainer in Egypt right now who's a *New York Times* multimedia guy when he's not training for us and so his job is to go and let's say a story breaks out in an African country and the *Times* will send their correspondent there. They'll also send him to do the multimedia part of it. So the traditional reporter is still free to just spend his or her time making sure that they're getting the story right, that kind of thing, while they have him there to do some filming, take some pictures, get some audio, do graphics, all that stuff. But that's the *New York Times*, not everybody has that ability. (Interviewee 1, ICFJ)

The BBC similarly tries to avoid overly heavy workloads for its reporters in the field, yet does require them to work multimedia:

> Obviously we're not going to say: 'You've got to work three times as hard, because you've got three platforms.' We just say we pick the most sensible things to do. Maybe you don't need to do fifteen two-ways on News 24. Maybe you do eight and write an online piece as well. (BBC)

However, in many cases the typical backpack journalists are freelancers who have to ensure they can sell their material. The pressures of having to work crossmedia, making a living off it and having to guarantee a constant flow of stories can be problematic for a freelancer on the road without a regular income:

Well he/she's [the backpack journalist] a 'jack of all trades', where left to his/her own devices, he/she is really under so much pressure to deliver stories, that I once again have to view this critically. [. . .] But additionally it's a bit of a question, you can always say 'backpack journalism': What have we got here? Now is it somebody who holds a salaried position and then travels there for a month? Or is it somebody who is independent and just goes there? That once again makes a rather large difference because an independent [journalist] relies on selling his/her material. But can generally only sell it when he/she's already able to say what it is. As a salaried [journalist]—one can say: 'Okay, you've got a month. Come up with a few nice stories!' That's a huge difference! (ZEIT ONLINE)

More generally the AlterNet interviewee notes that being a backpack journalist imposes challenges that might be too heavy to carry for a single reporter:

It's one thing to take a little camera and shoot five minutes of an interview and upload it. That's fine, but I mean, if you try to weave together a story all by yourself under bad conditions? I don't think anyone could expect people to do that. Pretty hard! (AlterNet)

All in all the comments of the interviewees do leave the impression that backpack journalists do add information layers to stories that traditional foreign correspondents might miss. However, backpack journalism just as well as parachute journalism does not compensate for declining numbers of foreign correspondents and overseas bureaus. Besides this, traditional foreign corresponding, backpack and parachute journalism essentially do have one characteristic in common: None of them can cover a story in all its complexity or reach out to the whole range of potential sources a global information sphere provides.

The sphere of network journalism then does not only demand different correspondent profiles but also a widening of information circles. Networking with more sources enables journalists to deliver more viewpoints and more story angles. Offering a mix of viewpoints gathered via the web is one option. As discussed earlier in this chapter, one of the criticisms raised against traditional foreign corresponding is that reporters often concentrate on breaking news, but do not follow up on events once a news story is off the day-to-day agenda. The BBC, for example, tries to make up for this lack of follow-up coverage through its online presence where it reaches out to local communities:

We do go back, the New Orleans hurricane for example. All sorts of things we go back and say: 'What's happening there now?' Because we're conscious of the fact that people feel we go, do a big story, and then never go back. So we are—through the audience as well actually—trying to go back and say: 'Are things better or worse' or whatever. (BBC)

The BBC's user-generated content desk is just one platform in cyberspace that aims to follow up on stories and to provide various story angles through user participation. But the BBC is of course not alone. The vast space of the World Wide Web hosts an uncountable number of platforms that provide alternative sources of information from virtually any connected corner of the world, with bloggers or citizen journalists supplying local coloring and viewpoints. Some of these pages do carry the potential to fill the gap left behind through the closing of overseas bureaus and they also contribute material a backpack or parachute journalist might not be able to access on the ground. An increasingly globalized world demands a mix of global, local *and* glocal perspectives and the Internet is becoming a gateway to access such information.

The move onto the web to receive information from other parts of the globe also accentuates the change in the character of international reporting in the network journalism sphere: Here, users can choose from a number of news websites that provide news told from diverse perspectives. News from supposedly 'other' spots of the globe is embedded into different and often more 'local' contexts. These are viewpoints often missing in the coverage provided by foreign correspondents, who embed news stories within frameworks of 'otherness'.

10.3. USING GLOBAL NEWS FLOWS: COLLABORATING WITH NON-STANDARD NEWS SOURCES

> So ideally you wouldn't have a journalist who just arrived there from New York and is trying to capture what's the situation in Iraq that has really hundreds of years of back-story to it that they might not know at all. So we try to find journalists or sources on the ground who have a much broader understanding of the situation.
>
> (Democracy Now!)

Seib explains that among the currently available international coverage 'parochialism flourishes, as if the politics and culture of a news organization's home country were all that matter' (2004: 2). Traditional foreign reporting often does not take into account to mix national, global or local perspectives on news stories. However, through the new source access opportunities, foreign news coverage in a globalized sphere can potentially reach farther and go beyond frameworks of reporting about a country from a foreigner perspective. In the network journalism sphere, news coverage of supposed 'foreign' issues calls for fresh approaches in terms of a transnational framework. Such fresh approaches could contribute to a better understanding of the dynamics at play in a globalized world. The Executive Editor at MediaChannel, for example, argues that decisions made in the US might very well impact the situation in Iraq or Afghanistan or in locations around Africa and news coverage should reflect this. He suggests that in some cases a stringer operating out of centers of (global) decision making might bring more depth to a story than the on-the-spot reporting provided by a foreign correspondent or parachute journalist:

> If I was in Iraq and I wanted to cover the war, I would go to Washington and cover it from there, because that's where the decisions are being made about their country. [. . .] In other words, when I worked in Africa years ago we discovered: There was more information about Africa in America than in Africa about Africa. So if you want to know what's happening in Africa it's not enough simply to be there, but also know: What is the World Bank doing? What is the International Monetary Fund doing? What's happening at the United Nations? In other words: You need a textured picture and in a globalized world often it's not the ideal like what's happening here also relates to larger issues. (Interviewee 1, MediaChannel)

Globalization thus pushes supposedly local issues into a global context. This needs to be taken into account when it comes to angles from which a story is produced and how it is put into a larger context—and this is an angle neither a parachute nor a backpack journalist or a foreign correspondent can necessarily provide. They might be able to add important pieces to the information puzzle, but cannot deliver a complete picture of a story. Foreign news stories play out in a global arena and include a whole complex of story angles and local or global perspectives. They cannot be covered from just one specific spot on the globe or by using just one angle as path to a story. In order to add depth and to contextualize a story within a global setting, news organizations are challenged as to how to operate within a developing transnational sphere. Who to choose as sources and who to connect with in order to gather information is one aspect of this changing dynamic in international reporting.

The online sphere does support this move into the transnational sphere, yet according to the MediaChannel Executive Director, journalists still lack strategies of 'who' to implement and how to organize this transnational information network:

> I still think that that is something that has yet to be really tapped fully. That there is more of a global exchange. It's already happening, people now actually start to be able to pick up other sources online. But I keep feeling like [. . .] I know there's 20 guys like me in Europe and 50 guys like me in . . . There is tons of people doing it. But it's like: 'I don't know them!' And that's a little weird! Or like: I'm on listservs of political bloggers in the United States for example. Now I know those lists are happening all over, but how come our list doesn't know about these other lists? They're yet to have that more global communication.

[. . .] I really want to promote more news journalists and media makers to connect more on a global level. Because when you have a global perspective, which I think is very crucial right now, a global perspective is one that makes every story different. The global perspective of an economic story, if you have a global perspective you can start to identify with people in other parts of the world and start to see how they're having the same issues. It allows you to get out of thinking in terms of within your country or your culture. And politically as well. (Interviewee 2, MediaChannel)

As a consequence of this, he proposes that journalists need to learn how to move within a globalized sphere of information exchange and eventually have to contextualize news content in a transnational setting. Taking the example of how US news outlets tend to report about Israel or Iraq he comments:

George Bush says this about Israel or about Palestinians. Now, we automatically put anything that's said about Israel or Palestine by politicians in the United States, it will be compared to other politicians in the United States. Most people in the United States don't know that our stands with Israel is radically out of line with the rest of the world basically. And we never talk about something like that. And when we talk about Iraq we don't talk about why aren't the other Gulf States more involved or in what ways are they involved. The Iraq War is political, so even when we talk about the Iraq War in the newspaper it's about the election. It's about the Democratic Party versus the Republican Party. [. . .] With more people writing and creating and analyzing from a global perspective, I think it would give us a radically different take on the world. (Interviewee 2, MediaChannel)

The central question then is: How can outlets strategically expand their networks? Forming relationships and using alternative news sources in order to span a global web of contacts is according to the interviewees the inescapable step that needs to be taken. Journalistic organizations need to reach out and develop a network of sources and hence provide global and local takes on stories. With the whole spectrum of politics, economy and society being pushed into, being contextualized and functioning within a global setting, journalistic practice inevitably needs to follow.

Forming partnerships with other journalistic outlets operating in specific regions can be one approach or as one ICFJ interviewee formulates it: It means that:

they [journalistic organizations] have to find new sources of information for international news. So that means perhaps sometimes forming partnerships with news organizations in other countries that are still covering parts of the world; means establishing relationships with stringers and freelancers in countries around the world. (Interviewee 1, ICFJ)

Such a move might compensate in part for the closing of international bureaus and this statement can be interpreted as a call for journalistic organizations to widen their networks and team up with a larger number of stringers who add angles and background to a story. Optional partner outlets are news agencies or international bureaus of journalistic colleagues. Yet, with a growing number of smaller news organizations emerging, with citizen journalists or media activists and bloggers operating in various parts of the world, there are many more options. The other ICFJ interviewee, for example, notes that small local organizations could function as stringers:

In South Africa there is a network, like a very grassroots news agency of community news media. [. . .] In Latin America there are people calling me for ideas of creating their own little news agencies based on the web, because now it is going to be easier to do it. I think we are going to see a lot of regional, small, community-based news agencies that are going to be created because of how accessible technology is. I mean, look at Yahoo News, Google News! This is an example of how information is going to be delivered in a non-traditional way! It's not a mainstream news agency, though it is being used by many people as their main source of information—even for the media! For the mainstream media! You don't need an AP or Reuters or Agence France or BBC! I mean you have non-traditional systems of news delivery. (Interviewee 2, ICFJ)

In order to form collaborations between news organizations, grassroots news agencies, bloggers or citizen journalists, though, an increased level of communication *between* these nodes in the information network is necessary. Sharing stories and viewpoints becomes an essential ingredient of international news coverage:

People who are media makers and journalists and what not, they can be sharing their stories and their resources on a global way. What I'm thinking of specifically: I'm on a list that's all US progressive more or less political bloggers. And my thought is, these people should be talking with people in Europe. Or some of these people should [. . .]. When you have a good list, it really does become a community. It really is a resource! People will say: 'Hey, I'm writing about this. Does this ring a bell with anyone or is this . . . ' If you have that happening with people who are blogging just in the United States then that's one thing and that benefits people in one way. When you have those people—you have people blogging or communicating on lists on a global level—you can start and use that as a resource. Those references and that context is going to work the way into stories so that in people's news it is going to be often more of a global perspective. And I think that that's the key. (Interviewee 2, MediaChannel)

I would add: This is only possible if all sides start to understand that they are moving within the same sphere of information exchange. In this sphere, improved methods of information exchange are key. Forming global networks might eventually add various perspectives to a story. Listservs as mentioned in the quote above eventually were the first forms of such collaborative information exchange models on the web. The ZEIT ONLINE Editor:

> I can remember the Kosovo War very well. I had subscribed to a computer game mailing list. Completely different subject, but there was a participant who lived in Belgrade. He wrote daily updates on the situation in Belgrade vie email. Along the lines of: 'The coal-burning-power plant just blew up.' And similar stories. That wasn't any different, just a divergent format because it wasn't quite as easy back then to simply build a website. And he wrote for a specific public. That was essentially like a closed blog, but it completely turned the game mailing list into an unbelievable discussion mailing list on the sense and absurdity of war and related topics. [...] There were Americans, British, there were French, there were Italians, there were Germans—incredibly mixed! And unsurprisingly this was a very exciting type of public, formed by this. Nowadays he'd most likely create a blog and report on what's happening. Back then he did it that way. (ZEIT ONLINE)

The information the gamer provided in the closed environment of the mailing list back then, a blogger could provide today via the Global Voices Online network, or a user through the services of the BBC or a citizen journalist through sending a video to Current TV. Sources on the ground—be it local journalists, bloggers, citizen journalists or users—are gateways to information and an increasingly important source for journalists. They add layers to stories and in some cases might supply coverage from spots hardly accessible such as Zimbabwe:

> The BBC aren't allowed to report from Zimbabwe. But last night on the ten o'clock news John Simpson, our foreign editor, did a special report on Zimbabwe in which he read out three emails from people inside Zimbabwe saying how horrific it was now. So places like that, it's the only way to get news out! And it covers areas. (BBC)

One other example also illustrates that the BBC is ultimately wandering down the path of increased collaboration with users of its services on the ground, especially in remote areas. In this case it used a rescue worker to get first-hand information after a natural disaster on the Philippines:

> There was a mudslide in the Philippines, a huge mudslide; a school wiped away, horrific story about a year ago. And the area was so remote. It took two days, 48 hours, for TV crews and reporters to get there. Within about half an hour of that happening we had an email from somebody, a charity worker, saying: 'I've got the phone number of somebody who's working on the mudslide, a rescue worker. And you can speak to him.' And we did. He was all over the news and on the online stories. And the crews got there two days later. [. . .] In a way doing international coverage is easier, because it's more useful, because it takes so long to report. Because you can't be everywhere. (BBC)

Delivering local perspectives and mixing them with traditional foreign corresponding might ultimately lead the way to a multi-layered style of transnational news reporting. This style of reporting does do justice to an increasingly globalized sphere and takes into account many more viewpoints and story angles.

Providing a range of viewpoints on a story to get a better picture of the situation on the ground is especially crucial in times of war when national bias often does lead the way for the tone of coverage. Aday et al (2005) note in their cross-cultural analysis of television coverage of the Iraq War in 2003 that the supposed value of 'objectivity' often goes out the window when it comes to war reporting. Instead, ideology becomes the main driving force and journalists often privilege official sources or uncritically echo opinions of military representatives or politicians.[1] These findings correspond with a comment made by the AlterNet interviewee. He highlights the dangers of relying too heavily on one-sided viewpoints:

> Well, you know, Judith Miller and some of the journalists, they brought us Chalabi and all the information that Bush used to justify invading Iraq. So we would have been better with them not being there! Because the fact that you're in a foreign country doesn't mean you're any closer to getting the truth and reporting it! The *New York Times* has been really good about Iraq, but I think increasingly it's really hard for them to get outside of the greenzone. And if you're embedded into a military unit: Jesus, you can't really write stuff that's very critical, because the people are protecting your lives! You got to have second thoughts about that! [. . .] That's why the Internet has made information more accessible. And especially in situations where outsiders have a hard time getting in and understanding what's going on. (AlterNet)

How in the case of the war in Iraq a mix of traditional foreign reporting and the use of alternative sources did add to the conversation will be the subject of the following pages. Examples of different forms of war coverage will illustrate the emerging diversity of viewpoints accessible in the network journalism sphere: With correspondents, parachute journalists, independent backpack journalists or Iraqi bloggers at work, the case of the Iraq War stands representative of how news flows can function today.

10.4. THE CASE OF COVERING THE WAR IN IRAQ

> The case of Iraq totally changed the landscape of how news is reported! When reporters can't leave the greenzone, there is a big problem in what reality the audience and the public is seeing. So bloggers are totally instrumental; bloggers and vloggers in giving a certain insight. [. . .] That window into the world of what everyday Iraqi civilians are going through is something that still isn't being reported on as much as it should be, I think.
>
> (Current TV)

How news reached global audiences out of Iraq during the military campaign in 2003 and in the first years after illustrates how communication flows are changing. With a growing number of news deliverers covering the conflict from different angles and sharing their stories online, more sources are accessible for anyone who seeks information about the situation.

One case in point are Iraqi bloggers who reached out to global audiences and gathered millions of users in front of individual computer screens. The success story of Iraqi bloggers is partially a result of the difficulties correspondents working for traditional media organizations in Iraq had to face:

> The foreign correspondent in Baghdad has created what's a new type of journalism called 'Hotel Journalism'. In other words: These people are stuck in hotels, they can't get out, because it's so dangerous. And as a consequence we're getting a very narrow view of what's happening there. They are kind of all reporting on what each other are saying. [. . .] I think a lot of these people are brave and they are well intentioned, they are trying to get at what's going on. It's just not easy.
> (Interviewee 1, MediaChannel)

Stuck inside the greenzone, direct access to stories was and mainly still is restricted. Palmer and Fontan (2007) conducted interviews with journalists and fixers in Iraq who work for French and British news outlets and found that local knowledge and background to stories is mainly provided through the lens of the fixers. Due to the security situation and language barriers, gathering first-hand information is extremely difficult for Western journalists. They do not blend in with the local population, often lack cultural background and are highly dependent on fixers and Iraqi journalists. This bears a number of risks: Mistranslations, for example, often go undiscovered and fixers are in control to form certain views (Palmer and Fontan, 2007: 13). They are well aware of the content that fits best with certain national agendas and do anticipate what kind of information journalists look for as they know that 'foreign newsgathering is a routinized process where only certain categories of information are going to be relevant, as dictated by Western news values' (Ibid.: 18).

In addition to these mainly cultural problems, the lack of financial resources and declining numbers of staffers for international operations add to access difficulties. The World Wide Web can come as an important tool in this respect. It offers the opportunity to connect with locals outside of the greenzone and to receive first-hand information from Iraqis:

> As bureaus are being cut [. . .] people don't have people to throw at Baghdad. You don't have people to throw at Kabul. People don't have people to throw at Darfur. So how do you find out what's going on there? Well, you're going to have to use the resources you have on the computer. You're going to have to use more of them. And you're going to have to be careful about how you use them. But the advantages are [. . .] if you're a small paper or small TV station or radio station [. . .], television, newspapers, magazines: You've got to rely on these, because you just don't have the resources anymore to do it if you want to have feet on the ground. (PEJ)

Such optional sources of information can be citizen journalists or bloggers. Especially at the height of the war in 2003, in the aftermath the following years and in some cases up to now, Iraqi bloggers shared their account of the situation and provided perspectives not reported by foreign correspondents. The Democracy Now! interviewee reflects:

> I think the Iraqi bloggers . . . for me it's an amazing story. Right now, especially for any Western journalist, they are so constrained as to what they can do in Iraq. [. . .] Many of them can't even leave the greenzone. And you really can't report on a war if you're spending all the time with the military and with the occupiers. But the bloggers who have perhaps more than anyone else really given a sense of what it's like living in Baghdad, living in Nadjaf during a time of war. So I think, it has opened the eyes, I'm sure, of journalists around the world as to what day-to-day life is for Iraqis. And it's also allowing Iraqis to speak in their own voice, not just in sound bites or short quotes in the newspaper. But allowing them day after day to really explain what's going on in their country and how the war is affecting them personally. (Democracy Now!)

The Iraqi bloggers provided voices from inside Iraq and organizations such as MediaChannel used them as an important information resource. For example, the organization worked together with an Iraqi blogger who from August 2003 until October 2007 wrote under the pseudonym Riverbend about the conditions in Iraq after the war:

> She calls herself Riverbend because she lives at the bend of a river. And she's basically reporting on the war, writing about the war from her own experience inside her family. So it's an insight-out approach. But she's Iraqi. She's also a very, very good writer. So she's able to offer comment and discussion of the lives of ordinary Iraqis who are invisible in most of the media. We never see them, we never hear from them. So here's a war, [. . .] obviously there's more than two sides or many sides. But we're only hearing from about one. We're hearing about what the USA is doing and maybe the Iraqi government, which is totally unrepresentative. And that's supposed to be Iraq! But what about all these people who are not in the government, who are living through this nightmare every day? And she is their voice. She's one of the voices of that community and it's the legitimate voice and an important voice. But you label her and call her 'blogger'; suddenly she doesn't have the credibility of somebody else who may in fact have been wrong about everything he's done. (Interviewee 1, MediaChannel)[2]

The personal tone of blog entries such as the ones written by Riverbend does collide with journalistic ideals of 'neutral' or 'factual' reporting. However, her writings shed a different light on the situation. Iraqi bloggers like her added a different perspective to news stories and they provided an extra layer of information to the 'conventional' content provided by foreign correspondents.

Another and probably the most prominent spokesperson in this respect was the so-called Baghdad blogger who wrote under the pseudonym 'Salam Pax'.[3] He blogged the 2003 breakout of the war from inside Iraq and his writings did not only bring him to fame in the blogosphere, but news media around the globe drew upon his material and gained him readers in many countries of the Western world:

> That guy, the reason why we all loved him, is because he sounds like a real person. [. . .] It was journalism, but it was also storytelling and sometimes I think that's a little bit different! When I watch American journalism, very often it's very cold and analytical. It's full of facts, which is good, but when you see a blogger like that, there's all that stuff plus there's this humanity behind him. And that really brings you into the story. It makes you care! I think that this notion of being 'objective' has gotten brought way too far. Where for some reason journalists think that they aren't allowed to get involved or have an opinion. (Ourmedia)[4]

Salam Pax did also inspire other Iraqis to start blogging such as a dentist from Baghdad who started 'Healing Iraq', a blog that is at the time of writing this book still alive and updated on a regular basis. The Indymedia volunteer followed this blog when the war broke out and he was intrigued by the many layers of information provided by this particular blogger:

> So, this was a guy [. . .] who as soon as the invasion happened, started this amazing blog! And he would have maps of like the Armedian neighborhood in Baghdad. And he would say: 'This is what is happening right now in my neighborhood. There are people firing guns over here, here and here. And there are militias on the other side here.' And he would draw all this and then he would have pictures of it happening underneath there. It was amazing! (Indymedia)

Bloggers such as Salam Pax, Riverbend and the dentist from Baghdad can be found in many parts around the globe and report from many spots hard to reach or at times even inaccessible for journalists. Their accounts can be an extraordinarily useful resource for journalists and they add interpretative angles foreign correspondents might miss:

> Foreign journalists, first of all, they are in danger. Secondly, the military is not going to let them see very much. So, in situations of crisis like that it often becomes essential to have citizen journalists giving information out. It's been true in China, it's been true in Latin America [. . .]. And it's just one piece of the larger picture. (AlterNet)

Going back to the example of Iraq, other sources providing information pieces, adding content as well as contexts, were journalistic projects such as *Alive in Baghdad*, a weekly news program that regularly streamed videos online until late 2009.[5] The project was initiated by independent journalist Brian Conley, who traveled to the Middle East in 2005 covering Iraqi life. A year later he went back equipped with digital production devices and trained Iraqis to produce weekly news bulletins for a global audience on the life in Iraq beyond the greenzone. The project also collaborated with traditional news organizations and produced work for outlets such as the BBC or Sky News. *Alive in Baghdad* gave an insight into rarely covered lifeworlds and went to areas where foreign correspondents are rarely found.

Other journalists providing alternative viewpoints to the coverage of traditional foreign correspondence were independent journalists such as Kevin Sites and Christopher Allbritton. They both traveled as backpack journalists reporting out of Iraq, especially during the height of the conflict. Kevin Sites, for example, gained fame for his reporting on his vlog kevinsites.net. He was one of very few journalists not embedded with military troops and provided multimedia-reporting packages. After working in Iraq, the former NBC News and CNN correspondent went on to work for an online news program at Yahoo News called *Kevin in the Hotzone* where he covered armed conflicts around the globe as a solo multimedia reporter. Equipped with not more than a bag full of digital devices including a laptop, two digital cameras, a satellite modem, a satellite phone and a standard mobile phone, he has ever since been on assignments in the Middle East and elsewhere.

Leaving for Iraq in 2002, the former AP, *New York Daily News* and *Time Magazine* reporter Christopher Allbritton also posted stories from inside Iraq. He initially went into the country financially supported by the readers of his 'Back to Iraq' blog and stayed on and off in Iraq until 2006. His reports did catch the attention of a number of news organizations and he ended up not only blogging on his own website, but filing reports to the *Boston Globe*, the *San Francisco Chronicle* and *Time Magazine*. The stories published on 'Back to Iraq' added background that traditional correspondents did not provide and his insights widened the contextual framework about the Iraq conflict. For his current blog 'InsurgencyWatch' Allbritton now reports from Pakistan and Afghanistan and uses the same reader-funded model he started for 'Back to Iraq'. About himself he writes:

> I'm a firm believer in mainstream newspapers as a source of great information, but I'm also realistic. With fewer and fewer newspapers sending staffers overseas (or even using stringers and freelancers), the ability for Americans to get good foreign news and analysis is suffering. (Allbritton, 2010: Online)

With his blogs he aims to fill this gap in order to ensure that what happens in countries such Iraq, Pakistan and Afghanistan remains in the attention zone of his users. For the Indymedia interviewee, reporters such as Sites or Allbritton break with the conventional frameworks of war coverage and they are an essential resource of information that deserves attention. Looking in retrospect at the coverage Allbritton provided from Iraq, he notes that 'Chris Allbritton should be setting the agenda in Iraq! Because he actually seems to be doing reporting and actually talking to people, instead of sitting in the greenzone filing stories from his hotel room' (Indymedia).

Another way to provide a broader scope of perspectives from Iraq is to embed user-generated content in foreign corresponding footage. The BBC, for example, uses this material to complement the content provided by its own reporters: 'The BBC has a team there, but they can't leave the greenzone. Very rarely do they go out. It's just not safe. But ordinary people in Iraq can tell their own story' (BBC). The result of such collaboration during the height of the Iraq War and in the years after was featured on the BBC website, which carried a host of special reports put together by BBC editors. The content is gathered from users and covers the life stories of people in Iraq. Just a few examples that can still be found on the site are features like

'Fleeing Iraq' (a collection of stories from Iraqi refugees) or 'Iraqi Voices' where Iraqis tell their story of day-to-day life in the country.[6]

The Iraq War is one of the first cases in the recent history of journalism where traditional news organizations have started to realize the potential of networking with alternative information providers, be it users, bloggers or freelance backpack journalists. They all added context and local coloring that often was missing in conventional foreign news coverage. And even though the PEJ interviewee notes that working with alternative information sources differs significantly from working with foreign journalists, he also stresses that they are a tremendous resource, especially in times of foreign bureau cut downs:

> And there are definitely things that are lost in that relationship. It's not the same as like saying: 'You're my reporter and I know you. And I know your work and I know I can trust you. I know where your strengths are; I know where your weaknesses are. I know when you give me something what I'm going to get.' But I don't have that any more. You're not there anymore. So having these people out there can be a great benefit to media organizations. (PEJ)

The interviewee at Current TV argues that finding the citizen journalist or the blogger to collaborate with to expand the margin of perspectives might at times even be more useful than sending an organization's own reporters into the field:

> We had one of our reporters who wanted to go to Iraq. He followed a convoy last year and he wanted to go back and check on that convoy. And I didn't approve that story, because I said: 'What new information are you going to get? Not only is it expensive, it's risky, all that sort of stuff, but beyond that what real story beyond what this convoy is doing are you going to get that's different? And so let's use our energy and resources elsewhere to expand on other stories and let's find that citizen who is in and outside of the greenzone and let's find that blogger and let's find that vlogger who wants to submit something for Current. (Current TV)

Overall, the case of covering the war in Iraq and its aftermath does illustrate that establishing networks with users, bloggers or independent backpack journalists can help create a rich pool of information. The case exemplifies the opportunities the network journalism sphere provides and it serves as grounds for the assumption that an evaluation of current collaboration models at news organizations becomes necessary. An 'opening up' of internal networks, allowing more information channels to enter the production chain of a media outlet, does not need to happen at the cost of credibility. It does ask of news organizations, though, to deliberate who they choose as collaborators:

You're talking about the reputation of your news organization. That is the most valuable commando that you have as a news organization, it's your reputation. If you damage it you're really hurting yourself. But again, I think that these people are valuable—number one—, and number two: it's more necessary than ever. You have to find a way to use them and to make it work, but the way I would go about doing it I think is: Look at their work, ask them to file some reports for you, see if things check out. And then it's like anything else. It's like if you're a reporter: Over time I start to trust you more and more. If you've done many things right and I don't have problems with your work and you bring me something that's sensational I'm going to say: 'Okay, I've trusted your work before, this is what you say happened. Maybe I'll ask you for some clarification.' If I don't know you and you come to me and say: 'Oh my God, I've got this unbelievable story for you' my first reaction is probably going to be: 'Right, that's unbelievable!' I don't think I would believe it. And maybe somebody else will go with your story and you're right and that's wonderful, but I can't play with the reputation of my news organization! That's too important.' (PEJ)

Strategies are needed to set rules on how to embed alternative information flows into conventional newsgathering and production processes. And such strategies are more important than ever, as otherwise stories about war or crisis and especially from countries and regions that are hard to access most likely will lack appropriate coverage.

On the other hand, bloggers—just as the stories provided by the news agency or the correspondent in the greenzone—deliver only one part of the complex settings around foreign news stories. As one interviewee warns:

Usually those kinds of things [blogs] are not telling me the whole story. They're from a very narrow focus of 'what is my life like', somebody who's writing that kind of blog isn't getting the opinion of, you know, what do the Sunnis think, what do the Shiites think, what do the Kurds think, what does [. . .] the US coalition think. All that kind of stuff that I get from traditional media. So, to me it's a balance. I love that stuff. Some of those blogs that I read are just gripping, they're fascinating. And there is stuff I don't get in traditional media. [. . .] It adds to the voices. It gives us information we weren't getting before. But I still read the traditional—not everybody does. [. . .] I don't think they are [bloggers] giving me the full context and they are [. . .] often not able to do investigative reporting. Let's say you're reading a blog from a Shiite [. . .] in Iraq. They wouldn't be able to talk to the people in the Sunni community. And so I guess I could read lots of different blogs and make sure that I'm getting a balance, but it's dangerous if you're getting your information only from blogs, you run the risk of getting one side of the story and not getting the full context. (Interviewee 1, ICFJ)

The foreign reporting provided by news organizations thus should not only rely on bloggers. It is the information mix just as well as the mix of sources that makes the news coverage multi-layered and delivers a complex and more accurate picture of the stories being told. Journalists play a very important role in this process:

> Dave Winer said a while ago: 'You don't need reporters in Iraq! You don't need reporters in Iraq, because there's going to be a thousand bloggers and you run an aggregation engine over that and that's better!' Now all that collection of voices: Very powerful and very engaging. But having one person on the ground and a desk back in the UK and people who are committed to actually distill that, to make sense of it, to make human judgments based on years and decades of experience really, really adds value and I think is very, very important. (Guardian)

The task of journalists then is to draw together the information they receive from their correspondents just as well as from bloggers, citizen journalists, users or officials such as military staff or politicians. It is neither only the correspondent nor only the blogger who delivers the full picture—required is a mix of various angles, viewpoints and background that adds context to stories unfolding in a globalized world. Or as one interviewee claims:

> I want both. To me the whole thing is that there's just more sources and I think that's good as long as we can figure out a way to adequately understand what we're seeing, reading whatever. I want both. I would love to get some 16-year old blogger on Haifa Street in Baghdad. I'd love to read that! Would I trade that for being able to read the AP story on Iraq that day? No, probably not. I want them both! And from that I'll start formulating my own opinion. (Interviewee 2, MediaChannel)

The story of the Iraq War coverage is therefore also a story about the importance of shaping collaborative networks between traditional journalists and alternative news providers. In times of globalization news stories can hardly be grasped through the lens of the supposed 'foreign'. With the help of digital technologies and the World Wide Web, various angles have become accessible. Information transmitters such as satellites or broadband connections do not stop at the border of the greenzone. These devices prolong the scope of journalists; they help to reach the many people who want to tell their story and who provide pieces of information that help to better understand the complex settings unfolding in a globalized sphere.

11 Reconceptualizing Journalistic Outlets as Information Nodes

Journalists have always been in demand of sources who share and deliver information. Without sources news production would be an impossible task. However, as so far argued in this book, the emergence of non-linear global information flows fundamentally affects the work of journalists and their 'conventional' collaboration models. The argument presented here is that the underlying dynamics driving these processes of change are fostered by digital technologies and by the emergence of the network society. But what is the role of journalistic outlets within the sphere of network journalism? Where should they position themselves in the context of increasingly decentralized information flows and how can journalists effectively use the optional sources who offer multiple layers of information to a story?

Tapscott and Williams (2008) argue that in today's world, collaboration has become the inevitable business operation that affects every industry and demands new work models:

> For the business manager, the number one lesson is that the monolithic, self-contained, inwardly focused corporation is dead. Regardless of the industry you compete in, or whether your firm is large or small, internal capabilities and a handful of b-web partnerships are not sufficient to meet the market's expectations for growth and innovation. (Tapscott and Williams, 2008: 314)

Applied to journalistic work this means that professional news organizations have to adapt to the rules of openness and collaboration or they will perish. In this remaining empirical chapter, the main arguments that have lead this book will be summarized and combined with suggestions as to how journalistic organizations can adapt to the sphere of network journalism.

11.1. THE FORMATION OF A NETWORK OF MULTIPLE RELATIONSHIPS

> First of all you have to want to broaden and diversify your news offerings. Not everybody does that. They find it threatening, because they

don't think the audience is interested or whatever. They are also very absorbed in their own Egos and their own institutional Ego. But if you do want to, you can do it!

(Interviewee 1, MediaChannel)

Today's journalism sphere—to use the words of the AlterNet interviewee—is a 'flattened' one in which traditional news disseminators have to deal with more competitors from the independent as well as the alternative media sphere. As digital technologies make it easier to access more sources, the restructured information flows support the extension of the journalistic network—especially internationally:

> Networking is not exactly the smallest part of a journalist's job, and in particular networking amongst colleagues to mutually exchange information and so forth. That's just an element of it. That today this predominantly takes place online simplifies the process. That has to be acknowledged perspicuously. If I want information from Argentina, I get information from Argentina. I know people in Argentina. If I want information from Russia, I can call somebody there whom I trust. I can also send him an email—preferably encoded. Hence, there are these options. Put it this way: Journalistic opportunities to network internationally have improved exponentially, and for me it's the case where I can honestly say that in countries currently exhilarating for me I either have somebody on site locally or I have someone sitting somewhere else who is extremely knowledgeable [on a situation]. Therefore if I have any questions about a specific topic, I can ask. My personal network, for my journalistic work in Germany as well as internationally is in fact so diverse, that it isn't just comprised of journalists. More often than not it also includes bloggers. (ZEIT ONLINE)

Strategically forming relationships with potential news gatherers and disseminators within this global network journalism sphere may assist to control the information flows. Developing collaboration models with bloggers or citizen journalists is one part of this. The transformed sphere calls for a plan of action to organize a news outlet around these new global news flows. However, such plans can only succeed if journalistic organizations understand that ultimately the sphere in which they move has radically changed. This demands, as one of the ICFJ interviewees argues, less 'antipathy' from traditional journalists toward alternative news disseminators and vice versa. According to him, traditional media are

> standing on an island and this is probably going to be very accurate with global warming: The island is getting smaller and smaller and smaller and at some point you've got to change and figure out some other way of surviving, because pretty soon there is not going to be an

island anymore and that's the situation traditional media are in. Many traditional media people are just in denial! [. . .] There are cases where it is working. There are cases where the two sides are trying to work together. But I still see a lot more division than I do [see] coming together. (Interviewee 1, ICFJ)

Recent research into journalistic practice supports the interviewee's remarks. In their study of interactivity features in traditional newsrooms, Paulussen and Ugille (2008: 37), for example, identify a number of current professional newsroom practices as the main problem. They point out that (1) strong hierarchies in present newsroom cultures often stand in the way of collaboration, (2) newsroom practice often lacks negotiations among staffers, for example between IT personnel and editors and (3) journalists struggle to change an often rather skeptical attitude toward the use of alternative sources and more collaborative approaches because they fear higher workloads and in addition complain about a lack of time and resources. Similarly, Schmitz Weiss and de Marcedo Higgins Joyce (2008, 597) have found that budget and resource constraints are the main arguments journalists raise with respect to this. Paulussen and Ugille summarize:

Although the interview transcripts are full of quotes concerning the increased importance of interactivity, we cannot but conclude from our interviews and observations that handling user generated content (blogs, forums, etc.) or interacting with users do not seem to be part of the daily routine activities in the newsroom. (Paulussen and Ugille, 2008: 35)

Based on the findings presented here I add that the reason new approaches toward newsgathering, production and dissemination seem to be hard to adopt is an even more fundamental one. The conflicts between traditional organizational structures and fresh approaches toward collaboration and thus the problems of adapting new models of journalistic practice are rooted in the main argument presented here: The dynamics and the power of networks are often not understood.

Many journalistic organizations lack awareness of the impacts the evolving network journalism sphere has on their work and traditional top-down organization models do not pay tribute to the new ways information flows. The hierarchical structures do barely leave space for bloggers, citizen journalists or activists. Instead, new source and collaboration options are mainly greeted with fear and interpreted as an add-on to workloads. But, as one interviewee stresses vividly, these alternative news providers now are 'a fundamental part of the new communication chain, whatever you want to call it. And every news media—mainstream or no mainstream—will have to rely on [them] if you wanted to survive as a media in the 21st century' (Interviewee 2, ICFJ).

In accordance with his assertions, the ICFJ interviewee pledges that journalists need to understand the degree of impact the restructured information flows have and proposes that journalists have to take bloggers or citizen journalists 'serious':

> They got to understand the power of the communication chain now and that there are good things that will happen because of that. First it's recognizing. I don't think we have reached that point. I think especially the large media begin to recognize that. And they are facing it in different ways. First it was very timid. They would create their webpage; they would allow some people to interact now, because they realized they cannot ignore these people. They begun, as you know, getting their bloggers, they selected their bloggers and now they are part of the mainstream. They are co-opting some of them and now they see that this is not enough! [. . .] How should the mainstream or the professional journalists react to this? I would say that more and more they would have to incorporate these citizen journalists, or bloggers, or audiences into their news sections. [. . .] There is a little bit of that. But I don't think it's fully fletched yet. (Interviewee 2, ICFJ)

Other interviewees argue accordingly. The ZEIT ONLINE Editor, for example, views the number of alternative news disseminators as a procreative addition:

> I believe it to be complementary. It just doesn't work any other way! You can't compare it in that sense. It can only be mutually fertile. Because if an interesting blog-entry appears somewhere, if all else fails one can always say to the correspondent: 'How about it? Can you investigate this?' More often than not he'll have a better grasp of it than me on site. As a result I can tell him: 'This sounds quite interesting, please check it out!' And that's how it really works. (ZEIT ONLINE)

Similarly reacts the BBC Editor:

> I see it all as complementary. I think people want their news from lots of different sources. They'll come to the BBC site and find out maybe the overview of what's happening, maybe they'll send in some comment or messages. And then they'll probably have their favorite blogs that they get on RSS or whatever they do. And they have multiple sources. And if we can help make sense of some of that then that's a good thing. I don't see us as in competition with people who are doing the blogs and things. (BBC)

Strategic embedding of collaborative actions can help to guarantee a multiplicity of voices and reporting from various angles. A journalistic outlet can benefit from the new possibilities and potentials if it embraces the logic of interactivity that Tapscott and Williams phrase as 'the new art and science of collaboration we call wikinomics' (2008: 3). According to them, 'to simply intensify existing management strategies' is insufficient:

> This is more than open source, social networking, so-called crowd-sourcing, smart mobs, crowd wisdom, or other ideas that touch upon the subject. Rather, we are talking about deep changes in the structure and modus operandi of the corporation and our economy, based on new competitive principles such as openness, peering, sharing, and acting globally. (Tapscott and Williams, 2008: 3)

MediaChannel's business model is based on exactly these premises. According to its Executive Director, the future of journalism lies in the creation of collaborative networks:

> That's what MediaChannel is [. . .]; it's thirteen hundred affiliated groups. It's a whole network of organizations and that's what I'm trying to argue for to the blogosphere and these others that we have to find ways of working together, because that's what's going to give our voice more clout and power in the marketplace. But it's a hard thing to do, because we have a nation of 350 million individualists who don't want to work with other people necessarily. That's part of the tradition of this country [United States]. And so it's difficult to do that. And often also there's competition among these different groups and they're competing with each other and they're attacking each other and there is sectarianism and the right wing and the left wing doesn't talk to each other and all the rest of it. So you do the best you can, but at least our philosophy is what we call 'Post-Particip'. In other words: We don't want to just be covering the world through the eyes of the Democratic Party or the Republican Party. We want to go deeper, more insightful, more independent, more analytical, more investigative. (Interviewee 1, MediaChannel)

Despite the difficulties described by the interviewee in fostering such collaborations, the improvement and enlargement of networks is becoming an important part of journalistic work.

In search of models that could serve as an example of how to reorganize work structures in line with the changing environment, a look at the current news practice of alternative journalism outlets can be useful. Gillmor (2006), for example, proposes that traditional media can learn from the production and dissemination models employed in the alternative media sphere:

> Journalists will use the tools of grassroots journalism or be consigned to history. Core values, including accuracy and fairness, will remain

important [...], and professionals will still be gatekeepers in some ways, but the ability to shape larger conversations—and to provide context—will be at least as important as the ability to gather facts and report them. (Gillmor, 2006: XXV)

Outlets such as Global Voices Online are good cases in point. The platform understands how to create and sustain global collaboration networks, how to foster interaction and how to aggregate information. It pushes voices and commentary on the global news agenda otherwise often ignored and allows users to selectively pull the information they seek. The approach of Global Voices Online is one model of how to handle content streaming through the sphere of network journalism that could be used as an example for the revision of operational modes at traditional news organizations.

The Senior Associate at PEJ also advocates for increased interaction between journalists and alternative news providers such as bloggers or citizen journalists and suggests integrating the latter especially in regard to global news coverage:

Do I see a partnership with some of them? Yes, I do. I really do. I think it's where we're going to head in fact. [...] I actually have a lot of respect for what they [alternative news providers] can bring, because the fact of the matter is: Even the biggest news organization can't have feet on the ground in every location. And the idea that you would have: Listing posts. People you can rely on. [...] The idea of using them would be that: 'I can't be there. You can be there. So what I want to do is establish a relationship with you. I need you to give me this information. I'm going to edit you. You need to understand that. But we'll pay you some token, some money, you supply me with some content.' (PEJ)

To collaborate with alternative sources could help a news organization to span a web of stringers around the globe. As mentioned above, this is how MediaChannel works, incorporating as many voices as possible from as many sides as it can reach:

I've always thought it would be very inexpensive to actually have what we call 'Inside-Out-Journalism'. This is what we did on our program on human rights. We had submissions from journalists in all different countries. I went for example to the 'Human Rights Conference' in Vienna. But I also met journalists from other countries and they sent us reports as a result of my meeting with them! So when we covered Sarajevo we did so with the filmmakers of Sarajevo who are covering their own city, who have better access, they know the language et cetera et cetera. It was better coverage than what the other newspapers had for the most part. (Interviewee 1, MediaChannel)

How to access sources, who to contact and also in what order sources should be approached are important questions in this regard. During the China earthquake in May 2008, for example, first news accounts of the disaster were not delivered by news agencies, but via the microblogging tool Twitter. As outlined in Chapter 4, cases like this are an indication that the order of whom to contact on a story, where to receive breaking news and where to get background information is not set as it used to be. An ICFJ interviewee describes how the gathering process for news used to travel down a fairly determined path:

> Before, journalists would have to start with the official sources, with the mainstream sources, with the people who are the experts and so on. Now, if you think about it, this is the last place I would go for the information. [. . .] So, where do you start? You have got to start from the people. You have got to start from the eyewitnesses. You have got to start from the citizen journalists, from the blogging, from the people in the field, from the local angle. And then you have to go for the official, and the traditional, and the experts, and the global. So, before we would go from the official, from the global to the local. Now we have to go to the local, to the grassroots, to the wider picture, to the official and to the global connection. [. . .] Now the people, the local, manage information and they are able to share it easier. Before it was more difficult. (Interviewee 2, ICFJ)

Hence, awareness that the digital sphere offers access to much more information needs to be established and—taken from there—strategies for collaboration need to be developed. And every journalistic outlet has to review which role as a news organization it wants to take within a restructured sphere of information.

11.2. THE ROLE OF JOURNALISTIC OUTLETS IN THE NETWORK JOURNALISM SPHERE

> The techniques, the methodologies used by journalists, identifying information, looking for it, processing it, delivering it and reacting to it: I think it's going to change definitely. It has changed already. I see it as a more people-oriented profession.
>
> (Interviewee 2, ICFJ)

In the sphere of network journalism, the roles of journalistic organizations are under revision. Picard stresses that journalists used to distinguish themselves from others and to add value through their 'search and research skills' (2009: 4). However, as he explains, digital technologies are much more than just distribution and content processing tools. They are also content gathering and creation instruments—and they are most importantly instruments that not only journalists themselves can use, but their users or citizen journalists as well. In accordance with this, Picard demands:

> Journalism must innovate and create new means of gathering, process-ing, and distributing information so it provides content and services that readers, listeners, and viewers cannot receive elsewhere. And these must provide sufficient value so audiences and users are willing to pay a reasonable price. (Picard, 2009: 6)

The news organizations chosen as case examples in this book do try to provide such added value and they have chosen organizational work struc-tures that reflect the changing realities of news production. Journalists here become central networkers within the transformed sphere of global information flows. Journalists at the BBC's user-generated content desk, for example, are now a contact point in the production and dissemination pro-cesses. They are central nodes knitting together information that reaches the outlet and they create and sustain partnerships with users. This is not necessarily a new task, yet fostered by the increasing amount of accessible information, this process has become ever more important and it includes networking with sources formerly ignored:

> I think a journalist is still what he's always been. You're searching for the truth, you're telling the story as accurately as you can with the in-formation you have. And you obviously have your legal skills and your understanding of a story to tell it in the best possible way. What user-generated content is giving is more tools to tell that story. [. . .] And I think the role of the journalist is changing. It definitely is changing. They have to have more awareness of how to tell their story. And this is another way they can tell their story! They have to realize that the audience can feed information to them. And they use that to tell their story in the best possible way. (BBC)

Paying tribute to the complex realities of today's news flows, the BBC has thus created a new job profile: The journalists at their Interactivity Desk are solely responsible for networking with users, producing user-generated features and distributing user-generated content for stories across all BBC platforms. The main objective of the staff here is:

> to check it [the incoming information], to be forensically sort of: 'Is this what it is?' It is that: Their telephone number, is it in America? That photograph, does it look like all the other stuff? Is it on the agencies, is it really their picture? That's their job as journalists. So it's a different type of job, but it's still journalism. (BBC)

The journalists here are fact-checkers and networkers, responsible for generating and filtering content out of vast amounts of non-linear information floating into their newsrooms and they found the basis for the creation of a wide network of stringers.

Similarly, Current TV has assigned a group of staff to facilitating a conversation and creating a relationship with citizen journalists. Its Vanguard Department produces original features and in accordance with this administers a global interaction network with citizen journalists. The interviewee explains how this collaboration works:

> I have a team that works on the citizen journalism and then we also have the original end, all with the aim of speaking to, with and about this demographic [their young viewers]. So in a way our professional end of journalists is: young roving reporters who are content modeling. Sort of being a model for citizen journalists. And also calling out to citizen journalists for help! So we do kind of blend the two. (Current TV)

She also provides an example for such collaborative efforts in producing a story:

> We might have a reporter that's out doing a story on migration. Migration is a big theme that we cover. And it's a very big issue; immigration is a big issue on the US–Mexico border. But Current is really an international network and we see ourselves as an international community having an international conversation. So while we might cover a story on the Mexico–US border, we might also have a reporter who is covering the African exodus to Europe. So we can see some of the similar issues that are happening around the world. But at the same time we would ask our citizen journalists who have a really unique access to some of these stories that we might not have access to, to bring those stories into the conversation. [. . .] And it fits into this bigger picture of what the whole department is doing. It's trying to report on these big global issues with the help of our citizen journalists. So we try to set the stage for what the big forces are at play, and then our citizen journalists are filling in those pieces in the puzzle. Often at times they are creating new pieces of the puzzle that we never thought of. (Current TV)

The advantages the establishment of a network with citizen journalists has are greater access to more spots around the globe as well as gathering more stories and getting an idea of what topics users are interested in. This type of journalistic work also suggests that the role of journalists in the news-gathering, production and dissemination process is altered as more and more information is in circulation. The job of journalists is increasingly to filter out the best and most important pieces. The AlterNet interviewee describes it as follows:

They're sanity keepers, because if we considered every single person who thought that they should be writing at AlterNet, we would never get it done! So there's a universe around you with the people whose writing you know is good or you can trust them to do what they said you're going to do. You can trust them to back up their sources. They are reliable. And then sometimes you give new people a chance! It's always new blood coming in. But the new people that you've never worked with before, you're more cautious and you're more careful or you may go back and check out other things they've written or you talk to somebody who has worked with them. So it's all very intricate and maybe informal. It may not be written down. But the way that anybody deals with too much is to start with the familiar and be comfortable with that and then hopefully go into wider circles, because you want to get variety, you want to get other points of view or you're finding something you never even thought about. (AlterNet)

News organizations thus could be central nodes in a densely populated information sphere, providing guidance through the masses of content in circulation. Journalists become the navigators through vast amounts of information in this process. They pick and match information pieces; they aggregate, select and organize information flow. They filter and apply valence, put sources in order of importance, depending on who at a certain point in time provides the most valuable information, be it an official or an alternative source.

With more outlets aggregating and disseminating news, organizations wanting to succeed in the network journalism sphere then need to provide a competitive package that ultimately has to consist of a larger spectrum of voices and angles to stories. In accordance with this, the BBC, for example, views its role as an ever more important one today: 'One thing is people don't have lots of time and there's so much out there. So what broadcasters and newspapers can do is point you to the best. [. . .] Recommendation, things like that. It's all bringing the best to the top' (BBC).

Traditional media organizations are still powerful agenda setters, but they now compete with many more information disseminators. Allowing other news disseminators to join in, to open up to a variety of partakers, is an important part of the process:

If somebody has access to stories that other people don't have . . . you get that story in somewhere, because people want to be the competitors, so what have you? So there is a bright future for citizen journalism, but I think what we need is media transformation. In other words: The media system needs to be reformed and changed. [. . .] Citizen journalism is just one piece of a larger puzzle of different forces that could hopefully transform the media to have it play more of a democratic role in our society. More of an informative role than it's playing right now. (Interviewee 1, MediaChannel)

Global news flows then are an indicator for the transformation of the journalism sphere that demands a reorganization of the staff body and—as the BBC or Current TV models suggest—the establishment of departments that absorb and distribute these information flows. One ICFJ interviewee asserts:

> I think it would benefit them [news outlets] to do that, because again, they have to adapt, they have to change or they're going to lose all their readers and if we can convince young readers that traditional news media are a voice you can trust and that you can still get the new media information, the blogs, the citizen journalism that you want, but you have somebody who you trust. Who is telling you: 'This is the good stuff. This can be believed'. Then I think that that's worth it for the news organization. They're keeping readers; they're getting younger readers that they will lose otherwise. (Interviewee 1, ICFJ)

Additional training on the use of digital tools is a necessary action in respect to this. In order to know how to find the most valuable information pieces, journalists need instruction on devices that can assist them. Digital technologies help to use the power of crowdsourced collaboration in favor of journalistic work. They also assist to monitor the web and it is crucial that journalists know how to apply such tools. This not only includes a good knowledge of aggregation instruments such as RSS that help scan the web or of tools such as Twitter. It encompasses instructions on the use of social networks such as Facebook for journalistic purposes just as well as knowledge of how to master search engines effectively or how to use analytical instruments such as Google Trends, to name just a few tools that help journalists navigate through the network journalism sphere (for an overview of useful tools see Briggs, 2010). Websites such as Journalism.co.uk should become mandatory reading for journalists as they provide educational support on digital technology trends and recent developments in journalism.[1] Knowledge of tools will not only make navigating through information easier, but as the ZEIT ONLINE interviewee suggests, using the necessary tools can shift the perspective on a supposed 'information overload'.

> I became a net-user in 1995 and it has steadily increased since. But I find it has grown to be much more pleasant to navigate. The net hasn't developed into [something] less clearly arranged. It simply expanded. Just look at search engines from 1998. They certainly still were search engines! In this day and age you almost have find-engines. That's a huge difference! Even if to date Google only indexes a very small fraction of the net, it's still the case that Google currently plays a relatively

paramount part in finding information. Or other search engines, but the classic one is Google. But I don't think it has gotten any worse to navigate. I, myself, use social bookmarking systems for support. They simply work very, very well. [. . .] Because it allows me to have a memory for topic strands. (ZEIT ONLINE)

Conveying digital technology training for journalists will provide them with the necessary tools to navigate successfully through the networked sphere.

What is more, awareness for the mass of useful content accessible needs to be boosted:

> One of the things that we have to be aware about and journalist training has to change accordingly, is that the more material you get in from the public, the more you have to check it! So my take on all this is: You don't go into this whole new participation thing thinking: 'We don't need journalists!' You actually need journalists to make the most of this content. Because the material you get in, you need to check it. Is it right? Is this person really in Virginia in the High School or are they just living somewhere else making it up as to hoax you? Is that picture really from where it is? And that's the role of journalists to check it. And like any skill: The more you do, the better you get at it. (BBC)

And the better you might as well get not only in aggregating the amount of information floating through the net, but also in deciding which platform is the most appropriate to disseminate the content. Print, broadcast and online platforms do function according to different rules. Space or time constraints as a journalist will find in a newspaper limited to a specific amount of columns and pages or in a broadcast bulletin constrained within a strict time frame are not existent online. Neither the space of a newspaper column nor the three-minute feature on television or radio news can directly compete with the options provided within an online space. With regard to newspapers, the ZEIT ONLINE interviewee remarks accordingly: 'Yet paper is first and foremost a limitation! It is a constraint in room. I cannot set links on paper. I cannot let any form of interaction take place on paper' (ZEIT ONLINE).

Thus not only should journalists use alternative news disseminators as complementary, but they should also use different media platforms as complementary. The Ourmedia volunteer suggests that traditional platforms such as television or radio, for example, could serve as breaking news outlets, whereas their online counterparts provide in-depth reporting:

> And maybe that's what's going to happen is that mainstream media is going to be more about these anomalies that are happening around the world. And the web is going to be more the depth. Like: 'Here is the

story of a family in Africa'. You probably won't see that on TV, but on the Internet it's there. And it would be a minute long; it could be ten minutes long. Online there's no limitations of anything. It's just the limitations of taste and peoples' patience. (Ourmedia)

This is a call to create awareness for the opportunities conventional dissemination platforms *in accordance* with the opportunities of online platforms offer. Traditional outlets could reposition themselves as the central information nodes within the sphere of network journalism. They gather, aggregate, organize and contextualize information flows:

Apart from the technologies there and the millions of ways you can contact people or listen whether you podcast, vodcast, listen on your PC, watch TV on your little PDA or whatever: We could be a prism through which all this is channeled. And so the best comes out. We can maybe say: 'This is what's out there and the blogs and maybe we can lead you to the best.' And I think that's a positive thing for broadcasters! [. . .] Because one thing is: people don't have lots of time. And there's so much out there. So what broadcasters and newspapers can do is point you to the best! The recommendation, things like that. It's all bringing the best to the top. (BBC)

News organizations such as the BBC can act as a coordination 'supernode'. Their financial means and their size just as well as their long-standing traditions and reputations as reliable news providers place them in a good position to attract large user numbers.

Accordingly, with well-trained, tech-savvy journalists who know how to handle non-linear content flows, outlets might be able to profit from the increasing amount of information in circulation—including information disseminated by bloggers or citizen journalists. A trusted traditional news organization then could be the guide, providing, for instance, the best information gathered from a variety of sources, including alternative media. One ICFJ interviewee suggests:

That means that the news organization on its website—probably not doing this in the paper-paper—is saying: 'Here is the best stuff coming out of China right now. These are the people who really know. They've called things right before.' So some—and it doesn't even have to be a traditional media organization. That's where I'm going to go. I would be more likely to trust when the *New York Times* tells me: 'These are the blogs out of China that have the most credibility, that have been right, they're looking at all sides' or something like that. (Interviewee 1, ICFJ)

This reconfiguration of journalistic outlets and the acceptance of non-linear news flows into the newsrooms also needs to be accompanied by an understanding that online journalists or journalists gathering and evaluating user-generated content or journalists collaborating with non-traditional news disseminators are by no means 'second-degree journalists':

> That's often the point I discuss most with my print colleagues, who believe online [journalism] to be 'Quickly, quickly! Faster, faster! A quick fix job!' We witness this in our own online editorial department, in particular in that area, we see it very, very prevalently. Those stories most readily accepted by the user are those that require a lot of effort. With a fair bit of time invested in them. And they are received unproportionally well. Concurrently it pays not to publish three smaller reports, but instead one big story. Users have come to expect this. This could be due to our unique profile. But I basically don't think so. I think many users are happy about receiving good stories extra on top of the news. Ultimately it's the combination that counts. And if the topic happens to resurface, they just type it into Google or whichever is the leading search engine in the future. Then they will fall straight back onto us. (ZEIT ONLINE)

In accordance with this, the interviewee also stresses that the payment for online journalists should reflect that they add valuable contributions:

> Online journalism has been underfunded for a long time and also very much understaffed. This has been also reflected in the quality. You have to openly admit that: If I do not have time and do not have money, I cannot write a good article! That simply does not work. I need the time to make phone calls, to drive there if necessary. (ZEIT ONLINE)

The aspect of appropriate payment does touch the very heart of the discussion involving citizen journalism, bloggers and traditional journalists. Professional journalists do get paid to fulfill the role of the information provider; media activists or citizen journalists in general work without payment. In this context, the often articulated fears of critics of the digital information sphere such as Keen (2007) or Carr (2005) proposing that the profession of journalism will be replaced by untrained 'amateur' reporters who lack skills and competences seem to be exaggerated:

> You have people who are actively motivated. If you're looking at Indymedia it's much more almost as: 'If you want, you have the stories to tell us'—very active there. And I think that's good. People have an outlet and it part-time provides an alternative to the mainstream. But I think what you're left with in terms of professional media is: We are committed and obliged. All our salaries depend on us producing *The Guardian* and everything that's around it every single day! And if it means we need to send a reporter to Iraq, we'll send a reporter to

Iraq. If it means sort of sitting there and covering politics, we cover the broad spectrum of things and we are obliged to do it. And our sense of obligation to do it every day and therefore to be completely relied upon and hopefully trusted in what we do is really where we are. And you can get fragments of that in different places, but I think what newspapers do and professional media organizations do is: They write the way across the spectrum of content on a continuous basis every single day. And I think that bloggers do a bit, but it's not the same. (Guardian)

Journalists then still have a vitally important role to play in the sphere of network journalism—yet they need to understand that this role needs adaptation. The PEJ interviewee stresses:

I think that what's going to happen with the citizen journalist is going to be less ultimately of a revolution than it is an evolution! The mainstream media will adopt some of the better stuff and will find ways to use it and incorporate it into what they do. And it will make the mainstream media better. I think there's no question on that. But it's not [. . .] going to be the utopian version of 'Everybody is a journalist' and 'Oh my God, did you see what Bob down the street or some guy two towns over . . . he is doing incredible reporting on issue X!' That's not going to happen! Because Bob's got a job, and he's got a life and he can't just be doing journalism all the time! Ultimately until you get paid to do something, I don't see how you have the time to do it properly, unless everybody is just independently wealthy and can go out and just be a journalist in their spare time, because they find it interesting. There are just not many people who can do that. (PEJ)

The institution of journalism thus is as important as ever, but the roles of journalists have to match the structures of the sphere of network journalism. This also includes that news organizations not only collaborate with sources outside of their own organization. It also includes that journalists need to develop crossmedia skills and collaborate with journalists working for different platforms *within* their own organization.

11.3. MULTIMEDIA NEWSROOMS

The times when journalists specialized to work for one specific media platform are coming to an end. Huang et al. argue that 'many news practitioners' functions are gradually changing or are expected to change as media convergence rolls on. As a reporter in a converged media environment, knowing how to write is probably no longer enough' (2006: 86). Multimedia qualities thus grow to be essential for journalists working in the network journalism sphere. Exemplary for this, the BBC Editor states:

> The phrase we use now is Video-Audio-Text. Because television is on the web! Radio is on the web! You're telling your story on whatever platform is the best one to get it out on. And there is a chap who's now editor of *The Telegraph* who talks about 'Ownership of the Story'. It's the story you own, not the medium. You're covering Iraq and you're doing it in all these different ways and the audience can reach it. But it's the story that is the important thing, not the fact you're three minutes on the 10 o'clock news. (BBC)

Almost no news outlet performs journalism on only one dissemination platform any longer. Newspapers such as the *Guardian* now disseminate podcasts, independent radio outlets such as Democracy Now! carry text video versions of their news bulletins online, newspaper weeklies distribute video pieces online such as ZEIT ONLINE or radio and television broadcasters such as the BBC produce 'video-audio-text material' for their online platform. These are already steps toward convergence and point down the road toward the creation of multimedia newsrooms. And even though many organizations seem to still view their outlets strictly as a newspaper, a radio station or a TV station, the times when one outlet produced content for just one single platform are over.

In the wake of convergence, though, journalists often state fears of a decline in quality. The Ourmedia volunteer argues:

> I think that that's going to increasingly just keep making journalism bad. Because journalists are being asked to do more and more and getting paid less and less. They're expected to not only write, but also run the camera and edit, whereas before that was done by different people. Back in the old days you might have been expected to do one story a day or one story every couple days. Now they're expected to blog all day long as well as do these stories. It's not possible! (Ourmedia)

Research into the practice of multimedia newsrooms does at large reflect the fears voiced by the interviewee. A number of studies are concerned with the impacts of convergence operations on journalistic practice (e.g., Avilés and Carvajal, 2008; Boczkowski, 2004; Erdal, 2009; Huang et al., 2006; Silcock and Keith, 2006) and similar to the general fears of journalists in the wake of changes to current news practice as stated above they find that time pressures and heavy workloads are among the main concerns of journalists. Deuze, for example, summarizes that

> journalists tend to be cautious and skeptical towards changes in the institutional and organizational arrangements of their work, as lessons learnt in the past suggest that such changes tend to go hand in hand with downsizing, lay-offs, and having to do more with less staff, budget, and resources. (Deuze, 2008: 8)

Similarly argue Avilés and Carvajal (2008) or Huang et al. (2006: 876 et seq.), who found that journalists are greatly concerned about being expected to do more work for less money, mainly to the financial benefit of a media company.

What is more, even though the strict divisions in convergent newsrooms are supposed to fade, journalists still do see each other more as internal competitors than partners in the production of news. Silcock and Keith (2006) found that journalists involved in converged newsroom operations often encounter language and culture-based challenges. Converged print and broadcast newsrooms, for example, often operate in front of a backdrop of differing newsroom cultures and different work routines. One result of this is that instead of sharing content, some stories or angles are withheld and thus the notion of two competing newsrooms still holds up. Guided by stereotypes of journalists working for another platform within an outlet, Singer (2004) and Deuze (2008) also assert deep 'cultural clashes'. Especially print reporters are according to Deuze highly critical toward their colleagues in broadcast and even more so toward their colleagues working for online arms of a news outlet (2008: 9). These 'cultural differences' among news staff are according to Singer (2004: 16) the result of differing ideologies, work routines and organization structures.

Erdal (2009)—who reports about the obstacles of differing journalistic cultures at the Norwegian public service broadcaster NRK—similarly observed that even though the main management strategy there is to foster teamwork across various platforms, strong hierarchies within multimedia newsrooms prevail, with online journalists often being the last in line (Ibid.: 225). He finds that 'it proved difficult to get from just sitting side by side to actually cooperating' (Ibid.: 222). However, Erdal's study also provides a positive glimpse of convergence when he suggests that: 'The question of what defines quality journalism may slowly be changing, as the ideal of the highly specialized radio or television professional is complemented by the versatile crossmedia reporter' (Erdal, 2009: 227).

To summarize and analyze the findings presented in these first studies of multimedia newsrooms: The main problem seems to be a lack of knowledge about how other media platforms work. This could be the point of intervention: building trust *among* journalists working in converged newsrooms. One way to go about this is to teach at least a minimal degree of practical tools needed to work on different media platforms. In addition, Silcock and Keith conclude that 'an organization's ability to deal with cultural conflicts may ultimately have some effect on its ability to profit from convergence' (2006: 624). Drawing upon this ability will be the key to making multimedia newsrooms work.

So despite the difficulties visible in convergence operations, studies like the ones undertaken by Erdal, Huang et al. or Silcock and Keith in combination with the statements gathered throughout the interviews for this book do provide valid grounds for the assumption that the integration of platforms is a necessary step to take in journalistic practice. Converging formerly distinct media platforms promises to work in favor of the journalistic end product. However, convergence operations will only succeed with appropriate staff training that equips journalists to think across media.

The case of the BBC is one example in this respect. In April 2008, the organization was one of the first of its size that converged into a multimedia newsroom.[2] At the time of the interview in 2007, the preparation of converging BBC newsrooms was already visible in the structural coordination of disseminating content within the outlet. Staff at the Interactivity Desk, for example, reflected the plurality of dissemination options at the BBC, with journalists originally trained on radio, as well as on the BBC's various television channels working side by side on the same desk.

Drawing together staff from different arms within the BBC does ensure that the journalists know what kind of content might be useful for a certain platform. Thus, new teams are created within the BBC, specialized on generating content for all platforms the organization encompasses. The interviewee explains the procedures of disseminating news within the BBC—an example of how content crisscrosses through the various arms of the outlet: 'We have an internal wire that we tell everybody what we're doing. So you can call them stakeholders if you want. They all look at what we're doing and they try and get stuff for their program. (BBC)

The material the user-generated content desk gathers feeds into national channels as well as into the BBC World Services, be it radio or television:

> So we work like a hub. It's a hub! We're at the center getting all this stuff and it all goes out to all sorts of people. And it's taken a while to get them up to speed. I mean a lot of people didn't want to, you know: 'Oh, there's another thing to think about. I'm so busy, I can't think about this. But I actually think it helps me. If I do this, then I've got access to the story.' I think people have now bought into it internationally. But it certainly happened more quickly domestically. I think people who were in the domestic channels realized more quickly how important this stuff was. (BBC)

Other news outlets that still hold up the boundaries between dissemination platforms do seem to start realizing as well that journalists do not eventually have to work within just one journalistic medium:

> The interesting thing that's happening in print is photographers at print media organizations are increasingly not photographers any more. They're 'videographers'. And they've found a way to get the screen grasps from the videos to such nice resolution that they can actually use them for photos in the paper if they need to use them. So in terms of the great convergence aspect of it all: I think it's really interesting and I think that increasingly the line between print and audio and video will

break down. And you'll have—I hate phrases like this—'Multi-Plat-form-Content-Providers'. But that's what they're going to be. And they really are going to be out there giving you everything. And that's really interesting. [. . .] The *New York Times* site right now is better than it was two years ago. It's just much more interesting. [. . .] It's a better site. It's a better site; it's a richer site. There's a lot more there. (PEJ)

Similarly, many journalists working for the *Guardian* are not only equipped with pen and paper anymore:

There are quite a few reporters on the *Guardian* who would rather not go anywhere without an additional camera. It's not because they're obliged to take photos, but actually sometimes it's just quite handy. [. . .] They're not great photographers, they are never going to be great photographers; they're not obliged to take photos. But actually there are just times when it would be handy to do it. And I think the natural progression for all these things is not that you give people sort of tons and tons and tons of stuff! But I think the best journalists will use the best tool to tell the story. (Guardian)

The *Guardian* is also using audio material quite a lot. This has proven to be an inevitably useful tool for its print and online journalists:

We had an incidence with Peter Mandelssohn a few weeks ago, where we interviewed him. He said on the *Today* program that we misquoted him. Fine! We put the audio up on the website and: 'No, we didn't misquote you! This is exactly what you said!' And I think at that point a journalist [. . .] starts to go: 'Actually this is going to help us do our job better!' And I think the ordinary people running around using loads of different media in a completely mindless way to create video that no one is really interested in is one thing. But I think to give creative people the tools to tell the story in the best possible way is not just sort of a 'nice' thing. I just think that is part of the evolution of journalism. And I think text is very powerful, but it is just one way of doing things. (Guardian)

The solution to guarantee that this evolution runs as smoothly as possible can only be found in advanced training for journalists as well as in reassigning journalists and reorganizing newsrooms in order to work most effectively across various dissemination platforms. As Huang et al. (2006: 94) stress based on the findings of their study on multimedia newsrooms: There need to be resources as well as time dedicated to education and training of multiplatform reporting skills for staff as well as training students of journalism. Journalists might still be trained for a specific area of expertise, but do need at least a basic understanding of how other arms of an outlet function and they need to understand that they are not in competition with their colleagues, but work as a team for the better of the product.

Accordingly, the Senior Program Director at ICFJ foresees the creation of new departments that work interconnectedly:

> We will see new positions created in the mainstream media and in the non-mainstream media. [. . .] Such as journalists that handle just the citizen journalists and the blogging. Or a journalist that would be extremely specialized in new media. He is just going to be working on the whole package issue. Like the 'backpack journalist'. You will probably going to have backpack journalists, reporters. Literally! That's going to be their title. You probably are going to see more positions such as journalists for new strategies. Or innovation journalists. You will probably also going to see whole new departments for the 'parachute foreign correspondents'. Full fletched departments for that. However, I think the core values of journalism and the importance of credibility will still be extremely important. [. . .] If there is something that is going to remain, it is going to be the seek for credibility, the thirst for credibility! From the people and from the media and from anybody working in the media industry. How do we get that? We will see! I think it is being reinvented. (Interviewee 2, ICFJ)

Part of this reinvention is a repositioning of journalistic outlets within the larger framework of the evolving network journalism sphere that presupposes the awareness of the evolution of revised structures. As the term 'network' already suggests, news organizations need to reposition themselves and define their place within a dense net of information providers. Each organization constitutes just one information node within a wider system of nodes and each organization is just one part of today's information flows. As what kind of node an organization wants to act within the complex system of news production and dissemination is up for the specific outlet to decide. In accordance with this, news organizations consider which niche as an information provider they want to fill. Tailoring a specific type of audience or specializing on a certain topic area could be one way to go about this:

> So the way of news networks to react to that is going be getting more specialized. They say: 'Well, everybody is now sharing this and providing this. Maybe we are going to be the leaders on the specialized news'. Bloomberg for example: Economic news. How many people can do that? I don't think that many. (Interviewee 2, ICFJ)

With the proliferation of smaller news organizations and through the growing amount of news disseminators, such specialization can eventually be the outcome of the flattened, decentralized network journalism sphere.

Current TV is an example of such an organization positioning itself as a niche information node that addresses especially young audiences and concentrates on background information and story angles provided by its own staff in collaboration with citizen journalists. Take the example of the coverage on the Virginia Tech shooting once more, where Current TV never set a foot on campus as opposed to news organizations focusing on the breaking news angle of the story:

> We all knew what happened. You can go through the facts of what happened and that is what certain outlets are there for. That is what I go to if I want immediate breaking news. I know where to go. But if I want to get a real personal take and kind of like a deeper look from the voice and point of view of somebody in our demo: That's what you're going to get when you're going to come to Current. (Current TV)

Current TV occupies just one niche within the information market. Within the restructured sphere of network journalism, then, the role of journalists is inevitably reshaped through the reorganization of the news sphere into a conglomerate of decentralized information nodes that can operate within niche markets, yet also collaborate with other nodes. The platform itself on which news is disseminated becomes irrelevant to a certain degree. More importantly, the tools and sources journalists use to process the information will lead the way to the platform on which a specific sort of content can best be delivered—and the next generation of journalists growing up in a multimedia environment might not even bother to think within restrictions of one specific medium:

> If you just talk about the collection of people in Journalism College now, who are in their early twenties, they will all be grown up. To them, editing a video-package will be just intuitive. There's nothing special about it. It's just part of what they do. Why wouldn't they? And so this video-text-audio, I think that's just going to become part of the mix over time. (Guardian)

And this 'media mix' of smaller and larger information nodes, the mix of traditional journalistic platforms, blogs, citizen journalism and media activist sites or user-generated content providers, is eventually transforming journalistic practice into an interactive collaboration.

12 Conclusion

A new globalized geography of journalism is taking shape, based on the structure of the network. It is a journalism in which boundaries between traditional media outlets of print, radio and television and between national and foreign journalism are blurring and merging online. To quote Castells, a network is a 'highly dynamic, open system, susceptible to innovating without threatening its balance' (2000c: 501 et seq.). A network journalism structure does not eliminate 'balance', but requires 're-balancing'. Journalistic practice is currently in this state of 're-balancing'—it is adapting to the new dynamics of information exchange. Journalistic practice used to be a closed operation, with only a few partakers contributing to newsgathering, production and dissemination. These processes have now been shifted into an open, dynamic space and each chapter in the empirical part of this book has addressed different aspects of the digital challenge as well as the opportunities involved in this shift.

Within the network journalism sphere, an uncountable number of information nodes are emerging. These information nodes vary in size and include traditional journalistic organizations as well as citizen journalism platforms, media activist platforms, bloggers and user-generated content providers. Each of these nodes positions itself in a specific niche. Each one takes a distinctive place in the network journalism sphere. The variety of forms these nodes can take indicate that the global information sphere has become by far more complex, with more information deliverers taking part in the news production processes around the globe. They all contribute to the vast network of information production and dissemination.

The journalistic system in the network age thus constitutes a complex collection of information nodes, within a sphere in which collaboration and cooperation between news organizations and news distributors becomes essential. Only teamwork allows a degree of control over these 'chaotic' non-linear information flows. Collaboration and cooperation, and the creation of partnerships, become the ingredients of successful journalistic practice. Journalistic organizations must adapt to the dynamics of this network journalism sphere.

The interviewees who took part in the study presented here appeal to journalists to understand the new dynamics and find ways to reposition themselves within a globalized network of information nodes. These sources suggest that if news organizations do not adapt to the emerging structures of network journalism, they might run the risk of perishing. If journalistic outlets ignore the transformation of the journalistic production environment, they will eventually become isolated, and might fail to survive in a network society in which users increasingly search for news 'on demand' and—not least—for guidance through the vast amounts of information in circulation. In the era of network journalism users can personalize news services, and the recommendations of peers become yardsticks as to what content and which platform will be accessed.

The role of journalistic organizations in this reconfigured sphere of information exchange could be to guide their users. They can position themselves as 'supernodes'. This can only be achieved, though, if news organizations concentrate on providing competitive news packages that include the many story angles and viewpoints criss-crossing through the information space. Cooperation and collaboration with alternative sources, searching for the other angle, for the other 'truth' and for the fresh perspective is becoming ever more important in this respect.

This book, then, can be read as a voice in support of a new model of journalistic organization, a call to action for journalists to revise the tools they use for their work as well as to renew their networks in order to navigate through today's restructured, decentralized information flows. This demands an attitude change on many levels. Mainstream journalists and alternative news providers are not necessarily competitors in the sphere of network journalism, but rather collaborators or complementary information providers. Users are not silent absorbers of news, but have the potential to be individual information nodes.

Acknowledging that users can be active in the news production process and that the 'wisdom of crowds' is a core principle of the network journalism sphere then demands time and resources to build and enhance networks with potential collaborators. It is not an easy task, for sure, but it is doable as the many examples outlined in this volume prove.

This book was written with the aim of conceptualizing the evolving network journalism sphere. It has aimed to reveal significant changes in the structures of global journalism today, and to create awareness of the challenges that lie ahead, as well as the opportunities. However, this is merely the starting point for further research.

To name just three other aspects affected by the transformation processes outlined here that urgently need more attention: Journalism education will need to be restructured, new business models need to be put in place and questions of media literacy in regard to users need to be addressed.

In regard to the first, the reorganization of journalistic practice calls for new approaches to journalism education and training. Journalists need to know not only how to use digital technology, but develop an understanding of the wider impacts processes such as globalization have on the way people think and act in a network society. In addition, curricula in journalism courses should now include alternative journalism as a regular teaching module (Atton, 2009: 284). And it is important to recognize that not only might some alternative news providers be valuable information resources, but the way they gather, produce and disseminate information may be leading the way toward the future of journalism. Platforms such as NowPublic or Global Voices Online are excellent case studies in this respect. The work of the Voices of Africa Media Foundation demonstrates how the story of Africa can be covered from angles often ignored in traditional media. These new information deliverers teach us how to deal with alternative sources and show that in many cases the blogger, the citizen journalist or the user can contribute much more than just a picture flicked 'by accident'.

Secondly, and since all this is not going to be possible without adequate financial means, more research and investigation into future business models is urgently needed to ensure the economic survival of news organizations. Studies such as Currah's (2009) *What's Happening to Our News* underline that increasing commercial pressure is undermining the business models journalism used to build upon and news organizations have to date not found the silver bullet into a bright future. The way to a sustainable future can only be paved on the basis of an understanding of the fundamental transformation the journalism sphere has undergone.

Thirdly, users will need to be educated to navigate the global news sphere. I would not go as far as to say 'that learning to be journalists is in fact a key life skill for private citizens this century' (Duffield, 2006: 5). However, Duffield is right to remark that users of news will need to be trained in how to cope with 'vast floods of information, like a journalist' (Ibid.). With more users signing up for social networks and with an increasing amount of information in (global) circulation, a call for media literacy education is necessary. Users need to learn the ground rules of the network sphere— from issues of how to protect their privacy or how to move securely within social networks to issues of knowing how to estimate and value information as well as to identify 'reliable' sources in the online sphere.

To conclude, network journalism takes place on many levels. Network journalism describes the reconfigured relationships of professional journalists with their sources, be it in the integration of user-generated content to collaborations with bloggers or the development of partnerships with citizen journalists. It also describes the way in which journalists interact across media platforms and connect with their colleagues in a multimedia environment. And above all, network journalism suggests a structural model of the journalistic environment today in which news organizations function as information nodes.

First steps in the adaptation process of journalistic organizations adjusting to the network journalism sphere include the adoption of alternative media tools such as blogging and the incorporation of interactive features such as online forums and user-generated content platforms. Journalistic organizations are beginning to realize that the way their users deal with content, how they search for it and where they engage with it is changing and that they have to modify the ways in which they present information to their users accordingly. Journalistic organizations are also beginning to realize that transnational news flows demand new approaches toward reporting from afar.

If they adapt successfully, the role of journalistic outlets here can be not only to identify and distribute information that is credible, but to enable access to a wider mix of viewpoints, and to guarantee their users the most valuable pieces of information—be it the best blog entry, the best citizen journalism piece or the best documentary filmed by one of their own correspondents. Core values such as reliability, credibility and accurateness will be even more important in the sphere of network journalism, given the range of voices and the multiplicity of perspectives available on stories.

To end with Castells: 'Networks are open structures, able to expand without limits, integrating new nodes as long as they are able to communicate within the network' (2000c: 501). This is exactly what journalistic outlets should be: open to expand and open to integrate contemporary (global) information flows. Journalistic practice today is taking place in an interactive sphere, where collaboration is key and the sharing of information and knowledge a core value.

Notes

NOTES TO THE INTRODUCTION

1. This quote is taken from an interview conducted in 2007 that is part of a series of interviews conducted for my PhD thesis. An analysis of the information I gathered throughout these interviews with thirteen media practitioners will be presented in Part II of this book.
2. For the story behind the video see the *New York Times* article titled 'Honoring Citizen Journalists' by Stelter (2010: Online).
3. Keen (2007) subtitled his polemic 'How today's Internet is Killing our Culture'. His statement culminates in the slander of comparing users and producers of web content to monkeys, drawing upon T. H. Huxley's theory according to which an infinite number of monkeys equipped with an infinite number of typewriters will eventually create a masterpiece—not without producing first and foremost a pile of useless content, though. Keen refers to an essay written by Jorge Luis Borges in 1939 that sums up Huxley's idea of the infinite monkey (Borges, 1999).

NOTES FOR CHAPTER 1

1. Or as McNair puts it: 'If the environment changes, so does content' (2006: 48).
2. Giddens refers to the advent of satellite communication and the launch of the first commercial satellite in 1969. The advent of instantaneous communication via satellite and its worldwide spread as well as the spread of its successors like personal computers and the Internet took place within only a few decades.
3. Namely, this work is inspired by the works of Appadurai (1996), Beck (2000), Featherstone (1990), Giddens (1999), Robertson (1992, 1995) or Urry (2003), who all view globalization as a concept with far-reaching consequences for *every* aspect of human life—and that includes journalistic practice and its outcomes.
4. For a striking rationale against technological determinism see Nye's article *Shaping Communication Networks: Telegraph, Telephone, Computer* (1997) as opposed to, for example, Negroponte's *Being Digital* (1995) that carries the underlying idea of digital technology being a natural force.
5. I do not want to peculate Schroeder's perspective here. He argues for a more sophisticated view of technological determinism, which comprises that technological determinism holds truth, but only to a degree as 'science and

technology *do* determine social change, but from a social science perspective, their role in society is never independent of *what* they do to change the natural and social worlds' (2007: 2 emphasis in original).

6. Briggs and Burke, for example, propose that technology has to be 'treated as social activity, involving people and products as well as patents' (2005: 151). Their illustration of the use of print technology in Russia and the Orthodox Christian world underlines this argument. It was not until the early 18th century and Tsar Peter the Great that print became a vital part of social and economical life in Russia. The first printing press had already reached Moscow in 1564, but was destroyed by the rulers at the time (Briggs & Burke, 2005: 13 et seq.). In addition, the press was finally founded in St. Petersburg no earlier than 1711: 'The fact that printing arrived so late in Russia suggests that print was not an independent agent, and that the print revolution did not depend on technology alone. Printing required favourable social and cultural conditions in order to spread, and Russia's lack of a literate lait was a serious obstacle to the rise of print culture' (Ibid.: 14). Elsewhere, the authors draw upon the invention of the telephone, which in 1876 was still viewed as unnecessary for society as such. The final breakthrough of the phone as mass communication tool was to come decades later (Ibid.: 117). Nye argues that the choices of inventors or consumers are the decisive elements. Telephone inventor Alexander Graham Bell, for instance, 'advertised it [the telephone] until the 1920s as an instrument of business and vital communication' (1997: 1071). Telephones were not sold to the public as a communication tool for almost two generations. Accordingly, Winston argues that a need has to be identified in order to push an invention through in society (1998: 67). Before the usefulness of the invention is not obvious and potential values are not credited, scientists will most likely turn away from developing their ideas further—and so will consumers if they do not see the advantages of a technological innovation. The case of the introduction of the computer supports this idea, as it was seen 'exclusively as a serious instrument of business, government, and the military for a full generation' (Nye, 1997: 1071).

7. Nerone analyzes the evolution of the Penny Press as an example of a journalistic development rooted in social and political change. Schudson uses the same example, arguing along similar lines (1978).

8. On this note, the works of James W. Carey are of invaluable importance. From the 1970s onward, he called for a rethinking of 'journalism history' and how it was practiced, proposing a 'cultural history'. He claimed to view 'communication as culture' (Carey, 1989). According to him, journalism aims at the maintenance of cultural norms and ideals that unite society (see also Kaplan, 2003). Analyses of journalism history such as Briggs' and Burkes' *A Social History of the Media* (2005) or Winston's *Media Technology and Society* (1998) are based on the idea of a close relationship between technology and the media (see also Anderson and Curtin, 2002; Brügger and Kolstrup, 2002, or Conboy, 2004). These historical analyses create a contextual framework for the analysis of developments in journalism over time.

9. According to this, media organizations can be attributed with the power to control the flows of information and act as 'missionaries of capitalism' (Herman and McChesney, 1997). Other proponents of 'cultural imperialism' are Mattelart (1979) or Schiller (1976, 1998).

10. Similarly, Straubhaar talks of 'hybridization' (Straubhaar, 2007: 5): 'In hybridization, global forces bring change, but that change is adapted into existing ways of doing things via a historical process in which existing local forces mix with new global ones, producing neither global homogenization nor authentic local culture, but a complex new hybrid with multiple layers of

culture, where older, traditional forms may persist alongside new ones. This situation is neither a complete resistance to rejoice about nor a complete loss of identity to despair about, but a complex contradiction of both continuity and change' (2007: 5 et seq.).

11. For an overview of various definitions of the concept of 'culture' see Hanitzsch (2007: 369).

12. One should also take into account that a culture of professional journalists might differ significantly from journalistic (sub)cultures such as peace journalism or development journalism (Hanitzsch, 2007: 368).

13. Weischenberg and Scholl (1998) similarly argue, drawing upon cross-national comparisons of journalistic attitudes that processes of professionalization in journalism are quite similar across different countries.

14. See McNair: 'The online sites established by print and broadcast media in the 1990s transformed the pattern of flow of journalistic communication by allowing print and broadcast news outlets hitherto constrained within national boundaries to achieve global reach, extending their relationships to anywhere and anyone on the planet with access to a networked computer and the relevant linguistic ability' (2006: 121).

15. As Rosenau points out: 'It is technology [. . .] that has so greatly diminished geographic and social distances through the jet-powered airliner, the computer, the orbiting satellite, and the many other innovations that now move people, ideas and goods more rapidly and surely across space and time than ever before. [. . .] It is technology, in short, that has fostered the interdependence of local, national and international communities that is far greater than any previously experienced.' (1990: 17)

16. The term 'cyberspace' as coined by Gibson aims 'to describe a 'virtual' landscape made up of all the information in the world' (Bell, 2007: 17). 'Cyberspace is entered as disembodied consciousness, by 'jacking in' to the network, and the landscape is a battleground over the ownership of and access to data, between corporations and hackers. Gibsonian cyberspace thus refers to visions of cyberspace which trace back to Gibson's vivid descriptions' (Ibid.: 17).

17. Similarly, Shirky points out: 'The internet augments real-world social life rather than providing an alternative to it. Instead of becoming a separate cyberspace, our electronic networks are becoming deeply embedded in real life' (2008: 196).

18. It should be noted that within this framework, places do not disappear, but as Castells points out, 'their logic and their meaning become absorbed in the network. The technological infrastructure that builds up the network defines the new space, very much like railways defined 'economic regions' and 'national markets' in the industrial economy; or the boundary-specific, institutional rules of citizenry (and their technologically advanced armies) defined 'cities' in the merchant origins of capitalism and democracy' (Castells, 2000c: 443).

19. Along these lines argue Halcli and Webster (2000), who critique that Castells might be too overenthusiastic in his novelty claim as well as with his argument of the 'network' as the central structure of social organization. According to them, Castells neglects that inherent conservative (social) structures and established inequality roasters in society still do have a major important role to play in shaping social realities.

20. Along these lines, Hirst and Harrison critique that Castells neglects longgrown relations that exist between the evolution of new technologies, modes of production and in fact the capitalistic system (Hirst and Harrison, 2007).

21. Mosco (2004) argues even more radically against a positivistic approach toward the evolution of digital technologies and the interplay between technology and social developments. He goes as far as to deconstruct what he views as supposedly too enthusiastic 'myths' around digital technology and cyberspace and views the belief in a 'new order' as a pervasion of every aspect of today's world of finance.

22. According to this model, media organizations act as the organ of elites disseminating their ideology and thus perpetuating the elites' dominant role in society. The 'control paradigm' 'is premised on economic determinancy, whereby ruling elites are presumed to be able to extend their control of economic resources to control of the cultural apparatuses of the media, including the means of propaganda and public relations, leading to planned and predictable outcomes such as pro-elite media bias, dominant ideology, even 'brainwashing'' (McNair, 2006: 3). The 'dominance paradigm' thesis can be identified in the works of, for example, Hall et al. (1978) or Herman and Chomsky (1988). For an overview of 'dominance paradigm' theories see McNair (1998: 21–28, 2006: 21–33) and Campbell (2004: 86–103).

23 For a discussion of *Four Theories of the Press* and its limits as a model for the journalism-state relationship in the information age see Campbell (2004: 31–43) as well as Ostini and Fung (2002).

24. The problem of accessability has been captured with the terminology of the 'digital divide', which brings major disadvantages to societies and countries that do not have or only have limited access opportunities to digital technologies. For discussions of the 'digital divide' see, for example, Castells (2002b: 247–275), Thussu (2000: 247–259) or vanDijk (2005). Norris or van Dijk, for example, also point out that social divisions are influenced by unequal societies and thus 'digital divides' do not necessarily only exist between different countries or regions around the globe, but can rather also be found within the borders of one country (Norris, 2004; vanDijk, 2005).

25. Similarly, following Appadurai, Bell explains that flows 'don't merely circle the globe like satellites; they land. Where they land, and what results from their landing, is similarly unpredictable (even though there are patterns and there is stability in parts). Where they land are the nodes in the network. But there are different kinds of nodes, some with greater capacity to control at least some flows, for example by refusing entry to some people, or blocking some media content from being accessible. 'Strong' nodes can act as magnets, drawing down some flows while also pushing others away, deflecting them elsewhere. Other nodes are relatively powerless, and are endlessly buffeted and battered as flows land' (2007: 70).

26. The mass media system as defined by Luhmann includes journalism, entertainment and advertising (Luhmann, 2000). This notion has been criticized widely. For a critical reflection see Görke and Scholl (2006: 650).

27. This concept is based on constructivist theories that maintain that reality as such can only be interpreted and thus 'constructed,' but not represented (Luhmann, 2000: 5 et seq.).

28. Luhmann is aware that influences from outside are possible. However the influences he thinks of are only concerned with interferences through spin or public relations efforts, for example in the case of the successes of military censorship of reports in Gulf War I (Luhmann, 2000: 8). Apart from these professional actors, it seems that according to Luhmann's understanding of the operations of systems, actors outside of the 'mass media system' have no power whatsoever to influence media, but instead are silenced as outsiders and condemned to the role of receivers.

NOTES TO CHAPTER 2

1. As Thussu points out: 'The establishment of the news agency was the most important development in the newspaper industry of the nineteenth century, altering the process of news dissemination, nationally and internationally' (2000: 20).
2. Campbell vividly explains: 'For journalism, the impact of both new trans-portation technologies and the telegraph revolutionised the way news was made. It is no accident that the global news agencies that still dominate the world, Reuters, Associated Press and Agence-France Press, had their origins in the nineteenth century (the former two associations began in direct rela-tionship to the new telegraph technology)' (2004: 4).
3. Innis views technology as a causal force transforming the structure of a cul-ture. Whereas I support his approach 'using historical situations as a social lab', as McLuhan has termed it in the introduction to Innis' *The Bias of Communication* (1951), I remain skeptical of overstating the impact of tech-nology as a 'force', as this argument does too closely relate to a technological determinism. Nevertheless, Innis also points out: 'A medium of communi-cation has an important influence on the dissemination of knowledge over space and over time and it becomes necessary to study its characteristics in order to appraise its influence in its cultural setting' (1951: 33).
4. For the sake of completeness it should be noted that papermaking was a tech-nique invented well before the printing press. First papers occurred as early as the second century AD and the technique of printing from woodblocks was already in use in China since the seventh century (see for example Füssel, 2001, or Mitchell, 2007). Five decades prior to Gutenberg's press, moveable metal type had also been successfully used in Korea, but the Koreans made little use of it (Willmore, 2002: 90).
5. For a history of the newsbook see Raymond (1996). He identifies newsbooks in England in the seventeenth century as precursors of journalism. According to him, the evolution of newsbooks 'can be seen to lead directly to the jour-nalism of the eighteenth century, when the newspaper became an established factor in British Politics; when the daily newspaper appeared, beginning with the *Daily Courant* in 1703; when leisurely journals, such as *The Tatler*, *The Female Tatler*, Swift and Sheridan's *The Intelligencer*, and *The Spectator*, began to fashion a literary discourse discrete from politics; and when the provincial newspaper developed' (1999: 15).
6. Rantanen makes a valid point in this respect, noting that a greater schol-arly attention to this period in history is of great value: 'Communication research often lacks a historical dimension. Most research concentrates on the twentieth century and thus fails to acknowledge that it was the first elec-tronic media of the nineteenth century, news agencies, that changed concepts of time and place and became early agents of globalization. The electronic media in the nineteenth century were the first to decouple time and distance by bringing news from remote places instantaneously' (2003: 438).
7. In Britain, William Cooke and Charles Wheatstone were credited with the invention of the first working electric telegraph in 1836, while Morse devel-oped his own version parallel to it and his code entered the scene in 1838 (Willmore, 2002: 92).
8. One example in this respect was the *New York Sun*. Blondheim notes that this newspaper was among the first dailies to use a steam-driven press, advancing the printing process and contributing to the improvement of paper. The *Sun* also excelled to 'accelerate the speed with which news reached its presses.

Chartering fast locomotives, dispatching carrier pigeons, even setting special editions in type on board express steamships that carried late news were characteristic of the newspaper's efforts' (Blondheim, 1994: 48).

9. Schudson's information source here is Stover (1961).

10. For example, at the penny press outlets in New York, which 'focused on the nearby and everyday, and for the first time hired reporters on a regular basis to cover local news. Reporters were assigned to the police, the courts, the commercial district, the churches, high society, and sports' (Schudson, 1980: 27).

11. Blondheim provides a detailed study of the foundation of the Associated Press and its relationship to telegraphy. With regard to the founding date of AP there is considerable discussion. However, the year 1848 has been generally accepted (Blondheim, 1994: 48 et seq.).

12. For a detailed history of Reuters see Read (1999). Read repeatedly also draws upon the aspect of technology and its role in the evolution of Reuters.

13. For an interesting account of how Julius Reuter used pigeons see Read: 'On 24 April 1850 he [Reuter] made an agreement with Heinrich Geller, an Aachen brewer, baker, and pigeon-breeder, to provide a total of 45 trained birds for a service between Brussels and Aachen. Twelve birds were to be always available at Brussels; all birds were to be returned by train each day to Brussels, ready to fly back the next day. This pigeon news service was started on 28 April. It obviously worked well, for under a contract on 26 July Geller agreed to assign all his pigeons (over 200) to Reuter's use' (1999: 11).

14. Putnis' article adds an interesting aspect to the discussion of the history of news agencies. He outlines how Reuters failed to establish itself as the leading distributor of news in Australia at the end of the nineteenth century. According to Putnis, this failure was the result of the resistance of major newspapers in the metropolitan markets of Australia to a 'globalization' of international news delivery. Instead, Australian newspapers created an alternative system of gathering international news that heavily relied on cooperation models among Australian-based news outlets. Additionally, the Australian press 'may have maintained some link with Reuters most of the time, but it also successfully asserted its independence and insisted on dictating the terms of its relationship with Reuters' (2006: 2). Australian newspapers also created London-based bureaus in order to keep their independence and to be able to focus solely on news of interest for the Australian population.

15. Namely, these are the four major Western-based news agencies AP, United Press International (UPI), Reuters and the direct successor to Havas, Agence France Presse (AFP). For an overview of studies of news flow, selection, agency content and agency structures see Boyd-Barrett (1980) as well as Boyd-Barrett and Rantanen (1998), where agencies are characterized as agents of globalization.

NOTES FOR CHAPTER 3

1. For more information on NowPublic.com, check the FAQ section on their homepage. Information on the Mumbai terror attacks are tagged on the website under the title 'Mumbai'.

2. For current statistics on the number of active Facebook users check Facebook's pressroom online.

3. Similarly, Straubhaar (2007: 18) and Benkler (2006: 22) point out that a greater number of actors take part in the production and dissemination of

news. Pavlik stresses the ability of what he defines as 'traditional sources', 'serving as primary news providers to the public, often bypassing the traditional news gatekeepers altogether' (2000: 236).

4. Accordingly Jarvis organized a meeting titled 'Networked Journalism Summit' at the CUNY Graduate School of Journalism in October 2007.

NOTES TO CHAPTER 4

1. See the article on Deutsche Welle Online by Bösch (2008). For similar accounts see the coverage provided on ZEIT ONLINE and their news pieces on Tibetans trying to draw attention to their situation via platforms such as YouTube or Twitter (Kleinz, 2008: Online).

2. See the Guardian.co.uk article by Sweney (2008: Online). For another account on the censorship imposed on mainstream media see the Associated Press news story published in the *International Herald Tribune* where it is pointed out: 'Information about the violence has come out through foreigners leaving Lhasa, Tibetan activist groups and phone calls to people in Lhasa' (International Herald Tribune/Associated Press, 2008: Online).

3. See the BBC's feature on 'Accounts from Lhasa and Beyond' (2008: Online).

4. One striking case of staged propaganda occurred when the Chinese government allowed a selected delegation of journalists from outlets such as the *Wall Street Journal, Financial Times, USA Today*, Al Jazeera and the Associated Press on a state-organized media trip into Tibet. The purpose of this visit was to show the world that the situation in Tibet had calmed down. During the press visit, a group of Tibetan monks managed to get through to the journalists, making claims that religious freedom in Tibet was suppressed and accused the Chinese government of lying to the outside world about the situation in Tibet. For more information on the story see the coverage on Guardian.co.uk (Watts, 2008: Online) or on the website of the *Financial Times* (Dyer, 2008: Online).

5. Among others, articles on issues of censorship with regard to China and the situation in Tibet can be found in the *New York Times* (2008: Online) or on the Guardian website (Kiss, 2008: Online).

6. Livingston and Bennett have conducted an analysis of CNN international desk stories from 1994 to 2001 asking if journalists with greater technological freedom through the uses of mobile devices such as videophones and other mobile transmission technologies would make less use of officials framing the story and executing gatekeeping functions. The authors conclude that 'event-driven news has not changed the core of the organizational gatekeeping process from its reliance on official sources' (2003: 372). 'When an unpredicted, nonscripted, spontaneous event is covered in the news, the one predictable component of coverage is the presence of official sources' (Ibid.: 376). What Livingston and Bennett do not analyze is the interplay between digital technology and the delivery of information material from a range of sources apart from official channels and how this impacts the organizational gatekeeping processes of journalistic outlets.

7. For the background on the deal between the government, the royal family and the press see for example the Telegraph.co.uk article by Pierce (2008: Online).

8. Matt Drudge was not the first one to report on the story of Prince Harry, but his Drudge Report is one of the websites with the highest traffic on the net ever since he broke the story on the Clinton-Lewinsky affair. The first outlet

to report on the story was the Australian magazine website New Idea on January 7, 2007, but it went largely unnoticed until Drudge picked the story up. For information on how the story broke see for example the Guardian. co.uk story by McMahon et al. (2008: Online) or the Telegraph.co.uk story by Gardham (2008: Online). A portrait of Matt Drudge and his Drudge Report can be found on Telegraph.co.uk (Harnden, 2008: Online).

9. For an account of how Twitter became the tool for breaking news in this case see for example the article on Telegraph.co.uk (Beaumont, 2009: Online).

10. Others have criticized that the loss of the gatekeeping function is also a result of the commercialization of news resulting in a decline of gatekeeping standards, with journalism flattening into 'infotainment' and driven by political spin (Kovach and Rosenstiel, 1999).

11. Bennett's work can serve as a basis for a reconfiguration of gatekeeping models in the information age. He suggests a 'multigated model' that concentrates on a collection of four factors or 'gates' that shape news content, namely (1) personal and professional judgment values of journalists, (2) organizational routines, (3) economic factors and (4) information and communication technologies. For a detailed outline of his model see Bennett (2004).

12. For an overview of audience behavior see the State of the News Media Report 2008 conducted by the Project for Excellence in Journalism (2008a: Online).

13. These examples will be illustrated and discussed in detail in Chapter 10 of this book.

14. The examples Castells uses in this context are mainly related to grassroots groups such as anti-globalization movements (Castells, 1999).

NOTES FOR CHAPTER 5

1. The interview study was part of my PhD project and approved by the Ethics Committee at the University of Otago in November 2006. All interview partners agreed to participate voluntarily. The reference code of the University of Otago Ethics Committee for the project is 06/175.

2. See for example the report *Understanding the Participatory News Consumer* conducted by the Project for Excellence in Journalism that researches how cell phone users access news (Purcell et al., 2010: Online). The research paper *Politics online* analyzes Internet use of Americans for news or information about the midterm elections, conducted by the Pew Internet & American Life Project (Horrigan, 2006: Online).

3. For an overview of some of Nielsen's databases on global Internet activity or online audience measurements, refer to their Netratings page. The 2010 *State of the News Media* report conducted by the Project for Excellence in Journalism contains an analysis of the Nielsen ratings of people's online behavior.

4. On the purposes and aims of expert interviews see Meuser and Nagel (2003). In the context of qualitative research, experts are viewed as informants. Researchers use their expertise knowledge on the object of investigation in order to gain insights (see Keuneke, 2005: 262; Hoffmann, 2005: 270).

5. Each of the interviews was roughly between 40 minutes and 60 minutes long (with the exception of one interview lasting up to 100 minutes) and was based on a semi-structured questionnaire that served as a guideline for each individual interview and allowed comparability of the responses. In order to guarantee openness to the responses of the interviewees, the questionnaire

contained open questions, allowing the interviewees to chart their thoughts and opinions in depth.

6. The reference systems of journalism's aims and purposes can be considered as similar, whereas journalistic systems, for example, in the Arab world are grounded on different premises. An outlet such as Al Jazeera, for example, would have been an interesting object to study with regard to its ways of networking with its Western counterparts such as ZDF in Germany or CNN in the US. Yet, Al Jazeera is operating within a vitally different environment characterized by a fairly 'young' tradition of commercial broadcasting as well as being strongly dependent on its host nation in terms of censorship. For a history of Al Jazeera and the development of an Arab journalism culture refer to Sakr (2007) or El-Nawawy and Iskander (2002).

7. The interviews were conducted in three blocks throughout the first half of 2007. The first interview block took place in Washington, DC, and New York City in January 2007 with interviewees based in New York City at MediaChannel.org, Democracy Now! and Indymedia and interviewees at the Project for Excellence in Journalism and at the International Center for Journalists, both based in Washington, DC. The second block of interviews was conducted in Europe in April 2007 and included visits to the BBC and the Guardian Media Group as well as a meeting with a staff member of ZEIT ONLINE. The interviews with BBC and Guardian staff members were conducted in London. The interview with the producer for ZEIT ONLINE took place during a conference in Berlin. A last block of interviews was conducted in San Francisco in late May and the beginning of June 2007. I met with staff from AlterNet.org, Current TV and Ourmedia.org. All interviews were record-taped and transcribed. The information provided here about the organizations and about the interviewees was gathered throughout the interviews and collected from the websites of each organization.

8. For further information on the history of the BBC refer to its website.

9. Peter Horrocks, the Head of BBC Newsroom, announced the reorganization of the BBC on November 12, 2007 (2007: Online).

10. The team-up was part of the BBC's so-called 'SuperPower Season', a program special that ran across all BBC platforms and was dedicated to underscoring how the introduction of the Internet has changed people's lives. For more information on the 'SuperPower Season' see the articles by Horrocks (2010: Online) and Herrmann (2010: Online). The cooperation between the BBC and Global Voices Online was also covered by various outlets, e.g. on the Guardian website (Bunz, 2010: Online) or on the editorsweblog.org (Conde, 2010: Online).

11. For more information on the launch of Guardian's Zeitgeist project check out the blog entry by Catt and Pickard on the Inside Guardian.co.uk blog (2010: Online).

12. Even though finances are handled by IMC's centers individually, all activities at each IMC center are funded through donations.

NOTES TO CHAPTER 6

1. For the general acceptance of the launch of the first free browser as marking the 'beginning' of the Internet as a mass medium, see McNair (2006: 118) and Lovink (2008). Lovink points out: 'The significant change of the past several years has been the 'massification' and further internationalization

of the Internet. In 2005, the one billion user mark was passed' (2008: x et seq.).

2. The interviewee is referring to an iPod, which was used to record the interview.

3. For further research, for example, on how young users access the Internet or use social networks such as Facebook and other alternative platforms for news, see the Pew Report on 'Social Media and Young Adults' (Lenhart, Purcell, Smith and Zickuhr, 2010: Online).

4. Stray conducted an interesting study in regard to original content provided by outlets online. He researched the so-called 'Google/China hacking case'. In February 2010, the *New York Times* broke a story about the hack attacks on a number of American companies that occurred in 2009. According to unnamed sources, these attacks could be traced back to a technical university and a vocational college in mainland China. Stray researched how many news outlets did provide original reporting pieces on the story after it broke and he found that: 'Out of the 121 distinct versions of last week's story about tracing Google's recent attackers to two schools in China, 13 (11 percent) included at least some original reporting. And just seven organizations (six percent) really got the full story independently' (2010: Online).

5. The interviewee refers to CNN's iReport platform where users can provide self-edited content.

NOTES TO CHAPTER 7

1. A number of research studies provide an overview of the work practices in such newsrooms. Thurman (2008), for example, analyzes user-generated content features at UK outlets based on in-depth interviews with editors at leading news media websites. Hampel (2008) provides an overview of the practices on the CNN user-generated platform iReport, a feature launched in 2006 that got its own stand-alone website in 2008.

2. Wardle and Williams also found in their study that 'there was no fixed definition of "UGC" [user-generated content] among journalists' (2008: 54). What they did find overall were six different types of 'UGC' in use at the BBC: 'Audience Content (including Audience Footage, Audience Experience, Audience Stories), Audience Comment, Collaborative Content, Networked Journalism, and Non-news Content' (Ibid.).

3. The student, Nikolas Macko, provided the BBC with an eyewitness account of the shooting that can be accessed on its website (BBC News, 2007: Online).

4. For more examples of how crowdsourcing works for journalists just as well as for corporations and in fields such as product development see the online article on *Wired* written by Howe (2006: Online). He gathers a range of cases where crowdsourcing became an inevitably useful tool for journalists and corporate companies alike.

5. The Reuters Social Media Guidelines are covered in the section on 'Reporting from the Internet' as part of the Reuters Handbook of Journalism, which is accessible online. The Social Media and Blogging Guidelines of the Radio Television Digital News Association can also be retrieved online.

6. For an overview of citizen journalist activities see Kelly (2009).

7. Frederick Douglass is one of the most prominent figures in the African American history of the United States. A former slave, he became a leader of the abolitionist movement and as a statesman, reformer and author he fought for freedom, emancipation and equal rights. He is notably famous for his

autobiography *Narrative of the Life of Frederick Douglass*, first published in 1845.

8 The interviewee mentioned throughout our conversation that Current TV targets a demographic group aged between eighteen and thirty-four.

NOTES TO CHAPTER 8

1. The so-called 'new journalism' movement in the 1960s was rooted within a group of US journalists 'frustrated by the fetishisation of the objectivity principle and the limits which (they believed) it placed on their work, broke free of the conventions of their profession and began to develop a subversive, 'anti-objective' style which became known as *new journalism*. The new journalism movement intentionally set out to undermine the notion of objectivity by combining the techniques of journalism with those of literature, and to demonstrate that all supposedly objective accounts of reality are highly subjective' (McNair, 1998: 73, emphasis in original).
2. The study conducted by Reese et al. (2007) is based on a content analysis of the six most prominent blogs in the United States and outlines perfectly how bloggers have understood to position themselves within an interactive sphere of information exchange, making use of the technological means as well as of the network in which they move.
3. Jochen Bittner used to run a blog on ZEIT ONLINE called 'Beruf Terrorist' (= Occupation: Terrorist). He stopped blogging in June 2007, but the blog, including an archive, is still accessible.
4. The ZEIT ONLINE blog 'Herdentrieb' (= Herd Instinct) is at the time of writing run by six staff members who are all economics and finance journalists.
5. The full report titled 'Press Accuracy Rating Hits Two Decade Low' is accessible online.
6. For the whole story go to the BILDBlog archive (2008: Online).

NOTES TO CHAPTER 9

1. The Indian actress Shilpa Shetti was the winner of the British TV show *Celebrity Big Brother UK* in 2007. She was involved in a large controversy when she allegedly became the target of racist bullying by other housemates during the show.
2. Nevertheless, it needs to be mentioned here that this engagement is restrained with regard to language skills as well as dependent on means of access such as Internet connections and can be restrained through censorship walls created, for example, by governments. The discussion of the digital divide mentioned previously has to be taken into consideration here.
3. As mentioned in the chapter on user-generated content, these comments can also feed into stories, yet then are checked out: 'So something that's going to be in use in either the television or radio is verified. Though the debates as a whole aren't' (BBC).
4. See Volkmer's (2006) edited volume on media usage and media memory across generations. For a vivid portrait of this generation, the documentary *Growing Up Online* produced as part of the American public television public affairs series Frontline is worth watching.

NOTES TO CHAPTER 10

1. Aday et al. (2005) base their research on a content analysis of news coverage at ABC, CBS, NBC, CNN, Fox News Channel and Al Jazeera.
2. According to her last blog entry dating back to October 2007, Riverbend fled to Syria. Her blog entries were published in two books and her publishers note on their website that they have not heard from her since. Her blog is currently resting, but still available online.
3. It should be noted here that the interviewee at ZEIT ONLINE has a word of warning with regard to using bloggers who write under pseudonyms. A lot of Iraqi bloggers, for example, choose to remain anonymous in order to protect themselves and their families from threats by opposing groups. However, this bears a certain risk for users: 'The minority of these bloggers provide an editorial department [on their websites], where I could quickly call to check: 'Do you even exist? Are you actually a real person or do you lead a purely virtual existence?' That doesn't work. That's what's so very, very difficult about that' (ZEIT ONLINE). This is a problem that needs careful consideration. However, if one takes into account the many pieces of false information and hoaxes that came out of mainstream news organizations, the problem might become relative in size. As noted in Chapter 8, accountability and trust in a source do develop over time and as long as journalists are aware that they have to handle online sources with a lot of care, developing collaborations with bloggers who choose to remain anonymous can be an option.
4. The blog of Salam Pax is resting but still accessible online. Stories about him and his work can be found, for example, in the *Guardian* (McCarthy, 2003: Online), at the BBC (Rice, 2004: Online) and the German weekly *Stern* (Stillich, 2003: Online) among many others.
5. According to the information on the website of 'Alive in Baghdad', at the time of writing this book the Iraqi Bureau Chief had been relocated to Sweden after receiving threats related to his journalistic work. He initially was hiding in Syria, which left the project without its leading staff member and caused significant problems for the grassroots outlet. Financial difficulties are adding to the problems of sustaining the reporting and the project is currently working on new approaches to secure regular coverage of the situation in Iraq.
6. At the time of the interview conducted at the BBC, it also had a staff member assigned to particularly work on Middle East interactivity.

NOTES TO CHAPTER 11

1. Here, journalists can, for example, find introductory information on topics such as how to master Twitter, how to use RSS and social media for news-gathering, how to do precision surfing using search engines or how to create podcasts.
2. See Horrocks' announcement of the restructurization plans on BBC in November 2007 (2007: Online). The articles of Stabe (2008: Online) or Robinson (2008: Online) reflect on the move into the new newsroom in April 2008.

Bibliography

Aday, Sean; Livingston, Steven; Hebert, Maeve (2005). 'Embedding the Truth: A Cross-Cultural Analysis of Objectivity and Television Coverage of the Iraq War'. *The Harvard International Journal of Press/Politics* 10(1), 3–21.

Albarran, Alan B.; Chan-Olmsted, Sylvia M. (eds) (1998). *Global Media Economics: Commercialization, Concentration, and Integration of World Media Markets.* Ames: Iowa State University Press.

Allan, Stuart (2004). *News Culture.* Second Edition. Maidenhead: Open University Press.

Allan, Stuart (2005). 'News on the Web. The Emerging Forms and Practices of Online Journalism'. In Stuart Allan (ed) *Journalism: Critical Issues* (pp. 67–81). Berkshire: Open University Press.

Allan, Stuart (ed) (2005). *Journalism: Critical Issues.* Berkshire: Open University Press.

Anderson, Benedict R. (1983). *Imagined Communities: Reflections on the Origin and Spread of Nationalism.* London: Verso.

Anderson, Christopher; Curtin, Michael (2002). 'Writing Cultural History. The Challenge of Radio and Television'. In Niels Brügger; Søren Kolstrup (eds) *Media History. Theories, Methods, Analysis* (pp. 15–32). Aarhus: Aarhus University Press.

Appadurai, Arjun (1990). 'Difference and Disjuncture in the Global cultural Economy'. In Mike Featherstone (ed) *Global Culture. Nationalism, Globalization and Modernity* (pp. 295–310). London/Newbury Park/New Delhi: Sage.

Appadurai, Arjun (1996). *Modernity at Large: Cultural Dimensions of Globalization.* Minneapolis: University of Minnesota Press.

Atton, Chris (2004). *An Alternative Internet: Radical Media, Politics and Creativity.* Edinburgh: Edinburgh University Press.

Atton, Chris (2005). *Alternative Media.* London/Thousand Oaks, CA/New Delhi: Sage.

Atton, Chris (2009). 'Why Alternative Journalism Matters'. *Journalism* 10(3), 283–285.

Atton, Chris; Hamilton, James (2008). *Alternative Journalism.* Los Angeles: Sage.

Avilés, Jose Alberto García; Carvajal, Miguel (2008). 'Integrated and Crossmedia Newsroom Convergence: Two Models of Multimedia News Production—The Cases of Novotécnica and La Verdad Multimedia in Spain'. *Convergence: The International Journal of Research into New Media Technologies* 14(2), 221–239.

Baldasty, Gerald J. (1992). *The Commercialization of News in the Nineteenth Century.* Madison: University of Wisconsin Press.

Bardoel, Jo (1996). 'Beyond Journalism. A Profession between Information Society and Civil Society'. *Journal of Communication* 11(3), 283–302.

Bardoel, Jo (2002). 'The Internet, Journalism and Public Communication Policies'. *Gazette: The International Journal for Communication Studies* 64(5), 501–511.

Bardoel, Jo; Deuze, Mark (2001). '"Network Journalism': Converging Competencies of Old and New Media Professionals'. *Australian Journalism Review* 23(2), 91–103.

Barnhurst, Kevin G.; Nerone, John (2003). 'US Newspaper Types, the Newsroom, and the Division of Labor, 1750–2000'. *Journalism Studies* 4(4), 435–449.

Barnouw, Erik (1966–1970). *A History of Broadcasting in the United States.* Three Volumes. New York: Oxford University Press.

Baur, Nina; Lamnek, Siegfried (2005). 'Einzelfallanalyse'. In Lothar Mikos; Claudia Wegener (eds) *Qualitative Medienforschung. Ein Handbuch* (pp. 241–252). Konstanz: UVK.

Beck, Ulrich (2000). *What is Globalization?* Translated by Patrick Camiller. Malden, MA: Polity Press.

Beckett, Charlie (2008). *SuperMedia. Saving Journalism so it Can Save the World.* Malden, MA: Blackwell.

Beckett, Charlie; Mansell, Robin (2008). 'Crossing Boundaries: New Media and Networked Journalism'. *Communication, Culture & Critique* 1(1), 92–104.

Bell, Daniel (1973). *The Coming of Post-industrial Society: Venture in Social Forecasting.* New York: Basic Books.

Bell, David (2007). *Cyberculture Theorists. Manuel Castells and Donna Haraway.* London/New York: Routledge.

Benkler, Yochai (2006). *The Wealth of Networks. How Social Production Transforms Markets and Freedom.* New Haven/London: Yale University Press.

Bennett, W. Lance (2004). 'Gatekeeping and Press-Government Relations: A Multigated Model of News Construction'. In Lynda Lee Kaid (ed) *Handbook of Political Communication Research* (pp. 283–314). Mahwah, NJ: Lawrence Erlbaum Associates.

Blanchard, Margaret A. (ed) (1998). *History of the Mass Media in the United States: An Encyclopedia.* Chicago: Fitzroy Dearbor.

Blondheim, Menahem (1994). *News over the Wires. The Telegraph and the Flow of Public Information in America, 1844–1897.* Cambridge/London: Harvard University Press.

Boczkowski, Pablo J. (2004). 'The Process of Adopting Multimedia and Interactivity in Three Online Newsrooms'. *Journal of Communication* June, 197–213.

Borges, Jorge Luis (1999). *The Total Library: Non-Fiction 1922–1986.* London: Penguin.

Boyce, George; Curran, James; Wingate, Pauline (eds) (1978). *Newspaper History: From the 17th Century to the Present Day.* London/Constable/Beverly Hills: Sage.

Boyd-Barrett, Oliver (1980). *The International News Agencies.* London/Constable/Beverly Hills: Sage.

Boyd-Barrett, Oliver; Rantanen, Terhi (eds) (1998). *The Globalization of News.* London/Thousand Oaks, CA/New Delhi: Sage.

Braman, Sandra (2004). 'Technology'. In John D.H. Downing; Denis McQuail; Philip Schlesinger; Ellen Wartella *The SAGE Handbook of Media Studies* (pp. 123–144). Thousand Oaks, CA/London/New Delhi: Sage.

Bridge, Gary; Watson, Sophie (eds) (2002). *The Blackwell City Reader.* Oxford: Blackwell.

Briggs, Asa; Burke, Peter (2005). *A Social History of the Media. From Gutenberg to the Internet.* Second edition. Cambridge/Malden, MA: Polity Press.

Briggs, Mark (2010). *JournalismNext: A Practical Guide to Digital Reporting.* Washington, DC: CQ Press.

Brügger, Niels; Kolstrup, Søren (eds) (2002). *Media History. Theories, Methods, Analysis.* Aarhus: Aarhus University Press.

Bruns, Axel (2005). *Gatewatching. Collaborative Online News Production.* New York: Peter Lang.

Bruns, Axel (2006). 'Towards Produsage: Futures for User-Led Content Production'. In Fay Sudweeks; Herbert Hrachovec; Charles Ess (eds) *Proceedings: Cultural Attitudes towards Communication and Technology* (pp. 275–284). Perth: Murdoch University. Retrieved April 1, 2008, from: http://produsage.org/articles.

Calabrese, Andrew (1999). 'The Information Age According to Manuel Castells'. *Journal of Communication* Summer, 172–186.

Campbell, Vincent (2004). *Information Age Journalism. Journalism in an International Context.* London: Arnold.

Carey, James W. (1974). 'The Problem of Journalism History'. *Journalism History* 1(3), 5–27.

Carey, James W. (1989). *Communication as Culture: Essays on Media and Society.* Boston: Unwin Hyman.

Castells, Manuel (1996). *The Rise of the Network Society.* Oxford: Blackwell.

Castells, Manuel (1999). 'Grassrooting the Space of Flows'. *Urban Geography* 20(4), 294–302.

Castells, Manuel (2000a). 'Materials for an Exploratory Theory of the Network Society'. *British Journal of Sociology* 51(1), 5–24.

Castells, Manuel (2000b). *End of Millennium.* Vol. III of *The Information Age: Economy, Society and Culture.* Oxford: Oxford University Press.

Castells, Manuel (2000c). *The Rise of the Network Society.* Vol. I of *The Information Age: Economy, Society and Culture.* Second Edition. Oxford: Blackwell.

Castells, Manuel (2001). *The Internet Galaxy. Reflections on the Internet, Business, and Society.* Oxford: Oxford University Press.

Castells, Manuel (2002a). 'An Introduction to the Information Age'. In Gary Bridge; Sophie Watson (eds) *The Blackwell City Reader* (pp. 125–134). Oxford: Blackwell.

Castells, Manuel (2002b). *The Internet Galaxy. Reflections on the Internet, Business, and Society.* Oxford: Oxford University Press.

Castells, Manuel (2004). *The Network Society. A Cross-Cultural Perspective.* Northampton, MA: Edward Elgar.

Castells, Manuel; Ince, Martin (2003). *Conversations with Manuel Castells.* Cambridge: Polity Press.

Chaffee, Steven H.; Metzger, Miriam J. (2001). 'The End of Mass Communication?' *Mass Communication & Society* 4(4), 365–379.

Chalaby, Jean K. (1998). *The Invention of Journalism.* London: Macmillan.

Chapman, Jane (2005). *Comparative Media History. An Introduction: 1789 to the Present.* Cambridge/Malden, MA: Polity Press.

Chapman, Jane; Kinsey, Marie (eds) (2008). *Broadcast Journalism: A Critical Introduction.* London: Routledge.

Coe, Lewis (1993). *The Telegraph. A History of Morse's Invention and Its Predecessors in the United States.* Jefferson, NC/London: McFarland & Company Inc. Publishers.

Collins Australian Dictionary (2003). Fifth Australian Edition. Pymble, NSW: Harper Collins.

Conboy, Martin (2004). *Journalism. A Critical History.* London/Thousand Oaks, CA: Sage.

Conboy, Martin; Raymond, Joad; Williams, Kevin; Tusan, Michelle (2006). 'Roundtable Discussion of Martin Conboy's "Journalism: A Critical History". London: Sage, 2004'. *Media History* 12(3), 329–351.

Corner, John; Harvey, Sylvia (eds) (1991). *Enterprise and Heritage: Cross-Currents of National Culture.* London/New York/Routledge.

Cottle, Simon (2009). *Global Crisis Reporting: Journalism in the Global Age.* Maidenhead/NY: Open University Press.

Cottle, Simon; Rai, Mugdha (2006). 'Between Display and Deliberation: Analyzing TV News as Communicative Architecture'. *Media, Culture & Society* 28(2), 163–189.

Couldry, Nick (2004). 'The Productive "Consumer" and the Dispersed "Citizen"'. *International Journal of Cultural Studies* 7(1), 21–32.

Cresswell, John W. (2003). *Research Design. Qualitative, Quantitative and Mixed Methods Approaches.* Second Edition. London/Thousand Oaks, CA,/New Delhi: Sage.

Currah, Andrew (2009). *What's Happening to Our News. An Investigation into the Likely Impact of the Digital Revolution on the Economics of News Publishing in the UK.* Oxford: Reuters Institute for the Study of Journalism. Retrieved January 10, 2010 from: http://reutersinstitute.politics.ox.ac.uk/about/news/item/article/whats-happening-to-our-news.html.

Dahlgren, Peter (1996). 'Media Logic in Cyberspace: Repositioning Journalism and its Publics'. *The Public* 3(3), 59–72.

Delwiche, Aaron (2005). 'Agenda-setting, Opinion Leadership, and the World of Web Logs', *First Monday* 10(12). Retrieved April 01, 2008, from: http://firstmonday.org/htbin/cgiwrap/bin/ojs/index.php/fm/article/view/1300/1220.

Deuze, Mark (1999). 'Journalism and the Web. An Analysis of Skills and Standards in an Online Environment'. *Gazette. The International Journal for Communication Studies* 61(5), 373–390.

Deuze, Mark (2001). 'Educating New Journalists: Challenges to the Curriculum'. *Journalism Educator* 56(1), 4–17.

Deuze, Mark (2003). 'The Web and its Journalisms: Considering the Consequences of Different Types of Newsmedia Online'. *New Media & Society* 5(2), 203–230.

Deuze, Mark (2004). 'What is Multimedia Journalism?' *Journalism Studies* 5(2), 139–152.

Deuze, Mark (2005). 'What is Journalism? Professional Identity and Ideology of Journalists'. *Journalism* 6(4), 442–464.

Deuze, Mark (2006). 'Participation, Remediation, Bricolage: Considering Principal Components of a Digital Culture'. *The Information Society* 22(2), 63–75.

Deuze, Mark (2007). *Media Work.* Cambridge/Malden, MA: Polity.

Deuze, Mark (2008). 'Understanding Journalism as Newswork: How It Changes, and How It Remains the Same'. *Westminster Papers in Communication and Culture* 5(2), 4–23.

Douglass, Frederick (2006). *Narrative of the Life of Frederick Douglass.* Project Gutenberg. Retrieved January 10, 2010 from: http://www.gutenberg.org/catalog/world/readfile?fk_files=216491&pageno=1.

Downing, John (2002). 'Independent Media Centers: A Multi-local, Multimedia Challenge to Global Neo-liberalism'. In Marc Raboy (ed) *Global Media Policy in the New Millennium* (pp. 215–232). Luton: Luton University Press.

Downing, John (2003). 'The IMC Movement Beyond "The West."' In Andrew Opel; Donnalyn Pompper (eds) *Representing Resistance: Media, Civil Disobedience, and the Global Justice Movement* (pp. 241–258). Westport, CT: Praeger.

Downing, John; McQuail, Denis; Schlesinger, Philip; Wartella, Ellen (eds) (2004). *The SAGE Handbook of Media Studies.* London/Thousand Oaks, CA/New Delhi: Sage.

Duffield, Lee (2006). 'Thinking like Journalists: How Journalists and the General Public can Work Together in the Information Economy'. In Lee Duffield; John Cokley *I, Journalist. Coping with and Crafting Media Information in the 21st Century* (pp. 1–52). Frenchs Forest, NSW: Pearson Education Australia.

Duffield, Lee; Cokley, John (2006). *I, Journalist. Coping with and Crafting Media Information in the 21st Century.* Frenchs Forest, NSW: Pearson Education Australia.

Edgar, Andrew; Sedgwick, Peter (eds) (2002). *Cultural Theory. The Key Concepts.* London/New York: Routledge.

Ellul, Jacques (1964). *The Technological Society.* Translated by John Wilkinson and with an introduction by Robert K. Merton. London: J. Cape.

El-Nawawy, Mohammed; Iskander, Adel (2002). *Al-Jazeera: How the Free Arab News Network Scooped the World and Changed the Middle East.* Cambridge: Westview.

Entman, Robert M. (1989). *Democracy without Citizens: Media and the Decay of American Politics.* New York/Oxford: Oxford University Press.

Erdal, Ivar John (2009). 'Crossmedia (Re)Production Cultures'. *Convergence: The International Journal of Research into New Media Technologies.* 15(2), 215–231.

Fagen, M.D. (ed) (1975). *History of Engineering and Science in the Bell System: The Early Years 1875—1925* (pp. 22–23). Prepared by Members of the Technical Staff, Bell Telephone Laboratories. New York: Bell Telephone Laboratories, Inc.

Featherstone, Mike (ed) (1990). *Global Culture. Nationalism, Globalization and Modernity.* London/Newbury Park/New Delhi: Sage.

Featherstone, Mike; Lash, Scott; Robertson, Roland (eds) (1995). *Global Modernities.* London/Thousand Oaks, CA/New Delhi: Sage.

Featherstone, Mike; Lash, Scott (eds) (1999). *Spaces of Culture. City, Nation, World.* London/Thousand Oaks, CA/New Delhi: Sage.

Flick, Uwe; Kardoff, Ernst von; Steinke, Ines (eds) (2000). *Qualitative Forschung. Ein Handbuch.* Hamburg: Reinbek.

Füssel, Stephan (2001). 'Gutenberg and Today's Media Change'. *Publishing Research Quarterly* 16(4), 3–10.

Garcelon, Marc (2006). 'The 'Indymedia' Experiment: The Internet as Movement Facilitator Against Institutional Control'. *Convergence: The International Journal of Research into New Media Technologies* 12(1), 55–82.

Garnham, Nicholas (2004). 'Information Society Theory as Ideology'. In Frank Webster (ed) *The Information Society Reader* (pp. 97–120). London/New York: Routledge, pp. 165–183. (First published in 1998 in *Loisir et Société* 21(1).)

Gibson, William (1984). *Neuromancer.* London: Gollancz.

Gibson, William (1995). *Neuromancer.* London: Harper Voyager.

Giddens, Anthony (1999). *Runaway World: How Globalisation is Reshaping Our Lives.* London: Profile Books.

Gilboa, Eytan (2002). *The Global News Networks and U.S. Policymaking in Defense and Foreign Affairs.* Paper published by the 'Joan Shorenstein Center on the Press, Politics & Public Policy' at Harvard University. Retrieved December 10, 2010, from: http://www.hks.harvard.edu/presspol/publications/papers.html#g

Gillmor, Dan (2006). *We the Media. Grassroots Journalism by the People, for the People.* Sebastopol, CA: O'Reilly.

Glesne, Corrine; Peshkin, Alan (1992). *Becoming Qualitative Researchers. An Introduction.* White Plains, NY: Longman.

Gordon, R. (2003). 'The Meanings and Implications of Convergence'. In Kevin Kawamoto (ed) *Digital Journalism. Emerging Media and the Changing Horizons of Journalism* (pp. 57–73). Lanham/Boulder/New York/Toronto/Oxford: Rowman & Littlefield.

Görke, Alexander; Scholl, Armin (2006). 'Niklas Luhmann's Theory of Social Systems and Journalism Research'. *Journalism Studies* 7(4), 644–655.

Gowing, Nik (1994). *Real Time Television Coverage of Armed Conflicts and Diplomatic Crises: Does it Pressure or Distort Foreign Policy Decisions.* Paper published by the Joan Shorenstein Center on the Press, Politics & Public Policy at Harvard University. Retrieved December 10, 2010, from: http://www.hks.harvard.edu/presspol/publications/papers.html#g

Habermas, Jürgen (1989). *The Structural Transformation of the Public Sphere: An Inquiry into a Category of Bourgeois Society.* Translated by Thomas Burger with assistance of Frederick Lawrence. Cambridge: MIT Press.

Halcli, Abigail; Webster, Frank (2000). 'Inequality and Mobilization in "The Information Age"'. *European Journal of Social Theory* 3(1), 67–81.

Hall, Peter Christian (ed) (2004). *Die Krise des Medienmarktes. Geld—Strukturen—Standards.* Mainz, Germany: Zweites Deutsches Fernsehen (Mainzer Tage der Fernseh-Kritik; 36).

Hall, Stuart; Critcher, Charles; Jefferson, Tony; Clarke, John; Robert, Brian (1978). *Policing the Crisis: Mugging, the State, and Law and Order.* New York: Holmes & Meier.

Hallin, Daniel C.; Mancini, Paolo (2004). *Comparing Media Systems: Three Models of Media and Politics.* Cambridge/New York: Cambridge University Press.

Hamilton, James W. (2003). 'Remaking Media Participation in Early Modern England'. *Journalism* 4(3), 293–313.

Hampel, Matt (2008). 'iReport: Participatory Media Joins a Global News Brand'. In *Media Re:Public. News and Information as Digital Media Come of Age.* Published as part of the Berkman Publication Series. The Berkman Center for Internet & Society at Harvard University. Retrieved January 10, 2010 from: http://cyber.law.harvard.edu/pubrelease/mediarepublic/downloads.html

Hanitzsch, Thomas (2007). 'Deconstructing Journalism Culture: Toward a Universal Theory'. *Communication Theory* 17, 367–385.

Hannerz, Ulf (1996). *Transnational Connections. Culture, People, Places.* London/New York: Routledge.

Hardt, Hanno (1990). 'Newsworkers, Technology, and Journalism History'. *Critical Studies in Mass Communication* 7, 346–365.

Hassan, Robert (2004). *Media, Politics and the Network Society.* Maidenhead/New York: Open University Press.

Hassan, Robert (2007). 'Network Time'. In Robert Hassan; Ronald E. Purser (eds) *24/7. Time and Temporality in the Network Society* (pp. 37–61). Stanford, CA: Stanford Business Books.

Hassan, Robert; Purser, Ronald E. (eds) (2007). *24/7. Time and Temporality in the Network Society.* Stanford, CA: Stanford Business Books.

Hassan, Robert; Thomas, Julian (2006a). 'Introduction'. In Robert Hassan; Julian Thomas (eds) *The New Media Theory Reader* (pp. xvii–xxvii). Maidenhead, UK/New York: Open University Press.

Hassan, Robert; Thomas, Julian (eds) (2006b). *The New Media Theory Reader.* Maidenhead/New York: Open University Press.

Held, David (1995). *Democracy and the Global Order: From the Modern State to Cosmopolitan Governance.* Cambridge: Polity Press.

Herman, Edward S.; Chomsky, Noam (1988). *Manufacturing Consent: The Political Economy of the Mass Media.* New York: Pantheon Books.

Herman, Edward S.; McChesney, Robert W. (1997). *The Global Media: The New Missionaries of Corporate Capitalism.* London/Washington, DC: Cassell.

Hirst, Martin; Harrison, John (2007). *Communication and New Media: Broadcast to Narrowcast.* Melbourne: Oxford University Press.

Hoffmann, Dagmar (2005). 'Experteninterview'. In Lothar Mikos; Claudia Wegener (eds) *Qualitative Medienforschung. Ein Handbuch* (pp. 268–278). Konstanz: UVK.

Høyer, Svennik (2003). 'Newspapers without Journalists'. *Journalism Studies* 4(4), 451–463.

Huang, Edgar; Davison, Karen; Shreve, Stephanie; Davis, Twila; Bettendorf, Elizabeth; Nair, Anita (2006). 'Facing the Challenges of Convergence: Media Professionals' Concerns of Working Across Media Platforms'. *Convergence: The International Journal of Research into New Media Technologies* 12(1), 83–98.

Inglis, Fred (2002). *People's Witness: The Journalist in Modern Politics*. New Haven: Yale University Press.

Innis, Harold (1950). *Empire and Communications*. Toronto: Dundurn Press.

Innis, Harold (1951). *The Bias of Communication*. Toronto: Dundurn Press.

Jarvis, Jeff (2009). *What Would Google Do?* New York: Collins Business.

Jenkins, Henry (2004). 'The Cultural Logic of Media Convergence'. *International Journal of Cultural Studies* 7(1), 33–43.

Jenkins, Henry (2006). *Convergence Culture: Where Old and New Media Collide*. New York: New York University Press.

Johnson, Michael L. (1971). *The New Journalism. The Underground Press, the Artists of Nonfiction, and Changes in the Established Media*. Lawrence/Manhattan/Wichita: University Press of Kansas.

Jones, Steve (ed) (1999). *Doing Internet Research: Critical Issues and Methods for Examining the Net*. London: Sage.

Kaplan, Richard L. (2003). 'American Journalism Goes to War, 1898–2001: A Manifesto on Media and Empire'. *Media History* 9(3), 209–219.

Kawamoto, Kevin (ed) (2003). *Digital Journalism: Emerging Media and the Changing Horizons of Journalism*. Lanham, MD: Rowman & Littlefield.

Keen, Andrew (2007). *The Cult of the Amateur. How today's Internet is Killing our Culture*. New York/London/Toronto/Sydney/Auckland: Doubleday/Currency.

Kelly, John (2009). *Red Kayaks and Hidden Gold: The Rise, Challenges, and Value of Citizen Journalism*. Published by the Reuters Institute for the Study of Journalism. Retrieved January 10, 2010 from: http://reutersinstitute.politics.ox.ac.uk/publications/risj-challenges/red-kayaks-and-hidden-gold.html.

Kester, Bernadette (2008). 'Working at the End of the Assembly Line: A Conversation with Joris Luyendijk about the Impossibility of Doing Western-style Journalism in Arab Countries'. *The International Journal of Press/Politics* 13(4), 500–506.

Keuneke, Susanne (2005). 'Qualitatives Interview'. In Lothar Mikos; Claudia Wegener (eds) *Qualitative Medienforschung. Ein Handbuch* (pp. 254–267). Konstanz: UVK.

Kovach, B.; Rosenstiel, T. (1999). *Warp Speed: America in the Age of Mixed Media*. New York: Century Foundation Press.

Lamnek, Siegfried (1993). *Qualitative Sozialforschung*. Second Edition. Weinheim: Beltz.

Lash, Scott; Urry, John (1994). *Economies of Signs and Space*. London, Thousand Oaks, CA/ New Delhi: Sage.

Lasica, J.D. (1996). 'Net Gain: Future of the News on the Internet'. *American Journalism Review* 18(9), 20–33.

Lasica, J.D. (2003). 'Blogs and Journalism Need Each Other'. *Nieman Reports* 57, 70–74.

Lawrence, R. (2000). *The Politics of Force: Media and the Construction of Police Brutality*. Berkeley: University of California Press.

Lee-Wright, Peter (2008). 'Virtual News: BBC News at a 'Future Media and Technology' Crossroads'. *Convergence: The International Journal of Research into New Media Technologies* 14(3), 249–260.

Lévy, Pierre (1997). *Collective Intelligence*. Cambridge: Perseus.

Livingston, Steven; Bennett, W. Lance (2003). 'Gatekeeping, Indexing, and Live-Event News: Is Technology Altering the Construction of News?' *Political Communication* 20, 363–380.

Lovink, Geert (2008). *Zero Comments. Blogging and the Critical Internet Culture*. New York/London: Routledge.

Luhmann, Niklas (1995). *Social Systems*. Translated by John Bednarz Jr with Dirk Baecker. Stanford, CA: Stanford University Press.

Luhmann, Niklas (2000). *The Reality of the Mass Media*. Translated by Kathleen Cross. Cambridge: Polity Press.

Luyendijk, Joris (2009). *People Like Us: Misrepresenting the Middle East*. New York: Soft Skull Press.

Marshall, David P. (2004). *New Media Cultures*. London: Arnold.

Marvin, Carolyn (1988). *When Old Technologies Were New: Thinking About Electric Communication in the Late Nineteenth Century*. New York: Oxford University Press.

Matheson, Donald (2004). 'Weblogs and the Epistemology of the News: Some Trends in Online Journalism'. *New Media & Society* 6(4), 443–468.

Mattelart, Armand (1979). *Multinational Corporations and the Control of Culture: The Ideological Apparatuses of Imperialism*. Translated by Michael Chanan. Brighton, Sussex: Harvester Press; Atlantic Highlands, NJ: Humanities Press.

Mäkinen, Maarit; Wangu Kuira, Mary (2008). 'Social Media and Postelection Crisis in Kenya'. *The International Journal of Press/Politics* 13(3), 328–335.

McChesney, Robert W. (1998). 'Media Convergence and Globalization'. In Daya Kishan Thussu (ed) *Electronic Empires. Global Media and local resistance* (pp. 27–46). London/New York/Sydney/Auckland: Arnold.

McCombs, Maxwell E.; Shaw, Donald L. (1972). 'The Agenda-Setting Function of Mass Media'. *Public Opinion Quarterly* 36, 176–187.

McCombs, Maxwell (2005). 'A Look at Agenda-setting: Past, Present and Future'. *Journalism Studies* 6(4), 543–557.

McLuhan, Marshall (1962). *The Gutenberg Galaxy. The Making of Typographic Man*. Toronto: University of Toronto Press.

McLuhan, Marshall (1964). *Understanding Media: The Extensions of Man*. New York: McGraw-Hill.

McNair, Brian (1998). *The Sociology of Journalism*. London/New York/Sydney/Auckland: Arnold.

McNair, Brian (2005). 'The Emerging Chaos of Global News Culture'. In Stuart Allan (ed) *Journalism: Critical Issues* (pp. 151–163). Berkshire: Open University Press.

McNair, Brian (2006). *Cultural Chaos. Journalism, News and Power in a Globalised World*. London/New York: Routledge.

Meyer, Philip (2002). 'Journalism's Road to Becoming a Profession'. *Nieman Reports* Winter, 107–108.

Meyrowitz, Joshua (1985). *No Sense of Place: The Impact of Electronic Media on Social Behavior*. Oxford: Oxford University Press.

Meuser, Michael; Nagel, Ulrike (2003). 'Experteninterview'. In Ralf Bohnsack; Winfried Marotzki; Michael Meuser (eds) *Hauptbegriffe Qualitativer Sozialforschung* (pp. 57–58). Opladen: Leske und Budrich.

Mikos, Lothar; Wegener, Claudia (eds) (2005). *Qualitative Medienforschung. Ein Handbuch*. Konstanz: UVK.

Mosco, Vincent (2004). *The Digital Sublime. Myth, Power, and Cyberspace*. Cambridge/London: MIT Press.

Moyo, Dumisani (2009). 'Citizen Journalism and the Parallel Market of Information in Zimbabwe's 2008 Election'. *Journalism Studies* 10(4), 551–567.

Nerone, J.C. (1987). 'The Mythology of the Penny Press'. *Critical Studies in Mass Communication* 4, 376–404.

Nerone, John (1990). 'The Problem of Teaching Journalism History'. *Educator*, Autumn, 16–24.

Negroponte, Nicholas (1995). *Being Digital*. New York: Knopf.

Norris, Pippa (2001). *Digital Divide: Civic Engagement, Information Poverty, and the Internet Worldwide*. Cambridge: Cambridge University Press.

Norris, Pippa (2004). 'The Digital Divide'. In Frank Webster (ed) *The Information Society Reader* (pp. 273–286). London/New York: Routledge.

Nyamnjoh, Francis B. (2004). 'Global and Local Trends in Media Ownership and Control: Implications for Cultural Creativity in Africa'. In W. Van Binsbergen; R. Van Dijk (eds) *Situating Globality: African Agency in the Appropriation of Global Culture* (pp. 57–89). Leiden/Boston: Brill.

Nye, David E. (1997). 'Shaping Communication Networks: Telegraph, Telephone, Computer'. *Social Research* 64(3), 1067–1091.

Örnebring, Henrik (2009). 'Comparative European Journalism: The State of Current Research'. Working Paper. *Reuters Institute for the Study of Journalism*. Retrieved January 10, 2010 from: http://reutersinstitute.politics.ox.ac.uk/publications/risj-working-papers.html.

Opel, Andrew; Pompper, Donnalyn (eds) (2003). *Representing Resistance: Media, Civil Disobedience, and the Global Justice Movement*. Westport, CT: Praeger.

Ostini, Jennifer; Fung, Anthony Y.H. (2002). 'Beyond the Four Theories of the Press: A New Model of National Media Systems'. *Mass Communication & Society* 5(1), 41–56.

O'Sullivan, Tim; Dutton, Brian; Rayner, Philip (1994). *Studying the Media: An Introduction*. London: Arnold.

The Oxford English Dictionary (1989). Second Edition. Volume X. Prepared by J.A. Simpson and E.S.C. Weiner. Oxford: Clarendon Press.

Palmer, Michael (2003). 'Parisian Newsrooms in the Late Nineteenth Century: How to Enter from the Agency Back Office, or Inventing News Journalism in France'. *Journalism Studies* 4(4), 479–487.

Palmer, Jerry; Fontan, Victoria (2007). '"Our Ears and our Eyes': Journalists and Fixers in Iraq'. *Journalism* 8(1), 5–24.

Paulussen, Steve; Ugille, Peter (2008). 'User Generated Content in the Newsroom: Professional and Organisational Constraints on Participatory Journalism'. *Westminster Papers in Communication and Culture* 5(2), 24–41.

Pavlik, John (2000). 'The Impact of Technology on Journalism'. *Journalism Studies* 1(2), 229–237.

Picard, Robert G. (2009). *Why Journalists Deserve Low Pay*. Address at the Reuters Institute for the Study of Journalism Weekly Seminar, May 6, 2010. Retrieved January 10, 2010 from: http://reutersinstitute.politics.ox.ac.uk/fellowships/visiting/current-visiting-fellows/robert-g-picard.html.

Pintak, Lawrence; Ginges, Jeremy (2009). 'Inside the Arab Newsroom. Arab Journalists Evaluate Themselves and the Competition'. *Journalism Studies* 10(2), 157–177.

Powell, Adam Clayton III (2003). 'Satellites, the Internet, and Journalism'. In Kevin Kawamoto (ed) *Digital Journalism. Emerging Media and the Changing Horizons of Journalism* (pp. 103–112). Lanham, MD: Rowman & Littlefield.

Putnis, Peter (2006). 'How the International News Agency Business Model Failed—Reuters in Australia, 1877–1895'. *Media History* 12(1), 1–17.

Raboy, Marc (ed) (2002). *Global Media Policy in the New Millennium*. Luton: Luton University Press.

Rantanen, Terhi (2003). 'The New Sense of Place in the 19th-Century News'. *Media, Culture & Society* 25(4), 435–449.

Raymond, Joad (1996). *The Invention of the Newspaper. English Newsbooks 1641–1649*. Oxford: Clarendon Press.

Raymond, Joad (ed) (2006). *News Networks in Seventeenth-Century Britain and Europe*. London/New York: Routledge.

Read, Donald (1999). *The Power of News. The History of Reuters*. Second Edition. Oxford/New York: Oxford University Press.

Reese, Stephen D.; Routigliano, Lou; Hyun, Kideuk; Jeong, Jaekwan (2007). 'Mapping the Blogosphere: Professional and Citizen-based Media in the Global News Arena'. *Journalism* 8(3), 235–261.

Regan, Tom (2000). 'Technology is Changing Journalism. Just As it Always Has'. *Nieman Reports*, Winter, 6–9.

Reich, Zvi (2008). 'How Citizens Create News Stories'. *Journalism Studies* 9(5), 739–758.

Rich, Bryan (2001). 'Digital Technology Could Lead Journalism Back to Its Roots'. *Nieman Notes* 55(2), 90–91.

Ritzer, George (1996). *The McDonaldization of Society: An Investigation into the Changing Character of Contemporary Social Life*. Thousand Oaks, CA: Pine Forge Press.

Riverbend (2005). *Baghdad Burning: Girl Blog from Iraq*. New York: The Feminist Press at CUNY.

Riverbend (2006). *Baghdad Burning II. More Girl Blog from Iraq*. New York: The Feminist Press at CUNY.

Roberts, Brian (2007). *Getting the Most Out of the Research Experience. What Every Researcher Needs to Know*. Los Angeles/London/New Delhi/Singapore: Sage.

Robertson, Roland (1992). *Globalization: Social Theory and Global Culture*. London/Newbury Park/New Delhi: Sage.

Robertson, Roland (1995). 'Glocalization: Time-Space and Homogeneity-Heterogeneity'. In Mike Featherstone; Scott Lash; Roland Robertson (eds) *Global Modernities* (pp. 25–44). London/Thousand Oaks, CA/New Delhi: Sage.

Robins, Kevin (1991). 'Tradition and Translation: National Culture in its Global Context'. In John Corner; Sylvia Harvey (eds) *Enterprise and Heritage: Cross-Currents of National Culture* (pp. 21–44). London/New York: Routledge.

Robinson, Piers (2002). *The CNN Effect: The Myth of News, Foreign Policy and Intervention*. London/New York: Routledge.

Rosenau, James N. (1990). *Turbulence in World Politics: A Theory of Change and Continuity*. Princeton, NJ: Princeton University Press.

Sakr, Naomi (ed) (2007). *Arab Media and Political Renewal. Community, Legitimacy, and Public Life*. London/New York: I.B. Tauris.

Schiller, Dan (1982). *Telematics and Government*. Norwood, NJ: Ablex.

Schiller, Dan (1999). *Digital Capitalism. Networking in the Global Market System*. Cambridge/London: MIT Press.

Schiller, Herbert (1976). *Communication and Cultural Domination*. White Plains, NY: International Arts and Sciences Press.

Schiller, Herbert (1984). 'New Information Technologies and Old Objectives'. *Science and Public Policy* 12, 382–383.

Schiller, Herbert (1998). 'Striving for Communication Dominance. A Half-century Review'. In Daya Kishan Thussu (ed) *Electronic Empires. Global Media and Local Resistance* (pp. 17–26). London/New York/Sydney/Auckland: Arnold.

Schmitz Weiss, Amy; Higgins Joyce, Vanessa de Macedo (2009). 'Compressed Dimensions in Digital Media Occupations: Journalists in Transformation'. *Journalism* 10(5), 587–603.

Schoenbach, Klaus; de Waal, Ester; Lauf, Edmund (2005). 'Research Note: Online and Print Newspapers. Their Impact on the Extent of the Perceived Public Agenda'. *European Journal of Communication* 20(2), 245–258.

Schroeder, Ralph (2007). *Rethinking Science, Technology, and Social Change.* Stanford, CA: Stanford University Press.

Schudson, Michael (1978). *Discovering the News. A Social History of American Newspapers.* New York: Basic Books.

Schudson, Michael (1995). *The Power of News.* Cambridge: Harvard University Press.

Schudson, Michael (2003). *The Sociology of News.* New York/London: W.W. Norton & Company.

Seib, Philip (2002). *The Global Journalist. News and Conscience in a World of Conflict.* Lanham/Boulder/New York/Oxford: Rowman & Littlefield.

Seib, Philip (2004). *Beyond the Front Lines. How the News Media Cover the World Shaped by War.* New York: Palgrave Macmillan.

Seidman, Irving (2006). *Interviewing as Qualitative Research. A Guide for Researchers in Education and the Social Sciences.* Third Edition. New York: Teachers College Press.

Shirky, Clay (2008). *Here Comes Everybody. The Power of Organizing without Organizations.* New York: Penguin.

Siebert, Fred S.; Peterson, Theodore; Schramm, Wilbur (1956). *Four Theories of the Press. The Authoritarian, Libertarian, Social Responsibility and Soviet Communist Concepts of What the Press Should Be and Do.* Urbana: University of Illinois Press.

Sigal, Leon V. (1973). *Reporters and Officials: The Organization and Politics of Newsgathering.* Lexington, MA: Heath.

Silcock, William B.; Keith, Susan (2006). 'Translating the Tower of Babel? Issues of Definition, Language, and Culture in Converged Newsrooms'. *Journalism Studies* 7(4), 610–627.

Sinclair, John (2004). 'Globalization, Supranational Institutions, and Media'. In John D.H. Downing; Denis McQuail; Philip Schlesinger; Ellen Wartella (eds) *The SAGE Handbook of Media Studies* (pp. 65–82). London/Thousand Oaks, CA/New Delhi: Sage.

Singer, Jane B. (1998). 'Online Journalists: Foundations for Research Into Their Changing Roles. In *The Journal of Computer-Mediated Communication* 4(1). Retrieved December 10, 2010, from: http://jcmc.indiana.edu/vol4/issue1/singer.html

Singer, Jane B. (2004). 'Strange Bedfellows: Diffusion of Convergence in Four News Organizations'. *Journalism Studies* 5(1), 3–18.

Smethers, Stephen (1998). 'Telegraph'. In Margaret A. Blanchard (ed) *History of the Mass Media in the United States: An Encyclopedia* (pp. 634–636). Chicago: Fitzroy Dearbor.

Smith, Anthony (1978). 'The Long Road to Objectivity and Back Again: The Kinds of Truth we get in Journalism'. In George Boyce; James Curran; Pauline Wingate (eds) *Newspaper History: From the 17th Century to the Present Day* (pp. 153–171). London/Constable/Beverly Hills: Sage.

Sosale, Sujatha (2003). 'Envisioning a New World Order Through Journalism: Lessons from Recent History'. *Journalism* 4(3), 377–392.

Stalder, Felix (1998). 'The Network Paradigm: Social Formations in the Age of Information'. *The Information Society* 14, 301–308.

Standage, Tom (1998). *The Victorian Internet. The Remarkable Story of the Telegraph and the Nineteenth Century's Online Pioneers.* London: Phoenix.

Stanton, Richard C. (2007). *All News is Local. The Failure of the Media to Reflect World Events in a Globalized Age.* Jefferson, NC/London: McFarland & Company.

Starr, Paul (2004). *The Creation of the Media: Political Origins of Modern Communications.* New York: Basic Books.

Stephens, Mitchell (2007). *A History of News.* Third Edition. New York/Oxford: Oxford University Press.

Sterne, Jonathan (1999). 'Thinking the Internet: Cultural Studies versus the Millennium'. In Steve Jones (ed) *Doing Internet Research: Critical Issues and Methods for Examining the Net* (pp. 257–288). London: Sage.

Stover, John F. (1961). *American Railroads*. Chicago: University of Chicago Press.

Straubhaar, Joseph D. (2007). *World Television. From Global to Local*. Los Angeles/London/New Delhi, Singapore: Sage.

Sunstein, Cass R. (2009). *Republic.com 2.0*. Princeton, NJ/Oxford: Princeton University Press.

Surowiecki, James (2005). *The Wisdom of Crowds*. New York: Anchor Books.

Tapscott, Don; Williams, Anthony D. (2008). *Wikinomics. How Mass Collaboration Changes Everything*. Expanded Edition. London: Atlantic Books.

Thorburn, David; Jenkins, Henry (eds) (2003). *Rethinking Media Change. The Aesthetics of Transition*. Cambridge/London: MIT Press.

Thurman, Neil (2008). 'Forums for Citizen Journalists? Adoption of User Generated Content Initiatives by Online News Media'. *New Media & Society* 10(1), 139–157.

Thussu, Daya Kishan (ed) (1998). *Electronic Empires. Global Media and Local Resistance*. London/New York/Sydney/Auckland: Arnold.

Thussu, Daya Kishan (2000). *International Communication: Continuity and Change*. London: Arnold.

Toffler, Alvin (1971). *Future Shock*. London: Pan.

Tomlinson, John (1999). *Globalization and Culture*. Oxford: Polity Press.

Tomlinson, John (2007). *The Culture of Speed. The Coming of Immediacy*. London/New Delhi/Singapore/Thousand Oaks, CA: Sage.

Urry, John (2003). *Global Complexity*. Malden, MA: Polity.

van Dijk, Jan (1999). *The Network Society: Social Aspects of New Media*. London/Thousand Oaks, CA: Sage.

van Dijk, Jan (2004). 'Digital Media'. In John D.H. Downing; Denis McQuail; Philip Schlesinger; Ellen Wartella (eds) *The SAGE Handbook of Media Studies* (pp.145–163). London/Thousand Oaks/New Delhi: Sage.

van Dijk, Jan (2005). *The Deepening Divide: Inequality in the Information Society*. London: Sage.

van Dijk, Jan (2006). *The Network Society: Social Aspects of New Media*. Second edition. London/Thousand Oaks/New Delhi: Sage.

Volkmer, Ingrid (1999). *News in the Global Sphere: A Study of CNN and its Impact on Global Communication*. Luton: University of Luton Press.

Volkmer, Ingrid (2003). 'The Global Network Society and the Global Public Sphere'. *Development* 46(1), 9–16.

Volkmer, Ingrid (2004). 'Im Zeitalter der weltweiten Vernetzung—Neue Herausforderungen fuer die Oeffentlich-Rechtlichen'. In Peter Christian Hall (ed) *Die Krise des Medienmarktes. Geld—Strukturen—Standards* (pp. 209–219). Mainz, Germany: Zweites Deutsches Fernsehen (Mainzer Tage der Fernseh-Kritik; 36).

Volkmer, Ingrid (2005). 'News in the Global Public Space'. In Stuart Allan (ed) *Journalism, Critical Issues* (pp. 357–369). Berkshire: Open University Press.

Volkmer, Ingrid (ed) (2006). *News In Public Memory: An International Study of Media Memories across Nations*. New York: Lang.

Volkmer, Ingrid (2007). 'Governing the "Spatial Reach"? Spheres of Influence and Challenges to Global Media Policy'. *International Journal of Communication* 1, 56–73.

Volkmer, Ingrid; Heinrich, Ansgard (2008). 'CNN and Beyond: Journalism in a Globalized Network Sphere'. In Jane Chapman; Marie Kinsey (eds) *Broadcast Journalism: A Critical Introduction* (pp. 49–57). London: Routledge.

Waisbord, Silvio (2004). 'Media and the Reinvention of the Nation'. In John D.H. Downing; Denis McQuail; Philip Schlesinger; Ellen Wartella (eds) *The SAGE*

Handbook of Media Studies (pp. 375–392). London/Thousand Oaks, CA/New Delhi: Sage.

Wall, Melissa A. (2003). 'Social Movements and the Net: Activist Journalism Goes Digital'. In Kevin Kawamoto (ed) *Digital Journalism. Emerging Media and the Changing Horizons of Journalism* (pp. 113–122). Lanham, MD: Rowman & Littlefield.

Wall, Melissa (2005). '"Blogs of War". Weblogs as news'. *Journalism* 6(2), 153–172.

Wardle, Claire; Williams, Andrew (2008). *ugc@thebbc. Understanding its Impact upon Contributors, Non-contributors and BBC News.* Cardiff University Report to the BBC Knowledge Exchange Programme and the Arts and Humanities Research Council, 16 September 2008. Retrieved January 10, 2010 from: www.bbc.co.uk/blogs/knowledgeexchange/cardiffone.pdf.

Watts, Duncan J. (2003). *Six Degrees. The Science of a Connected Age.* New York/London: W.W. Norton & Company.

Weaver, David (ed) (1998). *The Global Journalist: News People Around the World.* Cresskill, NJ: Hampton Press.

Webster, Frank (2002). *Theories of the Information Society.* Second Edition. London/New York: Routledge.

Webster, Frank (ed) (2004). *The Information Society Reader.* London/New York: Routledge.

Wegener, Claudia; Mikos, Lothar (2005). 'Wie lege ich eine Studie an?' In Lothar Mikos; Claudia Wegener (eds) *Qualitative Medienforschung. Ein Handbuch* (pp. 172–180). Konstanz: UVK.

Weinberger, David (2007). *Everything is Miscellaneous.* New York: Times Books.

Weiss, Robert (1994). *Learning from Strangers. The Art and Method of Qualitative Interview Studies.* New York: The Free Press.

Weischenberg, Siegfried; Scholl, Armin (1998). *Journalismus in der Gesellschaft: Theorie, Methodologie und Empirie.* Opladen: Westdeutscher Verlag.

Williams, Kevin (2006). 'Roundtable Discussion of Martin Conboy's "Journalism: A Critical History", London: Sage, 2004'. *Media History* 12(3), 336–342.

Willmore, Larry (2002). 'Government Policies Toward Information and Communication Technologies: A Historical Perspective'. *Journal of Information Science* 28(2), 89–98.

Winston, Brian (1998). *Media Technology and Society. A History: From the Telegraph to the Internet.* London/New York: Routledge.

Zelizer, Barbie; Allan, Stuart (eds) (2002). *Journalism After September 11.* New York/London: Routledge.

ONLINE SOURCES

Allbritton, Christopher (2010). 'About'. *Insurgencywatch.* Published online (no date), retrieved April 10, 2010: http://insurgencywatch.com/about/.

Amin, Salim (2007). 'Voice of Africa a Vision of Hope for Continent'. *The Sydney Morning Herald Online.* Published online August 27, retrieved July 24, 2010: http://www.smh.com.au/news/opinion/voice-of-africa-a-vision-of-hope-for-co ntinent/2007/08/26/1188066939921.html.

BBC News (author unknown) (2008). 'Accounts from Lhasa and Beyond'. *BBC News.* Published online March 18, retrieved July 24, 2010: http://news.bbc. co.uk/2/hi/asia-pacific/7302319.stm.

BBC News (author unknown) (2008). 'BBC Website 'Unblocked in China''. *BBC News.* Published online March 25, retrieved July 24, 2010: http://news.bbc. co.uk/2/hi/asia-pacific/7312240.stm.

BBC News (author unknown, quote Nikolas Macko) (2007). 'Student Describes Shooting Spree'. *BBC News*. Published online April 16, retrieved July 24, 2010: http://news.bbc.co.uk/2/hi/talking_point/6561733.stm.

BBC Press Office (2008). 'Live Report: BBC Russian Launches New Blogging Community on LiveJournal.com'. *BBC News*. Published online April 21, retrieved July 24, 2010: http://www.bbc.co.uk/pressoffice/pressreleases/stories/2008/04_april/21/russian.shtml.

Beaumont, Claudine (2009). 'New York Plane Crash. Twitter Breaks the News, Again'. *Telegraph.co.uk*. Published online January 16, retrieved July 24, 2010: http://www.telegraph.co.uk/technology/twitter/4269765/New-York-plane-crash-Twitter-breaks-the-news-again.html.

BILDblog (2008). 'YouTube überfuehrt "BILD-Leser-Reporter"'. *BILDblog*. Published online May 3, retrieved July 24, 2010: http://www.bildblog.de/2943/youtube-ueberfuehrt-bild-leser-reporter.

Blood, Rebecca (2004). 'A Few Thoughts on Journalism and What Can Weblogs Do About It'. *Rebecca's Pocket*. Published online April 15, retrieved July 24, 2010: http://www.rebeccablood.net/essays/what_is_journalism.html.

Bösch, Marcus (2008). 'Tibet 2.0—Blogger berichten aus dem Krisengebiet'. *Deutsche Welle Online*. Published online March 17, retrieved July 24, 2010: http://www.dw-world.de/dw/article/0,2144,3198777,00.html.

Bunz, Mercedes (2010). 'BBC Teams Up with Citizen Journalists' Network Global Voices'. *Guardian.co.uk PDA The Digital Content Blog*. Published online March 9, retrieved July 24, 2010: http://www.guardian.co.uk/media/pda/2010/mar/09/blogging-digital-media.

Carr, Nicholas (2005). 'The Amorality of Web 2.0'. *Rough Type*. Published online October 3, retrieved July 24, 2010: http://www.roughtype.com/archives/2005/10/the_amorality_o.php.

Carr, Nicholas (2007). 'Twitter Dot Dash'. *RoughType*. Published online March 18, retrieved July 24, 2010: http://www.roughtype.com/archives/2007/03/the_telegraph_o.php.

Catt, Dan; Pickard, Meg (2010). 'What's Hot? Introducing Zeitgeist'. *Inside Guardian.co.uk Blog*. Published online February 3, retrieved July 24, 2010: http://www.guardian.co.uk/help/insideguardian/2010/feb/03/zeitgeist.

Cohn, David (2007). 'Network Journalism Versus Citizen Journalism Versus the Myriad of Other Names for Social Media in the News World'. *Newassignment*. Published online September 6, retrieved July 24, 2010: http://www.newassignment.net/blog/david_cohn/sep2007/06/network_journali.

Conde, Mara (2010). 'BBC and Global Voices Announce Partnership'. *Editorsweblog.org*. Published online March 9, retrieved July 24, 2010: http://www.editorsweblog.org/newsrooms_and_journalism/2010/03/bbc_and_global_voices_announce_partnersh.php.

Cyberjournalist.net (author unknown) (2007). 'Press Release: CNN to Launch User-Generated Video Show On-Air'. *Cyberjournalist.net*. Published online May 14, retrieved July 24, 2010: http://www.cyberjournalist.net/news/004204.php.

Drudge Report (2008). 'Prince Harry Fights On Frontlines In Afghanistan'. *Drudge Report*. Published online February 28, retrieved July 24, 2010: http://www.drudgereportarchives.com/data/2008/02/28/20080228_164320_flashph.htm.

Dyer, Geoff (2008). 'Monks' Tibet Protest Gives Voice to Anger'. *FinancialTimes.com*. Published online March 27, retrieved April 01, 2008: http://www.ft.com/cms/s/0/3c19875a-fbf8-11dc-9229-000077b07658.html?nclick_check=1.

Facebook Press Room (2010). *Statistics*. Published online (no date), retrieved July 24, 2010: http://www.facebook.com/press/info.php?statistics.

Friedman, Jon (2008). 'Prince Harry Blackout Sets a Bad Media Precedent'. *Marketwatch*. Published online March 5, retrieved July 24,

2010: http://www.marketwatch.com/news/story/prince-harry-black-out-sets-bad/story.aspx?guid=9D914379-E94E-4B48-B2EF-11-D7042A1895&dist=SecMostRead.

Frontline (2008). 'Growing Up Online'. Documentary. *PBS.org*. Airdate January 22, 2008. Published online, retrieved July 24, 2010: http://www.pbs.org/wgbh/pages/frontline/kidsonline/.

Fulton, Kate (1996). 'A Tour of Our Uncertain Future'. *Columbia Journalism Review*. Published online March/April 1996, retrieved March 27, 2008: http://backissues.cjrarchives.org/year/96/2/tour.asp.

Gardham, Duncan (2008). 'Matt Drudge Expresses No Regret For Prince Harry Report'. *Telegraph.co.uk*. Published online March 01, retrieved July 24, 2010: http://www.telegraph.co.uk/news/main.jhtml?xml=/news/2008/02/29/wdrudge229.xml.

Gorman, Steve (2007). 'Al Gore Collects Interactive Emmy for Current TV'. *Reuters.com*. Published online September 17, retrieved July 24, 2010: http://www.reuters.com/article/technologyNews/idUSN1341763520070917.

Harnden, Toby (2008). 'Matt Drudge: World's Most Powerful Journalist'. *Telegraph.co.uk*. Published online March 03, retrieved July 24, 2010: http://www.telegraph.co.uk/news/main.jhtml?xml=/news/2008/02/28/wdrudge128.xml.

Herrmann, Steve (2010). 'SuperPower: BBC and Global Voices'. *BBC News. The Editors*. Published online March 8, retrieved July 24, 2010: http://www.bbc.co.uk/blogs/theeditors/2010/03/superpower_bbc_and_global_voic.html.

Horrigan, John (2006). 'More Americans Turn to the Internet for News about Politics'. Report published by the Pew Internet & American Life Project. *Pewinternet.org*. Published online September 20, retrieved July 24, 2010: http://www.pewinternet.org/PPF/r/187/report_display.asp.

Horrocks, Peter (2007). 'Multimedia News'. *BBC News. The Editors*. Published online November 12, retrieved July 24, 2010: http://www.bbc.co.uk/blogs/theeditors/2007/11/multimedia_news.html.

Horrocks, Peter (2010). 'BBC's SuperPower Season'. *BBC News. The Editors*. Published online March 8, retrieved July 24, 2010: http://www.bbc.co.uk/blogs/theeditors/2010/03/bbcs_superpower_season.html.

Horowitz, Bradley (2006). *Creators, Synthesizers, and Consumers, Elatable*. Published online February 16, retrieved July 24, 2010: http://blog.elatable.com/search?q=creators+synthesizers.

Howe, Jeff (2006). 'The Rise of Crowdsourcing'. *Wired*. Published online June, retrieved July 24, 2010: http://www.wired.com/wired/archive/14.06/crowds.html.

International Herald Tribune/Associated Press (2008). 'China Slams Foreign Media while Restricting Access to Tibet'. *International Herald Tribune*. Published online March 19, retrieved April 01, 2008: http://www.iht.com/articles/ap/2008/03/19/asia/AS-GEN-China-Tibet-Media.php.

Jarvis, Jeff (2006). 'Networked Journalism'. *BuzzMachine*. Published online July 5, retrieved July 24, 2010: http://www.buzzmachine.com/2006/07/05/networked-journalism/.

Karp, Scott (2008a). 'How Link Journalism Could Have Transformed The New York Times reporting On McCain Ethics'. *Publishing2.0*. Published online February 25, retrieved July 24, 2010: http://publishing2.com/2008/02/25/how-link-journalism-could-have-transformed-the-new-york-times-reporting-on-mc-cain-ethics/.

Karp, Scott (2008b). 'How Networked Link Journalism Can Give Journalists Collectively the Power of Google and Digg'. *Publishing2.0*. Published online February 29, retrieved July 24, 2010: http://publishing2.com/2008/02/29/how-networked-link-journalism-can-give-journalists-collectively-the-power-of-google-and-digg/.

Kiss, Jemima (2008). 'China 'unblocks' BBC news Site'. *Guardian.co.uk*. Published online March 25, retrieved July 24, 2010: http://www.guardian.co.uk/media/2008/mar/25/digitalmedia.chinathemedia.

Kleinz, Thorsten (2008). 'Zensierte Hoffnung'. *ZEIT ONLINE*. Published online March 18, retrieved July 24, 2010: http://www.zeit.de/online/2008/12/tibet-zensur-internet?page=all.

Lemann, Nicholas (2006). 'Amateur Hour: Journalism without Journalists'. *The New Yorker*. Published online August 07, retrieved July 24, 2010: http://www.newyorker.com/archive/2006/08/07/060807fa_fact1.

Lenhart, Amanda; Purcell, Kristen; Smith, Aaron; Zickuhr, Kathryn (2010). 'Social Media and Young Adults'. Report published by the Pew Internet & American Life Project. *Pewinternet.rg*. Published online February 3, retrieved July 24, 2010: http://www.pewinternet.org/Reports/2010/Social-Media-and-Young-Adults.aspx.

Mayfield, Antony (2008). 'Network Journalism: What's in a Word?' *TypePad*. Published online July 08, retrieved July 24, 2010: http://open.typepad.com/open/2006/07/network_journal.html.

McCarthy, Rory (2003). 'Salam's Story'. *Guardian.co.uk*. Published online May 30, retrieved July 24, 2010: http://www.guardian.co.uk/world/2003/may/30/iraq.digitalmedia.

McMahon, Barbara; Brown, Maggie; Dowling, Tim (2008). 'Apology for Royal Scoop of the Year'. *Guardian.co.uk*. Published online March 17, retrieved July 24, 2010: http://www.guardian.co.uk/media/2008/mar/10/pressandpublishing.television.

New York Times/Associated Press (2008). 'China Blocks YouTube After Videos of Tibet Protests Are Posted'. *New York Times*. Published online March 17, retrieved December 20, 2010: http://www.nytimes.com/2008/03/17/business/media/17youtube.html?scp=3&sq=china%20blocks%20youtube&st=cse.

PEW Research Center For The People & The Press (multiple authors) (2009). *Press Accuracy Rating Hits Two Decade Low*. Survey report published by the Pew Research Center for the People & the Press. Published Online September 13, retrieved July 24, 2010: http://people-press.org/report/543/.

Pierce, Andrew (2008). 'Prince Harry Fighting Taliban in Afghanistan'. *Telegraph.co.uk*. Published online March 1, retrieved July 24, 2010: http://www.telegraph.co.uk/news/main.jhtml?xml=/news/2008/02/29/nharry129.xml.

Project for Excellence in Journalism (multiple authors) (2008a). 'Audience'. *The State of the News Media 2008. An Annual Report on American Journalism*. Published online, retrieved July 24, 2010: http://www.stateofthenewsmedia.com/2008/narrative_overview_audience.php?cat=3&media=1.

Project for Excellence in Journalism (multiple authors) (2008b). 'News Investment'. *The State of the News Media 2008. An Annual Report on American Journalism*. Published online, retrieved July 24, 2010: http://www.stateofthenewsmedia.com/2008/narrative_cabletv_newsinvestment.php?cat=5&media=7.

Project for Excellence in Journalism (multiple authors) (2010a). 'Nielsen Analysis'. *The State of the News Media 2010. An Annual Report on American Journalism*. Published online, retrieved July 23, 2010: http://www.stateofthemedia.org/2010/online_nielsen.php.

Project for Excellence in Journalism (multiple authors) (2010b). *The State of the News Media. An Annual Report on American Journalism*. Published online, retrieved July 24, 2010: http://www.stateofthemedia.org/2010/index.php.

Purcell, Kristen; Rainie, Lee; Mitchell, Amy; Rosenstiel, Tom; Olmstead, Kenny (2010). *Understanding the Participatory News Consumer. How Internet and Cell Phone Users Have Turned News into a Social Experience*. Report published by the Pew Internet & American Life Project. Published online in March, retrieved July 24, 2010: http://www.pewinternet.org/Reports/2010/Online-News.aspx.

Radio Television Digital News Association (author and publication date unknown). *Social Media and Blogging Guidelines.* Retrieved July 24, 2010: http://www.rtdna.org/pages/media_items/social-media-and-blogging-guidelines1915.php?g=37?id=1915.

Reuters Handbook of Journalism (author unknown) (2008). *Social Media Guidelines.* Published in April, retrieved July 24, 2010: http://handbook.reuters.com/index.php/Reporting_from_the_internet#Social_media_guidelines.

Rice, Anita (2004). 'Baghdad Blogger: 'Elections Our Only Hope''. *BBC News,* Published online October 12, retrieved July 24, 2010: http://news.bbc.co.uk/2/hi/programmes/newsnight/3733104.stm.

Robinson, James (2008). 'On screen, Online and on the Airwaves: BBC News Comes Together'. *Guardian.co.uk.* Published online April 20, retrieved July 24, 2010: http://www.guardian.co.uk/media/2008/apr/20/bbc.television.

Rosen, Jay (2005). 'Bloggers vs. Journalists is Over'. *Pressthink.* Published online January 21, retrieved July 24, 2010: http://journalism.nyu.edu/pubzone/weblogs/pressthink/2005/01/21/berk_essy.html.

Rosen, Jay (2006). 'The People Formerly Known as the Audience'. *Pressthink.* Published online June 27, retrieved July 24, 2010: http://journalism.nyu.edu/pubzone/weblogs/pressthink/2006/06/27/ppl_frmr.html.

Samuelson, Robert J. (2006). 'A Web of Exhibitionists'. *Washington Post.* Published online September 20, retrieved July 24, 2010: http://www.washingtonpost.com/wp-dyn/content/article/2006/09/19/AR2006091901439.html.

Stabe, Martin (2008). 'BBC News Opens Multi-platform Newsroom'. *PressGazette.co.uk.* Published online April 24, retrieved July 24, 2010: http://www.pressgazette.co.uk/story.asp?sectioncode=1&storycode=40958&c=1.

Stelter, Brian (2010). 'Honoring Citizen Journalists'. *New York Times.* Published online February 21, retrieved July 24, 2010: http://www.nytimes.com/2010/02/22/business/media/22polk.html?_r=2&ref=business.

Stillich, Sven (2003). 'Wir müssen Hoffnung haben. Interview with Salam Pax'. *Stern.de.* Published online October 13, retrieved December 10, 2010: http://www.stern.de/digital/online/salam-pax-wir-muessen-hoffnung-haben-514341.html.

Stray, Jonathan (2010). 'The Google/China Hacking case: How Many News Outlets Do the Original Reporting on a Big Story? *Nieman Journalism Lab.* Published online February 24, retrieved July 24, 2010: http://www.niemanlab.org/2010/02/the-googlechina-hacking-case-how-many-news-outlets-do-the-original-reporting-on-a-big-story/.

Sweney, Mark (2008). 'China Blocks Media Due to Tibet Unrest''. *Guardian.co.uk.* Published online March 17, retrieved July 24, 2010: http://www.guardian.co.uk/media/2008/mar/17/chinathemedia.digitalmedia.

Sweney, Mark (2008). 'Wikileaks Defies 'Great Firewall of China''. *Guardian.co.uk.* Published online March 19, retrieved July 24, 2010: http://www.guardian.co.uk/media/2008/mar/19/digitalmedia.tibet.

The Sydney Morning Herald (author unknown) (2006). 'Kovco Died in 'Gun Bungle''. *Sydney Morning Herald.* Published online December 01, retrieved July 24, 2010: http://www.smh.com.au/news/national/kovco-died-in-gun-bungle/2006/12/01/1164777779394.html.

Watts, Jonathan (2008). 'Tibetan Monks Disrupt Chinese Show of Stability'. *Guardian.co.uk.* Published online March 28, retrieved July 24, 2010: http://www.guardian.co.uk/world/2008/mar/28/tibet.china.

Wikileaks Press Release (2008). 'Wikileaks Releases Over 150 Censored Videos and Photos of the Tibet Uprising'. *Wikileaks.org.* Published online March 18,

retrieved July 24, 2010: http://www.wikileaks.org/wiki/Wikileaks_releases_
over_150_censored_videos_and_photos_of_the_Tibet_uprising.

Yahoo! News (2008). 'What's in Kevin's Gearbag'. *Yahoo.com*. Published online
(date unknown), retrieved June 23, 2008: http://hotzone.yahoo.com/gear;_
ylt=AjWQ61YduyuDQzTQlgH.Il.LFMsF.

YouTube (2008). 'Autos Brennen Hamburg Demo 1.Mai Polizei Demo Teil 1'. *You-
Tube*. Published online May 01, retrieved June 23, 2008: http://youtube.com/
watch?v=5ALYMaPU8Og.

WWW.MATERIAL: RESEARCH SAMPLE

AlterNet.org
http://www.alternet.org
Background information on *AlterNet*: http://www.alternet.org/about/

BBC News
http://www.bbc.co.uk
Background information on BBC: http://www.bbc.co.uk/historyofthebbc//
BBC Interactive 'Have Your Say': http://news.bbc.co.uk/2/hi/talking_point/4784595.stm
'Fleeing Iraq': http://news.bbc.co.uk/2/hi/talking_point/6176457.stm
'Voices From Iraq': http://news.bbc.co.uk/2/shared/spl/hi/middle_east/02/voices_
from_iraq/html/default.stm

Current TV
http://current.com
Background information on *Current TV*: http://current.com/s/about.htm; http://
current.com/s/faq.htm

Democracy Now!
http://www.democracynow.org
Background information on *Democracy Now!*
http://www.democracynow.org/about/history
http://www.democracynow.org/about

Guardian.co.uk
http://guardian.co.uk
Background information on the Guardian Media Group: http://www.guardian.
co.uk/information/0,,711853,00.html; http://www.guardian.co.uk/information/
theguardian/story/0,,1038110,00.html; http://www.gmgplc.co.uk/; http://www.
guardian.co.uk/g24/0,,1820858,00.html
Guardian 'Comment is Free': http://commentisfree.guardian.co.uk/index.html

Independent Media Center New York City
http://nyc.indymedia.org/en/index.html
Background information on *Indymedia*: http://www.indymedia.org/en/static/
about.shtml
http://docs.indymedia.org/view/Global/FrequentlyAskedQuestionEn

International Center for Journalists
http://www.icfj.org/index.html
Background information on ICFJ: http://www.icfj.org/AboutUs/tabid/202/Default.
aspx

ICFJ Manual 'Fighting Words': http://www.icfj.org/Resources/ManualFighting-Words/tabid/425/Default.aspx
Background information IJNet: http://www.ijnet.org/Director.aspx?P=Home

MediaChannel.org
http://www.mediachannel.org
Background information on *MediaChannel*: http://www.mediachannel.org/word-press/about/; http://www.mediachannel.org/wordpress/about/faq/

Ourmedia.org
http://ourmedia.org
Background information on *Ourmedia*: http://ourmedia.org//about
Ourmedia partner organizations: The Internet Archive: http://www.archive.org/index.php

Outhink: http://www.outhink.com/
Revver: http://revver.com
Broadbandmechanics: http://www.broadbandmechanics.com/

Project for Excellence in Journalism PEJ
http://www.journalism.org
Background information PEJ: http://www.journalism.org/about_pej/about_us
PEW Research Center: http://pewresearch.org/

ZEIT ONLINE
http://www.zeit.de
Background information on ZEIT ONLINE: http://www.zeit.de/zeitverlag/zeit_online; http://www.zeit.de/news/index
ZEIT ONLINE blogs mentioned: Blog 'Herdentrieb': http://blog.zeit.de/herden-trieb/ Blog 'Beruf Terrorist': http://blog.zeit.de/bittner/

ADDITIONAL ONLINE REFERENCES

Alive In Baghdad: http://aliveinbaghdad.org/
Back to Iraq: http://www.back-to-iraq.com/
BILDBlog: http://www.bildblog.de
Blogs! Buch Blog / Blogbar: http://blogbar.de/index.php
Blogscope: http://www.blogscope.net/
BuzzMachine: http://www.buzzmachine.com
Center for Citizen Media: http://www.citmedia.org/
CNN I-Report: http://edition.cnn.com/exchange/ireports/spotlight.html
Cyberjournalist.Net: http://www.cyberjournalist.net/news/004204.php
Drudge Report: http://www.drudgereport.com
Globalvision: http://www.globalvision.org/
Global Voices: http://www.globalvoicesonline.org/
Healing Iraq: http://www.healingiraq.blogspot.com/
Indymedia: http://www.independentmedia.org/
InsurgencyWatch: http://www.insurgencywatch.com/
Journalism.co.uk: http://www.journalism.co.uk
Kevin Sites Blog: http://kevinsites.net
Livejournal: http://www.livejournal.com/
MediaShift: http://www.pbs.org/mediashift/

MoveOn.org: http://www.moveon.org/
MySpace: http://www.myspace.com/
Nielsen Net Ratings: http://en-us.nielsen.com/content/nielsen/en_us/product_families/nielsen_netratings.html
NowPublic: http://www.nowpublic.com/
NowPublic 'Mumbai terror attacks' coverage: http://www.nowpublic.com/tag/mumbai
OneWorld.net: http://www.oneworld.net
OhMyNews International: http://english.ohmynews.com/
Publish2 Blog: http://blog.publish2.com
Riverbend Baghdad Burning: http://riverbendblog.blogspot.com/
RoughType: http://www.roughtype.com/
Technorati: http://technorati.com/
TalkingPointsMemo: http://www.talkingpointsmemo.com
Twitter: http://twitter.com
Where is Raed?: http://dear_raed.blogspot.com/
Wikileaks.org: http://wikileaks.org/
Yahoo: 'Kevin in the Hotzone' http://hotzone.yahoo.com/

Index

A

ABC, 102, 244
accountability or accountable, 149,
    150, 158–168, 180, 244n3
activist, 70, 71, 74, 80, 97, 99, 101,
    115, 158, 159, 161, 175, 209;
    see also media activist
Afghanistan, 51, 69, 75, 76, 151, 159,
    185, 193, 203
Africa, 2, 9, 46, 68, 72, 191, 193, 194,
    196, 215, 219, 230
Agence France Press (AFP), 196, 237n2,
    238n15
aggregation site or website, 52, 75,
    77, 80, 92, 103; aggregate or
    aggregating information, 216,
    218, 219; news aggregator 101;
    blogging aggregation platform,
    147
agenda, 4, 48, 74, 76, 81, 99, 200, 203;
    setter, 49, 216; agenda-setting,
    5, 68, 69, 74–77, 84, 107; news,
    21, 28, 51, 68, 75, 104, 115,
    116, 140, 186, 212
Agha-Soltan, Neda: *see* Neda
Alive in Baghdad, 80, 202, 244n5
Al Jazeera, 4, 18, 34, 239, 241, 244n1
Allbritton, Christopher, 1, 80, 202, 203
alternative: journalism, 3, 188, 211,
    230; media, 63, 92, 96, 98, 101,
    113, 121, 139, 145, 152, 159,
    160–165, 208, 211, 219; news
    deliverer, 52, 71, 116; news dis-
    seminator, 166, 208, 210, 218;
    news or information provider,
    10, 72, 91, 93, 121, 144, 138,
    204, 206, 209, 212, 229, 230;
    news producer, 122, 167; news
    outlet, 89, 114, 116–118, 121,

163; source, 70, 74, 77, 78, 87,
    132, 137, 161, 193, 195, 198,
    204, 209, 212, 216, 229, 230;
    see also independent media
AlterNet, 10, 88, 92, 101, 102–103,
    164, 165, 172, 178, 179, 216,
    241n7
Americanization, 16
Anderson, Benedict R., 65
Appadurai, Arjun, 8, 17, 18, 233n3,
    236n25
Associated Press, (AP) 43–45, 46–50,
    83, 140, 196, 203, 206, 237n2,
    238n11
Atton, Chris, 3, 98, 113, 230
audience, 4, 5, 8, 19, 33, 41, 54, 57–59,
    63, 65, 77–82, 90, 94, 103,
    109, 115, 127–132, 137, 139,
    146, 153, 157, 159–161, 164,
    169–182, 187, 192, 199, 208,
    210, 214, 222, 226, 227; global,
    4, 21, 66, 187, 199, 202; *see
    also* user

B

Back to Iraq, 203
backpack journalist, 1, 183, 187–193,
    194, 199, 202, 204, 226
Bardoel Jo, 51, 56, 59, 60, 61, 62, 77,
    78, 79
Bardoel, Jo and Mark Deuze, 51, 56,
    59, 60, 61, 62, 77
BBC, 10, 18, 19, 57, 65, 70, 88, 92–94,
    113, 124, 125, 128–133, 141,
    151, 171, 174, 182, 189, 191–
    193, 196, 197–198, 202, 203,
    210, 214, 216, 217, 219, 222,
    224, 241nn7–10, 242nn2–3,
    244n6; BBC News Interactivity

Desk, 92–94, 127–133, 142, 171, 214, 224, 183, 193; Fleeing Iraq, 204; Have your Say, 70, 93, 94, 107, 128, 171–172, 175, 179; Iraqi Voices, 204

Beck, Ulrich, 8, 14, 16, 17, 21, 22, 233n3

Beckett, Charlie, 51, 56, 58, 62

Been There: *see* Guardian

Benkler, Yochai, 4, 5, 51, 52, 61, 81, 89, 238n3

BILDBlog, 165, 166

blog, the, 1, 56, 70, 71, 72, 79, 92, 107, 110, 112, 114, 117, 133, 135, 139, 141, 147–168, 172, 174–178, 187, 197, 202, 203, 205, 209, 210, 217, 219, 227, 231; weblog, 68, 72

blogger, 1, 2, 3, 4, 5, 8, 9, 31, 33, 52, 55, 65, 70–72, 74, 80, 89, 91, 118, 120, 124–126, 135, 138, 141, 146, 147–168, 175, 177, 183, 193, 194, 196, 197, 199, 200–202, 204–206, 208–210, 212, 219, 220, 221, 228, 230; blogging, 58, 137, 180, 213, 226; blogging guide, 106; blogosphere, 56, 58, 147, 148, 150, 157, 158, 162, 165, 166, 177, 201, 211

Boston Globe, 102, 167, 203

Boyd-Barrett, Oliver, 37, 42, 43, 47, 49, 53

Boxing Day tsunami, 4, 127, 128, 134–135, 187

Bruns, Axel, 2, 52, 170

C

Carey, James W., 36, 37, 42, 234n8

Castells, Manuel, 7, 9, 13, 15, 22–31, 51, 55, 62, 77, 80–82, 228, 231, 235nn18–20

CBS, 244n1

celebrity TV, 171, 243n1

chaos, 31; chaos: of a global news culture, 28; of the digital age, 82; *see also* cultural chaos

China, 69, 70, 71, 93, 202, 213, 219, 237n4, 242n4

citizen journalism or journalist, 2, 3, 4, 5, 31, 56–58, 61, 67, 70, 71, 79, 89, 91, 96, 98, 99, 100, 101, 105, 106, 107, 124, 125, 136, 138–146, 147, 152, 158–161,

163, 165–167, 175, 183, 193, 196, 197, 200, 202, 204, 206, 208–210, 212–217, 219, 220, 221, 226, 227, 228–231; participation, 72, 73, 101

CNN, 18, 19, 34, 65, 66, 70, 77, 98, 102, 114, 115, 119, 122, 127, 133, 143, 183, 187, 203, 239n6, 244n1

Cohn, David ,56, 57, 61, 62

collaboration, 5, 10, 54, 55, 82, 90, 129, 131, 141, 142, 155, 177, 193, 196, 197, 203, 204, 207–231; collaborate or collaborative, 47, 52, 57, 58, 59, 64, 78, 84, 91, 107, 111, 132, 206

Comment is free: *see* Guardian

connection: digital 2, 50, 74, 167, 183, 188; global 28, 30, 36, 107, 213

connectivity, 2, 4, 7, 13, 14, 18, 19, 21, 23–25, 27, 35, 37, 50, 52, 53, 56, 64, 154; connectivity or connect (users) 120, 129, 141, 156, 157, 174, 182; new or changing or transformed, 33, 34, 61–63, 71, 77–80, 84, 93, 107

consumer (of news), 6, 44, 53, 54, 65, 78, 80, 104, 107, 113, 119, 122, 132, 148, 160, 170–174, 176, 180, 181, 234, 240; consumption, 5, 60, 80, 81, 172, 174, 180

convergence or converged, 3, 53, 60, 90, 221–224; newsroom, 10, 81, 82, 223; global culture, 16; media space, 61, 97

control: distributed to users, 53, 60; editorial, 42; elite, 28; of information or news flows,50, 51, 208, 228; loss of, 67, 68, 69, 70, 73, 74, 76, 145, 154–155, 166; mechanisms, 161, 165; over the telegraph, 45, 47, 48, 49; paradigm, 27, 28, 236; state, 71

conversation (journalism as), 56, 57, 120, 122, 149, 150, 154, 166, 169, 171, 174–179, 182, 198, 212, 215; *see also* dialogue

credibility, 118, 158–168, 172, 201, 204, 219, 226, 231

crossmedia: to work across media, 82, 87, 189, 191; analysis of, 90; competence, 81, reporter, 223; 82; skills, 221; across platforms, 173, 214, 225, 230

crowdsourcing, 57, 130, 154, 177, 211, 217, 242n4
culture: global news, 7, 8, 27, 28, 29, 79, 84; journalism or journalistic, 3, 4, 9, 10, 19, 20, 22, 28, 29, 62, 83, 89, 91, 223; Arab journalism, 241; of real virtuality, 24
cultural: chaos, 3, 27, 29, 33; flows, 66; economy, 18, 19; imperialism, 16, 17, 234n9; production, 7, 16, 19
Current TV, 10, 88, 92, 96, 99–101, 142, 143, 144, 157, 159, 165, 172, 176, 179, 183, 187, 189, 190, 197, 204, 215, 217, 227, 241n7, 243n8
Cyberspace, 23, 24, 25, 26, 193, 235n16, 236n21

D

decentralization or decentralized, 4, 5, 21, 24, 29, 30, 32, 50, 51, 53, 55, 61, 63, 69, 76, 78, 84, 87, 98, 161, 161, 167, 207, 226, 227, 229
Democracy Now!, 10, 80, 88, 92, 96–97, 109–111, 114–116, 123, 141, 189, 193, 222, 241n7
Deuze, Mark, 3, 20, 28, 51, 56, 59–62, 68–69, 77, 80–82, 222–223
dialogue (journalism as), 58, 119, 166–167, 170–172, 174, 179; *see also* conversation
Digg, 59
digital: age, 3, 62, 77, 81–83, 170; camera, 4, 126, 203; capitalism, 26; divide, 60, 68, 72, 236n24, 243n2; native, 180; space, 2, 53, 55, 72, 79, 152
digitalization, 2, 3, 23, 50, 62, 108, 112, 183, 184; digitalization (introduction to newsrooms), 108–123
digital technology, 2, 3, 6, 7, 8, 13–15, 23, 28–30, 33–36, 53, 54, 56, 59, 61, 67, 68, 70, 73, 74, 78, 79, 87, 89–92, 107–111, 113, 116, 120, 122, 139, 144, 174, 183, 188, 206–208, 213, 217, 230; training, 218; tool, 4, 13, 23, 27, 62, 72, 80, 82–84, 87, 89, 92, 107, 108, 111, 114, 120, 173, 217

dissemination: information, 1, 33, 34, 39, 55, 68, 69, 71, 78, 157, 161, 166, 173, 228; journalistic, 2, 7, 22, 31; knowledge, 6; news, 4, 6, 21, 35, 38, 49, 50, 52, 56, 61, 68, 77, 79, 82, 87, 107–109, 113, 120, 171, 209, 215, 226, 228; modes, 8–10; platforms, 76, 146, 219, 222, 224, 225; technologies, 32, 139; production and, 2, 4, 6, 8, 10, 21, 22, 31, 50, 52, 55, 56, 78, 79, 82, 87, 91, 93, 107, 108, 120, 144, 173, 209, 214, 215, 226, 228
Douglass, Frederick, 139, 242n7
Drudge Report, 52, 75, 77, 239n8

E

Entman, Robert M., 75

F

Facebook, 2, 54, 65, 72, 93, 94, 111, 117, 169, 180, 181, 217
fact-checking, 53, 55, 68, 126, 148, 149, 161, 163, 164, 166, 177, 215
Featherstone, Mike, 14, 17, 233n3
Featherstone, Mike and Scott Lash, 67
Flickr, 72, 79
foreign correspondence or correspondent, 4, 65, 66–68, 70, 73, 74, 80, 84, 111, 183–199, 200–202, 226; foreign news, 42, 64–66, 183, 193, 194, 203–205; foreign reporting, 10, 21, 65, 66, 107, 183, 184, 193, 198, 203, 206
foreign policy, 3, 97
Four Theories of the Press, The, 28, 236n23
Fox News, 158, 244n1

G

Garnham, Nicholas, 25, 26
gatekeeping or gatekeeper, 5, 49, 52, 64, 67, 68, 69–74, 75–77, 84, 107, 114, 115, 117, 133, 212, 239n6, 240n11
geography, new of journalism, 8, 9, 10, 22, 29, 31, 33, 34, 79, 228
Gibson, William, 23, 24, 235n16
Giddens, Anthony, 14, 16, 19, 22, 27, 233n3
Gillmor, Dan, 52, 56, 211, 212
global or globalized: audience, 21, 187, 199, 202; complexity, 66;

communication, 21, 30, 37; cultural economy; exchange 14, 53, 65, 109; flow of news or information, 2, 9, 10, 18, 22, 25, 31–33, 50, 66, 71, 78, 112, 113, 120, 122, 124, 138, 183, 193, 207, 208, 214, 217, 231; information sphere, 55, 139, 168, 170, 192, 228; news culture, 7, 8; journalism or journalistic, 31, 50, 61, 62, 67, 229; news sphere, 10, 22, 31–35, 50, 53, 55, 56, 61, 77, 80, 83, 84, 89, 91, 92, 112, 116, 117, 120–122, 141, 151, 152, 230; 18; sphere, 3, 28, 67, 172, 193, 195, 198, 206; village, 16; world 8, 16, 17, 56, 193, 194, 206

globalization, 2, 3, 7, 8, 9, 13, 14–23, 26, 28, 30, 32, 34, 35, 62, 112, 183, 184, 194, 206, 230, 233n3, 237n6, 238n15

global and local, 17, 21, 34, 64–66, 109, 112, 138, 183, 193–195, 213; local-global axis, 17

Global Voices Online, 2, 9, 56, 72, 93, 141, 147, 197, 212, 230, 241n10

glocalization, 17, 19; glocal perspectives, 193; glocalized sphere, 22

Google, 59, 150, 155, 164, 196, 217, 218, 220, 242n4

grassroot, 57, 73, 97, 98, 120, 139, 140, 146, 179, 196, 211, 213

Guardian, 70, 94–95, 111, 134, 149, 150, 153, 154, 163, 164, 170–172, 175, 179, 220–222, 225, 241n7; Guardian Media Group, 10, 88, 92, 94, 95, 175; Been There, 175; Comment is free, 94, 95, 171, 175; Zeitgeist, 94

H

Haiti, 52, 94, 116, 187

Hallin, Daniel C. and Paolo Mancini, 20

Hanitzsch, Thomas, 19, 20

Hannerz, Ulf, 15, 17

Havas, 45, 47, 48

Healing Iraq, 202

Herdentrieb, 157, 243n4

Herman, Edward S. and Robert W. McChesney, 17, 234n9

heterogenization, 19, heterogenic movements, 17

homogenization, 16, 17, 234n10

Hudson River plane crash, 76

Hurricane Katrina, 192

I

impartiality or impartial, 20, 43, 144, 150, 151, 158

independent media, 89, 92, 96, 98, 100, 102, 105, 116, 141; *see also* alternative media

Indymedia or Independent Media Center, 10, 88, 92, 96, 97, 98–99, 113, 115, 116, 121–123, 138, 141, 143–146, 179, 220, 241n7

information: age, 6, 8, 9, 13, 19, 24, 27, 30, 31, 33–35, 50, 59, 64, 74, 107, 147, 155; society, 9, 25, 36; technology revolution, 24; string: *see* string

Innis, Harold, 37, 42, 47, 237n3

interactivity, 23, 33, 58, 60, 62, 92, 138, 154, 171, 173, 176, 178, 179, 182, 209, 211, 244; interactive, 2, 33, 34, 42, 161, 155, 166, 174, 177, 227, 231;

interaction, 14, 30, 33, 34, 54, 67, 73, 87, 89, 129, 154, 173, 174, 176, 178, 181, 190, 212, 215, 218; pattern, 9, 13, 23, 24, 26, 29, 32, 36, 61, 76, 173, 174, 176, 178

Interactivity Desk (BBC): *see* BBC

International Center for Journalists (ICFJ), 10, 88, 92, 104–106, 120, 162, 163, 196, 241n7

internationalization of news or international news 18, 37, 41, 42–49, 50, 65, 112, 116, 196

International Center for Journalists (ICFJ), 10, 105–106

Internet, 2, 5, 6, 7, 13, 18, 21–26, 29, 30, 31, 37, 51, 53–55, 57, 68, 71, 72, 83, 89, 90, 93, 105, 108, 110–112, 114, 117, 120, 121, 138, 141, 148, 163, 173, 174, 176, 180, 181, 184, 189, 193, 198, 219, 235n17, 240n3, 241n1

Iran, 1, 4, 9, 52, 64, 70, 93, 94

Iraq, 2, 80, 151, 185, 186, 193, 195, 220–222, Iraq War, 1, 80, 107, 111, 114, 158, 159, 183, 194, 195, 198, 199–206; Iraqi blogger, 80, 199–201, 244n3 iReport, 127, 133, 242n1

J

Jarvis, Jeff, 56, 57, 58, 61, 62, 155, 239n4
Jenkins, Henry, 90, 173–174
journalistic culture: *see* culture
journalistic practice, 2, 3, 5, 8, 9, 10, 13, 16, 20, 28, 37, 55, 68, 82, 87–93, 106, 108, 109, 132, 140, 147, 195, 209, 222, 224, 227–229, 231, 233n3

K

Karp, Scott, 58, 59, 62
Keen, Andrew, 5, 6, 82, 220, 233n3
Kenya, 68, 71, 72–74, 76

L

Lash, Scott and John Urry, 18
Lebanon War, 128, 171, 189
Lévy, Pierre, 54
LexisNexis, 164
linear: character of the telegraph, 47; flow of information, 30, 37; information flows, 49; media system, 4; news flows, 35, 50, 51; news flow structure, 62
London bombings, 1, 125, 128
Lovink, Geert, 52, 241n1
Luhmann, Niklas, 32–34, 236n26–28
Luyendijk, Joris, 186

M

mass media, 53, 65, 74, 139; mass media system, 5, 32, 33, 41, 75, 79, 236n26–28
many to many: communication of, 23; connection, 37; information flow, 29, 55
McCombs, Maxwell, 5
McDonaldization, 16
McLuhan, Marshall, 16, 237n3
McNair, Brian, 3, 7, 13, 19, 27, 28, 53, 55, 62, 71, 74, 87, 170, 235n14, 236n22, 243n1
media activist, 2, 8, 73, 91, 96, 98, 99, 107, 115, 124, 138–146, 147, 166, 196, 220, 227, 228; *see also* activist
MediaChannel, 10, 88, 92, 101–102, 113, 114, 153, 172, 200, 211, 212, 241n7
mobile phone: *see* telephone

monopoly of knowledge, 47
Morse, Samuel F.B., 40, 237n7
Mosco, Vincent, 236n21
MoveOn.org, 141
multi-directional: information flow, 17, 24, 55, 63, 121; information string, 33, 52, 64; roster of communication, 23; press-government-citizen gatekeeping relations, 77
multimedia: competence, 81, 82; coverage, 52 environment, 28, 227, 230; newsroom, 3, 10, 107, 221–227; reporter, 187, 188, 189, 203; multimedia, to work 191
multimediality 60, 62
Mumbai attacks, 4, 52, 70, 238n1
MySpace, 180, 182

N

nation, 36, 37, 65–66, 83; nation-state, 18, 21, 22, 28, 65–66
national: news exchange, 43, 47; news markets 48, 49
NBC, 203, 244n1
Neda, 1, 4, 64, 115
Negroponte, Nicholas, 15, 81, 233n4
network, 13, 24–27, 29–35, 36, 50, 55–59, 62–64, 77–79, 90, 122, 209, 226, 228, 235nn16–19, 236n25, communication, 21, 25, 37, 42, 47, 50, 181; information, 25, 37, 44, 64, 73, 78, 80, 194, 196, 228, 229; journalistic, 36, 43, 50, 78; news, 37, 38, 39, 42, 43, 49, 50, 78, 226; time, 2, 30
network journalism, 9, 10, 34, 35, 51–67, 68–84, 87, 89–91, 93, 107, 108, 117, 118, 122, 124, 129, 140, 142, 147, 149, 157, 158, 165, 167–169, 179, 181, 192, 193, 199, 204, 207–209, 212, 213, 216, 217, 219, 221, 226, 227, 228–231; networked link journalism, 58, 59; networked journalism, 56, 57, 58, 61; Networked Journalism Summit, 239n4
network society, 7, 9. 13, 22, 23–29, 30, 33, 34, 61, 62, 78, 79, 83, 174, 207, 229, 230
networked computer or computer network, 6, 26, 64, 235n14

news agency, 5, 9, 36–49, 50–54, 63, 66–68, 80, 83, 111, 121, 129, 140, 196, 205, 213, 238n14
newsbook, 37, 38, 39, 237n5
newsgathering, 1, 35, 40, 44–46, 49, 55, 56, 61, 73, 77, 83, 84, 87, 107, 108, 120, 126, 127, 130, 200, 205, 209, 215, 228; information, 38, 52, 54, 55, 70, 78, 80, 91, 108, 110, 121, 126, 214; of news, 5, 16, 31, 43, 45, 46, 50, 68, 129, 213
New York City Independent media Center (IMC): *see* Indymedia
New York Times, 4, 95, 151, 153, 160, 162, 167, 172, 191, 198, 219, 225, 242n4
node, 9, 10, 28, 30, 31, 33, 34, 56, 63, 69, 76–79, 82, 84, 87, 91, 122, 141, 165, 168, 181, 196, 214, 216, 226, 231, 236n25; information, 10, 31, 32, 34, 35, 50, 52, 68, 69, 73, 77, 87, 117, 124, 129, 137, 138, 142, 145, 147, 149, 181, 207, 219, 226, 227, 228–230; supernode, 78, 219, 229
non-linear news or information flows, 4, 5, 21, 24, 29, 32, 34, 50, 51, 55, 61, 63, 68, 78, 79, 84, 89, 91, 108, 207, 219, 228
nonmarket actor, 4, 52
non-standard source (news), 52, 68, 70, 74, 117, 161, 121, 193
Norris, Pippa, 236n24
NowPublic.com, 52, 141, 230, 238n1

O

objectivity or objective, 20, 143, 153, 198, 201, 243n1
OhmyNews, 4, 56, 141, 146, 161
one-way flow of information or news, 17, 51, 63, 77, 92
one-to-many: information flow, 55; path, 54
OneWorld.org, 102, 141
online journalism or journalist, 59–61, 94, 176, 220, 223, 225
open source, 58, 98, 211
Ourmedia, 10, 88, 92, 96, 97–98, 113, 115, 123, 144, 145, 241n7

P

Pakistan, 135, 203

parachute journalism or journalist, 183, 184–187, 192–194, 199, 226
Pavlik, John, 53, 55, 78, 81, 90, 239n3
Penny Press, 234n7, 238n10
podcast, 68, 93, 94, 96, 97, 107, 111, 219, 222
Prince Harry, 51, 68, 75, 76
printing press, 15, 38, 39, 41, 234n6, 237n4
production: chain, 28, 29, 77, 79, 80, 127, 144, 149, 155, 171, 183, 204; digital, 70, 107, 108, 111, 108–123, 202; information, 13, 78, 161, 228; journalistic, 1, 2, 5, 6, 7, 8, 9, 15, 22, 31, 58, 107, 119, 170, 179, 229; mode, 9, 25, 42, 54, 61, 235; news, 3–7, 20, 21, 27, 37, 43, 49, 52, 55–59, 68, 78, 79, 80, 82–84, 87, 91, 93, 113, 114, 118, 120, 121, 127, 162, 207, 209, 214, 215, 223, 226, 228, 229; process, 55, 57, 82, 110, 120, 130, 140, 157, 205, 228, 229
produser, 52
Project for Excellence in Journalism (PEJ), 5, 10, 88, 92, 104, 105, 241n7
public, the, 20, 36, 41, 44, 57, 62, 64, 75, 76, 108, 115, 119, 159, 171, 174, 199, 218
public relations, 28, 31, 51, 68, 236n22
public service: media or outlet, 5, 5, 51, 52, 54, 63, 64, 75, 78, 93, 111, 113, 115, 122, 129, 141, 144, 149, 160; journalist, 67, 70
public sphere, 5, 6, 28, 67, 68, 72, 74, 77, 82; alternative, 72
Publish2, 59, 80
push-pull medium, 54, 55, 63, 166

R

Radio Television Digital News Association, 137
Republican National Convention, 97, 115, 138
Reuter, Julius, 36, 45, 46, 238n13
Reuters, 42, 43, 45–46, 47–50, 83, 137, 140, 196, 237n2, 238n14
Riverbend, 80, 201, 202, 244n2
Robertson, Roland, 8, 15, 17, 233n3
Rosen, Jay, 157, 169
RSS, 80, 94, 95, 180, 210, 217

S

Salam Pax or Baghdad blogger, 201, 202, 244n4
satellite, 2, 16, 18, 21, 66, 67, 76, 109, 111, 188, 203, 206, 233n2, 235n15
Schiller, Dan, 25, 26
Schiller, Herbert, 25, 234n9
Schudson, Michael, 15, 16, 40, 41, 43, 44, 78
Seib, Philip, 53, 193
Shirky, Clay, 2, 54, 114, 161, 235n17
Sites, Kevin, 202, 203
social bookmarking, 180, 181, 218
social media, 73, 137, 182; and blogging guidelines, 137; policy, 137; tool, 2, 72, 97
social change, 23, 25, 27, 113, 234n5
social movement, 24, 116
social network or networking, 54, 58, 94, 96, 117, 137, 180, 181, 211, 217, 230; social network site, 1, 2, 111, 180–182
social structure, 7, 13, 22–25, 27, 56, 77, 235n19
space, 2, 3, 5, 8, 14, 15, 18, 19, 21–24, 29–31, 33, 34, 40, 41, 50, 53, 55, 56, 61, 65, 71, 72, 79, 122, 152, 157, 172, 180, 181, 193, 218, 228; information, 4, 9, 33, 78, 122, 168, 229; of flows, 29, 31, 82
spin, 28, 71, 74, 135, 161, 236n28, 240n10
Straubhaar, Joseph D., 14, 40, 53, 234n10, 238n3
string (information), 5, 7, 24, 29, 33–36, 50, 52, 62–64, 71, 73, 76, 79, 117, 121, 129, 163, 165, 167, 168
StudiVZ, 180
Sunstein, Cass R., 5, 6, 82
supernode, 78, 219, 229
Surowiecki, James, 55, 154
system (Luhmann), 32–34; centralized (media), 4, 162; closed (media/ journalism), 32, 33, 50, 51, 53, 62, 67, 75, 84, 88, 120, 166, 170, 180

T

Talking Points Memo, 177
Tapscott, Don and Anthony D. Williams, 54, 207, 211

technological determinism, 15, 26, 27, 233n4–5, 237n3
telegraph, the, 9, 35–37, 40–50, 70, 83, 237n7; telegraph technology, 35–37, 40–50, 83, 84; telegraphic news, 40, 45; telegraphic reporting, 44, 83
Telegraph, The (newspaper), 222
telephone (history of), 234; cell phone, 4, 51, 125, 126, 127, 136; mobile phone, 1, 2, 18, 71, 72, 74, 93, 110, 115, 125, 135, 136, 138, 203; satellite phone, 1, 203; smartphone, 2, 80
Thussu, Daya Kishan, 3, 6, 14, 37, 38, 42, 46, 47, 49, 53, 65, 237n1
Tibet, 52, 68, 69, 70, 71, 72, 73, 74, 76, 115, 239n1–5
Time Magazine, 160, 203
Toffler, Alvin, 170
Tomlinson, John, 13, 14
top-down, 87, 172, 180; communication order, 33; gatekeeping standards, 67; journalism, 8; organization models, 209; organization of journalistic work, 51; reporting methods, 92
transnational or transnationally: community, 67; connectivity, 8, 21; corporations, 25, 26; cultural exchange, 17; information, 20–21, 66, 112, 194; news, 21, 34, 66, 107, 109, 110, 183, 193, 195, 198; networks, 107, 183; sphere of participation, 117; state-society, 14
Twitter, 1, 2, 4, 8, 52, 70, 72, 76, 80, 169, 181, 213, 217

U

Urry, John, 18, 66, 233n3
user, 4, 6, 15, 18, 33, 37, 53–55, 57, 59–61, 63, 70, 72, 78, 80–82, 84, 87, 89, 90–92, 100, 107, 113, 124–138, 142, 154, 155, 156, 160, 167, 169–182, 183, 187, 193, 197, 203, 204, 206, 209, 212, 214, 215, 219, 220, 229–231; *see also* audience
user-generated content, 1, 3, 4, 5, 10, 31, 52, 92–94, 96, 107, 110, 122, 124–138, 142, 163, 165, 169, 175, 183, 193, 203, 209, 214, 220, 224, 227, 228, 230, 231

V

Virginia Tech Shooting, 51, 129, 130, 143, 218, 227
Voices of Africa, 2, 230
Volkmer, Ingrid, 3, 8, 16, 18, 22, 30, 53, 54, 55, 64–66, 77, 78, 81, 82, 243n4

W

Washington Post, 95, 105, 151, 160, 167
Watts, Duncan J., 63, 64
Weaver, David, 20
weblog: *see* blog
Webster, Frank, 25, 26, 27
Westernization, 16
wiki, 58, 72
Wikipedia, 52, 54, 76, 162
wisdom of crowds, 55, 57, 154, 178, 211, 229

web, 25, 31, 37, 42, 54, 58, 59, 122, 142, 149, 155, 168, 181, 195, 212
Web 2.0, 6, 70, 96, 178, 180
World Wide Web, 28, 52, 91, 94, 99, 109, 138, 150, 178, 179, 193, 200, 206
world society, 17, 21, 22
Wolff, 47, 48

Y

Yahoo News, 196, 203
YouTube, 68, 71, 72, 79, 93, 109, 111, 117, 122, 165, 166, 181

Z

ZEIT ONLINE, 10, 88, 92, 95, 96, 111, 154, 155, 156, 157, 170, 171, 179, 220, 222, 241n7
Zimbabwe, 68, 71, 72, 73, 74, 76, 197

398811